Henrietta Leyser is a fellow of St Peter's College and lecturer in medieval history at St Peter's and St Edmund Hall, Oxford. She studied history at Oxford University both as an undergraduate and as a graduate, and she has taught and lectured at universities in Great Britain and the USA.

Her other publications include *Hermits and the New Monasticism* and a topic book for schools about medieval women.

MEDIEVAL
WOMEN

A Social History of
Women in England
450–1500

Henrietta Leyser

PHOENIX
GIANT

A PHOENIX GIANT PAPERBACK

First published in Great Britain
by Weidenfeld & Nicolson in 1995
This paperback edition published in 1996
by Phoenix, a division of Orion Books Ltd,
Orion House, 5 Upper St Martin's Lane,
London WC2H 9EA

Second Impression 1997
Third Impression 1999
The author and publisher gratefully acknowledge
the following for granting permission to reproduce
extracts from: *Aelred of Rievaulx's Treatise: The
Pastoral Prayer*, translated by Mary Paul
Macpherson ocso (Cistercian Publications, 1971);
The Lais of Marie de France, translated by G. Burgess
and K. Busby (Penguin Books Ltd, 1986); *The Book
of St Gilbert*, edited by Raymond Foreville and
Gillian Keir (Oxford University Press, 1987); *A
Medieval Woman's Mirror of Honour*, edited by and
translated by C. Willard and M. Cosman (Bard Hall
Press, 1989); *Medieval Woman's Guide to Health*,
edited by Beryl Rowland (Croom Helm, 1981).

A CIP catalogue record for this book
is available from the British Library.

ISBN: 1 85799 735 2

Printed and bound in Great Britain by
Butler & Tanner Ltd, Frome and London

In memory of Karl
and for our children

Contents

Contents

Illustrations

The birth of the Virgin in a late medieval setting.
RCHME © Crown Copyright

Women and gossip depicted in an early fourteenth-century
stained glass window at Stanford, Northamptonshire.
RCHME © Crown Copyright

A guardian angel helping a woman carry out her devotions,
from the Lambeth Apocalypse.
Lambeth Palace Library, London / Bridgeman Art Library, London

St Anne teaching the Virgin to read.
Bodleian Library, Oxford

Susanna, thought to be the owner of the de Brailes Hours,
praying.
Bodleian Library, Oxford

A late medieval illustration from Richard II's Psalter of Poor
Clares in chapel.
British Library, London / Bridgeman Art Library, London

Chaucer's Wife of Bath from the fifteenth-century Ellesmere
manuscript.
Private collection / Bridgeman Art Library, London

Matrimony, as depicted on one of the faces of a late medieval
font at All Saints, Gresham, Norfolk.
Private collection

Preface

As an undergraduate reading history at Oxford at the start of the 1960s, it was only Richard Southern's inaugural lecture as Chichele Professor, delivered in 1961, that made me aware of what lay behind the syllabus we had to study. The discovery that history as an academic discipline was a nineteenth-century invention filled me with fascinated horror. Until then I had always assumed that the study of history, like any other subject I had ever learned, required a certain amount of groundwork, but that thereafter endless vistas of human experience lay before the student. Only listening to Southern did I discover that this was not at all what was in the minds of those who had in the first place devised the Oxford syllabus and who had indeed thereby managed to establish it as a respectable subject for university study. They had actually chosen to leave out 'that which is most interesting in the past in order to concentrate on that which was practically and academically most serviceable'.[1]

The Victorian syllabus, it hardly needs saying, had little place for women. Concentrating as it did on public life and constitutional developments there seemed to its framers barely an occasion to mention them. Even the great *Dictionary of National Biography*, begun in 1885 and designed for a wider public, could find room in its sixty-two volumes for only 3 per cent of women. All this is both well-known and being put to rights. History syllabuses, world-wide, include topics on women; the *New Dictionary of National Biography*, now under-

---

[1] R. W. Southern, *The Shape and Substance of Academic History* (1962), reprinted in F. Stern, *The Varieties of History* (1973), p. 418.

way, has a consultant editor for women on its staff. Women are, then, no longer in danger of being left out of history; but what is not yet clear is what precisely is their place within it. What are the grounds for the study of women as a separate topic? Should women's history make way for gender history?

In what follows I engage with this current debate only to the extent that in attempting to write a book of this scope at all I have shaped it in ways which seem to me to reflect work of great importance, much of it interdisciplinary, much of it still in progress, testimony to the continuing vitality and richness of women's history. My aims have been twofold: to provide an introduction to some of this work that will be of use and interest to both students and to the general reader, and secondly to try to present medieval women on their own terms; and here I must return to those Victorians. Their syllabus, as described by Richard Southern, may have been long dismantled but their ghosts are still around. On the one hand these ghosts (being male) still encourage historians, even when writing about women, to share assumptions created by men. And this, as Caroline Walker Bynum has taught us, will never give us 'the whole story': we cannot only look '*at* women; ... the historian ... needs to stand *with* women as well'.[2] The other thing these ghosts do is to transpose into the Middle Ages, as if it didn't have its fair share, some of the misogyny of the nineteenth century. That at least is the only explanation I have for the extraordinarily persistent caricatures of the attitudes of the Middle Ages towards women which still mar many discussions. In the famous debates about the authenticity of the correspondence between Abelard and Heloise, for example, those who argued not so long ago that Heloise could not have written the letters that bear her name either because she would not have been so clever, or so sensuous, were hearing voices that came not from the twelfth but from the nineteenth century.

Since in writing this book I have had in mind both general reader and student, as far as possible each chapter is self-contained and may be read with or without reference to the extracts from Primary Sources (pages 257–313). The bibliographies for each chapter, which appear at the end of the book,

---

[2] C. W. Bynum, 'Women's Stories, Women's Symbols', *Fragmentation and Redemption* (1991), p. 33.

include titles referred to in footnotes as well as suggestions for
further reading.

This book makes no claim to be original research; I have
tried to acknowledge how much I owe to the work of others
in the limited footnotes allowed by the format and in the
bibliographies, but if there are occasions when I have failed to
do so, I offer heartfelt apologies. I would like to thank my
family and many friends for their inspiration, advice and
understanding. I am particularly grateful to Caroline Barron,
Kate Cooper, Monica Green, Conrad Leyser, Henry Mayr-
Harting, Janet Nelson and Nigel Thompson who each read
chapters in draft and whose criticisms were of the greatest
value. Errors which remain are, of course, my own. I would
also like to thank students from the summer school at St
Peter's, Oxford, from 1991–4 and from the 1994 spring sem-
ester from Emory University, Atlanta, who allowed me to try
out sections of this book on them and for all their suggestions.
My thanks are due to the Faculty at Emory for their hospitality
and to the interloan library for its help and endless patience
with my requests. My debt to the Master and Fellows of St
Peter's College, Oxford, for their generosity and support in
the last few years is incalculable.

Between conception and completion this book lost its most
fervent supporter and its sternest critic. I dedicate it to his
memory and to our children.

Henrietta Leyser
St Peter's College, Oxford
March 1995

PART ONE

The Anglo-Saxons:
Studies in Evidence

CHAPTER ONE

Archaeology

The arrival of Germanic tribes in England in the early fifth century, following the departure of the occupying armies of Roman legionaries, has been immortalised for us through stories from the ninth-century *Anglo-Saxon Chronicle*. In these stories, epic heroes land along the south-east coast of England, on the shores of Sussex, Kent and Hampshire. They come in small bands, three to five shipfuls, brother with brother, father with sons. They kill natives, capture treasure, inspire terror. Historians tend to be sceptical now about the existence of those the *Chronicle* names; Hengist and Horsa, for example, alleged leaders and brothers are perhaps, like Romulus and Remus, the twins of Rome, to be regarded as archetypal founding figures rather than revered as historical personages.

Mythical or not, the cast of the *Anglo-Saxon Chronicle* is, in its invasion scenes, resolutely male. Women are conspicuous only by their absence. No one tells us whether shiploads of women arrived too. By contrast, following the Norman Conquest of 1066 the twelfth-century historian Ordericus Vitalis reported that Norman women were too afraid of the sea-crossing to join their menfolk. Such reluctance, whether in the fifth or the eleventh century, would have had political advantages for the newcomers. Intermarriage, quite as much as warfare is, or can be, a form of conquest. The extent of the slaughter of native British men in the fifth century will always remain incalculable, but it is hard to avoid the conclusion that whatever the estimate, women were more likely to have been enslaved than killed, set to work, as E. A. Thompson has argued, 'spinning, weaving, grinding corn, making pots,

3

fetching wood, water, and so on, as well as to serve as concubines'.[1] A scenario of this kind is supported by evidence
from Hampshire cemeteries: taller men appear in the post-
Roman record while the stature of the women remains
unchanged. The suggestion, though it can be no more, is thus
of an immigrant male population living alongside native
females.

'Sex and politics' with a different twist finds its way into the
ninth-century account of the Anglo-Saxon invasion attributed
to the Welsh ecclesiastic, Nennius. Woman here is both victim
and villain. Nennius's Hengist, 'an experienced man, shrewd
and skilful', spies out the land and then sends back home for
his 'beautiful and very handsome' daughter, Rowena. Once
she has arrived, Hengist organises a great feast for the British
leader Vortigern and, according to Nennius, 'he told the girl
to serve them wine and spirits. They all got exceedingly drunk.
When they were drinking Satan entered into Vortigern's heart
and made him love the girl ... he asked her father for her
hand, saying, "Ask of me what you will, even to the half of
my kingdom." ' Thereafter, in Nennius's narrative, the Anglo-
Saxons were unstoppable; the barbarians returned in force
since Vortigern, 'because of his wife', was their friend.[2]

It is the legendary character of accounts such as Nennius's
and to some extent also of the *Anglo-Saxon Chronicle*, which
has allowed the years between the departure of the Romans
and the establishment of the recognisable Anglo-Saxon kingdoms of the later sixth century to be called 'Dark Ages'. In the
absence of authoritative written sources, the work of archaeologists has been of fundamental importance to Anglo-Saxon
studies. Although much of the evidence here too is irrecoverable, there are still sites to be excavated; new techniques
and new questions, moreover, mean that what has already
been unearthed can now be reinterpreted. It is to the implications of these interpretations for the study of Anglo-Saxon
women that we must now turn. The focus will be on the richest
area of excavation, studies of cemeteries.

Cemetery evidence, it goes without saying, is not transparent.

---

[1] E. A. Thompson, *St Germanus of Auxerre and the End of Roman Britain* (1984),
p. 95.
[2] *Nennius*, ed. and trans. J. Morris (1980), pp. 28, 32.

Anglo-Saxon burial practices, like our own, are not simply a reflection of social reality. As Ian Hodder had pointed out, they may indeed invert, disguise and distort that reality; thus today, in Hodder's words, 'in many of our deaths we express an ideal of equality, humility and non-materialism which is blatantly in contrast with the way we live our lives in practice'.[3] That said, recent work by archaeologists has done much to decipher and translate the messages of graves and to establish categories for analysis. Following this work, we will need to consider three different types of burial: the 'normal', the rich and the strange. In each case we will need to take into account where abouts in the cemetery the grave is located, the position of the body in the grave and the nature of any grave goods. Corresponding questions apply also to cremations, a rite phased out only with the advent of Christianity at the turn of the sixth century. An attempt will be made first to give some descriptive examples of these types and, second, to consider broader implications.

The first thing to be noticed about 'normal' burials or cremations is that there is really no such thing. Each cemetery has its own quite particular story to tell. It is, however, generally possible to distinguish (and not just on skeletal grounds) between male and female inhabitants. In the case of cremations, for example, where the presence of charred bone still makes sexing possible, cinerary urns are likely to be decorated according to both gender and age. Thus, despite wide regional variations in design, urns with stamped concentric figures seem always to have contained women or children. Occasionally, a special zone of the cemetery was reserved for the burial of women, as, for example, at sixth-century Lechlade in Gloucestershire; sometimes in inhumations an identifying trait is the ritual position of the body. At Holywell Row in Suffolk, for example, men tended to be buried extended whereas a significant proportion of women are found with legs flexed.

A crucial question raised by the evidence of the Holywell Row cemetery is that of status and how this might interact with definition by gender. The evidence is highly complex[4] and will be discussed more fully later in the chapter. It is

---

[3] Ian Hodder, 'Social Structure and Cemeteries: A Critical Appraisal' in P. Rahtz, T. Dickinson and L. Watts (eds), *Anglo-Saxon Cemeteries* (1979), p. 167.
[4] See the analysis by E. J. Pader, 'Material Symbolism and Social Relations in Mortuary Studies', in *Anglo-Saxon Cemeteries*, pp. 147–57.

Anglo-Saxon England

▨ Celtic kingdoms

NORTH SEA

IRISH SEA

DALRIADA

GODODDIN

BERNICIA

R. Tyne

R. Tees

RHEGED

NORTHUMBRIA

Sewerby •

DEIRA

York •

ELMET

LINDSEY

• Chester

GWYNEDD

MERCIA

R. Trent

Shrewsbury •

Norwich •

MIDDLE
ANGLIA

EAST
ANGLIA

R. Severn

Bury St Edmunds • • Ixworth

Sutton Hoo •

POWYS

Worcester • • Bidford-on-Avon

Ipswich •

MAGON-
SAETE

Minster
Lovell • • Brighthampton

DYFED

Gloucester •

HWICCE

• Oxford

Colchester •

Cotswolds

• Long Wittenham

ESSEX

Lechlade •

London •

R. Thames

• Bath

• Camerton

Portway

Bifrons •

Kingston

Buckland

Glastonbury •

Salisbury •

• Worthy Park

KENT

Swallowcliffe
Down •

Winchester •

SUSSEX

WESSEX

Chichester •

• Dorchester

R. Tamar

ISLE OF
WIGHT

DUMNONIA

ENGLISH CHANNEL

sufficient to note here that in what is known as sector 1 of the Holywell Row cemetery, women buried in a flexed position had wrist clasps and ornaments on both right and left shoulders whereas extended women had no wrist clasps and ornaments only on the left shoulder. On the other hand, all the sector 1 women, flexed or extended, had accessories on the right side of the waist whereas in sector 2 such accessories were found only on the left side. The symbolic meanings here are far from clear; what does, however, seem to hold true for inhumations at Holywell Row and elsewhere – as yet we know little about cremations – is that the range of grave goods found with women is greater both in kind and in number than those found with men. Many of these objects are sex-specific – notably amethyst, cowries and keys for women as opposed to weaponry for men – but here again there are exceptions. Tweezers, for example, associated with women at the Chessel Down cemetery on the Isle of Wight, are at Long Wittenham in Berkshire found in the graves of men.

Each cemetery must be read, then, primarily according to the logic of its own rules. But there is a wider context, that of chronology, still to be considered. The earliest graves bear witness to those pagan beliefs of which we otherwise know so little. In these, the bones of animals, notably of sheep and goats, are found with both men and women; it is presumed, since the bones are articulated, that these were buried as a source of fresh meat to sustain the dead whereas other animals, such as dogs, were probably sacrificial offerings. Dogs, likewise horses, both high-status animals, were more commonly associated with men than with women; so far only one woman has been found buried with a dog, at Minster Lovell in Oxfordshire, while the closest we can get to a horse burial for a woman is at Buckland in Kent where the dead woman's treasures included the premolar tooth of a large horse. Boars' teeth and tusks, however, are found predominantly with women; beaver teeth with women and children. Such teeth and tusks were often perforated, having been worn as pendants, sometimes with expensive mountings, expressive of the value attached to them by their owners. Amulets of this kind seem to have been particularly favoured by women in the decades surrounding the conversion to Christianity, possibly indicating a need for extra protection in the face of the uncertainties caused by the new beliefs the Christian missionaries were spreading.

How far, and in what ways, these new beliefs affected ritual practices is hard to determine, but it is clear that the long-held notion that easily definable and recognisable alterations in burial customs were introduced by Christianisation is no longer tenable. Christians as well as pagans buried their dead with grave goods; conversely, pagans as well as Christians might choose an east–west orientation for their graves. None the less, the conversion period saw the playing out of significant dramas in which cemeteries acted as the stage. These struggles had as much to do with political ranking as with religious belief, though to try to separate the two would be a misguided enterprise. The principal parts in these dramas were taken by men, but this is no reason for ignoring the supporting roles played by women at times, indeed, these were clearly highlighted. It is as well to remember that whereas in the seventh century the graves of men – notably at Sutton Hoo in Suffolk – stand out both in terms of wealth, and, quite literally, as huge mounds in the landscape, in the sixth century the most splendid burials are of those of women.

Splendid female graves are thickest on the ground in Kent, itself the richest of the early Anglo-Saxon kingdoms. Here, in the mid-sixth century, a number of women were buried with particularly lavish quantities of jewellery, showing all the marks of the influence of their cross-channel neighbours, the Franks. The gold-brocaded armlets and headbands of these women and the arrangements of their brooches has led to speculation that here was a group of high-caste women, dressed in a way that underlined their special status. Veiled and perhaps distinctively clad in open over-gowns, such women may have been the instruments and ambassadors of Kent's pre-eminence in the early Anglo-Saxon world. Thus the presence of comparable graves elsewhere in England has led C. J. Arnold to suggest that marriage of these élite women into other dynasties was a hallmark of Kentish diplomacy.[5] Such marriage alliances came to be rivalled only by the novel Christian strategies of the seventh century when god-parenting by kings of neighbouring rulers provided an alternative means both of making alliances and of proclaiming dominance.

In the seventh century, alongside the new-style rich male burials, sumptuous women's graves are still to be found. What

[5] C. J. Arnold, *An Archaeology of the Early Anglo-Saxon Kingdoms* (1988), p. 178.

they yield now is evidence of the changing fashions brought by Christianisation, of ways in which the new faith could be displayed on women's bodies. As a missionary centre, home for the Italian monks sent by Pope Gregory I in 597, Kent continued to set trends, but its influence became more diffuse. For an example of the contrast between the sixth and seventh centuries we may look at the Gloucestershire cemetery of Lechlade.

Lechlade has been excavated only recently, in 1985; it was an excavation planned originally to last three weeks, supposedly of a prehistoric ceremonial area to be summarily investigated before Cotswold District Council began building houses on the site. It soon became clear that what was being unearthed was in fact a major Anglo-Saxon cemetery, in use from about 500–670 CE, possibly for as many as five hundred bodies, with women consistently buried in the north-western corner of the area. Here, in a wooden coffin (in itself a mark of some distinction since most corpses are laid out only clothed or shrouded) was found the sixth-century grave of a young woman thought to be between twenty-five and thirty, the average lifespan for a woman in this period. She had been buried with the right leg extended, the left leg slightly flexed, a beaver-tooth pendant by her ribs. But what was most remarkable was the richness of the woman's grave goods. 'Behind her skull', the archaeologists' preliminary report noted, was

a circlet of blue glass beads ... There was a large gilded saucer brooch on each shoulder with traces of woollen dress adhering to the back. A massive gilded, bronze, square-headed brooch held her cloak together. Amber beads and a string of tubular blue glass beads were thickly spread across her chest. A further heap of beads lay by her waist and had, perhaps, originally been kept in a bag ... [There was] even more jewellery – silver spiral rings on four fingers, bronze pins in her hair and a cosmetic brush. By her head a wooden or leather bottle was decorated with circular and triangular bronze plaques. Against this rested a bone spindle whorl and bone comb. A large ivory ring hung on the left side of her waist. This was the stiffener of a bag – when the ring was lifted the bag opened ... Inside were various metal rings which were probably kept as protective amulets. An iron chatelaine also hung from her waist...[6]

The contents and messages of this, and of comparable sixth-

---

[6] D. Miles and S. Palmer, *Invested in Mother Earth* (n.d.), p. 14.

century graves, must be compared with the women's graves of the seventh century in Lechlade. Here we again find signals of status: another coffin burial, for example, exceptionally surrounded by a ditch, of a woman we can reasonably, if not certainly, presume to be a Christian since she wore on her necklace a silver cross. Fashions, notably, have now changed. The accoutrements of this woman, and of her contemporaries beneath Lechlade soil, bear witness to Mediterranean influence. Regional styles have been discarded in favour of cosmopolitanism. The chunky square-headed brooches of the sixth century have been replaced by circular designs and by finely worked silver hoops, pins and necklaces. Mediterranean amethysts and garnets are favoured over Baltic amber. Prized possessions are no longer kept in little bags but in wooden caskets, such as the Franks had used in the sixth century, containing perhaps a thread-box full of scraps of textiles (hence the name) and a Red Sea cowrie, a treasure that may have represented the vulva, or purity, or both.

Mediterranean influence, mediated in the first instance through Kent, can be seen not only at Lechlade but also in the burial barrow at Swallowcliffe Down in Wiltshire. Here, in the seventh century, a woman of about eighteen to twenty-five years – quite possibly a Christian – laid in ostentatious splendour on a bed, had been interred in a Bronze Age barrow. While there is nothing Kentish about the bed – further examples of bed burials in England, all but one of them the graves of women, have been found in Wiltshire, Suffolk and Derbyshire – the grave goods suggest that, like the women of Lechlade, the Swallowcliffe woman was dressed in the latest Mediterranean style. Buried with her, in a fine 'modern' maplewood casket, were five silver safety-pin brooches, of a kind to be found only in seventh-century women's graves. The closest match to them comes from Kingston in Kent where a pair with similar engravings were found in a grave otherwise renowned for the beauty of its owner's polychrome brooch. Whether there was once other jewellery at Swallowcliffe seems certain – at some point the grave was robbed: of what we can only guess, but it has been suggested that a cross of gold and garnet cloisonné work, as found in the seventh-century bed burial of a woman at Ixworth in Suffolk, might have been among the objects stolen. Left behind by the robbers was a translucent glass bead with an opaque twist, technically superb and again with Kentish parallels.

The Swallowcliffe woman was also buried with an object that (to date, at any rate), is unique in an English setting: a spherical container, bronze, though originally with a silver coating, whose function is far from clear. A similar find in a ninth-century woman's ship burial in Norway poses the same question: what is the purpose of these objects? Earlier suppositions that these containers were censers seem now to have been disproved, closer examination of the workmanship suggesting that neither capsule was intended to be opened. Both do, however, work as sprinklers. If this interpretation is correct, then it would seem that the Swallowcliffe container should be understood alongside the perforated spoons and spherical balls found in a number of fifth- and sixth-century women's graves. This hypothesis will be considered after looking at the final category of graves: those containing 'strange' or 'deviant' burials.

'Deviant' burials may be defined as being those that arouse the suspicion that the dead person met a nasty end. Among those excavated, four women – one each at Sewerby in Yorkshire, Worthy Park in Hampshire, Camerton in Somerset and Buckland in Kent – were possibly buried alive. The skeletons of their bodies were contorted and prone. At Sewerby, the woman had been buried on top of a coffin burial of another much younger woman; a quern stone had been placed on her back as if to keep her in place but, as she had also been provided with a respectable range of grave-goods, there is no reason to assume that her burial was intended to be shaming. By contrast, at Worthy Park the burial was unaccompanied by any goods and a lesion on the right femur of the skeleton has given rise to the suggestion that here was a victim of rape (the injury is consistent with this possibility) who, by the norms of her society, deserved and met a shocking end. This is a highly speculative interpretation: the injury, apparently, could equally have been caused by rough horse-riding; moreover, we have no firm evidence to support the notion of this kind of penalisation for rape. Likewise, while it is possible that the double grave at Brighthampton in Oxfordshire is an example of a suttee-type burial, and that another at Bifrons in Kent contained a slave buried with her mistress, it makes no sense to isolate these cases from a broader ritual context.

11

How we are to understand this ritual context is as yet far from clear, but the recently completed excavation at Sutton Hoo has highlighted the need to make the attempt. When this great ship burial was first unearthed in 1939, and for decades thereafter, the big question was: who was the man so honoured in his death? Following the latest excavations, we can no longer think of it only as a kingly burial with its riches. Attention is also focused on the company this man kept. It is a mixed entourage, likely to have included at least one rich female burial (Mound 14) but of particular relevance, centred around a tree in the eastern sector of the cemetery, are the graves of men (perhaps with some women among them) who had been killed in celebration of a sacrificial rite. 'Deviant' burials of any kind are always likely to make headlines. In the light of the Sutton Hoo evidence, however, the assumption, sometimes made, that the victims were simply expendable or devalued women, can no longer be allowed to pass.

It is now time to consider not only how, and with what, women were buried, but to look more fully at the range of meanings their graves imply. Archaeologists warn us to proceed with caution. In her analysis of the cemeteries of Holywell Row, Suffolk, and Westgarth Gardens, Bury St Edmunds, Elaine Pader has concluded that although women's graves here – as elsewhere – may seem to be better furnished than those of men, we should not be misled by such superficial impressions; the fact, she suggests, that females often appear to be wealthier than men by artefact-count and quality might be totally irrelevant.[7] Their artefacts have different meanings. Inventories and estimates miss the point. More significant, to Pader, is the Holywell Row correlation between the graves of women and children. Whereas men were buried with shields, symbols of their majority, women, she argues, were buried as if they were minors, their frequently found flexed skeletons indicative of the marginal position they may have held within the community. Women, as other archaeologists have suggested with remarkable condescension, amassed amulets, trinkets and 'junk' because they were perhaps 'naturally more superstitious than men',[8] they collected bits of material to put in so-called thread-boxes 'like many modern needlewomen ... hoarding

[7] E. J. Pader, *op. cit.*
[8] D. Wilson, *Anglo-Saxon Paganism* (1992), p. 115.

any little scraps that might come in useful'.[9] What are we to make of such dismissive arguments?

Warnings not to exaggerate the functions and status of Dark Age and medieval women must always be heeded; there are times, however, when the bells ring too loudly. The intense competition for kingdom-building that was waged in sixth- and seventh-century England was led on the battlefield by kings, but female kin could and did take their share of the power and the glory. In 672, when Cenwealh of Wessex died, 'his Queen Seaxburh reigned one year after him'. The details of the story behind this annal of the *Anglo-Saxon Chronicle* are lost; but Seaxburh's year as ruler reminds us to take seriously the contribution of women to the success of their dynasties and kin groups. The *Chronicle* in the annal for 640 records the accession of Eorcenberht to the kingdom of Kent and gives the name of his wife, also called Seaxburh, and of his daughter Eormengota, 'a holy virgin and a wonderful person'. In time Seaxburh and Eormengota both became abbesses; as will be seen in Chapter Two, the responsibilities wielded by such women are inconceivable without there being already a strong tradition of female command and spiritual expertise on which to draw. To this hypothesis, grave-goods, buttressed by ecclesiastical literature, lend support. In calling upon it, it may be difficult not to seem to be re-creating some kind of 'wise-woman' stereotype; the risk must none the less be taken.

At this point we need to return to the objects buried with women and to consider, following Pader's criteria, what the artefacts in question may 'mean'. We can begin with what are known as 'girdle adjuncts'. Women's clothing, as Gale Owen-Crocker's study has shown, was always belted or girdled.[10] In the seventh century it became fashionable to attach chatelaine chains to belts and to festoon them with a variety of objects, but in the absence of such a chain appropriate possessions might be suspended from girdle hangers or simply tied on or stuck through girdle or belt. Knives, the most common of all grave-goods, buried with men, women and children, are generally reckoned to be the equivalent of penknives rather than weapons, and of functional rather than symbolic value.

[9] E. Crowfoot, quoted in A. Meaney, *Anglo-Saxon Amulets and Curing Stones* (1981), p. 184.
[10] G. Owen-Crocker, *Dress in Anglo-Saxon England* (1984), pp. 43–8.

Women's keys and fire-steels, on the other hand, despite their practical uses, need to be considered for other meanings, especially since the keys in question were designed not to open locks but to lift latches. A finger could have done the job as efficiently, but not as ceremoniously; it does not seem fanciful, therefore, to suggest that latch-lifters may have acted as the seemingly absent token of maturity for women, a sign of their role as guardians of a house and its possessions, and possibly also – the suggestion is Audrey Meaney's – as a sign of their sexual claims. The phallic associations of keys for the Anglo-Saxons is, as Meaney points out, confirmed by two riddles preserved in *The Exeter Book* of *c.*1000 – 'it had touched the known hole which it ... had often filled before'; 'girded with rings, I must thrust hard against hardness'.[11] Fire-steels, similarly, will have denoted a responsibility that was both necessary and rich in symbolic meaning. In many societies it has fallen, and still falls, to women to keep the home fires burning. As recently observed in certain regions of Portugal, after the first bath of a new baby 'people are careful to throw the water ... in the fireplace if the child is female, and out of doors if it is a male. Thus the little girl will be homely and a "friend of the hearth" ...'[12]

The symbolic meanings of fire, even in an age of microwaves, are not difficult to grasp. The associations conjured up in the medieval mind by spinning and weaving may perhaps to the twentieth-century reader be more elusive. Spiders' webs still seem creepy but weaving is simply folksy. But spinning and weaving, which have given 'spinsters' and 'wives' their appellations, have been the pre-eminent tasks for women of every class, from slave to aristocrat, in all the early civilisations of which we know – Egypt, Palestine, Greece, Rome. Anglo-Saxon England is no exception. In all probability every home had its loom; spindle whorls, shears and weaving batons are found regularly in women's graves. Indispensable as was the work of weavers, however, the activity itself was deeply feared, according to the *Penitential of Burchard of Worms* (*c.*1010):

Have you ever been present at, or consented to, the vanities which

[11] Cited in A. Meaney, *op. cit.*, p. 179.
[12] J. de Pina-Cabral, *Sons of Adam, Daughters of Eve: The Peasant World-view of Alto-Minho* (1986), pp. 83–4.

women practice in their woollen work, in their weaving, who when they begin their weaving hope to be able to bring it about that with incantations and with their actions that the threads of the warp and of the woof become so intertwined that unless [some-one] makes use of these other diabolical counter-incantations, he will perish totally? If you have ever been present or consented you must do penance for thirty days on bread and water.[13]

There was also white magic to be had through women's work: to treat the Anglo-Saxon suffering from pains in the jaw the recommended procedure was to 'take the spindle with which a woman spins, bind around his neck with a woollen thread and rinse the inside with hot goat's milk; he will soon be well.'[14]

The magic of spinning and weaving to which such texts attests, leads us directly (with the help of the work of Audrey Meaney) to thread-boxes. So far, at least three dozen of these have been found in seventh-century, probably Christian, women's graves. Similar boxes have been found on the Continent, but the English examples are different in their design and somewhat larger in their capacity: as receptacles they remain, however, tiny – on average 6 centimetres in diameter and 12 centimetres tall. Bits of thread were kept in them, together with scraps of material and herbs. Interpretations as to the uses or significance of thread boxes vary. Are they workboxes for needlewomen; reliquaries containing scraps of holy clothing of the kind which the tenth-century King Athelstan liked to collect, allegedly taken, by way of example, from 'the garment which our Lord himself wore ... from the head-dress of the mother of God ... from the clothes of St John the Apostle ...';[15] or 'first-aid boxes' containing herbs and bandages endowed with both magical and medicinal properties? Their size, the rich and varied nature of the contents, and the absence of any needles makes the first interpretation seem unlikely; the second and third are possible and not mutually exclusive. Thus a thread-box in a baby's grave in the seventh-century cemetery at Updown, Kent, looks distinctly like a reliquary, containing as it does what may be the earliest fragment of silk known in England, while cures of classical origin known from later Anglo-Saxon sources but possibly intro-

[13] Cited in A. Meaney, *op. cit.*, p. 185.
[14] Cited in M. L. Cameron, *Anglo-Saxon Medicine* (1993), p. 132.
[15] Cited in A. Meaney, *op. cit.*, p. 186.

duced much earlier demand cloth, thread and herbs. The woman who needs help in childbirth, for example, should have 'eleven or thirteen grains of coriander seed in a clean cloth tied with a warp thread held against her left thigh';[16] the woman who has been struck dumb should be provided with a powder of pennyroyal wrapped in wool. Such herbal remedies were easily Christianised, mixed with holy water, or lichen from a crucifix, and administered with prayer (scoffers might like to note that lichen has antibiotic properties).

An attempt to find any one explanation for the appearance of thread-boxes is likely to be not only doomed but also misguided: uncertain though we may be about pagan habits of thought, we do know that Christianity relished and encouraged layers of meaning. The four ways of reading scripture – literal, allegorical, moral and tropological – bred complexity and introduced a rationale for the adaptation of old habits. The Christian religion stridently condemned amulets, which represented 'the filth of the ungodly'; at the same time new stones, seemingly with special qualities, were being introduced. Whereas, according to the Roman Pliny writing in the first century CE, amber had been worn by simple peasant women in Gaul as a protection against tonsillitis, amethyst, according to Christian exegesis, was the twelfth apocalyptic gem, sharing its colour with the cup of passion and the wine of heaven. Bishops wore it in their rings; Anglo-Saxon women, particularly of Kent, abandoned amber for necklaces of pear-shaped amethyst beads. It is thus not impossible that thread-boxes, similarly, are a Christian replacement of a pagan cultic object, in this case, Meaney suggests, of crystal balls.

Crystal balls appear in Anglo-Saxon women's graves from as early as the fifth century. As many as twenty have been found in Kent, only six elsewhere, though it should be noted that commoner crystal beads may have shared some of the properties of the more prestigious balls. These balls are usually to be found placed between the woman's knees. In eight cases they are coupled with a perforated spoon; hence their possible connection with Swallowcliffe, though the earlier date for most cases confirms a pagan rather than a Christian context. Although a wide variety of sources make it clear that crystal, through its associations with the sun, light and purity, main-

---

[16] Cited in M. L. Cameron, *op. cit.*, p. 176.

tained magical qualities, the function and meaning of the spoons and the Swallowcliffe capsule remain controversial. A possibility that the spoons were used for sieving wine, and hence that they emphasise the role of women as ritual dispenser of drink, has been countered by those who argue that the bowls of the spoons are too shallow and the holes too big, and who favour instead prophylactic sprinkling as the use for both spoons and spherical container. But in either case, the point of relevance is the burial of these objects with women and the responsibilities and powers they may be supposed to represent.

Tania Dickinson's recent assessment of a late fifth- to sixth-century Warwickshire grave entitled 'An Anglo-Saxon "Cunning Woman" from Bidford-on-Avon' can serve as some kind of a conclusion to this chapter, as well as a pointer to other categories of artefacts not discussed above and to questions yet to be asked. The Bidford woman was buried with twelve miniature bucket pendants of a not uncommon kind, but unusually filled with textile fragments, the precursor in this respect of thread-boxes. The pendants were either placed or sewn into a bag, together with a disc pendant, and seem to have been worn around the neck. They were accompanied by the unparalleled find of an antler cone, together with a highly distinctive 'scalpel-like' knife whose bone handle was decorated with double bull's eyes. Two brooches, an iron pin and amber and glass beads also formed part of the assemblage. While unable to explain whether the buckets and the antler cone denote drinking symbolism, or whether they have other magical associations, Dickinson proposes that here is an example of a woman who had been buried with more than her share of bits and pieces. This fits with Audrey Meaney's observation that while women frequently have amulets, in any one cemetery there is likely to be someone who had a special collection: 'The odd mixture of amulets and "junk" may be the stock-in-trade and sign of women possessed of special powers.' Such 'cunning women' 'would have practised primarily beneficent magic, healing, protecting, and divining the future'.[17] Christian holy women, as will be seen in the following chapter, did much the same thing.

[17] T. Dickinson, 'An Anglo-Saxon "Cunning Woman" from Bidford-on-Avon' in M. Carver (ed.), *In Search of Cult* (1993), p. 53.

A postscript is called for. Cemetery evidence does not suggest that it was exclusively women who had amulets or worked magic; runic inscriptions on swords, boar motifs on helmets and decorative belt buckles will have been designed to give protection to their male owners. Moreover, while it remains true, in Meaney's words, that there is 'no getting away from the fact that Anglo-Saxon men did not have the kinds of amulets their women-folk demonstrably had',[18] recent researchers have been anxious to suggest the possibility of a 'third sex'. Grave 9 at Portway, Hampshire, is here indicative. It is a grave which seems to have been special in several respects: there was a large flint nodule on the chest of the occupant and, most striking of all, female-type jewellery on a male skeleton. The grave also contained carbonised grains of bread wheat (of significance in the light of the veto on burning corn at times of death in the *Penitential of Theodore*). It may be of relevance that the ninth-century *Penitential of Silos*, a text containing much Insular material, also condemns the practice of women burning grain, 'where a man has died', and likewise men who 'in the dance wear women's clothes and strangely devise them and employ jawbones (?) and a bow and spade and things like these . . .'[19] In the light of such texts, the evidence of the Portway grave and related work on burials from other cultures, it may be that we need to be less ready to assume that 'female' artefacts will always or only be buried with female bodies.

---

[18] A. Meaney, *op. cit.*, p. 240.
[19] *Medieval Handbooks of Penance*, ed. J. McNeill and H. Gamer (1990), p. 289.

CHAPTER TWO

History and Hagiography

The coming of Christianity to Anglo-Saxon England breaks the silence of the centuries of the settlement. Christianity brought with it literacy; the possibility and excitement of the new learning generated a flurry of book-making and writing. Scholars wrestled with a new alphabet, a new language, new forms of computation. Already, within a hundred years of the arrival of the mission headed by St Augustine, sent by Pope Gregory I in 597, a centre of monastic scholarship had been established at Jarrow in Northumbria. It was here that the monk Bede, near the end of his life, finished the writing in 731 of one of those books destined to become, in the words of King Alfred, 'most necessary for all men to know' – *The Ecclesiastical History of the English People* (hereafter *EH*). It is this account, more than any other, which has coloured our perceptions of the stages and the progress of the conversion. Described as (and indeed designed to be) 'a gallery of good examples',[1] the *Ecclesiastical History* lovingly depicts not only the men but also the women whose lives Bede considered worthy of emulation. Despite the many whom Bede, from his northern fastness of Jarrow, omits, it is still through his eyes and through his portraits of these men and women that any consideration of the conversion must begin.

Bede's *Ecclesiastical History* is dedicated to a king; in his preface, all the thanks go to men: to the priest Nothhelm who has searched through the archives of Rome on his behalf, to the abbots, bishops and monks who have provided him with

---

[1] J. Campbell (ed), *The Anglo-Saxons* (1982), p. 78.

the stories and records on which his work is based. His narrative is punctuated by the succession lists of bishops and kings. It is a tale structured around good men and their good deeds. And yet within the conventions of this framework it is clear that the momentum of conversion is significantly accelerated by women because, or so it would seem from the stories Bede has chosen to tell, the adoption of Christianity was for them much less problematic than it was for the men of their world. 'Dark Age' kings, and clerics, too, as Bede does not hesitate to show us, are deeply, indeed at times fatally, troubled as to how to reconcile the ethics of the new religion with barbarian codes of behaviour. The ecclesiastics have to decide what is an appropriate lifestyle: can they ride horses and feast with kings, or should they preach on foot, teaching their followers how to fast? Kings have to wrestle with the demands of a faith that expects them to give lavish alms to the poor in preference to booty to their followers and which even tells them to love their enemies.

How to adapt apostolic precepts of poverty to the dignity expected of officeholders, how to eschew war but still protect kingdoms, are questions which Bede's *Ecclesiastical History* highlights but does not answer. The fate of King Sigeberht of East Anglia, the king who hoped to escape the dilemmas of his office by becoming a monk but who is dragged by the East Anglicans out of his monastery and on to the battlefield where he refuses to carry arms and perishes at the hands of the still pagan Mercians, is a story Bede tells without comment. 'Good and religious man' though Bede considers him, Sigeberht is not regarded as a martyr whereas Oswald of Northumbria, killed in action against the same enemy, becomes a saint. Try as he might, Bede could find no fitting place in Anglo-Saxon society for a pacifist king.

The paradoxes and strains of Christianity which so trouble Bede's men seemingly impinge not one whit on his women. They take up its challenges with alacrity and with evident success. They become saints apace, exercising power in life and in death: in life in positions of influence as abbesses, in death through miracles worked at their shrines. Yet it is not any woman who can play this part; royal blood is an essential prerequisite. The high profile such women achieve would indeed seem to be explicable only if Christianity was in fact offering a continuation, albeit with significant variations, of roles in which aristocratic women were already well versed. With this in mind let us turn to such women as Bede presents them. We begin, as he does, with Christian women and the implications of their marriages.

Married women in Bede's narrative both precede the mission sent by Pope Gregory and help to ensure the survival of its teaching. The king of Kent, Aethelbert, who received the missionaries into his kingdom, alarmed though he is said by Bede to have been at the possibility that they might be magicians come to bewitch him, was none the less not a stranger to the new religion. His wife, Bertha, a Frankish princess, had been given to him in marriage on condition, Bede tells us, that 'she should be allowed to practise her faith and religion unhindered' (*EH I*, 25). A bishop, who had been sent to England with her, held services at the old Roman church of St Martin, just outside Aethelbert's capital, Canterbury. It was at St Martin's that Augustine and his mission set up their base, and there that within no time at all Aethelbert himself was baptised. This auspicious beginning is rerun, with extra flourishes, when the time comes for Aethelburh, the daughter of Aethelbert and Bertha, to marry. Her partner is to be the still pagan king of Northumbria, Edwin, but Aethelburh, in Bede's words, is 'not to be polluted by contact with the heathen'. Before she can join Edwin he must promise 'that he will put no obstacle of any kind in the way of the Christian worship which the maiden practised; on the contrary, he will allow her and all who come with her, men and women, priests and retainers, to follow the faith and worship of their religion after the Christian manner' (*EH II*, 9). And he will himself consider conversion.

Edwin, in fact, dithers and it is only after a thwarted attempt on his life and the birth of his daughter, Eanflaed – born at Easter and christened at Pentecost – 'the first of the Northumbrian race to be baptised' – that Edwin at last promises his own adherence to Christianity. His great-niece Hilda, still a young girl but destined to play a key role in Northumbria, is one of those to be baptised with him when he finally takes the plunge on Easter Day 627. Pope Boniface V meanwhile, in an attempt to hasten the event, had been writing chivvying letters both to Edwin and to Aethelburh: Edwin must convert. Aethelburh receives a present of an ivory comb together with a stern reminder that as a Christian wife she has a duty to soften and inflame the king's heart, to pour knowledge of the mysteries of her faith into his mind, to fulfil the testimony of scripture that 'the unbelieving husband shall be saved by the believing wife' (*EH II*, 9–10). Aethelburh's mother, Bertha, though Bede does not mention it, had had a papal letter in a similar vein, taking her to task for not exercising more influence over Aethelbert. She is to waste no time in making up for her past negligence.

Two marriages, two conversions, two daughters, two papal letters; and there is more to follow. First in Kent and then Northumbria there are pagan comebacks. In Northumbria Edwin is killed – his wife and children flee to Kent (where Christianity has by then been re-established) and there his daughter Eanflaed grows up; Northumbria is re-Christianised by Irish missionaries from the island of Iona under the leadership of Bishop Aidan who bring with them their own traditions, most troublingly a different system for calculating the date of Easter. Eanflaed returns as bride of the new king, Oswiu. The daughter she in turn bears (Aelfflaed) will be offered, as we shall see, when still a baby, to the new Christian God as a thank-offering for the victory in battle that secures the survival of the Northumbrian kingdom. The baby will become abbess of the great double monastery of Whitby. In widowhood her mother Eanflaed joins her there. But first Eanflaed, her court and her supporters impose on the north, through the decision of a synod held at this same monastery of Whitby, the Christian calendar and customs of their native Kent. This calendar is in line with that of Rome; henceforth Easter in Northumbria will no longer be celebrated according to the calculations of 'remote' peoples, but together with Christians 'throughout the whole world' (*EH III*, 25).

In contrast to these triumphant women of Northumbria and Kent, 'bad' women scarcely figure in Bede's *Ecclesiastical History*; there is a whiff of scandal at the Northumbrian monastery of Coldingham – 'feasting, drinking, gossiping and other delights' (*EH IV*, 25) instead of prayer and reading – but divine vengeance in the form of fire soon puts a stop to that. The 'bad ways' of Queen Iurminburgh, second wife of Ecgfrith of Northumbria, recounted with relish in the *Life* of Wilfrid, Bishop of York, are passed over by Bede in discreet silence. In Wilfrid's *Life* Iurminburgh's rivalry with Wilfrid, her jealousy at his power and influence reaches a peak when she steals his reliquary and wears it 'as an ornament both in her chamber at home and when riding abroad in her chariot'.[2] The tale, despite its exemplary ending (the return of the reliquary and ultimate conversion of Iurmingburgh to holy living), still has about it an air of verisimilitude. It reveals tensions of a kind made familiar in Francia where aristocratic women, as portrayed by the historian bishop Gregory of Tours (*c*.540–94), alternately love and hate their episcopal leaders. But unlike Gregory, Bede is more concerned to make than to break reputations; tale-telling is not a part of his agenda. To be sure, the wife of Redwald, king of East Anglia, gets sharply rebuked for encouraging her husband's polytheism – after his conversion to Christianity she insists that he continues to venerate his heathen gods – but aside from the recognition here of queenly influence over cultic practice, this same woman is represented by Bede as the epitome of virtuous barbarian values. Redwald, about to betray Edwin, whom as an exile he has harboured, is dissuaded from doing so only by her argument that this would be a shocking sacrifice of honour.

Bede's tales of the influence of Redwald's wife would seem to underscore that the behaviour of her – to Bede – more laudable Christian counterparts was no new departure. Queen Aethelburh on her arrival in Northumbria as bride to Edwin must have been responsible, like Redwald's wife, for a two-altar system as she worshipped her Christian god while Edwin clung to his paganism (there was indeed much to be said in the early days for hedging bets since the efficacy of the Christian god had yet to be proved). Later, in a situation comparable to that in which Redwald, his wife and Edwin figured, it would be Queen Eanflaed who would persuade her husband King Oswui to make reparation for dishonourable behaviour in the shameful murder of his co-king Oswine. It is in the light of such models that we must view not just the absence of scandal in Bede's work but also the presence of quite so many holy women. For we have to consider not only the parts played by wives, whether 'believing' or 'unbelieving', but also the very active role given to the figure of the abbess.

Bede's exemplary abbess is Hilda of Whitby, great-niece to King Edwin of Northumbria, and mother to all who knew her,

<hr/>

[2] *The Life of Bishop Wilfrid, by Eddius Stephanus*, ed. B. Colgrave (1927), ch. XXXIV, p. 71.

'blessed not only to herself but to the many who desired to live uprightly' (*EH IV*, 23). Her father had been poisoned by a British king and it is likely that Hilda was subsequently brought up at Edwin's court; she was certainly there on the occasion of Edwin's conversion to Christianity when she too was baptised, probably aged about thirteen. In Bede's *Ecclesiastical History*, we hear of her next in her early thirties in East Anglia on the point of departure for Francia to join her sister at the monastery of Chelles, a house favoured by Anglo-Saxon aristocratic women since they had as yet no such institutions in their homelands. The probability is that Hilda was by now a young widow; all that is certain is that before she could set out for Chelles a summons came to her from the Northumbrian bishop and missionary, Aidan, asking her to return home and giving her land where she could follow the monastic life.

The monastic life in Anglo-Saxon England, as led by both men and women, has recently been the subject of much research and discussion. It has become increasingly clear that monasteries were founded not as retreats from the world but as a means of both Christianising and ruling it. The glories of their buildings proclaimed the might of their founders and the majesty of their new God. Bede's own monastery of Jarrow was built with all the most up-to-date splendour; a double monastery such as Abbess Bugga founded in Wessex was renowned for the glories of the church, glistening with its 'many ornaments': 'a golden cloth with … twisted threads' over the altar; 'a golden chalice covered with jewels'; a Cross made of 'burnished gold, adorned … with silver and jewels'.[3] Such magnificence was part and parcel of a monastery's function; it had to act as beacon of both royal and divine power. It needed to look the part. Not for nothing did Bede claim that the original name for Whitby, *Streanaeshealh*, meant 'bay of the light-house' (*EH III*, 25).

Anglo-Saxon monasteries, such as Whitby, were frequently 'double houses', that is, they were communities founded for men and women under the command of an abbess rather than an abbot. Bede mentions nine such houses, but the recent estimate by Roberta Gilchrist suggests that throughout the country there may well have been as many as fifty. In every known case the first abbess was of royal birth. Her duties were

[3] *Aldhelm: The Poetic Works*, trans. M. Lapidge and J. Rosier (1985), p. 49.

not only to pray for the salvation of her kin but also to organise her house so as to provide a spiritual and administrative centre for the surrounding countryside. In the aftermath of the conversion the pastoral responsibilities that would later be assumed by parish churches under diocesan control seem to have been regularly exercised in this way. Whitby itself established a number of dependent communities throughout Northumbria in order to fulfil these pastoral obligations. As late as the eleventh century, as Alan Thacker has shown, evidence of this early activity at Whitby can still be found. Despite Viking attacks on the monastery, Whitby remained the centre of a valuable estate, retaining the ownership of around forty ruined oratories.[4]

Whitby's first abbess was Hilda. Within a year of her return to Northumbria Aidan had appointed her abbess of Hartlepool, a foundation renowned as the work of the nun Heiu, a pioneer of whom we know little except that she was 'said to have been the first woman in the Northumbrian kingdom to take the vows and habit of a nun, having been ordained by Bishop Aidan' (*EH IV,* 23). Hilda's rule at Hartlepool, following Heiu's retirement to live elsewhere, was characterised by Bede in terms of her friendships with men, relationships of the kind which later generations, bred in a different climate, would do their best to foreswear. Hilda worked assisted 'by many learned men' – 'for bishop Aidan and other devout men who knew her visited her frequently, instructed her assiduously, and loved her heartily for her innate wisdom and her devotion to the service of God'. In 657 she was entrusted with Whitby where 'not only ordinary people but also kings and princes sometimes sought and received her counsel when in difficulties' (*EH IV,* 23).

To students of Anglo-Saxon history and its literature, Whitby has become famous for two reasons: it was the scene of the great synod of 664 where the vexed question as to the correct method of calculating the date of Easter was at last settled and it was where the cowherd Caedmon, inspired by God and encouraged by Hilda, composed the first Anglo-Saxon poem, his much-famed verses 'in praise of God the Creator' (*EH IV,* 24). There is no need either to unravel the

---

[4] A. Thacker, 'Monks, Preaching and Pastoral Care in Early Anglo-Saxon England', in J. Blair and R. Sharpe (eds), *Pastoral Care Before the Parish* (1992), pp. 143–4.

intricacies of the Easter controversy, or to delve into recent analyses of the mythology behind the Caedmon story, to understand how Hilda is placed in these two stories in a pivotal role. It is a role derived not only from the nobility of Hilda's birth but also from the status of Whitby, under Hilda, as educational centre and seminary. 'She compelled those under her direction', so Bede tells us,

> to devote so much time to the study of Holy Scriptures and so much time to the performance of good works, that there might be no difficulty in finding many there who were fitted for holy orders, that is, for the service of the altar. We have in fact seen five from this monastery who afterwards became bishops, all of them men of singular merit and holiness; their names are Bosa, Aetla, Oftfor, John and Wilfrid. (*EH IV*, 23)

Bosa, Aetla, Oftfor, John and Wilfrid: these were monks of Whitby with great futures, but their origins, unlike that of their abbess, may have been of the humblest. It is worth remembering that in the age of the conversion there seems to have been something of a shortage not so much of person-power, but precisely of man-power. Despite the evident enthusiasm for monasticism on the part of a number of aristocratic young men – Benedict Biscop, the founder of Bede's own monastery at Jarrow, being the most obvious example – there still seems to have been a dearth of clergy in seventh-century England, a situation which Bishop Aidan attempted to remedy by buying up slaves so that they could be trained for the priesthood, just as, some decades later, manumitted slaves would be sent to join the mission in Germany. We also need to remember that England's best-known heroes of the conversion, St Cuthbert, Bishop and hermit of Lindisfarne, and Bede, were themselves both men of no fixed social identity. Nothing at all is known about Bede's parents and there is uncertainty about Cuthbert's. One of the reasons for the comparatively early success of the *Rule of Benedict* (*c*.540) in England may have been because it was a rule so well suited to native circumstances, directed, as Henry Mayr-Harting has shown, towards the 'systematic obliteration of all class distinctions within the monastery, and of all signs of the monks' previous standing in the world. Basic and repeated is the insistence that there should be no respect of persons.'[5] Slave-born and free-born must be taught to live

---

[5] H. Mayr-Harting, *The Venerable Bede, The Rule of St Benedict and Social Class* (Jarrow Lecture 1976), p. 3.

together. It was evidently a lesson well-suited to English monasteries where manumitted slaves might find themselves
living side by side with nobility. None the less, it would be
unrealistic not to suppose that there was much to be said for
entrusting authority to an aristocratic abbess who, by virtue
of her birth, would have had the authority to exercise
command over the men in her care, to persuade them, as Hilda
did, to hold their property in common and to live together 'in
peace and charity' (*EH IV*, 23).

Such men not only had to learn to live as a community; they
were also, as we have seen from Bede's description of Whitby,
expected to take to scholarship. Though this may have
appealed to some – men such as Aldhelm of Malmesbury who
could even find tackling fractions an exciting challenge – it
still went against the (male) barbarian grain. As Patrick
Wormald has pointed out, barbarian suspicion of the effects
of learning was tenacious and of long standing; hence Pro-
copius's tale of the outcome of the attempts of Amalasuntha,
daughter of Theodoric the Ostrogoth, to organise a Roman-
style education for her son. The Goths would have none of it:
'letters', they said, 'are far removed from manliness . . . the man
who is to show daring and be great in renown ought to be free
from the timidity which teachers inspire and take his training
in arms'.[6] It is interesting to compare this Gothic reaction with
the experience of nineteenth-century missionaries in Africa
who found that groups of boys would rush into the school-
room, 'proudly gaze at the alphabet board and with an air of
disdain mimic the names of letters pronounced by the school-
master and repeated by the girls, as if it were a thing only fit
for females'.[7] Certainly, in Anglo-Saxon England it seems to
have been the women who took to the bookish life with particular enthusiasm, seeing themselves perhaps as the suc-
cessors of the holy women who had sat at the feet of St Jerome.

Excavations at the monastery of Whitby and at the newly
discovered sites of Flixborough in Humberside and Brandon
in Suffolk, both of which were almost certainly double monasteries, have uncovered plentiful evidence of busy *scriptoria*
where nuns would have copied manuscripts. We do not know

[6] P. Wormald, 'The Uses of Literacy in Anglo-Saxon England and its Neighbours',
Transactions of the Royal Historical Society, 5th series, 27 (1977), p. 98.
[7] F. Bowie *et. al.* (eds), *Women and Missions: Past and Present* (1993), p. 113.

of any women authors, as opposed to scribes, in these communities although the possibility that the *Life* of Pope Gregory, the earliest native hagiography, was composed at Whitby by a woman rather than by a man is at last being seriously entertained. But while the questioning of the gender of the authors of anonymous works is an exercise both salutary and necessary, it is not on such tendentious grounds that the claim for the importance of the contribution of women's literacy to the progress of the conversion needs to rest.

At this point we must move south to Wessex, where at Wimborne in the early eighth century – at about the time that Bede was at work in Jarrow on the *Ecclesiastical History* – a devout couple were at last blessed with a longed-for child, Leoba. In thanksgiving Leoba is dedicated to God, a dedication which in the terms of her *Life* (written within some sixty years of her death) is seen to entail learning. (It is not without interest that it was Leoba's mother's nurse who, having foretold Leoba's birth by interpreting a dream, insists on this course of action.) As soon as she was old enough Leoba was sent to join the monastic community of Wimborne 'to be taught the sacred sciences.' At Wimborne,

> the girl grew up and was taught with such care by the abbess and all the nuns that she had no interests other than the monastery and the pursuit of sacred knowledge. She took no pleasure in aimless jests and wasted no time on girlish romances, but, fired by the love of God, fixed her mind always on reading or hearing the word of God. Whatever she heard or read she committed to memory and put all that she had learnt into practice.[8]

For Leoba, then, word and deed are inseparable. One night she has a dream; as if she were herself one of those thread-boxes found in women's graves, she finds herself pulling out of her mouth a stream of purple thread which, as it fills her hands, she proceeds to wind – with some desperation since the thread is endless – into a ball. As at the time of her conception, an old woman is called upon to interpret the dream, 'an aged nun ... known to possess the spirit of prophecy'. The interpretation was allegorical. The nun tells the disciple whom Leoba sends to her:

---

[8] 'Life of Leoba', ed. and trans. C. Talbot, *The Anglo-Saxon Missionaries in Germany* (1954), pp. 212–13.

These things were revealed to a person whose holiness and wisdom make her a worthy recipient [i.e. Leoba] because by her teaching and good example she will confer benefits on many people. The thread which came from her bowels and issued from her mouth signifies the wise counsels that she will speak from the heart. The fact that it filled her hand means she will carry out in her actions whatever she expresses in her words ... By these signs God shows that your mistress will profit many by her words and example, and the effect of them will be felt in other lands afar off whither she will go.[9]

'Other lands' turn out to be Germany where Leoba is summoned to join the mission of her kinsman St Boniface, at his insistence, and for many of the same reasons, one may suppose, that had made the help of Hilda seem desirable to Aidan. Boniface, monk and bishop, as was Aidan, had set himself the task of converting the pagans of Germany, hoping to include the 'old Saxons' who were of 'the same blood and bone' as the Saxons of England.[10] High on the list of obstacles which Boniface encountered were shortage of helpers and shortage of books and although women could not of course become priests, they could still do much to remedy both defects. Hence the appeal of Boniface to his kinswoman, Leoba: 'when she came, the man of God received her with the deepest reverence, holding her in great affection, not so much because she was related to him on his mother's side as because he knew that by her holiness and wisdom she would confer many benefits by her word and example.'[11]

Boniface appointed Leoba abbess of Bischofsheim in Mainz where she became 'one of the lynch-pins of his mission',[12] renowned for her teaching, for her 'zeal for reading', for her knowledge not only of scripture but also of 'the writings of the Church Fathers, the decrees of the Councils and the whole of ecclesiastical law'.[13] She is described as a woman 'so extremely learned' that even when seemingly asleep she would know if the nun whose duty it was to read scripture to her had skipped over a single word or syllable. Her disciples became abbesses, as Hilda's followers had become bishops, and, like Hilda, she is said to be a fount of wisdom for all in

[9] *Ibid.*
[10] C. Talbot, *op. cit.*, p. 96.
[11] 'Life of Leoba', p. 214.
[12] H. Mayr-Harting, *The Coming of Christianity to England* (3rd edn 1991), p. 268.
[13] *Ibid.*, p. 215.

authority: 'the princes loved her, the nobles received her, the bishops welcomed her with joy. And because of her wide knowledge of the Scriptures and her prudence in counsel they often discussed spiritual matters and ecclesiastical discipline with her.'[14]

Despite hints of homesickness Leoba's commitment to Boniface and his mission was such that she stayed in Germany for the rest of her life, long after Boniface himself had met martyrdom at the hands of the Frisians. On what proved to be his last journey he is said to have given Leoba his cowl and to have commended her to the monks of Fulda, telling them that she was to share his tomb 'so that they who had served God during their lifetime with equal sincerity and zeal should await together the day of resurrection'.[15] This was not, in the event, a wish that was respected; despite the impeccable precedent from the *Dialogues* of Gregory the Great for a joint tomb for St Benedict and his sister, the monks of Fulda seem to have felt that they had made enough concessions to Leoba in her lifetime in allowing her – alone among women – entry into their monastery to pray.

The note of misogyny which creeps in at the end of Leoba's *Life*, with the refusal of the monks to respect Boniface's wishes concerning Leoba's burial and their insistence on the rigorous and exceptional conditions that surrounded her visits to their monastery, should not mislead us into assuming this to have been always an issue. Especially close though the relationship between Leoba and Boniface undoubtedly was, it was not as unusual as Leoba's *Life* implies. As we know from Otloh's *Life of Boniface*, Leoba was in fact only one of the select group who joined Boniface's team – and not even, initially at least, its most prominent member; Otloh's narrative lists 'truly religious women, namely the maternal aunt of St Lull named Cynehild, and her daughter Berhtgyth, Cynethryth and Tecla, Leoba and Waldburg, the sister of Willibald and Wynnebald. But Cynehild and her daughter Berthgyth, very learned in the liberal arts, were appointed as teachers in the region of Thuringia.' Moreover, the rich collection of letters exchanged between Boniface, his friends and his disciples (generally known as the 'Boniface correspondence' even though its scope

[14] *Ibid.*, p. 223.
[15] *Ibid.*, p. 222.

is wider than that) bears vivid testimony, in the words of
Christine Fell, to the 'friendly co-operation between men and
women in religious communities';[16] testimony, moreover, that
such co-operation was reckoned to be not something special,
but rather the order of the day.

The men and women of the 'Boniface correspondence' are
bound together not only by a mutual aim – the furtherance of
Christianity – nor, though this was the case for a number of
them, by their shared experience of life in exile from England,
but equally by their common literacy and intellectual pursuits,
their delight in 'the liberal arts'. They wrote to each other as
much to display new-found skills as to invite criticism. The
one surviving letter from Leoba to Boniface dates from her
Wimborne days; it is a letter requesting not only Boniface's
prayers but also his help with her verse composition, her
teacher up to now having been her mistress Eadburga. From
the sample of verse Leoba adds to her letter, it is evident that
Eadburga had taught her pupil from Aldhelm of Malmesbury's treatise on the writing of Latin verse, the standard
work to which both men and women of any intellectual pre-
tension had recourse. But to infer from this letter that it was
customary for women to submit their work to men for criticism, and not vice versa, would be wide of the mark. Abbess
Cyniburg, for example (abbess possibly of Inkberrow in
Worcestershire), received a plea from the missionaries Lull,
Denehard and Burghard to correct the *rusticitas* of their letter
to her; conventional politeness this may have been, but there
is more to it than that. As Fell has pointed out, the whole letter
is written with 'love and deference',[17] in a tone that suggests a
relationship comparable to that we may suppose to have
existed between Hilda and those of her pupils who went on
to become bishops.

Elegant composition was one thing; quite another was the
problem of how to provide missionaries and seminaries with
the necessary books. This was a task to which women contributed their fair share. The monastery of Chelles, for which
Hilda, according to Bede, had once been destined and where
her sister was a nun, was a notable source, 'many volumes of

[16] C. Fell, 'Some Implications of the Boniface Correspondence', in H. Damico and
A. Hennessey Olsen (eds), *New Readings On Women in Old English Literature* (1990),
p. 31.
[17] *Ibid.*, p. 32.

books' being disseminated by its abbess Bertila (c.660–710). Bertila had been appointed abbess by the founder of the monastery, the Frankish Queen Balthild, herself of Anglo-Saxon birth, and she maintained, according to her *Life*, a number of links with England:

Faithful kings from the parts of Saxondom across the seas [i.e. England] would ask her through trusty messengers to send them some of her followers for teaching or sacred instruction (which they had heard that she possessed to a marvellous degree), or even those who might establish monasteries of men and women in that region. For the good of their souls, she did not refuse this religious request; rather, with the counsel of the elders and the encouragement of the brothers did she send, with a thankful heart, chosen women and very devout men thither with great diligence, with both saints' relics and many volumes of books, so that through her the yield of souls increased even in that people and, by the grace of God, was multiplied.[18]

In England, Leoba's teacher Eadburga was among those upon whom Boniface relied for his texts: he thanks her for 'the useful gifts of books and vestments' which she has already sent and asks her to continue 'the good work' she has begun of copying out for him in letters of gold the Epistles of St Peter.[19] And he sends her the gold to do the job. It is Boniface's hope that such a glorious edition will help to inspire the pagans to whom he is preaching the holy scripture with reverence and love but from an earlier letter to Eadburga it is clear that her 'gifts of spiritual books' brought to Boniface himself 'consolation' in his 'exile in Germany', 'for no man can shed light on these gloomy lurking places of the German people and take heed of the snares that beset his path unless he have the Word of God as a lamp to guide his feet and a light to shine the way'.[20]

Eadburga's deeds will henceforth, like the words of St Peter, 'shine in gold' to the glory of God;[21] yet however laudatory is the praise lavished on her intellectual efforts, or indeed on those of her pupil Leoba or of Hilda, it must still pale in comparison with that heaped upon the nuns of Barking in

[18] *Life of Bertila*, ch. 6. Cited in P. Sims-Williams, *Religion and Literature in Western England, 600–800* (1990), p. 110.
[19] C. Talbot, *op. cit.*, p. 91.
[20] *Ibid.*, p. 88.
[21] *Ibid.*, p. 92.

Essex by Aldhelm of Malmesbury in the time of their abbess Hildelith.

To call the nuns of Barking 'bluestockings' would be something of a bad joke, chastised as they were by Aldhelm for the variegated colours they chose to wear. Such strictures apart, Aldhelm's treatise *On Virginity*, written at the request of the community, is fulsome in its acclamation of the nuns' virtue and learning; at the same time it provides us with the fullest account we have of the curriculum which a double monastery might follow.

Aldhelm's nuns are as industrious as 'the highly ingenious bee ... roaming widely through the flowering fields of scripture.' They 'energetically plumb' the prophets of the Old Testament; 'scrutinise with careful application' the precepts of Mosaic law; 'explore wisely' the fourfold interpretation of the Gospels; 'rummage through old stories of the historians and the entries of chroniclers' before they move on to 'sagacious inquiry' into the 'rules of the grammarians and the teaching of experts on spelling and the rules of metrics.'[22] They consult patristic commentaries, and have at hand works such as Gregory the Great's *Moralia in Job* and Cassian's *Collationes Patrum*. If Aldhelm is to be believed they learn their lessons well; 'the mellifluous studies of the Holy Scriptures' are 'made manifest in the extremely subtle sequence of [Abbess Hildelith's] discourse'; her nuns write 'with a rich verbal eloquence' that elicits Aldhelm's admiration.[23]

Of course, Aldhelm's treatise is not, fundamentally, about scholarship or learning; it is about virginity, that 'special attribute' ... 'believed to be next kin to angelic beatitude'. But as has often been pointed out, there is something of a problem here for Aldhelm. Many of the nuns for whom he is writing were not virgins; they were just as likely to be widows or 'retired' wives. Among those to whom *On Virginity* is dedicated is a certain Cuthburg, generally thought to be a sister of King Ine of Wessex, who in mid-career separated from her husband Aldfrith, king of Northumbria, to join the community at Barking before going on to found one at Wimborne. This scenario was envisaged and provided for by ecclesiastical legislation, but there was still the possibility in such a com-

[22] *Aldhelm: The Prose Works*, trans. M. Lapidge and M. Herren (1979), p. 62.
[23] *Ibid.*, p. 59.

munity that 'ex-wives' might be disparaged by 'true virgins'. Aldhelm's response to this situation is to take over and then adapt the traditional tripartite division of the female life-cycle: virginity, widowhood and marriage. The hierarchy now includes the state of 'chastity', reserved for the once married who have chosen to move on to the higher form of life which a monastery is known to offer. And in any case, explains Aldhelm, virginity is not to be defined literally: 'pure virginity is preserved only in the fortress of the free mind rather than being contained in the restricted confines of the flesh.'[24]

The implications of Aldhelm's treatise are of more than local interest. The *amour propre* of the nuns of Barking was not all that was at stake. The special status a nun enjoyed as the bride of Christ was not just a matter of personal pride and concern; the relationship had implications for the nun's earthly family quite as much as for her heavenly future. The holiness of such women redounded to the honour of their male kin and the lineage they shared. Kingdoms acquired through bloodshed and treachery could be redeemed by the prayer of virgins. For fathers and brothers, a daughter or sister in a convent was not a woman 'disposed of' but a woman put to work to add sanctity and legitimacy to newly, often nefariously, acquired lordships. For royal women it was thus a privilege and a duty to consecrate themselves to the new God; it was a way both of signalling this allegiance and of ensuring his support.

No early Anglo-Saxon kingdom of any standing could afford to be lacking in royal women saints. The East Anglian record is particularly impressive. Four daughters of King Anna came to be thus venerated: Aethelthryth, Aethelburh, Sexburga (widow of the king of Kent) and Withburga. However, it is Aethelthryth of whom we know the most since it was she who attracted the attention of Bede. Twice married, once to Tondberht of the South Gyrwe and for twelve years to King Ecgfrith of Northumbria, throughout both matches Aethelthryth kept her virginity intact. Her long-held wish was at last granted, so Bede tells us, when Ecgfrith gave her permission to leave him and become a nun; within a year of taking the veil she returned to her native kingdom where she founded and took charge of the monastery of Ely (possibly the first double monastery in eastern England between the Thames

[24] *Ibid.*, p. 129.

34

and the Humber). There she lived with perfect humility and in great austerity, never wearing linen and strictly rationing her hot baths, until her death seven years later.

After a further sixteen years the new abbess (who was in fact her sister) decided to transport Aethelthryth's bones to a place of honour. The old coffin was opened; Aethelthryth was found to be not only incorrupt but even miraculously healed of a gaping wound she had had when buried. In honour of this 'queen and bride of Christ' (*EH IV*, 20) Bede exceptionally breaks into verse; Aethelthryth is placed in the company of the virgin martyrs and fitted with a harp to accompany songs to her heavenly bridegroom. The clothes in which her body had been clad have assumed curative powers.

The twentieth-century reader is likely to find Aethelthryth's story implausible or incomprehensible, or both. (S)he is likely to feel a much greater affinity with the scholarly (possible widowed) Hilda about whose personal habits we know nothing but whose work bears practical fruit even to the extent that the harp in her story is put into the hands of the cowherd Caedmon as an instrument for missionary teaching rather than for heavenly twanging. And yet, despite Bede's admiration and respect for Hilda and the assurance he gives us that on her death she was taken straight to heaven, he does not mention her cult or any associated relics or cures. Hilda is loved and remembered in the *Ecclesiastical History* as a 'mother of all', a figure who inspires affection but whom no quasi-legendary character attaches. The power of the virginal Aethelthryth, on the other hand, is such that even after the Norman Conquest four hundred years later hers is still a name to conjure with.

The contrast between the hagiographical treatment given to Aethelthryth and the seemingly historical character of Bede's account of Hilda has not passed unnoticed though its meaning has been disputed; it is possible that what we have are simply different links in the chain attempting to hold together newly formed (and as yet very fragile) kingdoms. In the making of this chain both 'mothers' and 'virgins' are needed; the roles are not mutually exclusive. At the risk of simplification, it seems reasonable to understand the former in terms of a pagan tradition of womanly influence and behaviour; the latter as being in the process of development under the influence of Christian teaching. Thus, although for the better part of the

Middle Ages virginity would come to be a necessary pre-requisite for female sanctity, in the age of the conversion this was not yet so, though with his paean for Aethelfryth, Bede can be seen as pointing the way forward.

As Roberta Gilchrist has recently suggested, this new 'discourse of celibacy' operated differently for women than it did for men; male priests became 'accessible to others' through their vows of virginity whereas women became 'private spaces inaccessible to others'.[25] In the age of the conversion this was a transformation that was not as yet apparent. At Whitby, Hilda and indeed her successor as abbess, Aelfflaed, are both described by Bede as 'maternal'; they act as mediators in politics, Hilda notably in her hosting of the disputants in the Easter controversy, Aelfflaed some years later at the Council of Nidd where – 'always the comforter and best councillor of the whole province' (according to the *Life of Wilfrid*)[26] – she helps to bring to a peaceful conclusion the long-drawn-out conflict between Bishop Wilfrid and her king. Neither Hilda nor Aelfflaed would be out of place in a Dark Age epic. Their monastic vocations are, like the marriages in such epics, arranged with an eye to the peace of the kingdom. The timing of the recall of Hilda (a Deiran princess) to the north is no coincidence, coming as it does in the wake of King Oswui of Bernicia's attempts to reunite the two provinces of Northumbria, Deira and Bernicia, after the defeat of his Mercian neighbour Penda and his elimination of Oswine, his Deiran partner. Aelfflaed's entry into the religious life is part of the same drama. She is vowed to God by Oswui in return for victory against Penda together with land – six estates from Deira and six from Bernicia – for the building of monasteries.

On her death Aelfflaed was buried at Whitby, alongside her parents, Oswiu and Eanflaed, and her grandfather Edwin. A monastery such as this was a family concern, founded for its spiritual welfare and entrusted to its kin-group. Time and again an abbess was succeeded by sister or daughter. Aelfflaed herself for a while shared the governance of Whitby with her widowed mother. For women such as these, running a monastery may have been similar in many respects to the

[25] R. Gilchrist, *Gender and Material Culture: The Archaeology of Religious Women* (1994), pp. 18–19.
[26] *Life of Bishop Wilfrid, op. cit.*, ch. LX.

tasks which any noblewoman in the world would have been expected to undertake: presiding over the women's quarters of a secular hall, receiving guests, accepting the responsibility of foster children. The stories Bede tells of the affection felt by the nun Frigyth for Hilda, or of Edith of Barking for the little boy Aesica who was 'learning his lessons in the dwelling of the maidens' (*EH IV*, 8), is testimony to the familial atmosphere of these institutions. Likewise the abbess of a double monastery was entrusted with the care of a vast number of dependants, with the welfare of her servants and with the education – a new kind of fostering – of postulants and children, as well as with the duties of hospitality and the administration of estates. Aelfflaed, in Bede's *Life of Cuthbert*, is depicted in just such a guise; while giving a meal to Cuthbert, Bishop of Lindisfarne, at one of her monastery's estates where he has some to con-secrate a church, a shepherd falls out of a tree and mortally injures himself; next day Aelfflaed's urgent concern is that Cuthbert will pray for the shepherd during the Mass for the dedication of the church.

Introducing Aelfflaed in his *Life of Cuthbert*, Bede calls her 'a holy handmaid of Christ ... who as one of the joys of her virginal state, had charge of a great number of nuns. She looked after them with motherly love, adding to her royal rank the yet more noble adornment of a high degree of holiness.'[27] Virginal, maternal, royal and holy: it was a daunting job description for the aspirant female saint of the seventh century but a remarkable number took on the challenge. And yet, already in Aelfflaed's time, there were changes afoot. Though described by Bede as a teacher, it is unlikely that her role in this respect measured up in any way to Hilda's. The need had passed. The arrival of Archbishop Theodore in 669 with Abbot Hadrian, and the opening of their school at Canterbury, her-alded a new era. Theodore's known disapproval of double monasteries, moreover, even though he took no active mea-sures against them, can have done nothing to improve their morale. One by one their functions were usurped; kings came to rely less on the charisma gained from the sanctity of their great abbesses, more on unction bestowed by bishops and on masses said by priest-monks. But it would be anachronistic to lament the demise of double monasteries without at the same

---

[27] 'Life of Cuthbert', ch. 23, trans. J. F. Webb, *The Age of Bede* (1983), p. 72.

time recognising the burden of running them. The 'Boniface correspondence' includes a letter from a certain Abbess Eangyth asking for Boniface's support for the pilgrimage which she and her widowed daughter wished to make. Her position in England was more than she could bear; her pastoral responsibilities – her 'care for the souls of those of either sex and of every age which have been entrusted to us' – were too heavy; far from having royal support – significantly those in power do not seem to have been related to her – she was subject to harassment and taxation. She yearns to give up her post and set sail for Rome.[28]

Whether Eangyth and her daughter reached Rome we do not know; Boniface's reply to her has not survived. We are, however, aware that in general Boniface's views on women making pilgrimages seem to have undergone a change. The sympathy he shows in a letter to Abbess Bugga, intent on such a journey – 'do what God's grace shall inspire you to do'[29] – was replaced some years later with disapproval and anxiety. He tells the Archbishop of Canterbury

that it would be well and favourable for the honour and purity of your church ... if your synod and your princes would forbid matrons and veiled women to make these frequent journeys back and forth to Rome. A great part of them perish and few keep their virtue. There are very few towns in Lombardy or Frankland or Gaul in which there is not a courtesan or a harlot of English stock. It is a scandal and disgrace to your whole church.[30]

Strong words; whether they are evidence of genuine 'scandal and disgrace' or of a new, misogynistic climate is hard to tell. But it seems likely that in what may be called the second phase of the conversion, in the organisation of the Church's administrative structures under Archbishop Theodore and beyond, changed perceptions of women were used to justify a diminution of their activities and in their role. When Augustine had written to Gregory the Great seeking advice on various points of missionary strategy, one of his questions had been whether a menstruating woman could take communion; the Pope had replied that it was a matter of choice. The ruling of the eighth-century *Penitential of Theodore* on the same issue was

[28] *St Boniface: The Letters*, ed. and trans. E. Emerton (1940), pp. 36–40.
[29] C. Talbot, *op. cit.*, p. 84.
[30] C. Talbot, *op. cit.*, p. 133.

quite different: 'Women shall not in the time of impurity enter a church or communicate – neither nuns nor laywomen; if they presume [to do this] they shall fast for three weeks.'[31] This emphasis on ritual impurity on the one hand justified the eventual exclusion of women from assisting in the celebration of Mass, and on the other it heightened admiration for those women who had against all the odds preserved their virginity and thus, in some sense at least, had overcome the demands of the flesh.

What would come to be of paramount interest was not – as it had been for Aldhelm – virginity of the mind; nor, as for Bede, actual virginity (as in the case of Aethelfryth), but rather the struggles of any virgin persecuted or pursued. Thus when the stories of Anglo-Saxon saints came to be rewritten after 1066, to suit Norman tastes, the bestsellers are not about how men and women worked together in the period of the conversion, but about conflicts between them. In such retellings Aethelfryth has literally to escape from the clutches of Ecgfrith; only the miraculous interpositioning of the sea saves her from his evil grasp. St Cuthbert, meanwhile, albeit buried in a shroud made for him by an abbess friend, becomes in Norman England a saint whose hatred of women is such that none dare approach his tomb for fear his curse should fall upon them. But within these parameters, there was, as we shall see in Chapters Nine and Ten, still room for interactions of quite different kinds.

---

[31] J. McNeill and H. Gamer (trans.), *Medieval Handbooks of Penance* (1990), p. 197.

CHAPTER THREE

Law Codes

For an account of the origins of Anglo-Saxon law codes we must turn once again to Bede's *Ecclesiastical History.* King Aethelbert of Kent, 'the first [English] king to enter the kingdom of heaven' according to Bede, died in 616, twenty-one years after the date of his conversion. In his obituary notice Bede records Aethelbert's law-making as one of his greatest achievements: a fine display, to Bede, of the king's new status as a Christian ruler with access not only to heaven but also to earthly benefits, to the uses of literacy and the inheritance of Rome. He writes:

among other benefits which he conferred upon the race under his care, he established with the help of his counsellors a code of laws after the Roman manner. These are written in English and are still kept and observed by the people. Among these he set down first of all what restitution must be made by anyone who steals anything belonging to the church or the bishop or any other clergy; these laws were designed to give protection to those whose coming and whose teaching he had welcomed. *(EH II, 5)*

These laws have long been famed both as the earliest set of written laws of any of the new Germanic kingdoms of post-Roman Europe and as the first known document to be written in the Anglo-Saxon language. They make, none the less, baffling reading particularly for anyone coming to them with expectations drawn from a knowledge of later law codes or indeed from Bede's description. And, as we shall see, what they have to tell us about the position of women in Anglo-Saxon society is far from clear.

Aethelbert's code is made up of ninety clauses; the first

clause alone relates to the Church, to the penalties incurred for damaging its property or disturbing its peace. Nowhere in the remaining eighty-nine clauses does there at first sight seem to be any hint of the influence of Christianity (a subject to which we will return). The immediate impression is that the laws are concerned not with moral norms but with the provision of a tariff of compensations; they seem, despite the ecclesiastical context in which Bede has set them, to be no more nor less than Germanic custom transmitted to writing. Thus the code is concerned with the cost of reparation in cases of wounded honour and physical injury, with attaching a price not just to homicide but to grievous bodily harm of every imaginable kind, from the seizing of your enemy by his hair to the gouging out of his eyes or the removal of the nails from his big toe. Seventh-century Kent was emphatically not a society that believed in 'an eye for an eye'; it believed strongly in unequal rights. Thus the king's *fedesl* (something like a fatted calf) might be considered more valuable than a man's life; it all depended on which man: what was his class? was he free, half-free or a slave? Every man and woman knew his or her worth; this was known as *wergeld*. Compensation for injuries suffered, or for death (payable to the surviving kin), were calculated accordingly.

The clauses in Aethelbert's code relating specifically to women are based on the same principles. There is *prima facie* no evidence here of Christian teaching. Women in this society may be abducted – whether forcibly or as a form of elopement to thwart an arranged match is not clear – but in any event cash payments settle the outcome. If the woman is a slave, 50 shillings will be paid to her owner in compensation, and a further sum is due to buy his consent; if the woman is betrothed 'at a price' to another man, 20 shillings shall be paid as compensation; if, on the other hand, the woman is then returned, the abductor faces a fine of 35 shillings, with a further 15 shillings owed to the king. A separate tariff applies to abducted and assaulted widows, depending on their class. Likewise, casual sexual encounters are not so much condemned as priced; the price depends upon the status of the woman concerned, a status derived from her occupation and from that of her owner. Thus a fine of 50 shillings was due for sleeping 'with a maiden belonging to the king', 25 shillings for sleeping with a woman from the special class of slaves employed to grind grain, 20 shillings if the woman in question was a nobleman's cup-bearer.

A matter of some importance – but equally of dispute – in determining the status of women in early Saxon society is to whom the compensation should be paid: to the women or to her master? Similar problems of interpretation attach to the discussion of adultery in clause 31:

If a freeman lies with the wife of another freeman he shall pay his (or her) *wergeld* and get another wife with his own money and bring her to the other man's home.

Quite apart from the fact that it is unclear which *wergeld* is meant – that of the husband, the adulterous freeman or the wife – there is a marked contrast with the solution proposed here and the various forms of death and torture meted out to adulterous wives in Germany as described (and admired) by St Boniface in a letter to King Aethelbald of Mercia. All the same, clause 31 has been censured as exhibiting 'a crude view of marriage', regulating, as it seemingly does, the practice of wife-purchase; according to this interpretation a woman is simply a chattel to be bought and sold as convenient. Other explanations are, however, possible. Getting married was costly, and it was in the interests of the woman that this should be so. From the groom a morning gift, the *morgengifu*, was necessary, either in the form of money or in land. This was not a way of buying the woman but rather endowing her; the *morgengifu* was hers to keep, to do with as she chose. It gave her security in the event of her husband's death. Should she, on the other hand, leave her husband for another man it was not then unreasonable to expect the new lover at least to ensure that the first husband could afford to find himself another bride. Similarly, the husband who took a bride, paid her her morning gift, and then found that there had been some 'fraud', was entitled to take the woman back to her natal home and to demand the return of his gift. It is not clear here quite what constituted 'fraud'; the main anxiety, probably, was to protect the man from the possibility of endowing a woman who was already pregnant with another man's child. The concern was almost certainly not with sexual morality and the virginity of the bride but with property.

Property and not propriety is likely, too, to lie behind the much-debated clause 73 of Aethelbert's code:

if a freeborn, lock-bearing, woman misconducts herself she shall pay 30 shillings as compensation.

The key word here (in more senses than one) is 'lock-bearing': this has often been translated as if it were a description of long and, by implication, wanton hair. The 30 shillings becomes than a fine for lascivious behaviour. But, as Christine Fell has recently argued, it is more realistic to take the literal meaning of 'lock-bearing', even if less colourful; the reference then concerns those women with keys – whom we have already met in cemeteries – and how they are to be punished for dishonest dealings with the goods entrusted to them. That Anglo-Saxon women could be expected to have sole responsibility for certain 'locked places' is made quite clear from the eleventh-century law code of King Cnut. In this instance a woman cannot be asked to share her husband's guilt in a case of theft unless the stolen goods are found in any of the places for which she has the key.

The lack of any influence of a Christian sexual ethic among the newly converted Anglo-Saxons has been noted by Margaret Clunies Ross who has shown that in the early sources there is only one Anglo-Saxon word, *haemaed*, used for sexual intercourse, irrespective of context.[1] Only gradually are compound words such as *unrihthaemed* and *wohhaemed* formed to describe 'unlawful' or 'wrongful' intercourse. Even then, the gravity of sexual offences remained contingent on status and rank. Penalties for fornication varied depending not only on whether the woman concerned was married or betrothed but also on the value of her *wergeld*. It is clear, moreover, that even after Christianity had become well-established, Christian sexual teaching was little heeded, least of all by kings who perhaps found Old Testament models of behaviour more congenial than the precepts of St Paul. Even if they did not all behave as badly as the mid-eighth-century Aethelbald of Mercia – of whom St Boniface was informed that he had 'never taken a lawful wife ... but had been driven by lust into sins of fornication ... in various monasteries with holy nuns,'[2] none the less throughout the period Anglo-Saxon kings regularly had more than one wife.

[1] M. Clunies Ross, 'Concubinage in Anglo-Saxon England', *Past and Present* 108 (1985), pp. 3–34.
[2] C. H. Talbot (ed. and trans.) *The Anglo-Saxon Missionaries in Germany* (1954), p. 121.

Although in a number of instances it would seem that kings practised serial monogamy, Cnut, after 1016 king of Denmark and England, had both a recognised queen, Emma, and a recognised concubine, Aelfgifu (of Northampton). The arrangement has been described as if it was peculiarly Scandinavian in origin – Aelfgifu was Cnut's wife 'according to Danish custom' – whereas in all likelihood there were plenty of Anglo-Saxon precedents for his behaviour; a different Aelfgifu appears as a witness to a charter of King Edmund, described as 'Aelfgifu the concubine of the king'. In Northumbria in an earlier period, the seventh century, King Oswui is succeeded by Aldfrith, his son by an Irish concubine. In Ireland itself concubines took their place in a polygenous network. Seventh-century Irish lawyers made room for primary wives and secondary wives, for a variety of unions that might, or might not, be official. As in England the lawyers' main concern was with property and the rights of heirs. These were ranked according to the status of the mother; the male progeny of a chief wife could be called sons, whereas a so-called 'woman of recognition' had 'womb-kindred' and a woman whose liaison was unofficial had only 'belly-kindred'. While in England there is no evidence of polygeny, the practice of having both a wife and a concubine is unlikely to have been restricted to kings. The resigned tone of an eleventh-century penitential says as much: '[Concerning] the man who has a legal wife and also a concubine let no priest give him the eucharist nor any of the rites which are performed for Christian men unless he turns to repentance. And if he has a concubine and no legal wife, he has to do as seems [best] to him about that; however let him see to it that he keeps to one whether it be the concubine or the wife.'[3]

To talk of 'concubines' and 'wives' is to evoke a pool of women shared between men. We are reminded here of Claude Lévi-Strauss's description in *The Elementary Structures of Kinship* of women as objects, circulated between clans, lineages and families; women, 'like words', were things to be exchanged. The arrangement was, however, 'a duet';[4] and if on these occasions men provided 'the main substance of a lineage', women 'provided the connections'.[5] Many marriages

---

[3] *Penitential of Pseudo-Egbert*, cited in M. Clunies Ross, *op. cit.*, pp. 23–4.
[4] C. Lévi-Strauss, *The Elementary Structures of Kinship* (1969), p. 496.
[5] T. Charles-Edwards, *Early Irish and Welsh Kinship* (1993), p. 87.

of Anglo-Saxon women, particularly of the aristocracy, were undoubtedly political arrangements, designed to establish just such ties. None the less, as we have seen in the instance of Queen Aethelfryth, marriages were not regarded as indissoluble and it was not always the wife who was discarded. In Aethelbert's code the woman who wanted to end her marriage faced no legal obstacles. After clause 77, defining the man's right to return the 'fraudulent' woman, come clauses that spell out the property claims of the wife who wishes to leave her husband; she may do so – and no grounds are specified – taking with her half the goods and all the children; if the children stay with the husband then the wife herself receives a child's share.

In the later seventh-century laws from Kent, made in the reigns of Kings Hlothere and Eadric (possibly joint rulers from 673–c.685), further provision is made for mothers, in this case widows, faced with the task of bringing up children on their own: 'if a man dies, leaving a wife and child, it is right that the child should accompany the mother and one of the child's paternal relatives who is willing to act shall be appointed as guardian to take care of the property until the child is ten years old.' The seventh-century laws from the Wessex of King Ine make similar arrangements. Clause 38 reads: 'If a man and wife have a child and the husband dies the mother keeps the child and brings it up: she shall be provided with six shillings for its care, a cow in summer and an ox in winter; the kinsman are to look after the property until the child is grown up.' While such laws may be designed in the first instance to protect children, the interests of mothers are still respected; moreover it is worth pointing out, following Christine Fell's discussion of these passages in *Women in Anglo-Saxon England*, that it is both sons and daughters who are the object of concern. The word used for 'child' in the laws is 'bearn'; like 'bairn' this is not a gendered word; it may refer to boy or girl.

To understand early Anglo-Saxon marriage law it may be instructive to compare it with codes that we have from Wales. This is not to suggest that there are necessarily any direct parallels or borrowings – though this is not impossible – but the more discursive evidence from Celtic sources, intractable and difficult to date though it may be at times, gives a richer picture than the terse solemnities of the Anglo-Saxons. The Welsh laws of Hywel Dda, a tenth-century king, contain particularly detailed instructions for divorce settlements. The earliest manuscripts of these laws date only from the thirteenth century, however, and there seems no reason to doubt that the law code which bears the Welsh king's name includes much archaic material. Whatever its precise date, the wealth of detail contained in the laws makes it worth while to give some indication of its contents.

According to the laws of Hywel Dda, if a marriage breaks up in the first seven years without good reason – which includes leprosy, impotence and bad breath – the woman is entitled to a fixed sum known as her *agweddi*. The amount will depend on her birth status. After seven years, on the other hand, 'though three nights be wanting from the seventh year and they separate, it is right for them to share everything in two halves'. Pigs go to the man, sheep to the woman; eldest and youngest son to the father, middle son to the mother; milking vessels, except one pail, to the woman; all drinking vessels to the man. The man gets the hens and one cat; the woman gets all the flax and linseed and wool, all 'the opened vessels of butter and the opened cheese' and 'as much as she can carry of flour by the strength of her hands and her knees from the larder to the house'. The minutiae of the settlement are endless but lest the impression be given that the arrangements represent no more than hard-headed bargaining let us move to the bedroom:

The bedclothes which are over them to the woman, and those which are under them to the man until he takes a wife. After he takes a wife they belong to the woman, and if the wife who comes to the man sleeps on them, let her pay the woman from whom he separated her *wynebwerth*.[6]

The word *wynebwerth* is hard to translate; literally, it means face-shame. Another occasion on which it might be paid is as compensation by the husband to his wife for any sexual infidelity; but the wife can only accept such a pay-off twice. At the third offence she is expected to leave. To stay any longer would be to risk having to endure further insults and this would be deeply shaming. She may, however, claim a final *wynebwerth* if any new wife sleeps on her matrimonial bedclothes.

[6] D. Jenkins (ed. and trans.), *The Law of Hywel Dda* (1986), p. 45.

There are those who would claim that laws such as these are in fact designed to protect the honour not of the woman but of her clan. If we return to the laws of Anglo-Saxon England we will indeed find that in ways which may seem unacceptable to late twentieth-century sensibilities women remained linked to male kin-groups, whether natal or marital; at marriage women moved from the protection and guardianship of one man to a new role of submission to another. A woman's duty as stated in clause 57 of the laws of King Ine of Wessex is 'to obey her lord.' To understand this relationship we must look at it alongside comparable bonds that existed between men; it is just as important to consider the ways in which men and women shared certain experiences as it is to isolate what was specific to each. For both sexes, social relationships were bounded by class. For both too, the need to have a lord was paramount. At puberty a young girl might leave her father's house to enter into the *mund*, the care of her future husband. At the same age her brother would leave home to find a new lord whom he also would be obliged to honour and obey. To live without a lord was to become a social orphan, a dreaded fate. Moreover, although in most cases 'the lord' would be male this was not absolutely essential. If we look further at King Ine's laws we find that, should anyone from abroad be murdered during his stay and have no kin, then his *wergeld* was to be divided between the king and whoever gave the traveller his or her protection; this protector, as envisaged by the laws, might be either an abbot or an abbess. In confirmation we may cite the letter of the three monks who had gone to Germany to join the mission of St Boniface to their mentor in England, Abbess Cyniburg:

We also wish it known to your care and wisdom that if any of the three of us should visit Britain we should not seek to put ourselves in obedience to the government of anyone else but only in subjection to your benevolence for in you we have the most complete confidence.[7]

Abbesses, as we have already had occasion to see, could be formidable and powerful characters; doubtless they had special responsibilities and privileges – and arguably special dangers to face as well. If Margaret Clunies Ross is right,

---

[7] Cited in C. Fell, 'Some Implications of the Boniface Correspondence', in H. Damico and A. H. Olsen (eds), *New Readings on Women in Old English Literature* (1990), p. 33.

we should at this point return to the subject of abduction. Sometimes, as she has argued, abduction may indeed have served as form of elopement, a practice well attested in early Irish law and among many other Indo-European peoples, but it also had its uglier side. The conquest of countries and kingdoms is, as we well know, frequently accompanied by the rape of women and it is Clunies Ross's contention that in Anglo-Saxon England this took the particular form whereby a conquering lord might express territorial victory by demanding sexual submission from an abbess or her nuns. She cites as an example the entry of the *Anglo-Saxon Chronicle* concerning Earl Swein; after a raid into Wales in 1046 'he ordered the abbess of Leominster to be brought to him and he kept her as long as he pleased and afterwards allowed her to go home'.[8]

Turning our attention from the ungodliness of Earl Swein and the law codes of kings, we must now consider the question of the 'godly' influence of penitentials devised by ecclesiastics on laws and the formation of a new theory (whatever the practice) of sexual *mores* in Anglo-Saxon England. In time, the development of Christian kingship and the corresponding ambitions of rulers to establish a 'holy society' in which crime and sin are one and the same will make it difficult to distinguish between the two. This is especially noticeable in the case of laws promulgated after the Viking invasions of the ninth century, when it was thought that only righteous living would protect the English people of God from further attacks by heathens, but the foundations of a Christian society had been laid long before. Some hundred years after Aethelbert's conversion, his successor as king of Kent, Wihtred (*c*.690–725), became the first king to insist on the Christianity of his subjects, which resulted, first and foremost in the enforcement of Christian marriage laws: by 'the command of the king and his bishop and the decree of the books' (cl. 5) – and here ecclesiastical canons are meant – there were to be no more 'illicit cohabitations' or 'irregular marriages' (cl. 3); such unions were to be punished with fines, excommunication and, in the case of 'foreigners', with their expulsion from the kingdom. (cl. 4) Later clauses got round to prohibiting devil-worship by men or women – significantly it was not assumed that wives would be guilty here alongside their husbands or that they owned

---

[8] Cited in M. Clunies Ross, *op. cit.*, p. 31–2.

their property in common. According to clause 12 of the laws:

if a husband sacrifice to devils without his wife's knowledge, he is to
be liable to pay all his goods and *healsfang* (a proportion of his *wergeld*);
if they both sacrifice to devils, they are to be liable to pay *healsfang* and
all their goods.

Notably different in tone and prescription though Wihtred's
laws are from previous codes, there is still the possibility that
the influence of Christianity on earlier laws has been under-
estimated. A. W. B. Simpson has argued that the first code of
all, Aethelbert's, was in fact, and despite appearances to the
contrary, revolutionary in its intent, designed to introduce the
idea that it was just, honourable, and indeed Christian to
accept money payment for injuries received rather than to
respond to them with violence:

What the laws ... were concerned to introduce into society was a new
idea - that it was not wrong to take money instead of blood. This
represents a dramatic change, and we can see in the laws the attempts
inspired by the church to introduce a new and merciful alternative to
the tradition of retaliation.[9]

Simpson is far from convinced of the extent to which Aethelbert's legislation was ever enforced; it represented aspirations
rather than actuality. On this reading, the adulterous woman
of Kent may indeed have been vilified with the same intensity
that followed her in Old Saxony, notwithstanding the suggested tariff for peaceably settling the affair. Though subsequent kings throughout the Anglo-Saxon period continued
to attempt to put an end to private acts of vengeance, none
was ever able to eradicate altogether the notion that a victim
could take the law into his own hands. Reality and damage
limitation jostled together; in the laws of King Alfred (cl. 42),
he who 'finds another man with his wedded wife, within
closed doors or under the same blanket; or if he finds another
man with his legitimate daughter or sister or with his mother,
if she has been given in wedlock to his father, can fight the
intruder with impunity; if he kills the man his kin will not be
allowed to avenge him.' To the notion of monetary compensation for adultery the laws of Cnut make no concession
whatsoever: 'If a woman during her husband's life commits

⁹ A. W. B. Simpson, 'The Laws of Ethelbert' in M. Arnold *et al.* (eds), *On the Laws and Customs of England* (1981), p. 15.

adultery with another man ... her legal husband is to have all her property and she is to lose her nose and her ears.' (II Cnut, cl. 53).

Stillborn though it may have been, behind Aethelbert's legislation lies, according to Simpson, the example of Christian penitentials with their elaborate computation of the gravity of sins and the penance needed to attone for them. Aethelbert and his advisers may have been familiar with the early penitentials of the Irish but the first known English compilation is the *Penitential of Theodore* of the early eighth century. Whether such texts reflect actual behaviour any more accurately than do the laws of the period is debatable; there are those who consider it unlikely that the laity would have submitted to the *Penitential*'s view of marital relations, prescribing sexual abstinence during Lent and for three days before taking communion and forbidding a man to see his wife naked; others consider that the fervour of early generations of Christians is borne out by the testimony of the *Dialogue* of the eighth-century Archbishop of York, Egbert, to the eagerness of laymen 'with their wives and families' to be freed from 'carnal concupiscence' before receiving communion at Christmas.[10] The provision of the *Penitential of Theodore* for the particular circumstances of a country still in the throes of conversion and endemic warfare suggests that permissible compromises have been spelt out; where no allowances are made, none, whatever may have taken place were to be anticipated.

How far the *Penitential of Theodore* faithfully represented the views of Archbishop Theodore it is hard to tell. While not a first-hand work of the archbishop's, the Penitential is generally believed to have emanated from his circle. According to the preface it was compiled from the answers – themselves based on earlier penitentials – that Theodore gave to the Northumbrian priest Eoda. Theodore himself, within three years of his arrival in England as Archbishop of Canterbury in 670, had called his bishops together to meet at the Council of Hertford. The agenda, as reported by Bede, was concerned primarily with the behaviour of bishops, but the tenth and final decree was about marriage:

That nothing be allowed but lawful wedlock. Let none be guilty of

[10] Cited in H. Mayr-Harting, *The Coming of Christianity to England* (3rd edn 1991), p. 260.

incest, and let none leave his own wife except for fornication, as the holy gospel teaches. If anyone puts away his own wife who is joined to him by lawful matrimony, he may not take another if he wishes to be a true Christian; but he must either remain as he is or be reconciled to his own wife. (*EH IV*, 4)

The high profile here given to 'lawful wedlock' is an illustration of a concern commonly shared by early Christian leaders: what exactly was 'lawful wedlock'? How strictly were the new rules to be enforced? Augustine, writing back from his mission post in Kent to Pope Gregory, put the following questions: could two brothers marry two sisters? could a man marry his stepmother or sister-in-law? Similarly St Boniface wrote again and again to Rome from Germany for guidance on the permitted degrees of consanguinity and for a justification of the, to him, inexplicable ban on marriage between couples related only through the spiritual bonds created by god-parenting. It is not difficult to imagine that for many converts the complexities and peculiarities of such marriage laws were among the most distinctive, albeit troubling aspects of their new faith. Eadbald, son and successor to Aethelbert, had married his stepmother, Aethelbert's wife in his role as leader of a heathen reaction to the rules in Kent; his subsequent rejection of her was a sign that he had seen the error of his ways and a mark of his conversion to the true faith.

In his recent work, *The Development of the Family and Marriage in Europe*, the anthropologist Jack Goody has emphasised how very different were the marriage laws of the Christian Church from anything that had gone before: the indissolubility of the new marriage ties coupled with the obligation to marry 'out' rather than 'in', that is, to avoid marrying near kin, revolutionised both patterns of property-holding and systems of kinship. There is no need to accept Goody's thesis for the causes of this change - the need and greed of the new Church – in order to accept its radical nature. And such seems to have been the feeling in eighth-century England. Despite the orthodox line on marriage taken by Theodore and his bishops at the Council of Hertford in 673, the *Penitential of Theodore* is notable for the concessions it makes.The hardships which the new rules were likely to cause had already been recognised by Pope Gregory in his reply to Augustine; a hundred years or so later, whatever the official position, compromises were still necessary. If, for example, a woman leaves her husband, 'despising him' and after five years has still not returned, the man may, with the permission of the bishop, marry again; if either husband or wife has been captured in war, new marriages are possible after five years, though should the first wife or husband return then it is the first marriage that counts; an adulterous woman, rejected by her husband, may remarry after five years of penance; the man who has married more than once must abstain from eating meat during the three forty-day fasts of the year and on Wednesdays and Fridays; marriage to a relation of the fourth degree is not recommended but none the less it can pass.

The *Penitential of Theodore* is not a text that can easily be characterised. The twentieth-century reader is unlikely to find its attitude to women sympathetic: menstruating women are unclean; adultery by the wife but not by the husband counts as grounds for separation; should the husband wish for a reconciliation it will be on his terms – 'her punishment does not belong to the clergy, it belongs to her own husband'. But it is not enough to castigate this text for unfeeling misogyny, or relentless patriarchy; relative leniency is shown towards the poor woman who kills her baby; absolute freedom given to daughters to reject suitors chosen for them. In the last resort, however, the drawing up of a balance sheet of his kind, in so far as it is concerned with 'women's rights', is likely to prove an anachronistic exercise. The prime concern of the *Penitential*, no less than of the laws, was with the right ordering of Christian society: in the words of the prologue to King Ine's laws, with 'the security of the kingdom and the salvation of souls'. The source of all law, ultimately, was God; the many men and women whom the *Penitential* tells us flocked to consult Theodore were, we may surmise, less troubled by the inequalities of their situation in this life than that they should not be found wanting at the Day of Judgement.

CHAPTER FOUR

Vernacular Literature

Anglo-Saxon literature was, for the most part, written in verse.[1] Intended for public delivery, it represented not so much the voice of an individual poet as the values of his society (perhaps also 'of hers', though it cannot be said that we know of any Anglo-Saxon women poets). It drew, like the laws, on both Germanic traditions and newer Christian lore. Stories of saints taken from Latin sources, of Judith, for example, heroine of the *Apocrypha* or of the third-century Juliana, were refashioned in ways that endowed them with some of the characteristics of northern valkyries. The combination was awesome. Judith, 'shrewd of purpose ... of elfin beauty' (l. 13) beheads the villain Holofernes with dazzling serenity; Juliana, greedy for martyrdom, takes on the devil and through force of words renders him 'utterly impotent, bound fast with fetters' (l. 432). Where, one might ask, is there room in all this for the passivity that has been said to characterise depictions of Anglo-Saxon women?

The notion of a passive Anglo-Saxon woman derives from the idea that the only acceptable model for her was the Virgin. As Jane Chance has recently put it, 'the primary conventional secular role of Anglo-Saxon woman demanded her passivity and peace-making talent, an ideal perfectly fulfilled in the social and religious archetype of the Virgin Mary (who represented all ages of, and roles available to, Anglo-Saxon women)'.[2] In literary terms, this is the equivalent of the image of the woman-as-chattel which the laws have sometimes been

---

[1] Translations throughout come from S. A. Bradley, *Anglo-Saxon Poetry* (1982).
[2] J. Chance, *Woman as Hero in Old English Literature* (1986), p. xiv.

said to present. But, like that picture, it is not the only one that can be drawn.

Let us begin with that most famous of all Anglo-Saxon poems, *Beowulf* (the dating of this poem remains a thorny question which need not detain us here; it is at least certain from the manuscript evidence that it cannot be later than 1000). On one reading, this is the tale of an aged and white-haired king, Hrothgar, and of the beast Grendel who is terrorising Heorot, his beloved hall. This beast the hero Beowulf magnificently fights and fatally maims. Carefree celebrations follow with recollections of earlier triumphs, and horse-racing 'along the sandy-yellow road' (l. 917). The mood proves premature: the beast's mother emerges from the depths of a foul lake to seek her revenge; Beowulf despatches her, too. But the time will come when Beowulf himself has a kingdom whose peace is threatened by a mean-spirited dragon. Beowulf by now is an old man; he is no longer invincible. In kingly style he takes on the dragon, but in the fight he is mortally wounded. His followers mourn his death, recalling his heroic deeds; they cremate his body, bury his treasures, deliver their eulogies.

Even so bald a summary as this could lead to varied interpretations; to pursue them here is not our business. Rather, let us tell the tale again; let us tell the story this time of Beowulf the young hero who comes to the court of Hrothgar and his queen, Wealhtheow. It is Wealhtheow, 'the ring-bejewelled queen, distinguished for the quality of her mind' (ll. 622–3) to whom Beowulf promises, as he accepts from her a ritual drink of welcome, that he will kill Grendel or die in the attempt. His subsequent fight is successful. The court prepares for a party. Hrothgar's poet will recall a saga of bitter feud and of the grief of the woman caught at the heart of it who loses both her sons, her brother and finally her husband; as the story moves to a close Wealhtheow comes forward, again with the ceremonial cup, to where her husband is seated. She pleads, in the event of his death, for the safety of their sons, for their protection by their uncle, Hrothgar's brother. As the audience, we know what she can only fear: he will be the wicked uncle who will kill a nephew. But for now the peace is shattered from without, by Grendel's mother; a tense and desperate conflict ends in Beowulf's victory. He returns to his people, to the court of Hygelac, whom he is to succeed, to the land where in old age he will die, a dragon's victim, where his funeral will be celebrated by the song of a woman singing 'over and over again a melancholy tale . . . a dread of evil days and violent deaths'. (ll. 3152–3)

These analyses are not intended as suggesting ways of reading *Beowulf* 'as a man' or 'as a woman'. The incidents that have been highlighted are, in the text, woven together and must be understood as such. Hrothgar and Wealhtheow sit together, side by side, in Hereot. Their match has sealed a successful pact between warring dynasties, between Wulfings and Scyldings. Powerless Wealhtheow may be to safeguard the future of her sons – and there is more than a hint that her daughter likewise will be powerless, through her marriage, to bring the desired peace – but we would do well to recall that Hrothgar, until the coming of Beowulf, is equally so. For twelve years Grendel has terrorised his court and there is nothing he has been able to do about it. He 'agonises unceasingly . . . unable to avert those griefs.' (ll. 189–90) Beowulf himself, though he merits a hero's death, dies in weakened circumstances. In his hour of need all his followers except one skulk off into the woods. They return only when both Beowulf and the dragon are dead. To suggest, as some critics have, that this is a poem where men act and women weep would be to fly against the evidence. Men knew how they should act – there is in place in the poem an unambiguous heroic code – but there are times when they can't and times when they won't – and times when, in any case, the affairs of men and women seem to be determined rather by *wyrd* or fate – 'the grim preordained decree' (l. 1233). None the less, for a woman too, whatever her destiny, there is a function to fulfil. She must present herself as the symbol of the unity and concord of the court, of the communion of those who sit there; she cannot only seek but must also demand loyalty. This is how Wealhtheow, *folccwen* or queen of the people, sees Hereot:

Here every lord is true to the other, gentle of disposition and loyal to his lord. The thanes are obedient, and the people are entirely at the ready: the men of this court, having drunk to it will do as I bid. (ll. 1228–31)

To fulfil her role, Wealhtheow must dispense not only drink but also treasure. For Beowulf, as reward for his deeds, she gives cloak and torque and holds out to him the promise of more to come. When Beowulf returns home, bearing his presents, we are reminded that he is on his way to another ritual arena for the celebration and display of the values of bravery and generosity and loyalty. He is making for the court of Hygelac, of 'royal renown', and of his queen, Hydg: 'very young, yet wise and well-accomplished ... not niggardly nor over-frugal towards the Geatish people in gifts and precious treasures' (ll. 1925–30). We are not so far away here from the women with keys buried in cemeteries or enshrined in law codes, nor from the ideal queen of *Maxims I*:

A queen ... must excel as one cherished among her people, and be buoyant of mood, keep confidences, be open-heartedly generous with horses and with treasures; in deliberation over the mead, in the presence of the troop of companions she must always and everywhere greet first the chief of those princes and instantly offer the chalice to her lord's hand, and she must know what is prudent for them both as rulers of the hall. (ll. 83–90)

If men do not always play their part – Beowulf's followers, for example, or Hrothgar's brother – no more do women. As Beowulf continues to make his way home after his triumphs at Heorot we are reminded by the poet of Queen Modthryth. She will end her days 'renowned for goodness'; but it had not always been so. There had been a time when she punished the male gaze quite shockingly, arranging the execution of those who dared to look at her: 'Not one brave man among the close companions, but only the supreme lord himself dared look her in the eyes ... or else he could count on cruel chains, hand-twisted.' Such is not, we are wryly assured, 'a queenly custom for a woman to follow, even if she is unmatched in beauty, that the peace-weaver should exact the life of a dearly esteemed man on account of an imagined insult.' (ll. 1931–56)

Modthryth shares with Wealhtheow, Hildeburh and Grendel's mother – at first sight a strange assortment – the distinction of being described as an *ides*. The meaning of this word has been a matter of some debate among philologists. *Ides* is a word which has cognates both in Old High German and in Old Norse. Its use in the Old High German *First Merseburg Charm* is commonly cited by way of definition:

In days gone by, the *idisi* sat and they sat here and yonder. Some made firm the fetters, some hindered the host, and some picked apart the chains; escape from fetters, escape from foes.

The connotations here seem sinister, appropriate for the antics of a Modthryth, and maybe of Grendel's mother, but hardly suitable as an appellation for women of heroic virtue as both Wealhtheow and Hildeburh have been portrayed. But when we find that it is also used of Eve and of the Virgin we realise that it has to be a morally neutral word and that what it signifies is the possession neither or 'goodness' nor of 'badness' but of power; it is a pointer to a person of significance, whatever their moral calibre, to someone, in short, who is extraordinary. There is, further, more than a hint in its usage that the power to be exercised may have a supernatural dimension; to grasp its nature it has been suggested, therefore, that we need to keep in mind a cluster of associations from Tacitus's description in *Germania*, of the respect of Germanic barbarians for the spirit of prophecy thought to reside in their women, from the amulets and crystal balls of female Anglo-Saxon graves to the eerie valkyries and formidable viragos of the Norse sagas; and that somewhere along this line of descent lies the formidable trio of Anglo-Saxon poetry: Elene, Juliana and Judith.

To move from *Beowulf* to the ninth-century poems *Elene* and *Juliana* (attributed to Cynewulf) and to the anonymous *Judith* (probably tenth century) is, arguably, to change worlds. Whereas, whatever its date and provenance, *Beowulf* belongs to a northern world, heroic and pagan, barely touched by Christian teaching, *Elene*, *Juliana* and *Judith* make sense only in a Christian context. These women fight their battles under Mediterranean skies, far from the murky swamps of Grendel territory. Their behaviour is not socially patterned in the manner of Wealhtheow's; it is not in any literal sense exemplary. We can suppose that Bertha of Kent, had she been able, might have chosen to send her daughter Aethelburh north (to where, at Yeavering, she will be queen of a hall much like Heorot) with a copy of *Beowulf* to read on the journey rather than with *Elene*, *Juliana*, or *Judith*.

Here, briefly, are the stories of these poems.

Elene opens with the Emperor Constantine's vision of the Cross in the sky, 'the beautiful tree of glory' (l. 89); the vision vouchsafes both victory in the emperor's impending struggle against barbarian hordes and his conversion to Christianity. His zeal for his new-found faith is such that what he wants now is to find the Cross of the crucifixion, the True Cross. Who better to send to look for it than his mother, Elene? And off she goes, 'courageous of thought and zealous of spirit' (ll. 264–5). 'Never before nor since,' claims the poet, 'have I heard of a woman leading a finer looking force on the ocean tide on the sea-rode' (ll. 240–2). Once in Jerusalem she delivers a rousing speech to an assembled Jewish crowd, challenging them to find representatives who can tell her, 'magnificent warlike queen clad in gold' (ll. 330–1), what she needs to know. The field narrows to one, a certain Judas; we listen to Elene cross-examining him, leading to his eventual submission and conversion and to the finding of the Cross. But that is not where the story ends. Elene has by now herself become preoccupied with a quest. She initiates a successful search for the crucifixion nails; having found them, she has them made into a bridle for her son, who is henceforth to be ensured of victory in all his battles.

Juliana's story is set in the reign of Constantine's father-in-law, the pagan emperor Maximian. One of his governors is a certain Eleusius. Eleusius falls in love with Juliana, but Juliana is already a Christian and anxious to preserve her virginity. Her father, none the less, accepts Eleusius's courtship on her behalf; both father and suitor are outraged by Juliana's subsequent defiance and her refusal to even contemplate the match unless Eleusius converts. They resort to imprisonment and torture. Juliana remains steadfast despite the efforts of the devil and six hours a day of physical torment. She bests the devil, survives fire and boiling lead but dies at last at the point of a sword, a triumphant martyr, sure of the city of heaven, her soul despatched from her body into lasting bliss by the stroke of a sword. For his part, Eleusius sets off to sea, is drowned and heads for hell.

The opening of *Judith* is missing; we are thus led straight to the camp of the lecherous Holofernes where all day long he and his fellow Assyrians have feasted and drunk. Night is closing in. Holofernes asks for Judith to be brought to him for he means to 'defile her with filth and with pollution' (l. 58). He falls asleep in a drunken stupor and Judith seizes both sword and opportunity. She drags Holofernes by his hair into a suitable position and cuts off his head. She pops the head into her lunch-bag, returns to her people, the Israelites, and exhorts them to prepare to fight. It is only when the battle is well advanced that the death of Holofernes is discovered –

and proves the turning point. The Assyrians in terror turn to flight and most of them get killed.

The questions which critics of Anglo-Saxon literature have asked about these poems are legion: how far, for example, do they represent a flight from the heroic world of *Beowulf*? how far its confirmation? Is it the purpose of *Juliana* to promote a new Christian ethic based on the heroine's search for 'personal religious integrity' rather than concern for 'the welfare of her society'?[3] Or (as Earl Anderson asks) should we read *Juliana* as 'a display of conflict between the values of a pagan "shame" culture and those of the Christian "guilt" culture'?[4] What, if anything, should we make of the marital status of these women? Is it significant that they represent between them 'virginity, widowhood and conjugality'?[5] Are the poems to be taken as versified histories of great women or are they rather to be read as characters from 'typological narratives'?[6] These are questions to bear in mind but what we must now consider is the further light these poems throw on the representation of women and their roles, whether heroic, Christian, 'actual' or allegorical – or indeed a blend of all four.

Close examination of both content and vocabulary has shown that despite first impressions the worlds of Cynewulf and of *Judith* are not, after all, as far away from Heorot as their very different contexts have suggested. It is not simply that Wealhtheow, Judith, Juliana and Elene have certain characteristics in common – wisdom is attributed to all four, and each is radiant, shiny even, with gold or virtue or both – but, more importantly, each woman demonstrates her power through words. Recent work on heroines of folklore (such as Cinderella) has shown how subtly but decisively heroines can be reduced to plaster-status by taking words from their mouths, by shifting the balance of speech from woman to man.[7] This is not the fate of any of our Anglo-Saxon quartet. In *Beowulf* not only does Wealhtheow make her presence felt through her speeches of welcome and of praise; she also, by

---

[3] The question comes from C. Schneider, *Anglo-Saxon England*, vol. 7 (1978), p. 114.

[4] E. Anderson, *Cynewulf: Structure, Style and Theme in his Poetry* (1983), p. 91.

[5] J. Chance, *op. cit.*, p. 34.

[6] A. H. Olsen, 'Cynewulf's Autonomous Women', in H. Damico and A. H. Olsen (eds), *New Readings on Women in Old English Literature* (1990), p. 223.

[7] R. B. Bottingheimer, *Grimms' Bad Girls and Bold Boys: The Moral and Social Vision of the Tales* (1987).

her words, brings about Beowulf's action. It is, as we have already seen, in response to her greeting that Beowulf makes his promise to slay Grendel or to perish. Her role here as an 'inciting' woman has many parallels in Norse tales and in the Anglo-Saxon fragment *Waldhere* – though to grasp the power and longevity of the topos we could do worse than to recall Lady Macbeth.

Lady Macbeth, of course, lives long enough only to rue the results of her own tirades. As saints rather than sinners, Cynewulf's women go for victories that win them eternal glory – but the weapons they, too, use are words. Elene lectures the Jews relentlessly, browbeats Judas (though admittedly she has to resort to submitting him to a week of starvation as well) and, not content with the finding of the Cross, gives orders for the nails to be discovered. Significantly (as Alexandra Hennessey Olsen has pointed out)[8] Elene's desire for the nails amounts in the Latin version to no more than an eighteen-word sentence of request; Cynewulf has changed this into an imperious twenty-line speech. Juliana's rhetoric is even more impressive. There is nothing Juliana does but speak; and the effectiveness of her words stand in sharp contrast to the increasingly frenzied and futile actions of her persecutors. Most memorable are her encounters with the demon, sent to her cell to tempt her. As we saw at the opening of this chapter, Juliana paralyses him with her words; he becomes 'utterly impotent, bound fast with fetters'. This, as Helen Damico has emphasised, is reminiscent of the spell cast by the ides in the *First Merseburg Charm*.[9] For the demon, the effect is devastating. He is forced to confess his sinful deeds and evil ambitions. It is only through an act of mercy that Juliana releases him rather than exposing his weakness before Eleusius. He returns, before her execution, to cry out for revenge at his 'unmanning' – but beats a hasty retreat, fearful that even in her last hours she will humiliate him further.

But what of Judith? Does she not belong to a different tradition? Many critics have found her hard to place. What is in some ways most striking about her achievement in beheading Holofernes is the downbeat manner in which she does it. In

---

[8] A. H. Olsen, 'Cynewulf's Autonomous Women: A Reconsideration of Elene and Juliana', in H. Damico and A. H. Olsen, *op. cit.*, pp. 224.

[9] H. Damico, 'The Valkyrie Reflex in Old English Literature', in H. Damico and A. H. Olsen, *op. cit.*, pp. 185–6.

contrast with the account in the *Apocrypha* there is little or no build-up (even allowing for a missing opening); the decapitation presents practical problems – the body has to be suitably arranged, it takes two blows and it's all a bit messy – but is neither miraculous nor traumatic: Judith and her maid (who is given the head in its bag to carry) can walk away as if nothing had happened. There is much more of both action and excitement in the description of the ensuing battle. But it should not be forgotten that there is no description at all of a battle in the *Apocrypha* and that in the Old English poem it is Judith who rouses the army and urges them to prepare to fight, telling them to go forth at dawn in full armour, to cut down the enemies' commanders with their gleaming swords. Judith too, then, is an *ides* who plays her part by words as much as by deeds. We are reminded, whether intentionally or not, of the defence of Mercia against the Vikings led by Aethelflaed, Lady of the Mercians (d. 918), and of how 'her fame spread abroad in every direction'.[10]

The image of the persuasive woman has, we must remember, a biblical as well as a Nordic origin. When popes wrote to Anglo-Saxon queens to remind them of their duty to whisper Christian enticements into their husbands' ears, they were passing on St Paul's message in I Corinthians, 7 on the duties of the 'believing wife' towards her 'unbelieving husband'.[11] On the other hand Christian teaching, especially as developed by Paul, was wary of allowing women any place in public speaking; women in church were to 'keep silence and take their place with all submissiveness as learners' (I Timothy, 2: 11). Women's words, essentially, were dangerous: was it not through the words of a woman, Eve, that sin had entered the world? But if, as we have been arguing, Anglo-Saxon literature suggests that women's counsels were expected and respected, where did that leave the message of Genesis?

The Anglo-Saxon verse translation of Genesis, known as *Genesis B*, goes far in answering the problem of how to fit Eve into the vernacular tradition. The poet's story of the Fall is significantly different from his source. In the Anglo-Saxon version, the devil disguised as a snake but claiming to be an

---

[10] Cited in F. T. Wainwright, 'Aethelflaed, Lady of the Mercians', in H. Damico and A. H. Olsen, *op. cit.*, p. 51.

[11] S. Farmer, 'Persuasive Voices: Clerical Images of Medieval Wives', *Speculum* 61 (1986), pp. 517–43.

angel goes first to Adam to persuade him to eat the apple. Adam refuses – the snake doesn't look to him like any angel he's met before. Defeated, the snake moves off to Eve on whom he tries a new line of argument: he appeals to her as a wife whose duty it is to do the best for herself, for her husband and for the future security of any children they may have. God, claims the snake, will be furious with both Adam and Eve if they disobey this new command to eat the apple. It is Eve's responsibility to avert God's wrath. 'Coax Adam carefully,' the snake tells her, 'so that he carries out your counsel lest you should both be forced to prove abhorrent to God your Ruler' (ll. 575–7). Eve, in short, is depicted as playing both the role of the 'believing wife' and the role of peace-maker. 'Believing in the devil's words' and certain that to refuse the apple will be to anger both God and his supposed servant, she asks Adam, 'What will it avail you, such detestable quarrelling with your Master's messenger?' (ll. 671–2) 'She talked to him repeatedly ... the whole day' (l. 684); at last Adam's 'mind was changed' (l. 705). Terrible though the consequences were to be, yet the *Genesis B* poet still asks for our sympathy for Eve: 'she did it out of loyal intent' (l. 707).

What then of the Virgin? In patristic theology, it is her acceptance of God's plan that undoes Eve's assent to the devil. Mary is the polar opposite of Eve. Eve rebels, Mary complies, Eve is loquacious, Mary a model of silence; on this came to be built the ideal of the passive woman. But, however frequently and vehemently such an ideal may have been proclaimed, this is no proof of its universal acceptance. The Virgin herself, particularly in her early medieval manifestations, is far from being the gentle creature we have more recently come to expect. She too could be a battle queen, inciting her followers to victory – most famously at Constantinople in 627 when her appearance on the walls of the city saved it from Arab Conquest.

The cult of the Virgin in Anglo-Saxon England developed early – in part, it has been suggested, through the influence of Eastern Christianity brought to England by Theodore of Tarsus, appointed Archbishop of Canterbury in 667. A remarkable carving from early-ninth-century Mercia, at Breedon in Leicestershire, shows the Virgin holding not her baby but a book in her left hand; her right hand is raised, in priestly fashion, in blessing. Whatever the model for, and meaning of, this particular sculpture it is clear that the Virgin could have unexpected roles. In Anglo-Saxon poems the Virgin is represented in ways that accord well with traditions we have already seen, traditions of women who talk and for whom speech does not mean submission. In *Advent Lyrics III* Mary speaks with dramatic poignancy to Joseph to persuade him to give up his 'bitter grieving' at what he has taken to be proof of her infidelity and to accept rather her love for him, the miracle of Christ's conception and his role as his earthly father. The description of Mary in *Advent Lyrics IV*, and of her role in the salvation of mankind, no more suggests mere acquiescence in the plan than does Christ's hastening to the cross, literally to embrace the instrument of his crucifixion, in the Old English poem *The Dream of the Rood*. In *Advent Lyrics IV* Mary is even portrayed as in some sense the initiator of the Annunciation; suitably clad as an Anglo-Saxon bride ('ring-adorned') it is her gift of herself to God which prompts his response:

bride of the most excellent Lord of heaven ... Lady of the heavenly host ... you alone among all people having the courage of your persuasions, gloriously determined that you would offer your maidenhood to the ordaining Lord and grant it to him without sin. None comparable has come, no other above all mortals, a ring-adorned bride who with pure heart, then sent the sublime offering to the heavenly home. On this account, the Lord of Victory commanded his exalted messenger ... to fly hither and swiftly reveal to you the abundance of his powers, that in a chaste birth you were to bring forth the Son of the Lord God as an act of mercy towards men; and yet thenceforth keep yourself, Mary, ever immaculate. (ll. 278–300)

We come, finally, to those most enigmatic of Anglo-Saxon poems, *The Wife's Lament* and *Wulf and Eadwacer*. Both poems are elegies and in both the speaker is female; stylistically, they stand apart. Whether this is because of their elegiac character or because they were written by women is as uncertain as what they are actually about. On the face of it, *The Wife's Lament* is a song of the sufferings of a woman in exile, longing in bitter and obsessive despair for her lord: 'Woe is to the one who must wait for love to come out of longing' (ll. 53–4). An alternative reading, and one of many, would make it an allegorical poem in which the figure in exile, far from being an actual woman, is instead the city of Jerusalem. Interpretations of *Wulf and*

Eadwacer are still more contentious. Even to tease out a simple meaning is difficult. On one island is Wulf; the speaker of the poem is on another. The speaker yearns for Wulf; at the same time she expects Eadwacer to be listening; but who is Eadwacer? or Wulf? Is this, critics have asked, a poem about adultery; a charm against wens; or the dream of a female dog?

A recent interpretation of *Wulf and Eadwacer* by Dolores Warwick Frese places the poem not so much in a class of its own as in a context which Anglo-Saxon poetry has already made familiar.[12] It belongs, in Frese's view, neither to the realm of allegory nor of romance but rather to the tradition of the grieving mother. This is a theme that will be taken up in Christianity, in the mourning of the Virgin at the foot of the Cross, but its primary root in Anglo-Saxon culture is pagan. It springs from the world we have met in *Beowulf*, a world where feud made both the death of sons and their commemoration in death fall heavily on mothers. On this reading, the speaker in *Wulf and Eadwacer* is a mother mourning Wulf, her son, who has died on alien territory; Eadwacer is not a proper name but a 'Heavenwatcher' petitioned to guard Wulf in the afterlife. Thematically, then, we may link (as Frese does) the most obscure of all Anglo-Saxon poems with those verses from *The Fortunes of Man* whose evocation of family life has such immediacy:

It very often happens through God's powers that man and woman bring forth a child by birth into the world and clothe him in colours, and curb him and teach him until the time comes and it happens with the passing of years that the young and lively limbs and members are mature. Thus his father and mother lead him along and guide his footsteps and provide for him and clothe him – but only God knows what the years will bring him as he grows up. (ll. 1–10)

While it has been convenient to devote a separate chapter to literary sources, on no other grounds is this defensible. Many of the characters in *Beowulf* have at least as much claim to historicity as those of the early annals of the *Anglo-Saxon Chronicle*. Conversely, Asser, in his *Life of King Alfred*, can avail himself of legend as freely as the *Beowulf* poet; his vignette of the scheming Mercian princess, over-generous with poison,

---

[12] D. Frese, '*Wulf and Eadwacer*: The Adulterous Woman Reconsidered', in H. Damico and A. H. Olsen, *op. cit.*, pp. 273–91.

who ends her days destitute in the streets of Pavia, after failing to give the 'right' answer to a question which would have secured her a place in the sun, is both as colourful and as didactic as *Beowulf's* Modthryth.[13] No one, historian or poet or hagiographer, has a monopoly on good tales, whether of the wicked or the virtuous, the 'real' or the 'imagined'. What we cannot, of course, know is how far lives are shaped by such tales, whether 'fact' or 'fiction'; or how far models are taken from lives, or lives from models. The interplay is the point.

[13] Asser, *Life of King Alfred*, in S. Keynes and M. Lapidge (eds), *Alfred the Great* (1983), pp. 71–2.

PART TWO

The Eleventh Century

CHAPTER FIVE

1066 for Women

The year 1066, as every English schoolchild knows, saw the conquest of England by William, Duke of Normandy. The Bayeux tapestry lays out the sequence of events before us. It is a tale of male rivalry, ambition, action. The old king, Edward, dies, his wife Edith poised dutifully at his feet; the crown is seized by Harold Godwineson, brother of Edith and long the power behind the throne. William, alleging that the kingdom has been promised to him and that Harold is an oath-breaker, prepares to invade. Magnificent ships are built; wine, men and horses are piled in and the Channel is crossed. A makeshift castle is throw up, a sign of the military rule to come. Saxons and Normans meet at Hastings where the Normans fighting from horseback and with new weapons – deadly crossbows – wear down Saxon resistance and win the day.

The Bayeux tapestry teems with countless knights and at least one hundred and seventy horses. Apart from Queen Edith, only two women are depicted. One is the mysterious figure of Aelfgyva whose relationship with a clerk is evidently sexual; the tapestry caption says no more than 'where a clerk and Aelfgyva' but the naked figure below makes it clear that the reference is to some famous scandal. The other woman is an anonymous victim of war. As prelude to the battle, this woman and her child flee from a home set ablaze by ravaging soldiers. Other sources, such as *The Song of the Battle of Hastings*, remind us further of the cost of war for women; in this poem William the victor and Gytha, mother of the slain Harold, bargain over the rights to his burial.

It hardly needs saying that Gytha will have been one among many mourners. Casualties both at Hastings and at the battle

Genealogical table to illustrate relationships referred to in chapter 5

Women in italics
Dates are of reigns

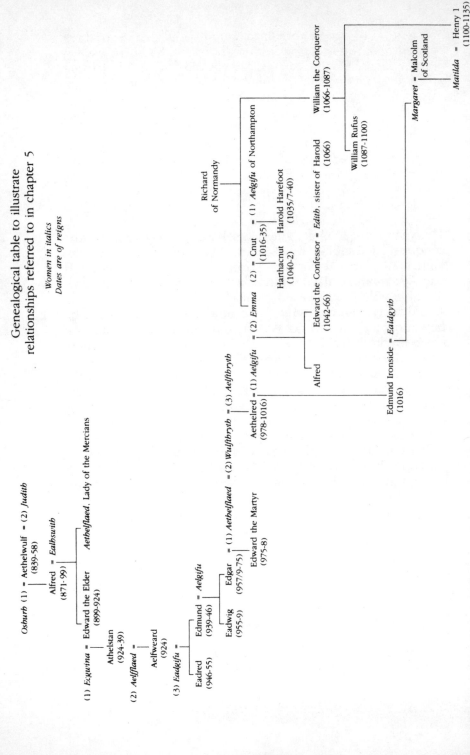

of Stamford Bridge in Yorkshire, fought only a matter of days
before against an invasion from Scandinavia, had been exceptionally heavy. Gytha herself lost not only Harold but three
other sons. Gytha and the Bayeux tapestry call to mind an
earlier battle, the Battle of Maldon in 991, a battle celebrated
this time for the heroic glory of the defeated Saxons who had
died at Viking hands. The deeds of Earl Brythnoth, the Saxon
leader, were recorded, like Harold's, in both poetry and
embroidery. A tapestry of the battle was commissioned by
Brythnoth's widow Aelfflaed, and given by her to the monastery at Ely where Brythnoth had been taken for burial.

The Bayeux tapestry may not portray many women, but it
was women who made it. The work of English needlewomen –
the aristocratic as well as the less nobly born – was already
famous throughout eleventh-century Europe. Queens, such as
Edith, were praised for their skills as embroideresses, alongside relatively modest workers like Leofgeat. According to
Domesday Book, Leofgeat lived in Wiltshire; in 1086 she held
the same land, measured at three and a half hides, which her
husband had held in 1066, when she herself is described as
doing gold embroidery for the king. Whether such women
also had a share in designing the tapestry we do not know;
but that it has connections with Canterbury is clear from its
iconography. Since Canterbury lay in what had once been
Harold's territory there is a certain irony in this. Whether or
not we subscribe to the theories of David Bernstein – who sees
hidden messages of comfort stitched into the fabric of the
tapestry through allusions to the biblical story of the Baby-
lonian Conquest of Judah[1] – we can at least acknowledge that
for many it may have functioned as a memorial to the dead in
the manner of Brythnoth's hanging at Ely rather than as a
panegyric to the victors. In the case of Brythnoth's hanging it
has been suggested that his widow Aelfflaed may herself have
contributed to its making; it is not beyond the bounds of
possibility that the Bayeux tapestry also had mourners among
its stitchers.

Such mourners had, of course, other destinies. The *Anglo-
Saxon Chronicle* for 1067 (D version), after having related the
Conqueror's campaigns to crush rebellions against him in the
West Country, goes on to record the dispersal of the losers

[1] D. Bernstein, *The Mystery of the Bayeux Tapestry* (1986), ch. 13, pp. 166–78.

in 1066 and their fates. Women feature prominently in his narrative:

in the course of the summer Edgar ... went abroad with his mother Agatha and his two sisters Margaret and Christina ... and [they] came to Scotland under the protection of King Malcolm and he received them ... then the aforesaid King Malcolm began to desire his sister Margaret for his wife ... the king pressed her brother until he said 'yes' [to the match] and indeed he dared not do anything else, because they had come into his control.

The marriage (divinely ordained, according to the chronicler) brings untold benefits to Scotland; the narrator describes Margaret's nobility of character and of birth; then, without a pause, he continues with the news that 'Gytha, Harold's mother, and many distinguished men's wives with her, went out to Flatholme and stayed there for some time and so went from there overseas to St Omer'.

Exile, marriage – or withdrawal behind convent walls, these were the choices facing the women of the Anglo-Saxon aristocracy. The one might not preclude the other. In the turmoil of the Conquest years a number of Anglo-Saxon women had evidently been committed to convents for safety, an eleventh-century form of evacuation. What happened if they wanted to leave in order to be married, or were expected to do so? Here a letter from the Archbishop of Canterbury, Lanfranc, to the Bishop of Rochester, is illuminating. Lanfranc writes:

Concerning the nuns about whom you wrote to me, dearest father, I give you this reply. Nuns who have made profession that they will keep a rule or who, although not yet professed, have been presented at the altar are to be enjoined, exhorted and obliged to keep the rule in the manner of their life. But those who have been neither professed nor presented at the altar are to be sent away at once without change of status, until their desire to remain in religion is examined more carefully. As to those who as you tell me fled to a monastery not for love of the religious life but for fear of the French, if they can prove that this was so by the unambiguous witness of nuns better than they, let them be granted unrestricted leave to depart. This is the king's policy and our own. *(Letter 53)*

The importance of this letter lies in the recognition that the marriage of William I's youngest son, Henry, with the Anglo-Saxon princess Matilda (to which we will return) was only one of a number of unions between the Normans (or 'French' as

Lanfranc calls them) and native heiresses. Such women were evidently in high demand both 'as peace-weavers and as channels of inheritance'.[2] Just as the rebel Hereward the Wake, famed as the leader of heroic Anglo-Saxon resistance to the Conquest in the fens around Ely, settles down at last (in legend at least) with a nice Norman girl, so, conversely, fierce Norman knights married to suitable natives might acquire new rights to their lands and a better chance of assimilation.

The intermarriage of Normans with Anglo-Saxon women explains not only the relative ease with which William I could impose his rule, but also the failure of the Conquest, in the long run, to establish French as the language of the country. Old English, after 1066, was eclipsed, but it was not forgotten. Old French, initially a symbol of status and power, ceased very quickly to be the mother tongue of all but a tiny minority; its use as a vernacular persisted at court but nowhere else. By the fourteenth century it had been overtaken even as a literary language by Middle English. This remarkable survival of English, to which we will be returning in the final chapter, may be attributed both to intermarriage and probably also to the influence of native wet nurses and servants who continued to speak in their 'mother tongue'. Thus Ordericus Vitalis, author of the *Historia Ecclesiastica*, the son of an English mother and a priest from Orleans, who was taught Latin as a young boy, spoke not the French of his father but English. Despatched to a monastery in Normandy at the age of ten he felt an exile, hearing, he tells us, a language he could not understand.

The research of Cecily Clark on women's names in post-Conquest England strengthens the case for supposing intermarriages on the pattern of that of Ordericus's parents to have been relatively common. Norman men's names even in the twelfth century are much more prevalent than Norman women's names.[3] This may not be conclusive evidence but it is none the less suggestive: and it follows that interpretations of the Conquest as an exercise of military might, of castle-building and the enfeoffing of knights, must be accompanied by a consideration of the identity of the wives, mistresses and servants of those knights, of the language they spoke to their

[2] E. Searle, 'Women and the Legitimisation of Succession at the Norman Conquest', *Proceedings of the Battle Conference* 3 (1980), pp. 159–70.
[3] C. Clark, 'Women's Names in Post-Conquest England: Observations and Speculations', *Speculum* 53 (1978), pp. 223–51.

children and of how this language may have shaped their perceptions of their new inheritance.

Alongside this picture of an informal power exercised through women it has become customary to place another: the Conquest, or so it is argued, saw a serious reduction in women's rights. Whereas Anglo-Saxon women could make wills and hold land, and therefore bequeath chattels and property to whomever they chose, Anglo-Norman women could do neither. In a famous early-eleventh-century case from Herefordshire a certain Edwin sued his mother for land, only to be angrily rebuffed; 'not a thing' was he to get; everything – land, gold, furnishings, clothing – was to go to her kinswoman Leofflaed. The independence seemingly shown here by Edwin's mother, coupled with the rich details gained from the wills of Anglo-Saxon women, has in large measure contributed to a long-cherished view that here was a 'golden age for women'. The *locus classicus* of this view is to be found in Doris Stenton's pioneering work, *The English Woman in History*. According to Stenton:

The evidence which has survived from Anglo-Saxon England indicates that women were then more nearly the equal companions of their husbands and brothers than at any time before the modern age. In the higher ranges of society this rough and ready partnership was ended by the Norman Conquest, which introduced into England a military society relegating women to a position honourable but essentially unimportant.[4]

This argument is paralleled by the belief that as in the twelfth century the style of government changed from, in effect, palace rule to administrative kingship, the power of both queens and of aristocratic women up and down the country correspondingly shrank. An index of the change, or so it has been argued, can be seen in the way that chroniclers after the Norman Conquest recounted the deeds of the Saxon past. Thus in the hands of the twelfth-century historian William of Malmesbury the heroic Aethelflaed, Lady of the Mercians, scourge of the Vikings (and possible model, as we have seen, for the poem *Judith*), becomes a character so feeble that she is unable to bear the pains of childbirth. Not all historians would

---

[4] D. Stenton, *The English Woman in History* (1957), p. 28.

accept this reading of William of Malmesbury;[5] but there are many who would still agree with the verdict that after the Norman Conquest women lost status. A different emphasis, however, has recently been advocated by Pauline Stafford.[6] For her, 1066 is a much overrated date. In the first place, Stafford would have us pay closer attention to the Anglo-Saxon evidence: to note, for instance, that in the famous case from Herefordshire mentioned above, Edwin's mother is never given a name while Thurkil the White, to whose diligence we owe the written record, is named five times – and happens to be the husband of the lucky Leofflaed. Moreover, argues Stafford, eleventh-century changes took place in a context of societal developments in which generalisations about women are of dubious value and where 1066, at any rate, is simply 'not crucial'.

To engage with the 1066 debate we will need to consider, albeit selectively, queenship on the one hand, and the rules of inheritance as they affected women of the aristocracy on the other. The starting point must be queenship and the transmission of royal power in Anglo-Saxon England. This will necessitate political narrative, a genre it is vital not to eschew if we are to illustrate the full diversity of medieval women's roles.

Before the Viking raids of the ninth-century, England was still a country of many kingdoms.[7] The celebrated victory of King Alfred of Wessex against the Vikings at the Battle of Edington in 878 belongs to legend quite as much as to history but in either guise it serves well enough as the point of departure for the eventual unification of England some eighty years later. When Alfred himself died in 899 the throne passed to his son Edward the Elder (brother of Aethelflaed, Lady of the Mercians). We tend to think of such a succession, from father

[5] *cf.* B. Bandel, 'The English Chroniclers' Attitude Towards Women', *Journal of the History of Ideas* 16 (1955), pp. 113–18; J. Truax, 'From Bede to Orderic Vitalis: Changing Perspectives on the Role of Women in the Anglo-Saxon and Anglo-Norman Churches', *Haskins Society Journal* 3 (1991), pp. 35–51.

[6] P. Stafford, 'Women in Domesday', *Reading Medieval Studies* 15 (1989), pp. 75–94; *Unification and Conquest* (1989), pp. 172–9 and her 'Women and the Norman Conquest', forthcoming in the *Transactions of the Royal Historical Society.* My thanks to Pauline Stafford for allowing me to see a copy of this paper before publication.

[7] For Viking women, a topic not covered in this book, see J. Jesch, *Women in the Viking Age* (1991).

to son, as normal, but this was far from being the case in ninth-century Wessex where brothers had the same rights of inheritance as sons. Edward's accession did not pass unchallenged nor did it set a precedent. The problems caused by too many heirs – or too few – continued to beset accessions until the mid twelfth century. To die leaving no heir (as Edward the Confessor was to do) might seem a dereliction of duty; to die leaving minors or a choice of heirs born to different women – or indeed both – was arguably no less reckless. But it was in just such circumstances, as Pauline Stafford has shown, that the mothers in question were able to acquire considerable power both for themselves and for their sons. That they were able to do so is testimony both to their own attributes and to the personal and familial character of royal government in tenth- and eleventh-century England. If this power seems fragile, so too was men's. If women's power was particularly precarious, their lives at least were more secure. Royal women who got in the way had a better chance of being sent off to convents than of being murdered.

We begin with Eadgifu, daughter of a Kentish noble family and herself a holder of Kentish lands. In about 919 she married King Edward the Elder; her lands explain the match. When Edward married her he had already had two wives and at least three sons; by Eadgifu he had two more, Edmund and Eadred. On Edward's death, in 924, these children of Eadgifu cannot have seemed particularly close to the throne. But the premature deaths of two older half-brothers and the failure of the third to produce heirs gave Edmund the crown. After only five years of rule he was murdered and, in 944, his brother Eadred succeeded him. Despite both Edmund and Eadred being of age by the time they became king, Eadgifu held a highly visible place at court. She regularly signed royal diplomas, usually in second place to the kings and before their archbishops. Her friendship with Dunstan, then abbot of Glastonbury, and her partnership with him at the beginning of the monastic reform movement of the tenth century is beyond doubt, and for the success of the movement of the utmost importance. But then came 955 and Eadred's death. The new king, Eadwig, had no time for either his grandmother or Dunstan. Within months both had been exiled from the court.

Eadwig's reign was both troubled and short-lived; his brother Edgar rebelled against him and for two years the country was divided between them but, on Eadwig's death in 959, Edgar became sole king. Back to court came both Eadgifu and Dunstan and the lands confiscated from Eadgifu by Eadwig were restored to her. The extent of these lands shows the basis of her power. Besides her patrimony in Kent (much of which she made over to Dunstan, now Archbishop of Canterbury, for monastic use) Eadgifu also held land in Sussex, Surrey, Hampshire and Berkshire, for the most part given and bequeathed to her by Eadred. We may glimpse in these transactions something of the ways in which a queen's inheritance might both transmit favour and foster bitterness. In his will Eadred left to his mother estates which King Alfred had held in Amesbury, Wantage and Basing; in addition, she had long held Meon in Hampshire, another Alfredian property. The title deeds of this property she had entrusted to Edgar some time before his rebellion against his brother; Eadwig confiscated it from Edgar but, by 961, the land was again in Eadgifu's hands. On her death she bequeathed it to Edgar who in turn gave a portion of it to his other grandmother, Winflaed.

We last meet Eadgifu in Winchester in 966. She had come to celebrate the christening of a grandson, the first child to be born to Edgar's new wife Aelfthryth. Two other wives had already been set aside, a reminder, should one be needed, of the insecurities of queenly status. Fertility was not enough; a queen needed appropriate connections as well. Edgar already had a son by his first wife (now abbess of Wilton) but he had needed to make sure of influence in the south west of the country where Aelfthryth's family held lands in order to consolidate his newly won position as king.

In some respects Aelfthryth followed in Eadgifu's footsteps. She patronised the new monastic movement, giving land to houses of newly reformed monks and nuns and, for the latter, she commissioned a translation into the vernacular of the *Rule of St Benedict*. But for our purposes the most memorable thing about Aelfthryth is what made her different from previous queens. In 973, at Bath, Edgar held both for himself and for Aelfthryth a dazzling, imperial-style coronation. Here king and queen shared the ceremony of anointment. Just as Mary was now depicted in the *Benedictional of Aethelwold* as a crowned queen of heaven, so too was the status of Aelfthryth elevated. After the ceremony Edgar dined with his bishops and nobles; Aelfthryth, in a garment of silk sewn with pearls and gems, presided over a feast for abbots and abbesses. Queenship had become a shared and sacred office.

The history of the anointing of queens and of kings is obscured by lack of evidence; and despite the fanfare of 973 we cannot be certain that Aelfthryth was the first native queen to be anointed. Some sort of a precedent had undoubtedly been set by the anointment of the Frankish princess Judith before she was entrusted by her father to King Aethelwulf of Wessex (839–58), father of King Alfred. But it is only after Aelfthryth's anointment that the ritual becomes customary and the privileges of the status so bestowed become apparent. As a crowned and consecrated queen, Aelfthryth could and did continue to exercise power long after the death of Edgar in 975. It was also as such that she argued the case, on Edgar's death, for the accession of her son Aethelred in favour of his elder half-brother Edward born to an unanointed mother.

In this she was none the less overruled. Edward became king. Four years later on lands belonging to Aelfthryth at Corfe Castle he was murdered, a murder that was soon revered as a martyrdom. For nearly a year Edward's body remained undiscovered. No one was punished for the crime. The suspicion of Aelfthryth's complicity (if not necessarily of Aethelred's) hung long in the air. In spite of this Aelfthryth played a significant role in the new court, now the court of her son, King Aethelred. Although Aethelred was still only a boy of about twelve, he had already married Aelfgifu, the daughter of a northern earl, as part of his strategy to win support in the contest of 975. And yet Aelfgifu was never consecrated; there was evidently no room in the palace for more than one anointed queen at a time and this was the position filled by Aelfthryth. Aelfgifu had to be content with a back seat. She never appears in the witness-lists to royal diplomas and, although she gave birth to ten children, including four boys, even their upbringing seems to have been the responsibility of Aelfthryth. It was only after her death, and the death of Aelfthryth in 1002, that Aethelred took a new wife, Emma, a wife who was anointed and who, in contrast to Aelfgifu, made for herself a place well in the limelight of the political stage.

Emma was a daughter of Duke Richard of Normandy. Aethelred's marriage to her was designed to prevent Vikings from using Norman ports on their way to and from raiding in England. It is therefore somewhat ironic that on Aethelred's

death in 1016 Emma should have been married posthaste to
the Viking who had not only ravaged but ultimately conquered
England: Cnut. This time the bride brought with her, above all,
respectability: Emma was the legitimate, consecrated queen.
Cnut, on the other hand, had a well-earned reputation as a
'prince of pagans'; he badly needed a new image as a Christian
king, fit to take his place among the crowned heads of Europe.
The great cross of gold and silver encrusted with gems that
he and Emma gave to Winchester has been depicted in a
contemporary drawing. As T. A. Heslop has recently pointed
out, given the rarity of queen portraits of this date, this is
a remarkable drawing; 'it may also be significant,' Heslop
comments, 'that it is Emma who stands on the dexter side of
the cross, that is to say, she is at the right hand of Christ.'[8]

Emma would come to need all the prayers solicited on her
behalf by the churches which she and Cnut patronised. Her
marriage to Cnut brought with it a conflict of loyalties. By
Aethelred she already had two sons, Edward and Alfred. Cnut
for his part not only had two sons of his own, Swegn and
Harold Harefoot; he also had a continuing relationship with
their mother, Aelfgifu (whom some would identify with the
Aelfgyva of the Bayeux tapestry, a likely enough target for
slanderous rumour). A possible solution was for the claims of
all existing sons to be shelved and for the inheritance to pass
to any son Emma might have by Cnut. It was following this
line of argument that Edward and Alfred were sent out of the
country to be brought up in Normandy where they would
pose no threat to the claims of Harthacnut, Emma's child
by Cnut. On Cnut's death in 1035 Emma duly pressed for
Harthacnut's accession, swearing that Cnut had, in 1017,
promised her on oath that he would 'never set up the son of
any other woman to rule after him'.[9] Aelfgifu's children she
dismissed as illegitimate. In this she had the backing of
Godwine, raised by Cnut to be Earl of Wessex, father of
the Harold who would claim the kingdom in 1066, but
Harthacnut's absence in Denmark gave Aelfgifu and Harold
Harefoot the chance to seize power.

It is at this point that the plot thickens. Somebody – either

[8] T. A. Heslop, 'The Production of De Luxe Manuscripts and the Patronage of
King Cnut and Queen Emma', *Anglo-Saxon England* 19 (1990), p. 157, n. 16.
[9] *Encomium Emmae Reginae*, ed. A. Campbell (1949), p. 33.

Emma herself, or Harold writing a forged letter in her name – invited Edward and Alfred, Emma's sons by Aethelred, to return from exile. Edward joined his mother at Winchester but Alfred fell into the hands of Godwine who chose this moment to desert Emma for Harold. Alfred was tortured, blinded and died from the wounds. Harold was now unstoppable. Emma fled from the country, 'driven out', according to the *Anglo-Saxon Chronicle* 'without any mercy to face the raging winter'. She went to Flanders and there, in 1039, Harthacnut joined her. Harold Harefoot's death in the same year allowed him to renew, unchallenged, his claim to the English throne. Emma's ambition was realised; but not for long. On Harthacnut's death in 1042 the crown passed at last to her son Edward, who lost no time in making his feelings about his mother clear. Soon after his consecration as king, so the *Anglo-Saxon Chronicle* tells us, the king with his earls rode to Winchester; 'and they came unexpectedly upon the lady and deprived her of all the treasures which she owned and which were beyond counting, because she had been very hard to the king her son, in that she did less for him than he wished both before he became king and afterwards as well.'

The interest of Emma's reign lies not only in the events, but also in her apologia. Emma was a believer not just in action; she also took good care to see that her own version of her life would be heard. The *Encomium* of Queen Emma was written some time in 1041, in the brief period when Harthacnut was king; it is a masterly justification of her actions by a woman who was in danger of losing not only power but every shred of respectability, suspected as she was of complicity in the death of her son Alfred, treachery towards Edward, and vindictiveness towards Cnut's wife Aelfgifu. With consummate skill the author of the *Encomium* glosses over the time of her life when she was married to Aethelred; by this sleight of hand it looks as if Alfred and Edward are, like Harthacnut, her sons by the only husband she ever had, Cnut. And there is, of course, no hint of any bad behaviour on her part towards her sons; on the contrary, throughout the *Encomium* Emma is the model of a caring mother concerned only with their welfare.

Despite the *Encomium* Emma never achieved the saintliness ascribed to her successor as queen, Edith, wife of Edward the Confessor. Edith has managed to depict herself in something of the hue later used for Edward's canonisation. She appears chaste and modest, preferring to sit at the king's feet rather than by his side, keeping him well-dressed in embroidered robes. That Edith took a part in the shaping of both her own and Edward's reputation is evident from her commissioning of the *Life of Edward*, a work that in the wake of 1066 could still hope to salvage some glory for her kin. The eulogies of the *Life* underline Edith's traditional role as peace-weaver:

> By her advice peace wraps the kingdom round
> And keeps mankind from breaking acts of peace.[10]

The lines say both too much and not enough. Edith is, on the one hand, the perfect peace-weaver. Her marriage to Edward in 1045 sealed an alliance between the house of Godwine and Edward that lasted against all the odds throughout the reign. Godwine's role in the murder of Edward's brother, Alfred, was seemingly forgiven in return for his promise of support. As William of Malmesbury tells the story, on the death of Harthacnut, Edward was 'lost in uncertainty what to do'. Godwine had all the answers: he would secure him the throne in return for honours for his sons and marriage with his daughter.[11] Despite this being a barren marriage it was only during the conflict between her husband and her father in 1051–2 that Edith had to suffer the indignity of repudiation; with the restoration of Godwine came her own reinstatement at court. But symbol of peace though she was, in her last months as queen Edith found herself deeply embroiled in the quarrel that had broken out between her brothers Tostig and Harold, a quarrel which did much to weaken Harold's capacity to withstand William at Hastings in 1066.

After 1066 Edith joined the convent at Wilton, near Salisbury. It was a natural choice. Long associated with the nobility of Wessex Edith had been educated there and, as queen, she had richly patronised it. In the post-Conquest years the convent kept alive memories of Anglo-Saxon saints; but we should not think of it as a nostalgic backwater. It was the scene of significant dramas, dramas which, as Eleanor Searle has shown, go far towards explaining Norman strategies for gaining in one move acceptance and inheritance.[12]

---

[10] *Life of Edward the Confessor*, ed. F. Barlow (1962), p. 15.
[11] William of Malmesbury, *Gesta Regum*, ed. W. Stubbs (1887–9), bk II, ch. 13.
[12] E. Searle, *op. cit.*

Wilton in the 1090s had among its inmates both Matilda, daughter of Malcolm of Scotland and Margaret of Scotland, who could through her mother trace her ancestry back to King Alfred, and Gunnilda, daughter of the last Anglo-Saxon king, Harold. The eligibility of Matilda and Gunnilda hardly needs stressing. What was at stake was the choosing of their grooms. According to Malcolm's calculations Matilda was to marry Alan the Red, Lord of Richmond. However the match would have given power to Alan which neither the king of England, William Rufus, nor Alan's fellow barons were prepared to sanction, and Alan was refused his bride. Her father, in rage, rode to Wilton where he tore the veil off Matilda's head, telling her she had never been intended as a nun but rather as Alan's bride. Alan, meanwhile, thwarted in his desire for one heiress, consoled himself with the other. He too rode to Wilton where he abducted Gunnilda, but died before he could marry her. No matter, his brother took his place. And Matilda? Matilda in 1100 married the new king of England, Henry I. The prophecy of Edward the Confessor could now be fulfilled. On his deathbed Edward had foreseen terrible upheavals in the kingdom, a sign of God's wrath; but better times would come – 'when a green tree, if cut down in the middle of its trunk, and the part cut off carried the space of three furlongs from the stock, shall be joined again to its trunk, by itself and without the hand of man or any sort of stake, and begin once more to push leaves and bear fruit from the old love of its uniting sap, then first can a remission of these great ills be hoped for.'[13] Henry and Matilda's children would be that fruit.

'The fruit' were Prince William and Princess Matilda. To King Henry's lasting sorrow, William died – a drunken crew led to a fatal shipwreck in the English Channel when he was still only seventeen. Henry's queen, Matilda, was already dead. Henry remarried but he had no other heir; in 1127 he made all his barons swear that, should this still be so when he died, they would choose his daughter, Matilda, Empress through her marriage to Henry V of Germany, to succeed him. In the event, Matilda never got the throne; but this was not for want of trying on her part, nor was it ever said even by her opponents, that her sex was any kind of a disqualification. Yet to have suggested her as prospective queen was an unpre-

[13] *Life of Edward the Confessor*, p. 76.

cedented step on Henry's part. English queens had hitherto held power as queen mothers or, like two earlier Matildas – the wives of William I and Henry – as regents when their kings were in Normandy; they had never exercised power in their own right. This would seem an appropriate moment to consider changes in the nature of queenship before and after the Conquest, and what light the oaths of 1127 throw upon it.

In 1127, what mattered more than gender was legitimacy of birth. In pre-Conquest England, illegitimacy had not been a bar to the succession. Queen Emma, it is true, had attempted to use it in the *Encomium* as a way of discrediting the claims of Harold, by presenting him as the son of Cnut's concubine or even as the smuggled-in son of the concubine's servant, but even in the *Encomium* it seems to be recognised that just to be illegitimate might not be a sufficient disgrace. A more famous bastard king is of course William the Conqueror himself, whose victory at Hastings, a battle fought with papal blessing, would seem proof enough that illegitimacy of birth was for him no handicap. Yet, within a generation, his own son Henry I had made the decision to leave the kingdom to his daughter rather than to any one of his innumerable bastard sons. An illegitimate king of England had become unthinkable. Better a woman than a bastard; but better than either, it came to be thought, was succession by the eldest son. Though Matilda herself never became queen it was her son who became Henry II and under whose reign the principle of primogeniture triumphed.

The establishment of primogeniture and the new attitude to illegitimacy are part of changes in inheritance observable throughout continental Europe in the eleventh century, accelerated in England, but not caused, by the events of 1066. The position of queens became as a result much more secure. Serial marriages became a thing of the past; queens could now expect to keep their jobs for the duration of the reign and for their sons to succeed without challenge. Even allowing for family dramas and quarrels, of which there were plenty, no queen in the central Middle Ages would find herself in the position of an Eadgifu, Aelfthryth or Emma. Only perhaps with the Wars of the Roses in the fifteenth century and both Margaret of Anjou and Margaret Beaufort's relentless cherishing and championing of the claims of their sons to the throne, are we reminded again of the role thrust on royal women by the insecurities of late Anglo-Saxon politics.

Henry I's queen, Matilda, was the last-born English queen until Edward IV's marriage to Elizabeth Woodville in 1464. Queens thereafter were chosen as part of international diplomacy. As foreigners, in a country that was fast developing a new sense of national identity, they and the entourage they brought with them were a likely target for criticism. Perhaps this was part of the job. Together with the king's 'evil counsellors' they acted as some kind of shield for the king, taking on their own shoulders some of the criticism of his handling of affairs. But this was by no means their most marked function. Precisely because queens occupied so distinctive a space as both consort and outsider there were other tasks which only they could perform and which came to be seen as quintessentially their own. This is not, of course, to forget those queens who marked out for themselves quite different paths - queens such as Isabella in the early fourteenth century, who, together with her lover, overthrew her king and husband Edward II; but such crises quickly passed. With the accession of Isabella's son as Edward III, and his marriage to Philippa of Hainault, there was once again a royal marriage in working order.

By the time of Edward III, queens on earth were, like the Virgin, Queen of Heaven, firmly established in ritual (and usually in reality) as the intercessory partner in the kingdom. Eleanor of Provence, queen of Henry III, as sign and promise of her duty pleaded with the king at her coronation for the release of a man imprisoned for a transgression of the forest law. This was a ritual, possibly repeated at every coronation, which had widespread appeal and a message that was clearly understood; the inhabitants of the town of St Albans clamoured around Eleanor of Castile in 1275 asking her to secure for them the mercy of Edward I, telling her that they placed all their hope in her as surely as they trusted the queen of heaven. After her death Eleanor would be remembered as 'a devout woman, gentle and merciful, a friend to all Englishmen and indeed a pillar of the realm'.[14] The extent to which she was also, in certain circles, resented and reviled both as a

[14] William of Rishanger; cited by E. Hallam in David Parsons (ed.), *Eleanor of Castile, 1290–1990* (1991), p. 9.

foreigner and as a spendthrift need occasion no surprise, nor did it seriously disturb her other image. In an unparalleled display of public mourning Edward provided Eleanor with three tombs (entrails, heart and body each had a separate resting place) and twelve memorial crosses. The statues of Eleanor on the twelve crosses underlined her relationship to the Virgin in ways undreamt of in the iconography of the tenth-century *Benedictional of Aethelwold* associated with Queen Aelfthryth. In this period, the regality of the Virgin had been a necessary buttress to the still fragile position of the queen; by the fourteenth century, it was the compassion of the Virgin that was called upon in order to soften, though not to challenge, the arbitrary power of royal rule.

The Virgin, as Paul Strohm has pointed out, was not the only exemplar of queenly behaviour.[15] Every bit as important was the Old Testament figure of Esther. Whereas Mary is both queen and intercessor, Esther is at one and the same time wise counsellor to her king and abject suppliant. Ways in which these models could be used have been tellingly illustrated by Strohm from a number of examples, including Froissart's account of Queen Philippa's successful plea to Edward III for the release of six burghers of Calais, due to bear the brunt (with their lives) of the king's anger at their town's resistance to his siege. Philippa succeeds in her intervention as a woman who is noble, good and valiant; at the same time she is humble and pregnant, and (a point emphasised by Strohm) 'she just *happens* to be on the scene'. Kings are under no obligation to consult with their queens; when the occasion arises and they choose to listen to them, they can yield to their requests without loss of face and without any suggestion that a binding precedent has been set.

The evaluation of this relationship in terms of gender analysis is a contentious issue: how far the 'frail woman' topos which Philippa exploits is a sign of actual weakness or of actual power is likely to remain debatable; what cannot be disputed is that the rise of administrative kingship in no way dispensed with the role or value of queenship. Contemporaries were clear and explicit as to what they expected from an office they regarded as essential and complementary to that of their king. Shortly after the arrival of Ann of Bohemia, perhaps even

---

[15] P. Strohm, 'Queens as Intercessors' in *Hochon's Arrow*, pp. 95–119.

on the day of her marriage to Richard II in 1382, the citizens of London presented her with a bill, letting her know what the job amounted to:

Since it pertains to your most benign piety to assume in the innermost parts of piety the role of mediatrix between your most illustrious prince and most powerful lord and our lord the king, just as [did] our other lady Queens who preceded your most excellent highness in your realm of England, may it be pleasing to your most clement and pre-eminent nobility to mediate with our lord the King in such wise with gracious words and deeds.[16]

Fine flattery and rhetoric, but as Anne's intervention in the quarrel between Richard and his citizens some ten years later was to show, these are words we must remember in any evaluation of the role of medieval queens.

It is time to turn now to the women of the aristocracy, to see how they fared in post-Conquest England and whether their 'relegation' was as severe as Doris Stenton's judgement would have us believe. The problem, on first viewing, seems illusory: Anglo-Saxon women, as we have seen, held land in their own right. Among those recorded in Domesday Book is the Yorkshire woman Asa, to whose rights the jurors testified. Asa, they said, had held her land 'separate and free from the lordship and power of Bjornulfr her husband, even when they were together, so that he could neither give it, nor sell it, nor forfeit it. After their separation, she withdrew from her land and possessed it as a lady.' In Anglo-Norman England, tenure such as Asa's was an anomaly. Women no longer held land on such terms. But we must also remember that conditions of land tenure for men changed too. Under the Anglo-Norman rulers all land belonged to the king; it could be enjoyed but not owned by anyone else, and its use was conditional on the performance of military service. In the words of S. Milsom, 'when he first made his grant, his lord was not just allocating resources within his control ... he was securing for himself a man.'[17] This militarisation of tenure meant, in theory, that only men could hold land, a theory which, as Doris Stenton

---

[16] See Strohm, *op. cit.*, p. 105.
[17] S. F. C. Milsom, 'Inheritance by Women in the Twelfth and Early Thirteenth Centuries', in M. Arnold *et al.* (eds), *On the Laws and Customs of England* (1981), p. 62.

observed, would seem to indicate a huge shift in the balance of power between women and men.

But reality was rather different. Both before and after the Conquest men, like women, on the whole wanted to leave at least some land to every member of the family; but, following the Conquest, men, like women, lost the right to bequeath their land freely. What provisions, then, could parents make for their children, whether sons or daughters? There was, of course, no guarantee that they would have sons – or indeed children at all. Take the example of Payn Peverall, given the barony of Bourn by Henry I in 1122. Ten years later Payn died, childless, and his nephew William Peverall succeeded to the title. In 1147 William died while on crusade; his heirs were his four sisters, of whom one married but died childless and another had a son who in his turn died childless. There was nothing unusual about such a story and hence it was essential, both for the king and his barons, that the rules of inheritance should be modified in order to respect the delicate balance between the workings of fate, the demands of lordship and the needs of families. There were no easy answers; the implications for women can be hard to ascertain, not least because frequently, as Milsom has pointed out, there might be no law beyond existing practice. None the less one or two generalisations are possible.

Under the new rules women of the Anglo-Norman world could be heiresses. Initially, one daughter could be the sole inheritor but from the later twelfth century it became customary to divide inheritances among heiresses in equal shares (the fragmentation of estates this caused had by the later Middle Ages created a further set of problems). What heiresses could not expect to do was to marry whom they pleased. A clause in Henry I's coronation charter makes this clear: 'If on the death of a baron or other of my men a surviving daughter is the heir I will give her (in marriage) with her land following the advice of my barons.' It was precisely this custom which prevented the proposed marriage between Matilda and Count Alan the Red of Richmond. In time the system would lead to the compilation of a list of those whose marriages could, at a price, be fixed: the *Register of Rich Widows and of Orphaned Heirs and Heiresses* of 1185. But we must not be misled by the wealth of information we suddenly have about these women into imagining that they fell into some new category. Despite the differences in the way they held their land, we have no reason to suppose that the Anglo-Saxon heiress had any greater choice in her partner than her Anglo-Norman successor. On the contrary, in a text of uncertain date but from some time around 1000, it is clear that marriages must be acceptable to kin-groups and that it was men who made the settlements: 'if they reach agreement about everything, then the kinsmen are to set about betrothing their kinswoman as wife and in lawful matrimony to him who has asked for her, and he who is leader of the betrothal is to receive the security.'[18]

We must not forget, moreover, that the freedoms of both men and women to choose their partners were circumscribed by family expectations, or that both men and women occasionally disregarded them. In a case cited by Milsom, a tenant of the Earl of Winchester stipulated in his will that his two daughters should inherit his land only in the event of their marriage to two brothers. The elder daughter indeed married the elder son; the younger son, however, was unexpectedly presented with a church living and decided against marrying, with the result that the younger daughter, his intended bride, was dispatched to a nunnery. Unlike the nun of the lament – 'Poor me ... shut out of the fun / when life's barely begun' – the daughter in question was resourceful. She sent a message to a boyfriend who promptly arrived, married her in her convent, and then lay in wait so that, as she was being led away to a more secure institution by her outraged brother-in-law, he could abduct her.

The final outcome of the litigation set in motion by this stirring tale is lost to us. What we see underlined again and again in equally tangled cases is the notion that women transmit rather than own their property. The father who wishes to endow his daughter with a *maritagium* (her dowry) technically can only do so through her husband. If he dies before her marriage she will only have the promise of land, not its ownership. But her position in this respect is more favourable than that in which her younger brother may find himself. The daughter, once married, can make a claim for her dowry from the heir and it is a claim which church courts will support. Her brother, on the other hand, has no such redress against the heir; to secure his portion, his father must take his son's homage; but

---

[18] *English Historical Documents*, vol. I, p. 468.

the result here will be to alienate the land permanently from the original inheritance.

The complexity of twelfth- and thirteenth-century disputes to which such arrangements led must not beguile us into imagining that the dealings in the days when an Anglo-Saxon woman could seemingly leave her land to whomever she chose were necessarily more straightforward. A letter from Queen Aelfthryth should put us on our guard: 'Wulfgyth rode to me at Combe, looking for me,' wrote Aelfthryth, 'and I then, because she was kin to me ... obtained from bishop Aethel-wold that they [Wulfgyth and her husband] might enjoy the land for their lifetime ... And with great difficulty we two brought matters to this conclusion.'[19] Much here is hidden to us; but the implications would seem to be clear. Land-holding depended on having the right connections and patronage. A recent paper by Marc Meyer invites us to look more closely at the women who owned land in late Saxon England: on inspection, it turns out that the wealthiest of these are the women of the Godwine family.[20] Thus, of the land held by the 350 women who figure in Domesday Book as land-holders in the time of Edward the Confessor, about half was in the hands of just three women: Queen Edith (sister of Harold Godwineson), Gytha (his mother), and Edith (his concubine). These three are clearly not holding land as 'liberated women' in the twentieth-century sense but in order to support the political ambitions of the men of their clan, from which they too can hope to derive status and profit. Likewise, and here we return to the arguments of Pauline Stafford, we cannot be certain what lies behind those apparently enlightened wills of the tenth and eleventh centuries in which women appear to have full control over the bequeathing of their property. Are women, Stafford asks, doing anything here other than putting into effect arrangements which male kin have already made? The answer, probably, is not a great deal. Many of the extant wills come from widows, confirming, in all likelihood, their husbands' dispositions.

The question we must ask ourselves is: what we are to make of this? To argue, as one might, that the early eleventh century

[19] Cited C. Fell, *Women in Anglo-Saxon England* (1984), p. 106.
[20] M. Meyer, 'Women's Estates in Later Anglo-Saxon England: The Politics of Possession', *Haskins Society Journal* 3 (1991), pp. 111–29.

was not, after all, such a 'golden age' for women, or that 1066 was not, after all, such a disaster, are both conclusions to be resisted. In trying to understand the changes for women wrought by the eleventh century, judgements based on notions of supposed or of failed 'progress' are unlikely to help. New circumstances demanded and furnished roles that were different, rather than 'better' or 'worse', both for women and for men. In 1066 meanwhile 'the wheel of fortune', so beloved by those medieval moralists wishing to underline the instability of all earthly power, continued to turn as relentlessly as ever.

PART THREE

The High and Later Middle Ages: Family Roles

CHAPTER SIX

Sex, Marriage and Motherhood

Sexual Debates

Medieval women were classified according to their sexual status: men might be thought of collectively as knights, merchants, crusaders; women were virgins, wives or widows. They were also, of course, mothers. A professed reason for showing respect to women was indeed that everyone – Christ included – had come into the world through a woman. Those who chose to eschew marriage and motherhood in order to enter the religious life as virgins were always a tiny minority; they will be the subject of a later chapter. Our concern here is with women who married and had children.

However varied the experience of such women, however irrecoverable their personal voices, the meaning, morality and nature of their lives was a topic of ever-changing complexity and debate. How to understand woman's particular physiology, how to reconcile the alleged demands of her nature with Christian teaching, these were matters not simply of academic interest, but of everyday urgency. In the late twelfth century, for example, questions like the following were being asked in learned circles in Northern Europe:

some-one's wife has been ruptured in the navel through repeated child-birth. The doctors tell her that if she gives birth again she will die. Nevertheless her husband asks her for the debt [debt here means the marriage debt, i.e. sex]. Is she bound to render it, since she knows for certain that she will die if she conceives? She knows that if she renders the debt she will conceive, because she is still young. Item, one asks if she can procure sterility for herself not principally in order to impede child-birth but in order not to die in child-birth.

93

This particular conundrum, recently discussed by Peter Biller in *Woman is a Worthy Wight*,[1] was set by Peter the Chanter of Paris. Peter in turn was master to Chobham, sub-dean of Salisbury Cathedral and the author of an influential manual designed to give guidance to English priests in the exercise of their parochial duties. It is a manual to which we shall have reason to return; but for now let us examine the overlapping and at times conflicting worlds in which the putative woman with the ruptured navel found herself.

The medieval Church, or so it is often claimed, believed that the best way of dealing with sex was to give it up; only minimal investigation will reveal that its teaching on the subject was considerably more complex. Sexual intercourse as such was not the problem; it was a part of God's original plan. Although Adam and Eve did not have sex in the Garden of Eden, this was simply because they had not, as things turned out, had time for it; if they had not sinned by eating the apple – a sin of pride – they would necessarily have had intercourse – there would otherwise have been no way they could have obeyed God's order to 'increase and multiply' (Genesis 1: 27–8). They could not have chosen to be virgins in paradise or they would have been guilty of thwarting God's intentions. The causes of the Fall and the expulsion of Adam and Eve from the Garden of Eden had, then, nothing to do with sex. The problem was that after the Fall sex was no longer possible, as it would have been in paradise, without the disturbing accompaniment of lust. As the thirteenth-century theologian, Peter Lombard, explained:

if the first humans had not sinned there would have been carnal union in Paradise without any sin or stain and there would have been an 'undefiled bed' (Hebrews 13: 4) there and union without concupiscence. Furthermore, they would have commanded the genital organs like other organs, so they would not have felt any unlawful movement there. Just as we move some bodily members towards others, such as the hand to the mouth, without the ardour of lust, likewise they would have used the genital organs without any itching of the flesh.[2]

Post-lapsarian lust, the result of sin, was therefore what

[1] P. Biller, 'Marriage Patterns and Women's Lives: A Sketch of Pastoral Geography', in P. J. P. Goldberg (ed.), *Woman is a Worthy Wight* (1992), p. 75.
[2] Peter Lombard, cited in P. Payer, *The Bridling of Desire: Views of Sex in the Later Middle Ages* (1993), pp. 24–5.

caused sex to be so troublesome; such lust, unless rigorously controlled, could lead the unwary to eternal damnation. Only one legitimate outlet for sex was possible, and that was marriage. Views on the moral quality of married sexual activity might and did vary but there could be no doubt that marriage had been ordained by God (in contrast to monasticism which, as was sometimes pointed out, had been instituted by man) and that sex was its expected component. Even the rigorists adhered to the theory of mutual conjugal debt as defined by St Paul:

Let the husband render to his wife what is her due, and likewise the wife to her husband. A wife has no authority over her body but her husband; likewise, the husband has no authority over his body but his wife. You must not refuse each other except perhaps by consent for a time, that you may give yourself to prayer and return together again lest Satan tempt you because you lack self-control. (I Corinthians 7: 3–6)

This is the 'debt' to which Peter the Chanter was referring. But Peter, as we have seen, was concerned also with the competing authority of the physician; the physician, in the case quoted, being the one who is urging restraint. The Church in the Middle Ages had never held a monopoly on discussions of sexual lore; there had always been a separate tradition derived from Greek medical schools and subsequently enriched by Arabic learning. Given their wholly different bases, the medical and ecclesiastical worlds could and did at times collide (for example, on the propriety of dissecting bodies), although for the most part they lived amicably side by side. To the late-twentieth-century reader it may come as something of a surprise to learn that the putting of a plaster of hemlock on the testicles before coitus was recommended as a form of birth control; even more surprising that this advice comes from a best-selling book, *The Treasure of the Poor*, written by the future Pope John XXI.[3] (We might note that today such contradictions tend to centre around the subject of food rather than sex: any woman's magazine is likely to contain dietary advice followed by recipes which conform to none of the recommended rules.) In any discussion of sex and marriage there is of course that most unfathomable world of all, the world of practice. What notice, if any, did men and women take either of their doctors

[3] J. Riddle, *Contraception and Abortion from the Ancient World to the Renaissance* (1991), p. 138.

or their priests? How far did their theories influence behaviour? Before we can even begin to consider such questions we will need to look more closely both at prevailing theories of physiology and at theological teaching on marriage. For university men of the late twelfth and thirteenth centuries these were matters of paramount interest.

Medical theories about sexual difference were themselves by no means uniform. There were two chief schools of thought. The earliest, following Galen, advocated a female anatomy which corresponded with that of a man. The newer one, based on Aristotle, saw women as defective males: the parts that were outside in a man were inside in a woman. For the Galenists, both men and women produced seed, whereas on an Aristotelian understanding of reproduction women provided no more than 'matter for the semen to work upon'. Galen's views, however 'egalitarian' they might seem, had a double edge. On the one hand, a woman had to ejaculate her seed in order for there to be conception, and this she could not do without enjoying the act of intercourse; on the other hand, it then became impossible for a woman who had been raped and who became pregnant to reclamate.

There was also, despite the seeming symmetry of Galenist theory, a considerable difference in its teaching on the nature of male and female seed. Male seed was precious; it must be neither unreasonably stored up nor prodigally wasted. Female seed, on the other hand, was potentially lethal. Women needed regularly to purge themselves of their bodily excesses. Menstruation was a part of this process; so was intercourse; in cases of necessity, masturbation was recommended to avoid the dangers of stored-up seed. Such seed could lead to a condition of varying degrees of seriousness known as 'uterine suffocation'. The woman thus afflicted would have difficulty in breathing, she would have convulsions and fainting fits and she might go mad. John of Gaddesden, of the Faculty of Medicine at Oxford University in the fourteenth century, had this advice to give:

If the suffocation comes from a retention of the sperm, the woman should get together with and draw up a marriage contract with some man. If she does not or cannot do this, because she is a nun and it is forbidden by her monastic vow or because she is married to an old man incapable of giving her her due, she should travel overseas, take frequent exercise and use medicine which will dry up the sperm ... If she has a fainting fit, the midwife should insert a finger covered with oil of lily, laurel or spikenard into her womb and move it vigorously about.[4]

Absent from Galen's thought but none the less of lasting influence throughout the Middle Ages was the quite separate tradition, put to pernicious use in the hands of misogynists, that women's seed, and more especially menstrual blood, were dangerous not only to women, but to everything else as well. As recorded by Pliny in his *Natural History*, contact with menstrual blood turned new wine sour, crops touched by it became barren and fruit fell from trees, hives of bees died, dogs who tasted it got rabies. Such lore, combined with Old Testament taboos, led to the strict insistence that intercourse during menstruation was to be avoided at all costs; any child so conceived was likely to have red hair and to contract leprosy. The mere gaze of a menstruating woman might have dire consequences; children in their cradles could be poisoned by the glance of an old woman who still had her periods, the logic being that the retention of her menses gave her poisonous vapours let off through her eyes.

Just as longevitous as classical superstitions about menstruation was the teaching of Hippocratic theory, inherited from Greece, of the four humours; this too could be given a misogynistic slant. According to Hippocratic thinking, the world must be understood as divided into four elements: fire, air, earth and water. To these corresponded three categories: first: heat, cold, dryness and moisture; second, the bodily humours: blood, yellow bile or choler, black bile and phlegm; third, the temperaments: sanguine, choleric, phlegmatic and melancholic. Health was a matter of achieving the correct humoral balance. Men and women were basically different: men were hotter and drier than women, which accounted for their physiological and moral superiority. Women's lack of heat accounted both for physical weakness and for their slippery and untrustworthy nature. It also helped to explain why women were sexually much greedier than men: cold uteruses were ever in need of being warmed up by hot semen.

Misogynistic interpretations were never, however, the whole

---

[4] Cited in D. Jacquart and C. Thomasset, *Sexuality and Medicine in the Middle Ages* (1988), p. 176.

story. Even as wild claims for the damaging effects of menstruating women were being disseminated through late-thirteenth-century tracts, so too discussions were afoot as to whether or not the Virgin had menstruated; the consensus was that she had. Our concern now must be to try and determine how far such mixed messages on their sexual nature affected 'actual' women. What relevance, if any, did the classroom discussions of celibate males have for women in medieval England? Let us start with medicine.

Difficult though it is to know how women interpreted or internalised scholastic traditions, we have in the writings of Hildegard of Bingen (d. 1178), abbess of the Rhenish foundation of Rupertsberg, a rare example of a woman who combined traditional teaching on women's nature with an understanding of humoral theory in such a way that perceived weaknesses became strengths; thus it was to her own 'airiness' as a woman that Hildegard attributed her receptivity to the wind of the Holy Spirit. Other women of lesser literary brilliance may have done likewise. We do not know. Nor, it must be admitted, do we have much evidence for the dissemination in medieval England of Hildegard's medical writings other than a copy owned by John Erghome (d. *c.*1385), prior of an Augustinian friary at York, but her reputation as a visionary was certainly well known.[5] On the other hand it would be a mistake to imagine that for an abbess to be interested in medicine was in itself unusual. Equally, we have only the sparsest evidence for women doctors in medieval England but this includes the knowledge that at the convent of Wherwell in Hampshire in the mid-thirteenth century, the abbess Euphemia practised medicine.

Abbess Euphemia may, or may not, have limited her expertise to the treatment of other women. Meagre though the evidence is of female medical practice it is clear that women healers, and not only nuns, did sometimes attend men: female skills in nursing sick heroes were a commonplace in romance – examples can be found in *Tristan*, *Silence* and *Guigemar* – and they were also an actuality. Monica Green, for example, has found a 'wise woman' (*vetula*) in attendance at the Anglo-Norman court. Conversely, as Green has also demonstrated, women's health in the Middle Ages must not be understood

---

[5] I owe the reference to John Erghome to Monica Green.

simply as 'women's business'.[6] Firstly, not all women's health problems were of gynaecological origin; the much vaunted reason for assuming female care – modesty – would thus in a number of conditions have been of limited relevance. Secondly, while a woman in labour might indeed be attended by another woman, her midwife, this in itself did not preclude male interest in gynaecology.

The legend of a supposed 'woman's world' of medicine, debarred to men, centres around the figure of Trota of Salerno. Trota has suffered the extremes of fame; on the one hand, she has been denied historicity – Salerno is recognised without hesitation as the eleventh-century centre for the transmission of Greek medical learning to the West but the idea that there was a place there for a woman physician has been ridiculed; on the other hand, Trota has been accredited with works she never wrote. A definitive study of the 'Trotula' treatises by Monica Green is to appear shortly. What is already clear from the work of both Green and John Benton is that, ironically, the one authentic work of Trota's, *The Practice According to Trota*, was little known in Europe and never translated into any vernacular. The three treatises attributed to her, on the other hand, were widely circulated and in use up until the sixteenth century. According to Green, at least three dozen copies of Latin 'Trotula' texts and three Anglo-Norman translations as well as Middle English versions were in use in England for the treatment of women. These repay attention.

The most popular, known as Translation A, of which there are five extant copies, draws in the main on two of the 'Trotula' texts; it also includes extracts from the *Gynaecia* of Muscio, a work of gynaecology based on the writings of the second-century Greek physician Soranus of Ephesus, of considerable interest for its instructions for normal delivery and for malpresentations. To these texts Middle English authors added variations of their own. Alexandra Barratt has edited an illustrative passage in *Women's Writing in Middle English*. As an important *apologia* for the work, this merits an extensive quotation and the following sample, loosely rendered into modern English, will give an idea of its character:

Our Lord God when he had established the world with all creatures, he

[6] M. Green, 'Women's medical practice and health care in medieval Europe', in J. Bennett *et al.* (eds), *Sisters and Workers in the Middle Ages* (1989), pp. 39–78.

made man and woman as rational creatures, and bade them grow and multiply, and ordered that from these two should come the third. And he ordered that of the man, that is made of hot and dry matter, should come the seed and that the woman that is made of cold matter and moist should receive the seed so that by the balance of hot and cold, moist and dry, the child should be conceived, just as we see trees, corn and herbs may not grow without the right balance of the four elements.

And in as far as women are by nature more weak and cold than men and have great travail in child-birth they often suffer from a greater variety of illnesses than do men, particularly in those parts of the body that appertain to conception. Wherefore for the worship of Our Lady and of all the saints, my intention was to try diligently to translate from Latin and French into English various causes of their maladies, the signs that you will know them by, the cures that will help them following the treatises of various masters that have translated them from Greek into Latin. And because women of our tongue can better read and understand this language than any other and every literate woman may read it to any who is illiterate and help her and advise her in her maladies without showing her disease to any man I have composed and written this in English.

And if any man chances to read it I pray him and charge him on Our Lady's behalf that he read it not in any way that would show contempt or be slanderous of any woman, nor for any reason except their healing and help, dreading the vengeance that might fall to him as it has done to others that have revealed women's secrets in a slanderous fashion; certainly understanding that those women who are now alive have troubles no different from those once endured by women who now are saints in heaven.

Just as the maker of all things ordered trees to flourish and flower and afterwards to bring forth fruit, in the same way he has ordained to all women a purgation which is called flowers (i.e. menstrual flow) without which no child may be engendered or conceived ... Just as pollution (i.e. nocturnal emissions) purge excess humours from a man so do the flowers for a woman.[7]

The author continues with a description of the physical differences between men and women and with instructions on how to conceive male as opposed to female children – or indeed vice versa. What is clearly remarkable, as Alexandra Barratt has pointed out, is the sympathy shown towards women.[8] There is no suggestion in the story of the Creation of any blameworthy behaviour on the part of the first woman

[7] A. Barratt (ed.), *Women's Writing in Middle English* (1992), pp. 29–31. My translation.
[8] *Ibid.*, p. 28.

nor of her as a secondary creation, a kind of afterthought on God's part. Genesis has been blended with humoral theory to produce an origin story free from any hint of misogyny. Similarly, at the end of the passage quoted, menstruation is mentioned as part of the natural order of things. There is no evidence here of any of the dangers associated with menstrual blood, as we have seen described by Pliny and borrowed from him by later writers, nor any intimation that women's physiology bears the stain of original sin; the special problems of women have been shared by the saints in heaven, surely an invitation, if not a theological *sequitur*, to regard them as free from impurity.

We will return to the author of Translation A after considering briefly some of the remaining 'Trotula' treatises and related Middle English texts. 'Trotula' Translation B claims for its cures the authority of Galen and Hippocrates. Unlike 'Trotula A' it contains no special address to women; possibly it was owned by a male physician. What makes it distinctive is its inclusion of a number of cosmetic recipes, for hair and face, for example, as well as the advice that, before sexual intercourse, a woman should rub her breast, nipples and genitals with a powder made of dried roses, cloves, nutmeg, galingale and laurel. A recipe is provided for constricting her vagina if she is trying to give a false impression of being a virgin. The contents of 'Trotula C', also known as *The Book of Rota*, include a diagnostic test for infertility, to be used by both men and women, as well as advice on a whole range of matters, such as talking in one's sleep. But much better known than any of these 'Trotula' texts was a quite separate compilation, *The Sickness of Women*.

The Sickness of Women is based not, in the first instance, on Salernitan works but on a Latin medical textbook of the thirteenth century compiled by Gilbert the Englishman. It circulated in England in both a shorter and a longer version. The longer version includes a little of Muscio's *Gynaecia* together with illustrations designed to help midwives correct the position of the infant at the start of labour.

Taken together, these texts show, on the one hand, the persistence of medical lore handed down from Late Antiquity, on the other its constant adaptation. The Middle English manuscripts were copied as working texts, not as compilations of antiquarian interest. However bizarre some of the recipes may sound, there is evidence of their being both tried and tested. New herbs are added; case histories are recited. A late-twentieth-century audience, aware again of the claims of aromatherapy and alternative medicine, may be less sceptical than earlier generations about the recommended herbal baths and the plant remedies proposed. Other advice seems neither more nor less than common sense. On failure to menstruate, for example, *The Sickness of Women* comments:

> But if this illness is a result of anger or sorrow, cause her to be cheerful, give her refreshing food and drink, and get her used to bathing some-times. And if it is the result of too much fasting or overwakefulness, see that she eats good food and drink which will give her good blood and get her to enjoy herself and be happy and give up gloomy thought.[9]

Whatever the merits of the advice given in *The Sickness of Women* it is far from clear whether we are still dealing with a world of women's medicine as adumbrated in 'Trotula A'. As Green has pointed out, of the 'Trotula' texts which we have considered only 'Trotula A' and *The Book of Rota* contain any suggestion – other than in conventional prologues closely modelled on Latin sources – of having been written for a specifically female audience. Thus, while 'Trotula A' regularly gives advice in the second person, and so in one manuscript does the author of *The Book of Rota*, the shorter version of *The Sickness of Women* addresses its readers as 'Sirs'. Despite the available evidence of book ownership by women, including herbals and books of medicine, and of the relationship between women and vernacular texts (subjects to which we shall return), Green has not as yet been able to find a single specifi-cally gynaecological manuscript owned by a woman. This is not in any way to underestimate the role of women midwives or the less prominent part played by women doctors and physicians; but it is to suggest, following Green, that women's fertility was considered too important to be left solely in their hands. What we make of this is another matter; whether, for example, we regard the Prior of Bermondsey's expertise in matters of haemorrhage of the womb (as reported in *The Sick-ness of Women*) as evidence of enlightenment on his part, or meddlesome curiosity, is an open question. What we clearly cannot count on is the sympathetic tone set by the author of

---

[9] B. Rowland (ed.), *Medieval Woman's Guide to Health* (1981), p. 71.

Translation A. Beryl Rowland cites prejudices which are likely to have been common: John of Mirfield (d. 1407), a doctor at St Bartholomew's Hospital, London, complained about 'worthless and presumptuous women who usurp this profession to themselves and abuse it; who, possessing neither natural ability nor professional knowledge, make the greatest possible mistakes (thanks to their stupidity) and very often kill their patients.'[10]

Women practitioners might be derided either for their general ignorance or for the limited field of their expertise. It should, however, be noted that this kind of criticism was primarily based on the new professionalism which university training gave doctors. When medical faculties were first set up in the mid-thirteenth century, women were excluded – as they were from any university education – but they continued to practise medicine, as did many laymen. Both came in for abuse. University-trained physicians and surgeons resented the continued esteem shown towards those who had not passed through the system. They poured scorn on healers, whether male or female, who were not, in their eyes, properly qualified and who might take away some of their business, undercutting their prices. Guy de Chauliac, a fourteenth-century surgeon whose work was translated into English, was equally scathing both about German knights who, he claimed, used stones and incantations to cure wounds, and about women and the unlettered whose medicine, he maintained, consisted of appeals to God and his saints.

Guy's lampoons raise the question as to how far 'textual' medicine conflicted, or tallied, with the admonitions and teachings of the Church. Did the one represent, as Guy seems to suggest, 'learned' medicine, while the other encouraged 'popular' cures? Professional jealousy apart, how big a gulf was there between hospital and Church? On one reading the medical and the ecclesiastical worlds are quite separate; in the medical texts there is not much room for magic. Mention of the healing qualities of certain stones or herbs – perhaps as used by Guy's German knights – is the only sign of any belief in the curative powers of supernatural properties. No invocations are included to make the recommended substances – balsam wood, aromatic calamus, spikenard, galingale, mastic,

[10] *Ibid.*, p. 14.

saffron, pellitory – any more efficacious than they will be after the necessary cooking or pounding. On the other hand, the authors are on the whole on their guard to preserve ecclesiastical proprieties. In cases of 'suffocation of the uterus' it may, according to *The Sickness of Women*, be helpful to have sexual intercourse – 'but understand what I have to say: the relations must be lawful such as with her husband and no other; for certainly it is better for man or woman to have the greatest physical illness while they live than to be healed through a deed of lechery or any other deed against God's command.'[11]

Likewise, in one of the 'Trotula A' texts, the scribe refuses to discuss contraception lest 'some cursed kelots [loose women] would use it'. Abstinence was the only method he would advocate. A different manuscript contains plenty of recipes for contraceptives though a similar anxiety surfaces: 'such things should not be known to young fools but only to save good and wise women from peril.' Penitentials dealing with the same subject are, as one might expect, more rigorous; their concern not only with *coitus interruptus* but also with potions given or taken to prevent conception suggests that so-called 'poisons of sterility' were relatively easy to come by. In penitentials and medical texts alike, poverty is regarded as some kind of an excuse for the use of contraceptives. What none of the texts will condone is abortion; this is a practice proscribed in thirteenth-century England by both canon and civil law, though, given the choice in *The Sickness of Women* between the life of the child and the life of the mother, it is the mother who is to be saved.

We may still want to know to whom the women in medieval England in need of medical attention or advice on sexual or gynaecological matters would first have turned. Penitentials and medical texts may tell us of recommended practices or solutions which women should avoid, in short, what they should and should not do, but still leave us guessing as to what, in fact, they did.

It would be easy, but probably misleading, to assume that the kinds of treatment women followed depended on their class. Our evidence, incomplete though it is, suggests that women and indeed men of whatever station were catholic in their choice of palliatives. Stories of their recourse to holy men

[11] *Ibid.*, p. 91.

and of visits to shrines help to suggest both the complex brew of remedies they tried as well as the wide social spectrum to which they belonged. A saint such as Hugh of Lincoln, for example, bishop from 1186 until his death in 1200, was faced with a fair share of cases of infertility, adultery and sexual harassment demanding miraculous intervention. One cure, of a woman allegedly molested 'by a demon in the shape of a young man', although attributed to the intervention of Hugh's prayers was also, according to Hugh's biographer, Adam of Eynsham, expedited by judicious use of the herb St John's wort. Adam is anxious to justify such a prophylactic; since doctors consider the herb 'a sovereign remedy against poison', such as snake-bites, there is no reason why it should not also be effective 'against the assault of the ancient Serpent'. 'Nothing in the world,' concludes Adam, 'which can be hurt by the malice of the treacherous enemy has through the gracious mercy of our Saviour been left without an adequate remedy.'[12]

Many saints dispensed their favours reasonably equally between men and women; but occasionally saints with a marked penchant for one or other sex can be found. One such is the patron saint of Oxford, St Frideswide, whom Henry Mayr-Harting has shown to have been particularly adept at dealing with the problems of women.[13] A new shrine was built for Frideswide in 1180; for the next decade pilgrims flocked to it. Among those said to have been cured was Beatrix from Wiltshire suffering from a two-year headache brought on after having had sex with her husband; Helen, also from Wiltshire, who could not sleep now that her lover-priest had given her up; Cecily from Oxfordshire whose neighbours suspected that her pregnancy was feigned. The young women who sought help were, Mayr-Harting has suggested, particularly troubled by the expectations roused by the Church's new teaching on marriage in contrast to their experience of it. It is time to consider what this teaching was.

---

[12] Adam of Eynsham, *The Life of St Hugh of Lincoln*, ed. D. Douie and H. Farmer (1962), vol. 2, p. 123.

[13] H. Mayr-Harting, 'Functions of a Twelfth-Century Shrine: The Miracles of St Frideswide', in H. Mayr-Harting and R. I. Moore (eds), *Studies in Medieval History Presented to R. H. C. Davis* (1985), pp. 193–206.

Marriage

Despite the fulminations of the early medieval church against unchristian sexual practices – concubinage, adultery, incest, to name only a few – it was not until the twelfth century that there was in place either a consistent theory of what made a marriage or a regularly used wedding liturgy. Only in the wake of the reforms of the Gregorian papacy did the Church turn its attention to the intensification of the Christian life of the laity and to a consideration of marriage as a sacrament rather than as a civil contract. But in its attempt to develop a new theology of marriage the Church remained faithful to, and indeed renewed, its commitment to the idea that what made a marriage was the consent of the couple: no more and no less. Debate in the mid-twelfth century centred on whether sexual intercourse was necessary to cement the alliance. In support of the traditional viewpoint the Bolognese lawyer Gratian argued that it was. In Paris, Peter Lombard and his school, proposing a new definition – and it was they who won the day – argued that it was not. (Otherwise, it was asked, how would it be possible to regard Mary and Joseph as married, given that Mary retained her virginity throughout her life?) To the Lombard school, an exchange of words of commitment was therefore all that was needed: the statements 'I take you as my wife ... I take you as my husband' in themselves had legal and sacramental force. But a promise to marry was another matter. In that case, there was no marriage unless the promise was followed by sex. Sex alone, or the promise alone, were not binding.

By its adherence to this ideology of consent the Church manoeuvred itself into a curious corner. Anxious on the one hand to promote the state of matrimony as 'an excellent mystery', to be likened, in the words of the Sarum liturgy, to the 'sacramental and nuptial union betwixt Christ and Church', it was on the other hand bound by its own logic to accept the validity of clandestine arrangements. Everything was done that could be done to urge that marriages be celebrated in church; that banns be read three times in order that the proposed marriage be made public and open to scrutiny; none the less, marriages contracted out of church and in secret still retained their legitimacy.

The theory of marriage as advocated by Peter Lombard was

finally accepted into the law of the church by Pope Alexander III (1159–81). It was left to his successor, Innocent III, to make the Church's teaching on consanguinity and affinity more manageable by reducing the prohibited degrees from seven to four. Given that this new ruling had some chance of being observed it was imperative to Pope Innocent that it should be. In future, therefore, marriages were to be solemnised with proper publicity. Canon 51 of the 1215 Fourth Lateran Council lays out both the procedure to be followed and the logic behind it:

As the prohibition of marriage in the three remotest degrees is repealed, we wish it to be strictly observed in others. Hence, following in the steps of our predecessors, we absolutely prohibit clandestine marriages, forbidding also any priest to be present at such. For which reason we extend the particular custom of certain countries to countries generally, decreeing that when marriages are to be contracted they shall be published in the churches by the priests, a suitable period being fixed beforehand within which whoever wants and is able to may adduce a lawful impediment.

Henceforth, a marriage where all the formalities were observed might take the following course:

(i) Before betrothal, it was customary for the financial settlement to be agreed between the families of the bride and groom. A woman was expected to bring to her marriage a dowry which, in effect, represented her share of her family's inheritance. There was an expectation, though it was no more than this, that the bride's dowry would consist of goods and cash and that she in turn would be endowed with rights (dower rights) in her groom's lands. Not infrequently, however, the bride's dowry was made up of land which she might have inherited from her mother whose own dowry it had originally been. In a sense such land, which often lay separately from paternal holdings, can be seen as 'woman's land', earmarked for use in the marriages of daughters or, if the need arose, of younger sons. In at least two passages, the twelfth-century legal text attributed to Bracton implies that families routinely used women's land in this way. Odard of Bamburgh, for example, a twelfth-century sheriff of Northumberland, granted land to his daughter Gunhilda and her husband as a marriage portion; they gave the same land in marriage to their daughter Emma and her husband. It then descended to

Emma's heir, Christina, who gave it to her younger son, Simon.

Arrangements were not always so simple and the details of landed settlements could vary widely. In the case of 1288 from Baynards in Haddestone (Norfolk), examined by Elaine Clark,[14] a father made over to his daughter and future spouse seven acres of arable land, two more of meadow and a messuage. In fact the father, who promised to support the couple at least until after their first harvest, was to enjoy the profits of this land until his death, when they were also to receive two horses and an oxen and a plough. In another case, at Horsham St Faith near Norwich in 1319, a father made over a third of nine acres and of two messuages to his daughter and her future spouse. They were to pay the entry fine for the land to the lord of the manor and technically, therefore, became the legal tenants; in fact the agreement was that the young couple would only have the use of two acres of arable and re-surrender the land to the father who would pay all rents and fulfil all tenurial obligations.

(ii) After agreeing the marriage settlement a betrothal ceremony could be held, probably before witnesses; depending on the exact words used (see below) this ceremony might or might not be considered binding. As far as the nobility were concerned betrothal ceremonies could be arranged early in life, at any time after children had reached seven years – the age of reason – but in such cases only the actual marriage, solemnised when the bride and the groom had come of age – at twelve and fourteen respectively – had the full force of law.

(iii) Before the marriage took place – and there were certain times of the year when marriages were not permitted, such as the weeks of Advent and Lent – banns were read out three times in church with at least a day between each reading to allow time for anyone to come forward with incriminating information that might invalidate the proposed union.

(iv) Bride and groom met at the church door for the wedding service. Here the groom made an announcement as to the dower his bride was to receive and gave her, arranged on a book or a shield, gold or silver as symbol of her dower and the ring that, once blessed and asperged, he would place on her finger. Vows in the vernacular were then exchanged:

---

[14] E. Clark, 'The Decision to Marry in Thirteenth and Early Fourteenth Century Norfolk', *Medieval Studies* 49 (1987), pp. 505–6.

although a wife was expected to obey her husband, the bride's vow of obedience to her husband was not introduced until the Reformation, in 1549.

(v) The couple now entered the church. Prayers and Mass followed and, after the Sanctus, the couple knelt (under a pall) for a further blessing on their marriage. According to a custom described by Grosseteste, a thirteenth-century Bishop of Lincoln, any children already born to the couple at this point gathered under the pall and thereby gained legitimacy (lawyers, it may be noted, thought otherwise).

(vi) The wedding feast followed. Depending on the couple's social position and on local custom this could be more or less obligatory and more or less expensive. The manorial court might fine a bridegroom for his failure to provide the expected festivities. In 1294, for example, at Wistow in Huntingdonshire:

Robert Juwel was convicted by jurors of this, that by custom he ought to have given a meal to all the servants of the Court of Wistow on the day when he married his wife, and he did not do so. Therefore he is in mercy for unjust detention, 12d pledge, Robert atte Broke. And by the same pledge he will satisfy the same servants of the aforesaid meal.[15]

Some feasts cost the father of the bride almost as much as the value of the dowry. A poor couple, on the other hand, might be treated to a bride-ale to which well-wishers brought not only their own food but also contributed money to help them set up house.

(vii) The priest blessed the bridal bedchamber and bed. Little is known about this final scene other than from literary texts such as Marie de France's *Le Fresne* which depends for its dénouement on the heroine preparing the bedchamber where the celebrant would bless the newlyweds 'for this was part of his duty'.[16] However, there are hints that the practice was not just a feature of fiction: a Northamptonshire charter reveals a case where some of the dower was to be handed over only after the bride had been bedded.

Marriage liturgies had already been developed in Anglo-Norman circles in the eleventh and twelfth centuries. By the thirteenth century they were not then entirely unfamiliar; what was new, however, was the coherence of the doctrine behind

[15] Cited G. Homans, *English Villagers of the Thirteenth Century* (1960), p. 173.
[16] *Le Fresne*, trans. G. Burgess and K. Busby, *The Lais of Marie de France* (1986), p. 66.

them and the zealousness of the attempts to make the church the place in which to be married. What had once been private contracts were now to become public weddings. Within only a few years of Lateran IV there was English legislation to implement its decrees. Episcopal Statutes from Salisbury (1217 × 1219), whose provisions were to be repeated in the course of the century at Exeter, London and Durham, enjoined on parish priests the duty to check up on, and if necessary regularise, the union of parents presenting a child for baptism. From the mid-thirteenth century, directives for archidiaconal visitations make it clear that archdeacons too were now making it their business to investigate marriages that lay within their jurisdiction.

What, it might be asked was the problem? Nothing in the evidence we have suggests hostility to the new demands so much as indifference mixed with confusion. Marriages, traditionally, lacked precisely the formality which was now expected and, despite the efforts of bishops, archdeacons and priests, they continued to do so. Throughout the Middle Ages, couples married not just at the church door but all over the place, under trees, in fields, kitchens and inns. Here, for example, is a description of a marriage given by a witness in a court case heard in York in 1372:

One year ago on the feast of the apostles Philip and James just past, he was present in the house of William Burton, tanner of York, about the third hour past the ninth, when and where John Beke, saddler, sitting down on a bench in that house, called in English 'le Sidebynke', called the said Marjory to him and said to her, 'Marjory, do you wish to be my wife?' And she replied, 'I will if you wish.' And taking at once the said Marjory's right hand, John said, 'Marjory, here I take you as my wife, for better or worse, to have and to hold until the end of my life; and of this I give you my faith.' The said Marjory replied to him, 'Here I take you John as my husband, to have and to hold until the end of my life and of this I give you my faith.' And then the said John kissed the said Marjory through a wreath of flowers, in English 'Garland'.[17]

Such marriages, it must be stressed, were not illegal. Considered and described by the Church as 'clandestine', it was bound paradoxically both to discourage and to support them. Deplorable as it might be to be married in an inn rather than at the church door, it was still a marriage. The cases that came

---

[17] R. Helmholz, *Marriage Litigation in Medieval England* (1974), pp. 28–9.

before episcopal and archidiaconal courts did so not because the marriages in question were clandestine but because they had become contentious for some other reason. In such cases the couple (where appropriate) were urged to regularise their union at a suitable time and place, but they were not penalised for having previously failed to do so. It was on the whole (though diocesan practice might vary) only those who tried to manipulate the new system to their advantage who were in danger of excommunication; these were the couples who knew there was some impediment to their proposed union and therefore chose, as a kind of cover, the respectability of a church wedding but in a parish other than their own where, it was hoped, there would be no knowing neighbours to betray their secret.

Cases such as these, which might sooner or later be brought to the attention of ecclesiastical courts, would be likely to include couples who had gone against the new rulings on affinity. Despite modification, these rulings could still prove onerous: it remained illegal to marry anyone with whom you shared a great-great-grandparent. Nor was it acceptable to sleep with a man and then decide that whom you really wanted to marry was his brother: sexual intercourse created bonds of consanguinity even if it did not make a marriage. On occasion, the rules of consanguinity could, of course, prove useful. The discovery of a previously unknown relationship could suffice to dissolve an unsatisfactory partnership or provide an excuse for breaking off negotiations which were in any case not going too well. Jeremy Goldberg cites the case of a certain Agnes who didn't think much of the man her parents hoped she would marry; asked for her objections she said she didn't like the way her prospective in-laws called her 'lass';[18] a revelation of a sexual liaison between the man and a relative of Agnes was subsequently revealed and the whole match called off. None the less ecclesiastical courts were not overburdened by pleas of consanguinity despite the complexities which blood and sex could create. The bulk of the business of these courts was taken up with cases of bigamy.

The frequency of bigamy – or cases of 'pre-contract' – was in

[18] P. J. P. Goldberg, ' "For Better, For Worse": Marriage and Economic Opportunity for Women in Town and Country', in P. J. P. Goldberg (ed.), *Woman is a Worthy Wight* (1992), p. 117.

itself a reflection of the difficulties which clandestine marriage could cause. Given the informality of so many arrangements, it was possible for there to be uncertainty as to whether a marriage had in fact taken place, either because there had been no witnesses or because the couple themselves might not understand the nature of the promises they had made. In the older view of marriage, as we have seen, both words and sex were necessary to make the match a legitimate union; according to the new theology, a promise with or without sex, if in the present tense, effected a binding sacrament. But it was not always clear, to the couples themselves, whether '*Volo te habere* ...', 'I wish to have you ...' was a promise, a statement of future intent or a description of present actions. There is evidence not only of genuine confusion about the difference between an engagement and a marriage but also that occasions could arise when it might be advantageous to play on the ambiguity of the situation. Some examples will illustrate both points.

John Astlott and Agnes Louth came before the court at York in 1422. John was a merchant and on one occasion when he was due to go abroad on business Agnes came to him to beg him to propose to her before he left; her father, she said, was nagging her. John duly turned up at Agnes's house with a goose, in the hope that it would put her father in a good mood, and they exchanged vows. Off went John on his journey – and he lost a lot of money, as a result of which Agnes no longer wanted to marry him when he came home. As John saw it, however, they were married already and so he took Agnes to court.

We do not know the outcome of this case, though we do know that the case of Isabelle Roll against John Bullock, heard at York over a period of three years, from 1351–5, divided the bench. John was alleged to have said to Isabelle, 'If I take any woman as my wife, I will take you' and they had slept together. But subsequently John had married someone else. Did John's condition amount to the same thing as a promise?

Claims of pre-contract not only gave rise to legal headaches – and sometimes parental wrath – they could also encourage corruption. Alice Palmer, unhappy with her marriage to Geoffrey Brown, gave Ralph Fouler 5 shillings to testify that there was a previous arrangement between them. Geoffrey subsequently remarried but Alice, later regretting her action, in

1337 confessed what she had done and claimed her rights as
his lawful wife. An example of a premeditated swindle is
provided by the case of *Brok* v. *Nastok* which got as far as the
king's court in 1290 and has been discussed by R. C. Palmer.[19]
Here was an instance of a couple, Edmund de Nastok and
Elizabeth de Ludehale, who hoped to set up home together
but, inhibited by poverty – or perhaps prompted by greed –
they married clandestinely. Thereafter Edmund opened negotiations with Richard de Brok for the hand of his daughter,
Agnes, and a dowry was agreed; it was to consist of six horses,
ten oxen, twelve cows with calves, twelve steers with heifers,
eighty ewes with lambs, twelve rams, thirteen pigs, ten quarters of wheat, eleven quarters of rye, twenty quarters of oats,
three quarters of salt, a cape, two mantles, four robes, eighteen
blankets, other clothes, cloth and towels and 100 shillings. All
this was handed over to Edmund and he and Agnes subsequently married. At this point Elizabeth entered the picture
with a plea of prior contract. The plea was heard in the ecclesiastical court and granted. Edmund and Elizabeth clearly
thought they would be able to retain at least half of Agnes's
dowry, though Edmund also tried to claim that the goods had
not been part of the marriage contract. The plan misfired; the
jury decided that Edmund was liable for the value of the
dowry plus £16 in damages.

A rather different kind of case, but which also revolved
around profit, arose in 1317 between Agnes Smith and John
Toller. John had given Agnes 24 shillings if she would marry
him. Agnes then discovered that John had previously slept
with one of her kinswomen. On grounds of consanguinity the
proposed marriage was called off and John asked for his
money back. This was refused by Agnes on the grounds that
part of the original bargain had been that it was hers to keep
whatever the outcome.

Pre-contract might be the most usual grounds for dissolving
a marriage but it was not the only one. Marriages that could
be shown to have taken place under duress were deemed
invalid, for there could then have been no true consent, the
very essence of the union. But in such cases the complaint had
to be speedily lodged for subsequent consummation or
cohabitation might be deemed to have negated the original

[19] R. C. Palmer, 'Contexts of Marriage in Medieval England', *Speculum* 59 (1984),
pp. 42–67.

charge. The reality of the dangers posed by any threats was also an issue; thus the complaint of a young girl, told that she would be seized by the ears and thrown into a pool unless she agreed to a match, would be disregarded if it could be shown that there had been enough of a crowd present to have protected her. Cruelty subsequent to a marriage was not grounds for dissolution, though it could make possible a legal separation. Such cases rarely occurred – some would argue because the threshold for what constituted cruelty was by our standards low – but when they did, every effort was made to effect a reconciliation between the parties. The husband might sometimes, but not in all cases, be asked to give a pledge of his future good behaviour either in money or in goods or to find sureties who would guarantee it. In Canterbury, for example, in 1373 'Thomas Waralynton appeared and was sworn to treat Matilda Trippes his wife with marital affection with respect to bed and table, and to furnish her with those things which are necessary in food and other materials according to his ability. And the woman was sworn to obey him as her husband.'[20] At Lichfield, Staffordshire, in 1466, Helen Hyndman sought permission to leave her husband on the grounds that he played dice and was losing all their money; the husband was ordered to give up gambling and to treat his wife well or face a whipping.

It would be easy enough, from examples such as these, to make lists of victims and villains but there would be little point in the exercise unless it could be shown that judges consistently favoured one or the other sex. While it is possible that future work may indeed uncover evidence of gender bias, there is as yet no reason to suspect it. On the contrary, every effort seems to have been made to pay equal attention to both men's and women's stories. The woman threatened with a ducking in the pond fared neither better nor worse than one Robert Peper who sought an annulment of his marriage from Agnes Besete on the grounds that, caught in bed with her, the promise had been forced out of him. The logic applied in all cases was the same: objections to contracts had to be shown by men and women to be serious and sustained. For adultery, there was no double standard: in mid-fourteenth-century Rochester, for example, as punishment for adultery both man and woman

---

[20] R. Helmholz, *Marriage Litigation in Medieval England* (1974), p. 102.

could expect a whipping three times round the churchyard, three times round the market.

The Book of Rota contained, it will be recalled, a test for infertility to be used by men and women; there was no hint of any suspicion that childlessness would be attributed, as a matter of course, to the barrenness of the woman. The same even-handedness appears in matrimonial cases. Here infertility as such was not grounds for the dissolution of a marriage. Impotence, on the other hand, was. Despite the ruling of Peter Lombard that sex was not necessary to create a union, none the less the inability to have sexual intercourse and therefore to render the marriage debt to one's partner was held to be an adequate reason to seek an annulment. Marriage, after all, had been instituted to provide both men and women with a legitimate sex-life, 'such that the infirmity that is prone to foul ruin might be rescued by the uprightness of marriage'. So said the eleventh-century decretalist Gratian who went on to explain that sex did not exist only for the purposes of procreation:

it is clear that [couples] are not commanded to join together solely for the procreation of children. Yet marriage is not to be judged evil on that account, for that which is done outside of the generation is not an evil of marriage, but is forgiveable on account of the good of marriage which is threefold: fidelity, offspring and sacrament.[21]

A couple could, of course, choose not to consummate their marriage or to end their sexual obligations to each other, but without mutual agreement the value of the marriage debt was such that it had always to be met; if it was not, or could not be, the complaints of the aggrieved partner were to be seriously investigated. According to canon law, a woman's virginity might be inspected by matrons of good repute (as was the Virgin's, after the birth of Christ, by her midwife Salome in the medieval drama scene of the nativity based on an apocryphal Gospel); and by a custom possibly of English origin, men too were liable to be inspected. The earliest reference to this practice occurs, according to Jacqueline Murray, in the manual of Peter the Chanter's pupil, Thomas of Chobham. Here Chobham advocates a physical examination of the man's genitals by 'wise matrons', followed by a kind of bedroom trial:

[21] Gratian, trans. P. Payer, *The Bridling of Desire* (1993), pp. 185–6.

after food and drink the man and woman are to be placed together in one bed and wise women are to be summoned around the bed for many nights. And if the man's member is always found useless and as if dead, the couple are well able to be separated.[22]

Cases in which this kind of procedure was followed are rare but they occurred in both York and Canterbury. In a case of 1292 at Canterbury twelve women 'worthy of faith of good reputation and honest life' testified that 'the virile member' of one Walter de Fonte was 'useless'. In a comparable case at York in 1433 every effort was made to arouse the husband but to no effect. According to the court's report:

The ... witness exposed her naked breasts and with her hands warmed at the said fire, she held and rubbed the penis and testicles of the said John. And she embraced and frequently kissed the said John, and stirred him up in so far as she could to show his virility and potency, admonishing him for shame that he should then and there prove and render himself a man. And she says, examined and diligently questioned, that the whole time aforesaid, the said penis was scarcely three inches long ... remaining without any increase or decrease.

Whereupon 'with one voice' the assembled women cursed John for not being 'better able to serve and please' his wife and left the court.[23]

The court cases mentioned above are interesting not least for the light they throw on the uses made of church courts by couples from right across the social spectrum to solve their matrimonial problems. Those who appear in marriage disputes before the ecclesiastical courts come from varied backgrounds; peasants and artisans as well as the more nobly born could and did take advantage of the church's teaching on marriage. The message of the twelfth-century canonists that there could be no legal marriage without free consent was understood by all classes. The choice of spouse belonged to the individual whether commoner or royal (a daughter of Edward I, much to the king's fury, married without his permission). Words of consent could not be undone. In medieval England one of the best documented of cases is the love-match between Margery, daughter of that thrusting Norfolk

---

[22] J. Murray, 'On the Origins and Role of "Wise Women" in Cases of Annulment on the Grounds of Male Impotence', *Journal of Medieval History* 16 (1990), p. 243.
[23] R. Helmholz, *op. cit.*, p. 89.

family, the Pastons, and their bailiff Richard Calle. Despite the outrage of Margery's brother John that his sister should marry so far beneath her station – 'to sell candle and mustard in Framlingham' – and despite the intensity of the pressure put upon Margery, the Bishop of Norwich had no choice but to uphold the marriage.

Margery won her case, even though her mother threw her out of the house, dismissing her as 'but a brethele'; but Richard kept his job as bailiff and the eldest son of the marriage received £20 from his grandmother in her will. In this story, as Colin Richmond has said, 'we cannot help ourselves cheering for Margery' even if we acknowledge, with the bishop, the loss caused by the match to her kin and to her friends. Margery remains, in our eyes, a heroine, a 'gritty individual'.[24] There are others: we might recall Agnes Nakerer and the travelling minstrel John Kent with whom she fell in love and whom she clandestinely married. Agnes's mortified parents found her another groom but she would have none of it. The York court upheld her alliance with Kent despite his being described as a 'public minstrel and juggler, frequently, dishonestly and shamefully engaged in sport displaying his body for the sake of profit'.[25]

Agnes and Margery, Richard and John were, in the terminology of the courts, 'constant women' and 'constant men'; their rights were vindicated by their determination. Whether they lived happily ever after we do not know; it is perhaps not only as twentieth-century readers that we hope they did. However, we cannot assume that their stories are typical. What happened to couples of weaker mettle? How often were women of all classes forced into marriages against their will in contravention of the doctrine of the Church? What kind of pressures lay behind their unions? We will consider first the circumstances of the group particularly vulnerable to family bartering, the aristocracy.

If, in our eyes, the heroines are those women of resolve who chose their own partners, then the victims must be the heiresses abducted by land-hungry barons. John Giffard, in the reign of Henry III, was alleged to have forcibly removed

---

[24] C. Richmond, 'The Pastons Revisited: Marriage and Family in Fifteenth Century England', *Bulletin of the Institute of Historical Research* 58 (1985), p. 34.
[25] Cited in R. Helmholz, *op. cit.*, p. 133.

the wealthy Maud de Clifford from her castle at Canford, Dorset, and married her. Maud's protest was overruled and she had to stay with John. Abductions could, of course, also be arranged by women themselves as a way of outwitting arranged alliances; but acquiescence with family arrangements was the more usual course. There is no need to interpret such compliance every time as mere spinelessness; we must allow for expectations, neither fruitless nor valueless, on the part of young girls that husbands would be found for them who would bring both them and their families income and honour. Getting married was like finding a job: the working conditions were important, advice from those with experience was welcome and the testimonials of elders essential.

None the less, children in particular were pawns in the marriage game; faced with betrothal ceremonies they did not fully understand they may, like Margaret Beaufort, have invented their own stories to try to make sense of subsequent events. Margaret, betrothed at the age of six to John de la Pole, was re-betrothed when she was nine to Edmund Tudor. Years later she had come to believe that, faced with two suitors, she had had a choice of husband and that in her indecision she had been advised to pray to St Nicholas, 'the patron and helper of all true maidens, and to beseech him to put into her mind what she were best to do'.[26] This trust in the 'rightness' of an arranged marriage goes far to explain how resolutely child-brides might insist on the consummation of matches which a modern reader might assume unpalatable. Agnes, daughter of Henry of Essex, fought long and hard for the recognition of her marriage to a man perhaps forty years older than herself, arranged when she was only three. Her battle lasted all her teenage years. What precisely fuelled her tenacity we do not know; but the pressures on her to deny her wedding contract were so considerable that we can be confident that the persistent decision to resist them was hers.

It has often been assumed that the marrying off of daughters was something of a nuisance; that it was the son and heir in any family who really counted; and that if there were no suitable husbands around for spare daughters it was easy enough to find convent space for them. For various reasons this is a

---

[26] M. Jones and M. Underwood, *The King's Mother: Lady Margaret Beaufort* (1992), pp. 37–8.

seriously misleading picture. Even in families seemingly well-endowed with sons and heirs, there was always the strong possibility that these male children might not survive long enough to pass on the inheritance. Consider the case of William Marshal who died in 1219 leaving five sons and five daughters. By 1245 each of those sons had died, childless, and so the Marshal inheritance was shared among the five daughters.

From the late twelfth century, as we have seen, such daughters divided inheritances equally among themselves. And, even if they were not heiresses, daughters, like younger sons, could expect some form of endowment. Primogeniture, the right of the eldest son to the bulk of the estate, co-existed with what has been called 'diverging devolution' whereby provision of some kind was made for all family members. Such a system necessarily threatened to deplete the original estate and so made its replenishment a constant source of concern. Women contributed in equal measure to both processes. They thereby helped to create elaborate networks of kinship and affinity within which land circulated and social relationships were maintained. Scott Waugh's study of this system at work in the thirteenth century has shown its effectiveness and the care taken to maintain it.[27] One useful strategy was 'sister exchange'; thus, in 1237, Peter de Brus married his son and his eldest daughter to the daughter and son of Peter and Isabel de Mauley. A variation on the same theme was for sons to marry sisters: two of William Marshal's granddaughters married sons of Ralph de Mortimer. In the next generation, the two sons of one of these marriages each married a woman who could trace her ancestry, albeit circuitously, back to the Marshals. This system of 'social endogamy' set up, according to Waugh, a 'consanguineous group' which helped to take the sting out of the problems which demography and inheritance customs could cause.

Throughout our period, peace-weaving, too, remained an important and explicit motive for arranging marriages. William de Bohun in the fourteenth century married Elizabeth de Badlesmere, widow of the Earl of March despite, or rather because of, the part he had played in the death of March's father. The marriage had been arranged 'in order to put an end

[27] S. L. Waugh, *The Lordship of England: Royal Wardships and Marriages in English Society, 1217–1327* (1988).

to the enmities between the two families'. After the Barons' Wars of the mid-thirteenth century, the peace terms agreed between the former rebel, Robert de Vere, Earl of Oxford, and Roger Mortimer of Wigmore (the recipient of Robert's confiscated lands) included a marriage between Mortimer's daughter, Margaret, and Robert's son. Should the son in question die before the marriage could be celebrated then Margaret was to marry his brother. If it goes without saying that there is no evidence that Margaret was consulted, it must equally be remembered that neither were Robert's sons.

Marriage strategies were an important part of family politics for all sections of society, from the richest to the poorest. If we move now to the other end of the social scale, to peasants or villeins, we will find that peasant women had extra problems with which to contend. Before marriage, a peasant wife might have had to pay *merchet*, *legerwite* or even *chidewite*. Already we are in a thicket of terminology which must be explained even if it cannot be satisfactorily defined. These fines are a mark of villein status, seemingly an indication of the right of the lord of the manor to exercise control over female peasant sexuality. *Legerwite*, literally 'lying down', is a fine of Anglo-Saxon origin; in post-Conquest England it was the penalty for illicit sex, usually but not always premarital, and usually but not always levied only on the woman. *Chidewite* was the fine for having an illegitimate child. *Merchet* was the sum to be paid for a licence to marry.

On examination, however, it transpires that these fines were a kind of sporadic taxation only erratically imposed. When, for example, in 1316, the lord of the manor in Wakefield, Yorkshire, badly needed extra cash, an unprecedented collecting of fines – for both *legerwite* or for failure to pay *merchet* – followed. The reasons behind the imposition of such fines are not always so clear. In some instances, the manorial court's demand for payments of *legerwite* may have been an attempt to ensure that couples accused of adultery before an ecclesiastical court did not try to commute a sentence of flogging into a payment of cash which would then leave the manor. It has also been suggested that a tax on brothels can sometimes be detected behind *legerwite*. As for *merchet*, is this a tax on people or property? In some manors it seems to have been levied only on the richer peasants; but this was not the case at Spalding in Lincolnshire, where *merchet* was regularly levied and where, in one instance, all that was asked for was a few herrings.

The herrings are exceptional; what recent research has shown to be surprisingly usual was for women to pay their own fines, sometimes paying *legerwite* and *merchet* as a combined fine. Fathers and husbands are found paying fines too but the records from the courts of Wakefield, Spalding, and, in Huntingdonshire, Ramsey Abbey and Houghton-cum-Wyton all show years when the majority of *merchets* (the commoner of the two fines) were paid by the women themselves. This financial independence is significant not only because it confirms the notion that women had some say in whom they married, but because it indicates that women had savings. None the less, it is clear that peasant women could also be put under pressure to marry, in their case by manorial lords anxious to maintain the man and women power needed for the successful running of their estates.

In 1308, for example, the prior of Norwich granted 24 acres of customary land to a man and his wife on condition that within eighteen months they married one of their daughters to a bondsman of the prior, by whom it was then to be held. If the marriage failed to take place then the land was to revert to the prior and the parents would have to pay a fine of 40 shillings. At Horsham St Faith, also in Norfolk, where the lord of the manor was the prior of St Faith, some time between 1284 and 1290, nineteen men and twenty-nine women were summoned by the prior and told whom they were to marry; the spouses had been chosen by a jury of local men. If the marriages did not take place heavy fines – the equivalent of a labourer's wage for twelve days – might be exacted. The peasants, even after paying the fines, still had to marry, only now they could choose other partners. According to Elaine Clark, while there are no signs of protest against such a system there is plentiful evidence that the peasants preferred to pay and choose rather than to submit to a prearranged match.[28] In 1291, for example, also in Horsham St Faith, a mother was fined 6d for impeding the marriage of her daughter to the man chosen by the jurors; the girl herself was fined a further 3d, and the intended groom (who had already refused two other brides) had to pay the same amount.

The right to choose a husband was, then, as jealously

[28] E. Clark, *op. cit.*

guarded as it could be flagrantly ignored. It would therefore seem appropriate to end this section by looking at one of the twelfth century's most famous test cases, that of Christina of Markyate. Christina was the eldest daughter of Anglo-Saxon burghers of Huntingdon, an ambitious couple who hoped to better themselves in the new world of Anglo-Norman England. A good marriage for Christina would advance their social standing. Christina, determined to remain a virgin, thought otherwise. According to her *Life*, written by someone who knew her well, Christina was mercilessly treated by her parents in the attempt to force her into marriage with Burthred, the man of their choice. They tried to bewitch her; they tried to get her drunk; they pulled her hair, beat and stripped her, and encouraged Burthred in his attempts to rape her. At last, in a decision that was a triumph for the Church's new views on marriage, Christina was released from her betrothal to Burthred and allowed to fulfil her own vow to become a nun. Her experiences have suggested to Jocelyn Wogan-Browne that the model of tortured virgins presented by hagiography, and usually dismissed as distasteful and gratuitously violent, may not, after all, have been unsuitable reading for those young women of the twelfth century whose chosen groom was Christ.[29] These are women we will meet again in Chapters Nine and Ten; meanwhile we must return to those women who had chosen to marry and to fulfil the command to 'increase and multiply'.

Motherhood

A fifteenth-century tenant of the Haberdon meadow in Bury St Edmunds, Suffolk, might be expected to keep a white bull on his or her land for use in the town's conception ritual. Such a bull, suitably festooned with garlands, would be regularly led by the monks of Bury St Edmunds in procession from the meadow. Women who wanted to conceive would accompany the bull, stroking its sides, until the gates of the abbey were reached. At this point they would enter the church to make their prayers and offerings at the shrine of the Anglo-Saxon martyr St Edmund. This is a ceremony which offers a very

[29] J. Wogan-Browne, 'Saints' *Lives* and the Female Reader', *Forum for Modern Language Studies* 27 (1991), pp. 314–29.

different perspective on the woes of pregnancy and childbirth from the lurid account given by the author of the renowned treatise on virginity, *Holy Maidenhood*:

Your rosy face will grow thin, and turn green as grass; your eyes will grow dull, and shadowed underneath, and because of your dizziness your head will ache cruelly. Inside, in your belly, a swelling in your womb which bulges you out like a water-skin, discomfort in your bowels and stitches in your side, and often painful backache; heaviness in every limb; the dragging weight of your two breasts, and the streams of milk that run from them. Your beauty is all destroyed by pallor; there is a bitter taste in your mouth, and everything that you eat makes you feel sick; and whatever food your stomach disdainfully receives – that is, with distaste – it throws up again ... Worry about your labour pains keeps you awake at night. Then when it comes to it, that cruel distressing anguish, that fierce and stabbing pain, that incessant misery, that torment upon torment, that wailing outcry; while you are suffering from this, and from your fear of death, shame added to that suffering with the shameful craft of old wives who know about that painful ordeal, whose help is necessary to you, however indecent it may be; and there you must put up with whatever happens to you.[30]

Such a text, though sometimes seem as representative of medieval misogyny, stands in sharp contrast both to the processing women and their bull and to the idealised vision of the birth of Christ. Here Mary, as mother, not only retains perpetual virginity; she is also spared the pains of childbirth. It has frequently been suggested that this rosy picture of Mary presented medieval women with an unrealistic and confusing role model. It is far from clear that medieval women themselves were troubled by the chasm between their experience and Mary's; nor that they were unduly worried by the message of tracts such as *Holy Maidenhood* – tracts which, in any case, may have been written with only a select audience in mind. (see p. 214–5). Motherhood and not virginity was what most women expected. Mary, it was reckoned, had had her own share of suffering at the foot of the Cross; if their own was to be in childbirth, Mary and the saints would help them through it. A charm from an English manuscript of the mid-eleventh century – Junius 85 – bears witness to this:

Mary, a virgin, bare Christ; the barren Elisabeth bare John the Baptist. I

---

[30] B. Millet and J. Wogan-Browne (eds and trans.), *Medieval English Prose for Women* (1990), pp. 31–2.

charge thee, infant, if thou be male or female, by the Father, Son and Holy Spirit, that thou come forth ... The Lord, seeing the sisters of Lazarus weeping at his tomb, wept in the presence of the Jews and exclaimed, 'Lazarus come forth' ... Write this on wax which has not been used for any work, and bind it under the right foot.

Such Anglo-Saxon lore was not forgotten after the Conquest. Annotations in manuscripts are an indication that traditional remedies were still in use at least until the thirteenth century. Familiar prognostications are likely to have been handed down: the mother who walks slowly, for example, and has hollow eyes, will bear a son; if she walks quickly and has swollen eyes, the baby will be a girl, if she walks with her weight on her heels – a boy, on her toes – a girl. Bald's *Leechbook*, our prime source for Anglo-Saxon medicine, strikes us as a strange amalgam of superstition, both native and classical, and sound advice. In Chapter 37 of *Leechbook III*, 'a pregnant woman is to be earnestly warned that she should eat nothing salty or sweet, or drink beer, or eat swine's flesh or anything fat, or drink to intoxication, or travel by road, or ride too much on horseback, lest the child be born before the proper time.' Nor is she to eat 'bull's flesh or ram's or buck's or boar's or gander's or that of any animal that can beget' or the child may be hump-backed.

Alongside Bald, new manuals appeared in post-Conquest England bearing the imprint of the latest developments in medical science. We have already considered some of the 'Trotula' texts and *The Sickness of Women*. A work that was likewise very popular was the *Encyclopaedia of Bartholomew the Englishman*, probably so titled because England was Bartholomew's birthplace, though as a teacher and scholar his homes were France and Germany.

In his section on childbirth Bartholomew draws heavily on the newly available works of Aristotle and Galen, on translations recently made from the Arabic of classical medical texts by Constantine the African. Here too are recommendations that by modern canons seem eminently reasonable: the newly born child is to be kept from extremes of temperature or of light; limbs should be gently massaged; honey and salt, still recognised today as possessing antiseptic properties, are to be used, though in this case to 'reduce the humours'; the infant may be soothed by songs and by rocking. But behind all this lies an alien philosophy:

The mother is so called because she nourishes the newborn with her breasts. She takes care of the infant; while it is in the womb, it is fed with blood, but at birth, nature drives this blood into the breast, so that it is transformed into milk in order to feed the child. Although the mother conceives in passion, she gives birth in suffering and grief. She very much loves her infant, embraces, kisses and lovingly nurses and feeds it. After she has been impregnated, the mother no longer emits menstrual blood because, as Aristotle says, this blood is now used to nourish the creature. A mother suffers less from the conception of a boy-child and her colouring is therefore more beautiful and cleaner, and her movements lighter than during the conception of a girl as Aristotle and Constantine say. The closer the birth comes, the more the mother suffers and is fatigued by the motion of the foetus. It is a sign of impregnation, according to Aristotle and Galen, that mothers desire different things, the colouring changes, the area under the eyes turns black, the breasts are enlarged, and the uterus grows slowly in size. Because of the size of the growing foetus, she suffers nausea and vomiting, feels heavy and unable to work. During the birth, she is forced to cry out in pain, and is easily endangered, especially young women, whose limbs are stiff and inflexible. The more the mother suffers during the birth of the child, the more she enjoys it and loves to teach it more.[31]

This is a passage heavy with Aristotelian learning – and misogyny; the conception of a boy-child is clearly the preferred option. A gulf separates its world from that of Bald's *Leechbook* or the forbidding rhetoric of *Holy Maidenhood*, and even more so from the Anglo-Saxon charm to be written on wax. Here there is neither magic nor repulsion. An attempt to understand and explain the physiology of pregnancy lies at the centre of the work. This attitude also permeates the extensive treatment of pregnancy that we find in at least one version of *The Sickness of Women*.[32]

Childbirth in *The Sickness of Women* is not necessarily seen as traumatic; if all goes well and there is a 'natural' birth, then 'twenty pangs' or so will do. We have no way of telling how often the twenty pangs sufficed; necessarily we are far better informed about possible complications, though we do not know the extent of their seriousness. In sixteenth- and seventeenth-century England it has been estimated that one in every forty women died in childbirth and that as many as two

[31] M. Goodich (trans.), 'Bartholomaeus Anglicus on Child-Rearing', *History of Childhood Quarterly* 3 (1975), p. 80.
[32] This is the version translated by B. Rowland in *Medieval Woman's Guide to Health* and referred to hereafter.

hundred out of a thousand children died before the age of five. Improvements in maternal mortality rates around the millennium have been suggested – the introduction of iron cooking pots is said to have helped to counteract anaemia – but in the absence of parish records no satisfactory statistics can be compiled for preceding centuries. Mothers were advised to make their confessions before the onset of labour lest they die giving birth. Complications envisaged in *The Sickness of Women* begin with sixteen 'unnatural' presentations. In such cases, it is the responsibility of the midwife, with her hands anointed with wild thyme oil, lily oil or oil of musk, to attempt to turn or rearrange the baby or to enlarge the cervix as appropriate. The second form of complication relates to stillbirths. There is, as we have seen, no question in early medical texts but that it is the life of the mother and not the baby which is to be saved, should a choice have to be made.

On what may be called the theology of childbirth *The Sickness of Women* is silent. We must turn to other texts to understand the full extent here of the midwife's responsibilities. The unbaptised child who dies has no destiny other than limbo. The baptised child, on the other hand, is assured of heaven. Baptism was a sacrament which, in an emergency, could be bestowed by a lay man or woman; it was a duty therefore incumbent on all midwives in cases where the child seemed unlikely to survive. There was no need to wait until the baby was fully delivered; if there seemed the slightest likelihood of a stillbirth, then any protruding limb could be baptised. Priests were to ensure that midwives understood this; that clean water was available in case the ceremony became necessary and that they knew the correct form of words. The midwife in Robert Manning's *Handling Synne* loses the life and soul of the child she has delivered (and thereafter her job) through her ignorance of the proper procedure.

The unbaptised child, shut out from heaven, was in theory – and this is confirmed in *Handling Synne* – excluded from burial in consecrated ground; this might even be the case if mother and child had died together before the actual birth. In some instances the child was removed (by hooks and perforators) before the mother went to her grave. Yet more traumatic was the problem of deciding at what point a mother was indeed dead; from the early thirteenth century it became the practice to perform post-mortem Caesareans, even if there was only time to baptise the dying child. Claims about Caesareans in which both mother and child survived were first made in the sixteenth century; even then they were greeted with scepticism and dismissed as 'absurd, incredible and worthless'. In the thirteenth century the development of guilds of barber sur-geons, who were officially licensed to use surgical instruments, meant that in theory Caesareans fell within their province. In practice, however, they remained, throughout the Middle Ages, more usually a midwife's task. In the fifteenth-century manual, *Instructions for Parish Priests* by John Mirk, the priest is told:

> And if the woman then should die
> Teach the midwife that she hurry
> For to undo her with a knife
> In order to save the child's life
> And hurry that it christened be
> For that is a deed of charity.

The awesomeness of the Church's teaching on neonatal baptism, coupled with the limitations of medical skill, under-lines both the responsibilities of the midwife and the anxieties roused by her calling. She seldom acted on her own. She might be accompanied by a fellow midwife but in any case births were sociable occasions likely to be witnessed by friends and neighbours, though not, with rare exceptions, by men. The company provided a ready-made band of witnesses in the event of any criticism of the midwife's judgement, competence or conduct. Had she performed a Caesarean too soon – or too late? Had she baptised a child already dead in order to secure him or her burial in consecrated ground? Had she been an accomplice to fraud, accessory to a 'pretence' birth to a barren woman? (A woman in the *Life* of Hugh of Lincoln, desperate for an heir, feigns a pregnancy using a pillow and the birth by subsequently adopting a peasant woman's child.) The temp-tations and pitfalls for any midwife were such that the interest of priests in their training and instruction becomes easy to understand. At times we glimpse priests at the bedside during childbirth. Peter Biller has drawn attention to the report of one such priest, for whom the outcome was quite literally a miracle:

One of my parishioners was in labour in a difficult childbirth. One arm would not come out, and when it would not follow the hands of the midwives who were struggling to bring it out it swelled to equal the thickness of a man's leg ... the [mother] shrank at every touch, and whenever they [the midwives] applied their hands she cried out in dread. She went through almost a night and a day ... I profess I noticed there was no help for her unless the arm was cut off. Fortunately the hand was withdrawn and the foetus turned and presented normally: all through the intervention of St Thomas [of Canterbury]...[33]

Mothers themselves in the course of difficult labours would, as we have seen, have offered prayers to the Virgin and to saints. The patron saint of childbirth was St Margaret. No matter that she was martyred rather than married, her experience during torture of being swallowed and spat out by a dragon gave her unrivalled powers of empathy with the processes of birth and women in labour listened to readings from her *Life*. A similar process of association must account for the prayer in the Sarum liturgy to be said for a pregnant woman, addressed as it is to God 'who delivered Jonah from the whale's belly'. Up and down the country saints, both male and female, could be expected to help women in labour: at Burton-on-Trent in Staffordshire, pregnant women 'were very desirous' to have the staff of St Modwena 'to lean on'; at Rievaulx Abbey in Yorkshire, monks guarded the girdle of St Ailred, known as it was to be 'helpful to lying-in-women'. In 1538, the Bishop of Salisbury gave instructions that midwives in his diocese were not to use 'girdles, purses, measures of our Lady or such other superstitious things'[34].

There are earlier references to superstitious practices which, from the early Reformation, ecclesiastics were trying to eradicate: in *The Sickness of Women* mention is made of 'a girdle of hart's skin' and of the beneficial powers of the 'precious stone called jasper', though this text is on the whole marked by an absence of such prophylactics. However, this should not be understood as evidence of learned as opposed to popular – or rustic – medicine. The use of birth girdles cut across both time and class. Such a girdle already appears in Bald's *Leechbook*: in the case of a difficult labour the woman is to 'put on her girdle these prayers as it is said in these *Leechbooks*'. The survival of a prayer roll, 180 centimetres long – the length corresponded

[33] P. Biller, 'Childbirth in the Middle Ages', *History Today* (August 1986), pp. 42–3.
[34] See E. Duffy, *The Stripping of the Altars* (1992), p. 384.

to the supposed height of Christ – used as a birth girdle, is a telling example of their popularity; over-handling has made the roll (Wellcome MS 632) barely legible. At Westminster Abbey, the monks guarded the Virgin's own girdle, this had been given to them by Edward the Confessor and it was available on loan for aristocratic and royal births.

Royal births necessarily were surrounded with particular pomp and circumstance. None the less, the rituals and rites they followed were common property. Thus St Thomas of Canterbury, invoked by Peter Biller's parishioner, was also called upon by Henry III when his queen, Eleanor (a borrower of the Virgin's girdle), was expecting her fourth child: a thousand candles were lit around his tomb. Eleanor safely gave birth to a boy who was christened Edmund because the antiphon of St Edmund was being chanted on her behalf at the time when he was born. In most cases, the name chosen would be expected to be that of one of the godparents – every boy had to have at least two men and a woman as godparents, every girl two women and a man – but a favoured saint or a particular association might override this convention. At a Yorkshire christening, for example, 'there was a question among those in the church how [the baby] could be called Katherine as neither of her godmothers was called so and to this it was replied that for the love of St Katherine she was so named.' Queen Eleanor herself as a godmother had lifted her godchild from the font and 'named her Mary because she was born on the eve of the Conception of the Blessed Mary'.[35]

Baptisms (other than bedside ceremonies) were meant to take place within eight days of the delivery, but given the rate of infant mortality it seemed risky to wait even as long as a week. Baptism on the day of the birth was not unusual. The ceremony was more elaborate than a baby can expect today, entailing as it did three immersions in the font – one on each side and one face downwards. Mothers, for whom a 'lying-in time' was the norm, were not expected to be present. Newly delivered mothers were considered to be 'weak and sick and lacking in bodily strength' and, in reasonably affluent homes, an extra servant might be hired as a nurse to help out during this period. To the visionary St Bridget, in a work translated

---

[35] L. Haas, 'Social Connections between Parents and Godparents in Late Medieval Yorkshire', *Medieval Prosopography* 10 (1989), p. 17.

into Middle English, it was a sign of the miraculous nature of Christ's birth that the Virgin was none of these things, and indeed was even strong enough to go to the Temple on the eighth day for Christ's circumcision.

'Ordinary' mothers re-emerged, publicly, only at the time of their purification, or churching. The origins of this ceremony are to be found in the Old Testament (Leviticus 12: 1–5) but the distinction that is made there between the birth of a boy and a girl does not seem to have been observed in medieval England where purification took place approximately a month after the birth, irrespective of gender. Associated as this ceremony is with Old Testament taboos concerning menstruation, the purification of women has often been seen as part and parcel of clerical misogyny; it may therefore be worth pointing out that the related injunction not to resume sexual intercourse until then closely tallies with modern medical advice which likewise recommends this for at least a month after a birth. It also seems as if the service, marked by the mothers with gifts of candles before whichever altar in the church was dedicated to Our Lady, was seen by women themselves not as a reminder of their fallen nature but rather as a thanksgiving in imitation of Candlemas, the Virgin's own Feast of the Purification, and as a way of sharing in her maternity. The iconography of the Altar of Our Lady at Ranworth in Norfolk, where new mothers of the parish presented themselves, recalled not only Christ's birth but that of the Virgin herself and of her sisters and cousins. Churching was thus a joyous occasion, providing an opportunity for dressing up and for a party. Records for several of Queen Eleanor's purifications suggest that fine music, plenty of candles, a splendid feast and lavish almsgiving were the order of the day. By contrast, it was considered to be a mark of the exceptional humility of St Elizabeth of Hungary (in a Middle English *Life*) that at her purifications she wore neither jewellery nor expensive clothes.

For the poor, on the other hand, the experience of childbearing and childbirth might bring hardship. A frequently asked question is how far in these circumstances either contraception or infanticide was practised. Penitential manuals make it clear that by the early fourteenth century, possibly as a result of demographic pressures, the practice of *coitus interruptus* was considered sufficiently widespread to be troubling to confessors; recent research suggests that effective herbal abortifacients were also both known about and used. Individual cases of infanticide certainly occurred but there is no evidence to show that these were other than extraordinary. Examination of church court records by Richard Helmholz and of coroners and gaol delivery rolls by Barbara Hanawalt have brought to light only a very small number of examples.[36] The cases cited by Hanawalt include the finding in the River Thames near Oxford of a baby of unknown parentage who, it was assumed, had not been baptised since the umbilical cord had not been tied.[37] To judge from the more abundant continental evidence the motive behind such acts of infanticide was more often shame than poverty; it is possible that in England, where the stigma attached to illegitimacy seems slight, the social pressures that led women to kill their children were significantly reduced.

Charitable provision for unwanted children did exist, albeit on a small scale. Foundling hospitals took in abandoned children, or offered unmarried women beds where they could give birth and, in the event of their deaths, undertook to care for their children until the age of seven. But there was no monastic order in England (as there was in France) dedicated solely to the care of foundlings and orphans. The question must be asked, how are we to explain this difference, a difference which the work of Peter Biller on the penitentials of England and Europe has recently accentuated?[38] It is the English penitentials that Biller has found to be particularly concerned with abortion, infanticide, and with preventive measures to reduce infant mortality. Again and again both ecclesiastical and secular legislation drummed home the responsibilities of caring for children and the wickedness of in any way causing their death. Whether these measures were particularly needed or heeded can only be a matter for conjecture. In the light of current concerns about global population, it is perhaps worth pointing out that the notion that children are a liability rather than an asset depends upon

[36] R. Helmholz, 'Infanticide in the Province of Canterbury during the Fifteenth Century', *History of Childhood Quarterly* 2 (1974–5); B. Hanawalt, *The Ties That Bound* (1986), p. 102.

[37] B. Hanawalt, 'Childrearing among the Lower Classes of Late Medieval England', *Journal of Interdisciplinary History* 8 (1977), p. 9.

[38] P. Biller, 'Marriage Patterns and Women's Lives', in J. P. J. Goldberg (ed.), *Woman is a Worthy Wight* (1992), pp. 60–107.

their being viewed as consumers rather than producers; for agriculturally based societies, it is sometimes the producers who are in short supply.

This must be the place to mention briefly a debate of some relevance to our topic, albeit one that has perhaps already run its course: conducted under the heading 'Did medieval mothers love their children?' it is something of a cuckoo-child hatched in a nest built originally by Philippe Aries.[39] Aries's primary concern was with the concept of childhood. 'The idea of childhood,' he wrote, 'is not to be confused with affection for children'; but in much subsequent writing this is precisely what has happened. This is not to deny that there is much to be learned from questioning notions of maternal love; but it is an exercise peculiarly full of pitfalls. We cannot hope to fathom the emotions of 'bad mothers' and 'good mothers', whether we think we know them well, like the mother of Margery Paston (cf. p. 117), or whether they are strangers, like the mother of the unbaptised baby found in the River Thames. What we can do is to note how contemporaries expected mothers to behave and attempt to identify the feelings they recognised as 'maternal'. There are many examples, ranging from homely depictions of mothers playing hide-and-seek with their children (in the *Ancrene Riwle* of the early thirteenth century) or of Sarah, anxious mother of Isaac, in the biblical plays 'Let Isaac abide at home here / For I kept not he went in the wynde', to the grandiloquent words attributed by Ordericus Vitalis in Book III of his *Historia Ecclesiastica* to Matilda, wife of William the Conqueror, in justification of her support for the rebellion of her son:

O, my lord, do not wonder that I love my first-born with tender affection. By the power of the most High, if my son Robert were dead and buried seven feet in the earth ... and I could bring him back to life with my own blood, I would shed my life-blood for him.

'Unnatural' mothers, on the other hand, that is to say those who killed their children, rather than offering to die for them, were generally regarded by the courts who heard their cases as insane. Pleas of insanity were sufficiently unusual for this to be a striking form of defence. In a rather different category are the attempts by mothers to pass on the responsibilities of

[39] P. Aries, *Centuries of Childhood* (1962), p. 128.

child-care to putative fathers or share this with them. A case heard in the ecclesiastical court at Rochester in Kent provides us with an illustration of such a case, though we do not know the outcome:

And the woman placed the child on the ground in front of the judge, saying that she no longer wished to care for it, but that it should be taken by the father, who she asserted was the said Rowland. To which the man replied, denying it, and offered to undergo compurgation as to any carnal relations with her. Then the judge warned the woman to receive the child at her breast to nourish it with due sustenance under pain of major excommunication until the question of paternity was discussed.

It would be otiose to underline the topicality of such a case.

The Upbringing of Children

According to medieval theories based on *The Etymologies of Words*, the highly influential work of the seventh-century scholar Isidore of Seville, an individual was an infant until the age of seven, a child until fourteen, and an adolescent – or, more accurately, youth – until twenty-eight. Isidore's scheme suffered several adaptations, but his definition of infancy was seldom challenged. Until they were seven years old, children were considered both to lack moral reasoning and to be in need of particularly close attention; it was part of the duties of the godparents, as promised at baptism, to keep their god-children safe from fire and water during this time, and it was considered both usual and reasonable for children, both boys and girls, to stay for their first seven years in the care of their mothers, though thereafter boys of noble birth could be expected to be handed over for their education to a male tutor (and girls, sometimes, to a 'mistress'). Practice, however, might be very different from theory, depending on a wide variety of circumstances. An heir or heiress who became a ward of court might have to leave his or her mother, even if still a baby, to join the household of a guardian until the age of majority was reached. The mother herself could bid for this guardianship; there are even cases of mothers kidnapping such children, though whether from sentiment or for gain, given the value of an heir or heiress on the marriage market is questionable.

In general, noble women would not have expected close

involvement with the upbringing of their children; it was not unusual to entrust them either to nuns or to a foster home at an early age as part of their education. None the less, a writ of Henry III to Mabel, widow of Roger Torpell, makes poignant reading. Her son had died; now she must surrender her daughter:

To Mabel, late the wife of Roger Torpell. She must well remember that the king gave the custody of the land and heirs of the said Roger de Torpell, with the marriage of the heirs, to R. bishop of Chichester, the chancellor during the minority of the heirs, whereof because William the eldest son and heir has died, the king commands her, as she loves herself and her goods, not to eloign Acelota, sister and next heir of the said William ... but to deliver her to the messenger of the said bishop bearing these letters of the bishop testifying that he is the messenger.[40]

Among the peasantry, unburdened by such inheritance problems, the mother was likely to be appointed guardian by the lord of the manor if the father died but, particularly during the Black Death when a high proportion of children lost both their parents, children might be brought up by more distant kin and often by parish priests.

Returning to the theorists and the ideal world, we find that the mother should feed her children herself though in 'Trotula A', colostrum is not recommended; 'some men say it is good for [the baby] to drink the milk of nine women before he drinks his mother's milk' but thereafter 'his mother's milk is best for him'.[41] Bartholomew the Englishman, as we have seen, went so far as to define a mother in relation to her function as breastfeeder: 'the mother [mater] is so called because she nourishes the newborn with her breast [mamma].' None the less, among the aristocracy few women seem to have fed their own babies. They regularly employed wet nurses, usually bringing them into the household rather than sending the babies out to their homes (although, strangely, no evidence exists of wet-nursing in London, in contrast with medieval Florence where plentiful records of the practice have survived). The 'mother' in the *Life* of Hugh of Lincoln, in a nicely ironic ploy, was able to hand over her supposed infant to the actual mother to feed. In his

[40] S. Sheridan Walker, 'Widow and Ward: the Feudal Law of Child Custody in Medieval England', *Women in Medieval Society* (1976), p. 160.

[41] London, British Library, MS Additional 12195, ff. 157r–185r, at ff. 169v–170r. I owe this reference to Monica Green.

treatise Bartholomew moves quickly on from the mother to discuss the feeding role of a second person, the nurse, and to describe her related duties:

The nurse (nutrix) is so named because of her nourishing (nutriendo) power, since she is suitable for feeding the newborn child. A nurse, says Isidore [of Seville], feeds the child in place of the mother. Like a mother, the nurse is happy when the child is happy, and suffers when the child suffers. She lifts him up if he falls, gives him suck when he cries, kisses him if he is sick, binds and ties him if he flails about, cleans him if he has soiled himself, and feeds him although he struggles with his fingers. She instructs the child who cannot speak, babbling, practically breaking her tongue, in order to teach him speech more readily. She uses medicines in order to cure the sick child. She lifts him up on her hands, shoulders and knees, and relieves the crying child. She first chews the food, preparing it for the toothless child so he can swallow it more easily, and thus feeds the hungry child. Whistling and singing she strokes him as he sleeps and ties the childish limbs with bandages and linens, lest he suffer some curvature.[42]

The practice of swaddling, as described here by Bartholomew, seems to have been common to all classes. Thus Gerald of Wales (1147–1223) in his *Topography of Ireland* considers it a sign of the barbarity of the Irish that they 'do not put their babies in cradles or swathe them'; nor, he continues, 'do midwives ... use hot water to raise the nose or press down the face or lengthen the legs'.[43] Wet-nursing, as we have seen, was likely to have been confined to the middle or upper classes, except necessarily if the mother died or was unable to feed her child. An Anglo-Saxon charm to induce lactation in a woman who cannot nourish her child occurs in the treatise *Lacnunga*:

Take then in her hand milk of a cow of a single colour and then sip it with her mouth and then go to running water and spit the milk into it and take up in the same hand a mouthful of the water and swallow it. Then say these words: 'Everywhere have I carried for me the splendid strong kinsman; with this splendid well nourished one. I will have him for me and go home.' When she goes to the brook then let her not look around, nor again when she goes away; and then let her go into another house than that she started from and there let her taste food.[44]

References to peasants employing rather than acting as wet

---

[42] M. Goodich (trans.), *op. cit.*, p. 81.
[43] Gerald of Wales, *The Topography of Ireland*, trans. J. O'Meara (1982), p. 100.
[44] M. L. Cameron, *Anglo-Saxon Medicine* (1993), p. 181.

nurses are rare; one such was the cause of marital tragedy; Isabel, wife of Nicholas le Swon, as reported in the Bedford court rolls of 1300, was spending so much time away from home feeding a neighbour's baby that the enraged Nicholas drew his sword and killed her. Perhaps more typical of wet-nursing arrangements is the case taken from the rural aristocracy of Yorkshire and recently brought to light by Jeremy Goldberg. In 1366 a certain Elena refused to act as wet nurse for her former mistress since she did not want to jeopardise the health of her own baby. Eighteen months later Elena, who was still feeding her child, was again approached by her former mistress who by now had a new baby in need of a wet nurse; this time, Elena agreed.[45] Most alien for the modern reader must be the Lateran decree of 1179, reinforced in England by a proclamation of Henry III, forbidding Christian wet nurses from nursing Jewish babies because, it was alleged, Jewish parents forced the wet nurses to 'express' their milk after Easter lest their babies should ingest the Eucharist.

According to one of the Latin 'Trotula' texts circulating in England, the wet nurse should be young, with a pink and white complexion. She must keep away from spicy food, especially from garlic, take plenty of exercise and drink vinegar syrup and light wine. Apart from the difficulty of finding any one to fit the bill, there could be dangers to the mother who employed a wet nurse in the drying-up of her milk: William of Malmesbury attributes the death of William the Conqueror's eldest daughter-in-law to an infection brought on by the binding of her breasts. None the less, wet-nursing remained a favoured custom throughout our period. Reluctance to breast-feed may have stemmed in part from the belief that the lactating mother should not make love. Arguably, given that breast-feeding has a contraceptive effect as we now know, a system which enabled the better-off to have more babies than poor wet-nurses had something to commend it. Priests, however, saw nothing in its favour. Thomas of Chobham (and the writers of later English penitentials would follow him) considered a mother's refusal to feed her own baby tantamount to murder; no other milk could be as suitable; to reject God's gift of milk-filled breasts was a

[45] P. J. J. Goldberg, *Women, Work, and Life Cycle in a Medieval Economy* (1992), pp. 148–9.

kind of blasphemy that deserved a severe penance. The mother who claims that she is too delicate to feed her baby is to be greeted with scorn: 'was she not [already] so delicate when she underwent intercourse and the labour of giving birth?' But even Thomas is prepared to make concessions: if the mother 'truly cannot bear the labour, she should at least feed and wash the baby when she can, so that she does not seem . . . to overturn nature through never deigning to go near her own offspring'.[46]

Though it may sound as if Thomas was fighting a losing battle, the indications are that the advice of priests did not always fall on deaf ears. Thirteenth-century mothers and nurses would have heard, week in week out, sermons on the need to feed babies 'with care'. They were regularly told that they must not take babies into bed with them until they were about three years old because of the danger of 'over-laying' them. Paediatricians today deny that this can happen, but to medieval preachers it was a cause of considerable anxiety. Deaths in such circumstances aroused suspicion. A fourteenth-century penitential asks:

whether the child was stifled thus in bed by the sides of its parents . . . If, however, it was found dead in its cot, a lesser penance should be imposed, because it is presumed that this did not happen through sure knowledge but rather through some lack of care. For it is not to be assumed that a mother is forgetful of her child[47]

Preachers were insistent, too, on the need to ensure that cots were secure, that they could not be easily overturned, that babies were not left unattended, or near boiling water, or close to fire. That these were precisely the circumstances in which many babies did die should not necessarily be attributed either to their mothers' inattentiveness in church or to undue negligence on their part in the home. Coroners' rolls emphasise the precariousness of many children's lives whether or not they are at the mercy of a careless mother. Even the most securely tucked up baby might still fall victim to marauding sows.

Once weaned and out of swaddling clothes, what kind of education could children expect from their mothers? Here class is the all-important factor. As a general rule we must assume that children learned to imitate their parents' skills,

[46] Cited in P. Biller, 'Marriage Patterns and Women's Lives', *op. cit.*, p. 81.
[47] Cited in P. Biller, *op. cit.*, p. 82.

whatever these might be; for girls, whether noble or peasant, spinning was the most common accomplishment. We should not, however, be too quick to assume that daughters necessarily followed in their mothers' footsteps. We find in London, c.1286, Katherine 'la surgiene' working alongside her surgeon father and brother. Education for girls as well as boys might take place outside the home, whether in a local school, monastery or convent. Opportunities for girls were more limited than for boys, despite the lack of discrimination in the Statute of Artificers of 1406: 'every man or woman, of what estate or condition that he be, shall be free to set their son and daughter to take learning at any manner of school that pleaseth them within the realm.' Both boys and girls might also be sent to other households as foster children or as servants to learn either good manners or a trade. We will return to such girls in their capacity as wage-earners; these are the young women who are the supposed audience of the late medieval poem *How the Good Wife Taught Her Daughter*, where a mother purports to pass on the lessons her own mother's views on decorous behaviour:

And when thou goest on thy way, go thou not too fast,
Brandish not with thy head, nor with thy shoulders cast,
Have not too many words, from swearing keep aloof,
For all such manners come to an evil proof.

A striking example of a mother's concern for the education of her children (possibly including a daughter) may be found in the will of Katherine Hawte (1493), recently cited by Carol Meale. Katherine leaves lands and property to be sold; the money raised is to be used so that her children can be 'kepte to scole'.[48]

Tantalisingly, we can only guess at the extent to which women taught their children to read. The evidence points in this direction but it is episodic, starting with the famous story from Asser's *Life of Alfred*, of the young Alfred whose interest in books was first kindled by a book of English poetry which his mother read to him and his brothers. The book is promised to whichever brother can remember the poems. Alfred, needless to say, is the winner. We have to wait until the eleventh

[48] C. Meale, 'Laywomen and their Books in Late Medieval England', in C. Meale (ed.), *Women and Literature in Britain, 1150–1500* (1993), p. 131.

century to find another mother similarly occupied: Queen Margaret of Scotland reads both to her illiterate husband and to her large gathering of children. In the mid-thirteenth century we come to the rather different example of Denise Montchensy, for whom Walter of Bibbesworth composed a treatise so that she could teach her children the kind of French they would need for 'husbandry and management'. A poem based on Walter's work assumes that 'woman teacheth child on book'.[49]

The fourteenth century gives rise to a new kind of evidence: representations of St Anne teaching the Virgin to read become widespread throughout Europe, but seem first to occur in England. An early example can be found in a Book of Hours of the early fourteenth century where Anne shelters the Virgin with her cloak while the Virgin holds an open book. In the Fitzwarin Psalter of the late fourteenth century 'the female donor kneels before the Virgin's mother, St Anne, as she teaches the Virgin to read as if the donor too is anxious to benefit from the same instruction'.[50] As has often been pointed out, these illustrations must be viewed with an open mind. Are they what they seem at first glance? Are these scenes evidence of increasing domestic literacy or should they be seen as new iconographical symbols of the Incarnation? Do we have to choose? The one interpretation should not exclude the other, particularly in view of the suggestive ruling during the clamp-down on Lollardy in the fifteenth century that women are to teach only other women and children in a domestic setting. To deny that women undertook precisely the kind of teaching that is here allowed would seem perverse indeed.

The topic of women's literacy promises to be greatly illuminated by the work of Michael Clanchy (in progress). Mention should be made here of the works of the French writer Christine de Pisan (1365–c.1430), herself a mother of three small children whom she was left to support in her widowhood. Five of Christine's works were translated into English in the fifteenth century. *The Moral Proverbs of Christine*, a book for children, that was translated by Anthony Woodville, tutor of Edward V, and published by Caxton in 1478, was the first by

[49] N. Orme, *From Childhood to Chivalry* (1984), p. 16.
[50] V. Sekules, 'Women's Piety and Patronage', in N. Saul (ed.), *Age of Chivalry* (1992), p. 130.

a woman to be printed in England. Christine's most popular book, however, was *The Epistle of Othea*, in which she restates the classical belief that women (albeit goddesses) are to be credited with the invention of technology, agriculture – and literacy.

The last word, however, on mothers and the education of their children must go not to Christine, but to Heldris of Cornwall, the author of the romance tale, *Silence*, about a heroine who, with the connivance of her mother – and indeed father – is successfully raised as a boy.[51] This thirteenth-century tale, set in England, opens with events that lead the king to decree that in future no woman can inherit. Subsequently the king's nephew Cador falls in love with the beautiful and skilled Euphemie (who appears initially as Cador's doctor). Cador and Euphemie marry and the king promises to give them the duchy of Cornwall, provided they have a son. They accept the terms but work out a strategy for keeping the inheritance even if they have a daughter. Euphemie is to have only one birth attendant, a female cousin, who can be trusted not to divulge the sex of the baby; whether boy or girl Cador and Euphemie have decided that the child will be brought up as a boy. The baby is born – and it's a girl. Told that he has a son but later finding out the truth, Cador declares that 'he wouldn't have given a fig to have a son instead of a daughter for he never saw such a lovely creature'. The child is baptised Silence, a nappy being put on with great care (by Cador) and the priest instructed not to remove it because the infant is sickly. Silence is then sent off to be brought up far from the court, leaving Nature to fume: 'they have done this to spite me, thinking that Nurture is stronger than my work.' And Nurture does indeed do a good job.

As the years pass Silence becomes anxious – will she make a good knight? If the inheritance laws are changed and the deceit therefore becomes unnecessary, will she know how to behave as a woman? Since both men and women can be musicians she decides to run away with a band of minstrels so that she can acquire for herself instruments, 'harp and vielle', in place of what she does not know about sewing – 'working orphreys [embroidery] or ribbons'. The complications of the story multiply; its intricacies need not concern

---

[51] S. Roche-Mahdi (ed.), *Silence: A Thirteenth-Century French Romance* (1992).

us and the outcome will cause no surprise – the truth is revealed and Silence allowed to inherit as a woman. In this sense Nature can claim victory; but it is won only after Silence herself has outshone her male companions as both minstrel and later, perforce, as knight.

Despite recent attempts to read *Silence* as a work underpinned by misogynistic assumptions, the triumph of Nurture over Nature, in the form of Silence's successes as a hero, serves to demonstrate that, however different the parameters, medieval interest in debates about the roles which women and men were brought up to play could be every bit as keen as our own.

CHAPTER SEVEN

Women at Work

Peasant Women

In the corner of the room farthest from the door there is a very large wooden platform, the height of a table, on which are strewn rags and old clothes. This is the bed where the family sleep. The main difference in the winter between waking and sleeping is the cold. It is warmer sleeping under the rags and on top of the sheep; on the side of the wooden platform are two planks that lift up to make an entrance; every evening the seven family sheep rush into the pen under the bed. When the father returns, there will be seven bodies on the bed and seven sheep underneath.[1]

This is not, as the reader might at first suppose, a description of a medieval English peasant family; it comes from the twentieth-century observations of the writer John Berger who has lived for many years in a peasant community. It is quoted as an illustration of the particular pitfalls of writing about peasants, men or women: how to find an appropriate chronology, on the one hand, how to represent a lifestyle that it is easy to sentimentalise, on the other. Possibly there were sheep under the bed in 1500 as well as in 1066, but we also have to remember that although the population in England had trebled between the Norman Conquest and 1300, it was decimated by the famines and plagues of the fourteenth century. What this might mean for village life can be seen from Cecily Howell's work on Kibworth Harcourt in Leicestershire. Between 1280 and 1340 the same families lived and held land

[1] John Berger, cited in 'Another Way of Seeing Peasants', *Peasant Studies* (1982), p. 93.

in the village; by 1390 only sixteen families had been there for more than a few years; by 1440 it was only eight.[2]

Discussion of the English medieval peasant is further bedevilled by the question of definition: who is a peasant? In this chapter I have adopted the usage of Christopher Dyer: 'peasant is a convenient, if rather elastic term to describe many small-scale cultivators.'[3] Even with this broad definition problems arise due to the lack of evidence until the mid thirteenth century, and the controversy surrounding the interpretation of later evidence, in particular manorial court rolls. Further, since no two manors are alike generalisations are especially risky. Historians have by now banished the once favoured notion of an extended medieval kin-group and there is general agreement that the average peasant family was a small conjugal unit consisting only of husband, wife, and no more than two or three children. In the absence of parish records much about the formation of this family remains unclear. The age of marriage in particular is hotly debated. The relationship between number of children and number of pregnancies is another much discussed issue: poor nutrition will have reduced maternal fertility and, of the babies conceived, many will not have come to full term or survived infancy. As far as the older generation were concerned, grandparents were not on the whole expected to live with their married offspring. A settlement of 1258 from Taverham in Norfolk, for example, suggests that while this could still be a possibility it was an arrangement to be viewed with caution: by the terms of this particular agreement a father surrendered his holding to his son and new wife but only on condition that he could reclaim most of it should their life together not work out.

Before marriage, daughters might already have been given land. Whatever the inheritance customs of any particular manor, and however short the supply of land, parents consistently attempted to endow non-inheriting children – daughters quite as much as sons – with at least a smallholding. In a sample of pre-plague land transactions from the manor of Brigstock in Northamptonshire, studied by Judith Bennett, just

[2] C. Howell, *Land, Family and Inheritance in Transition* (1983).
[3] C. Dyer, *Standards of Living in the Later Middle Ages: Social Change in England, c.1200–1520* (1989), p. 22.

over a quarter of grants were to daughters.[4] These grants were not necessarily a form of dowry – they might be made several years before the daughters in question married – nor were they, on the whole, conditional. Cristina Penifader of Brigstock, for example, who married in 1317, had already been given land grants by her father in 1313, 1314, and 1316. Sometimes, on marriage, such land was returned to the natal holdings since the women were now considered to be provided for by their husbands. Bennett has also found examples of single women – who already had some capital and who must therefore have had some years of employment behind them – buying land for themselves.

For a young single woman, earning money in any way that required a significant capital outlay was clearly difficult; few could therefore become brewsters or bakers until later in life. To start with, the single peasant woman was more likely to get a job either as a wage labourer or as a live-in servant. Of the two options, going into service paid less, but it was more secure; wage labour, such as harvesting, might be seasonal, whereas service contracts were made for the year. Service was not, as it would have become by the end of the Middle Ages, a demeaning profession – children might often be described as the servants of their parents. Nor was hiring servants uncommon; it might be beyond the reach of poorer peasants but richer peasants could expect to be able to do so, with the result that there might be little or no difference in social standing between master or mistress and servant. There was likely to be work within a ten- to fifteen-mile radius of home, possibly even in the same village. In Halesowen, Worcestershire, according to Zvi Razi, about 10 per cent of the population were employed locally as servants.[5] In those less prosperous families where only one servant was employed it can reasonably be assumed that he or she would have a variety of tasks to perform; in richer establishments there was more specialisation of labour and skills might entail laundry- or dairy-work. A dairymaid's duties are described in the thirteenth-century text known as *Fleta:*

---

[4] J. Bennett, *Women in the Medieval English Countryside: Gender and Household in Brigstock before the Plague* (1987).

[5] Z. Razi, *Marriage and Death in a Medieval Parish: Economy, Society and Demography in Halesowen, 1270–1400* (1980).

It is the duty of the dairy-maid to receive from the reeve, by written indenture, the utensils belonging to her office and when she leaves to return them by the same indenture, in which the date of her commencing work is stated. Further, it is her business to receive milk, against a tally, by the number of gallons, and to make cheese and butter, and to take charge of the poultry and frequently to render account and to answer to the bailiff and the reeve for the produce resulting therefrom ... And when she can reasonably find leisure for such things, it is her business to winnow, to cover the fire and do similar odd jobs.[6]

Once married, a woman was unlikely to remain in service. It should not, of course, be assumed that every woman did marry, though it is generally reckoned that there were few who did not; estimates for Lincolnshire villages of the late thirteenth century suggest a celibate population of only 4 per cent. As a married woman, the peasant wife assumed a new identity as the *materfamilias*, the mother of the family, or *domina domus*, mistress of the house. As the lord's tenant she had a part to play in the household economy, with obligations, such as harvest boon work, to fulfil; her special responsibilities were likely to have included milking cows, sheep-shearing, the care of poultry and pigs and the growing of vegetables and herbs. There was no rigid division of labour along gendered lines and no tasks a peasant woman might not be called on to perform. She was a full partner in the management of the holding; husband and wife might work quite literally as a team, as in *Pierce the Ploughman's Crede*, the wife goading the oxen as the husband guided the plough 'with a long ox goad / In a clouted coat cut short to the knee / Wrapped in a win- nowing sheet to keep out the weather.' Lest such teamwork should seem no more than a poetic image, bearing little relation to reality, we should consider the implications of Richard Smith's work showing how the peasantry, from the late thirteenth century, came to adopt the practice of holding land in jointure, so that in the event of her husband's death land passed automatically to the wife, a recognition of shared enterprise.[7] From late-fifteenth-century Sussex, moreover, we have evidence of husbands and wives buying property together, the mortgage being paid off in part by the woman's

[6] Trans. E. Amt, *Women's Lives in Medieval Europe* (1993), p. 182.
[7] R. M. Smith, 'Women's Property Rights under Customary Law: Some Develop- ments in the Thirteenth and Fourteenth Centuries', *Transactions of the Royal Historical Society*, 5th series, 36 (1986), pp. 165–94.

work. In 1467, for example, William and Juliana Greenstreet bought two cottages and half an acre from Richard Crane. They promised to pay him £3 over the next three years. One of the houses was used as an ale-house; the brewer was Juliana.

The overworked peasant woman is a figure familiar through satire, folk-tale and clerical polemic. *Holy Maidenhood*, in advocating a life of virginity, asks: 'What kind of position is the wife in who when she comes in, hears her child screaming, sees the cat at the flitch and the dog at the hide, her loaf burning on the hearth and her calf sucking, the pot boiling over into the fire – *and* her husband complaining.'[8] It is therefore perhaps worth making the point that the household was not expected to be self-sufficient. Many women would make butter and cheese, but buy bread and ale (often from other women); they would spin, but they would go to market to buy cloth. And they might have time, despite – or through – their occupations in house and garden, to make some money as well.

Women who brewed occupy a large place in any discussion of women's work. Until the fourteenth century, when hops were introduced and beer could be made, the most common beverage was ale, made from barley. No-one drank water since, as Judith Bennett remarks it was regarded as unhealthy.[9] Ale could only be kept for a few days before going sour so fresh supplies were constantly needed. The thirteenth-century Assize of Bread and Ale had laid down national standards but the assize was soon used as a way of licensing ale-makers rather than simply controlling the quality of their product. In Brigstock, ale-tasters met every three weeks and, if necessary, fined the ale-sellers of the manor. Whereas nearly every brewer in Brigstock was a married woman, the ale-tasters were all men (though female ale-tasters elsewhere are not unknown). The same was true of Wakefield in Yorkshire. Brewing was laborious and time-consuming but it could be fitted in around other household duties; it required no regular commitment. Many brewsters, judging from the court rolls, brewed only intermittently, depending on financial need and their other occupations. No particular prestige or stigma seems to have

---

[8] Trans. B. Millet and J. Wogan-Brown, *Medieval English Prose for Women*, p. 35.
[9] J. Bennett, 'The Village Ale-Wife: Women and Brewing in Fourteenth-Century England', in B. Hanawalt (ed.), *Women and Work in Preindustrial Europe* (1986), p. 21.

been at stake – brewers came from both poor and relatively prosperous families. On the other hand, there were established networks of brewing families: a newcomer to Brigstock had little hope of setting up an ale-shop, which suggests that a certain respectability was needed to fill what was after all a socially important role.

Just how many ale-wives were at work in any village can be difficult to assess because of the practice of registering amercements in the husband's name, irrespective of who was the actual brewer. Helena Graham's recent study of the manor of Alrewas in Staffordshire cites by way of example the case of William Shepherd who was regularly amerced even though it is evident from the details of a particular case that the person making the ale was in fact his wife.[10] This is not to claim anything like a female monopoly for brewing; in areas such as Iver in Buckinghamshire, where animal husbandry left men with more time on their hands than in forested Brigstock, there were correspondingly more male brewers than females. Among ale-wives Margery Kempe (see pp. 164–5 below) has a particular claim to fame, despite the failure of her enterprise, but there were also male brewers of considerable wealth and standing, and it was with them that the future was to lie. When beer took over from ale, as far as its production was concerned, women lost out. Beer, unlike ale, could be kept; it could therefore be made in large quantities and there was no longer any necessity for small-scale home brewing. In a similar fashion, the thirteenth-century 'advance' from spindles to spinning wheels was not necessarily in the interests of women. Spinning wheels speeded up work, but, unlike spindles, they could not be carried around. They were an unsociable invention that would keep a woman in her place in a hitherto unaccustomed manner.

Spinning apart, there was much gregarious business to be done. Bread might be baked in a communal oven; clothes washed in the village stream. Surplus produce might be taken by peasant women to local markets. By the thirteenth century a weekly market was likely to be within reach of most villagers. Alrewas, for example, since 1290 had held the right to a market every Tuesday. The butchers and bakers at this market were

---

[10] H. Graham, ' "A Woman's Work ...": Labour and Gender in the Late Medieval Countryside', in P. J. P. Goldberg (ed.), *Woman is a Worthy Wight*, p. 141.

men but the small traders, the tranters or regrators, were predominantly female. Like the ale-wives of Brigstock, women tranters seldom appear as professionals; they turn up from time to time when need or opportunity arises. There is, all the same, some specialisation in what they sell. Eggs, poultry and dairy produce feature regularly among their wares; an ordinance from Lynn is directed to the 'mylk wymen'; an 'egg-monger' molested on her way to market at Winchester becomes the object of a miracle by St Swithun (he 'mends' her broken eggs). It is, however, difficult to know how many of these market traders were countrywomen in town for the day, and how many were forestallers, that is, townswomen selling at a profit produce they had previously gone out into the country to buy.

Women wage-labourers took on work in the same casual way. They could be found doing all manner of jobs – haymaking, mowing, breaking stones for road-mending – but such work was considered as casual labour rather than full-time employment. Their rates of pay were sometimes, but not always, lower than men's. We have evidence of both women thatchers and reapers being paid the same as men; we also know of cases where women were clearly regarded as cheap labour and paid accordingly. Walter of Henley's husbandry manual of the thirteenth century recommended keeping a woman for stock-taking since 'it is always advisable to have a woman there for much less money than a man would take'. The shortage of labour following the Black Death undoubtedly gave women a bargaining power they had previously lacked, though attempts were made to curb this. The Statute of Cambridge, for example (1388), laid down six shillings as the maximum annual wage for dairymaids or 'women labourers'; shepherds and carters, on the other hand, at the top of the scale got ten shillings.

Despite regional differences in the nature of the work of peasant wives there is always a consistent pattern. Work is adapted to suit family circumstances. Married women derive their work identity from their status as wives rather than from any other jobs they may take on; the tasks they take up are likely to be those left over by men. We must also remember that whatever the economic contribution of the peasant woman to her household she remained, as far as the governing of her community was concerned, an outsider. The wives of Brigstock, as Judith Bennett has made clear, on marriage relinquished any independence they had previously enjoyed. Those who had previously attended court as tenants now left such business to their husbands. There was no call for their regular attendance; there were no official positions of responsibility open to them. Women did not join tithings, the basic peace-keeping units of any village; they did not act as reeves or jurors and only occasionally acted as pledges. Although it is possible that in manors other than Brigstock, for instance at Broughton (Huntingdonshire), women may have had rather more autonomy in the management of property they had brought into their marriage, office-holding was still not an option. Our concern must be not so much to register late-twentieth-century dismay at this state of affairs as to question whether this exclusion was felt as a grievance by peasant women themselves.

Whatever their legal disabilities, peasant women should not be pictured meekly straining their ale, or bundling up spare leeks. Agnes, wife of John Sadeler, a leader of the rising of peasants at Romsley in Worcestershire in 1386, may have been exceptional but it is worth bearing in mind the significant part women would come to play in sixteenth-century grain riots and in the protests against enclosure.[11] Such collective action was not without precedent. The women of Swaffham in Norfolk in the late fifteenth century were counted on to join, vociferously, in the proposed campaign against the Duke of Suffolk's agents. Likewise, any reading of court rolls will suggest both the range of activities and the assertiveness of peasant women. By way of example we may look at the Wakefield court rolls of 1348–50 recently analysed by Helen Jewell.[12]

At Wakefield, ale-related fines were by far the commonest cause for women to appear before the court but other offences reveal a variety of occupations. Women lent money: Alice de Sourby was owed 20½d from a loan; Alice del Lone, 12½d; Margaret, daughter of Ellen, 2s 2d. They not only sold cloth and oats but also livestock: Alice, wife of William de Hallestead, had sold two oxen to Richard, son of John; William del

[11] R. Houlbrooke, 'Women's Social Life and Common Action in England from the Fifteenth Century to the Eve of the Civil War, *Continuity and Change* 1 (1986), pp. 171–89.

[12] H. Jewell, 'Women at the Courts of the Manor of Wakefield, 1348–1350', *Northern History* 26 (1990), pp. 59–81.

Bothem had bought a horse from Margery de Wolruñwall. Both Richard and William were being sued for money outstanding. Women raised the hue and cry, a procedure of complaint against wrongdoings whereby a false accusation will lead to the fining of the accuser rather than the accused. Out of thirteen recorded cases, in only four was the woman's complaint not upheld; there is no evidence here of any bias against women's testimony. Women themselves were by no means peaceful: Matilda, wife of Robert of Combirworth, was fined 3d for drawing blood from Magota, daughter of John; Agnes, wife of William Walker, was fined 12d for drawing blood from William de Pudsay. In an earlier Wakefield roll the case comes up of Amabel the Cowkeeper who in defence of the cattle in her care had fractured a man's skull. 'Disadvantaged', as Jewell points out, is not be equated with 'downtrodden'.

'Disadvantaged' still begs the question: from whose viewpoint? Continental historians writing about the medieval peasantry have taken a very different approach from their British counterparts. Robert Fossier, for example, sees the central Middle Ages as a time when peasant women came into their own. The emergence of settled villages, populated by nuclear families, and the building of long houses with a central hearth brought women quite literally into the middle of things: 'The return of the womenfolk to their own roof is surely the fundamental reason for the great increase in female influence that is characteristic of the years 1100–1300 ... The presence of the hearth within the house created an entirely new situation as far as peasant attitudes were concerned ... The women who tended the fire drew from it their power and influence.' ... 'in the village the man is in the fields or the woods: everything else is in the woman's hands and it is impossible to ignore this fact.'[13]

Long houses were the most usual form of peasant housing in England; Fossier bases much of his argument on the excavations at Wharram Percy in Yorkshire. Werner Rosener, in his work on the medieval peasant, quotes the late-eighteenth-century philosopher Justus Moser's opinion of such houses in Northern Germany:

The house of the common peasant is so perfect in its floor-plan that it can hardly be improved and can be taken as a model. The hearth is

[13] R. Fossier, *Peasant Life in the Medieval West* (1988), pp. 68–9; 18.

situated almost in the centre of the house, and is so placed that the peasant's wife, who spends most of her time sitting and working there, can see everything at once. No other type of building has such an ideal yet comfortable vantage point. Without having to get up from her chair, she can overlook three doors, greet people entering the house, offer them a seat, while keeping an eye on her children, servants, horses and cows, tending cellars and bedrooms, and get on with her spinning and cooking. Her bed is just behind the hearth, and from there she can exercise the same supervision, watching her servants, getting up for work or going to bed, listening to the cattle feeding and keeping an eye on the cellar and other rooms. Each task is linked in a chain with the others.[14]

Moser's peasant is perhaps unusually sedentary; but the scene evoked of the *domina domus*, however idealised it is, may still tell us something about the role of the peasant woman. If not, at the least it may provoke us to ask why our sources are so silent about precisely the kind of activities from which peasant women of other times and places have derived their power.

Peasant women in medieval England, as elsewhere, were responsible for cooking and washing; this in turn gave them the duties of keeping the fire alive, of fetching water and of going to the washing place. Washing, in particular, seems to be a job only done by women; in aristocratic households in medieval England, the one servant certain to be a woman was the laundress. Whether we also look at thirteenth-century Spain, nineteenth-century Brittany, or twentieth-century Portugal we find that food, fire, water, washing, all laden with symbolism are intimately bound up with perceptions of women, with their roles and with recognisably 'feminine' space. In Alto Minho, Portugal, where Joao de Pina-Cabral has found constant conflict and ambiguity in gender roles, the fireplace is 'the sacred core of the peasant household ...'[15] The power of fire is recognised as both good and evil; it purifies as well as destroys. Rituals connect not only fire with food, in particular bread, but also with birth; it is essential that the umbilical cord of any newborn baby be burned in the household fireplace as a way of destroying what is perceived to be its antisocial origins. Women and men in Alto Minho 'participate jointly' in agricultural tasks but here, as elsewhere, washing is

[14] W. Rosener, *Peasants in the Middle Ages* (1992), p. 70.
[15] J. de Pina-Cabral, *Sons of Adam, Daughters of Eve* (1986), p. 39.

one of the few things only a woman can do. No man ever goes near women while they are washing clothes. The washing place is women's territory; it is where they exchange news; it is, as in Brittany, the women's court. According to a Breton folklorist

The washing is rinsed, twisted, and beaten at the wash-house where the tongues are quite as active as the washer-woman's beetles; it is the seat of feminine justice with little mercy for the men-folk. Soaped from head to foot, soaped again, and rinsed down, they go through some bad times ...

And again,

The wash-house is one of the principal places of gossip in our region. Women of all ages meet there and soaping and beating their linen seems only a secondary activity, so enthusiastically do they exchange scandal, and tell each other of the loves, marriages, births and other major events of the district.[16]

In medieval Spain, in northern Castile, according to customs studied by Heath Dillard, 'any bridge over water that was used as an exit from a town was supposed to be at least wide enough for two women and their jugs ... to pass side by side'.[17] Springs and streams were not places where men were expected to be; thus at Plasencia, women were not allowed to act as witnesses in disputes – unless they had occurred at springs or bakeries.

'Women's tongues' are, of course, the ready butt of medieval misogyny: it was something of a commonplace that women were garrulous and talked more than men because their bodies were wetter so their tongues slipped around more easily in their mouths. It may be worth considering this particular insult in the context of women washing and gossiping. Gossipers are feared and reviled because of the power of their words. If we return to John Berger we find in his *Pig Earth* that it is gossip which gives identity to a community: 'Every village's portrait of itself is constructed ... out of words, spoken and remembered: out of opinions, stories, eye-witness reports, legends, comments and hearsay. And it is a continuous portrait; work on it never stops'; 'the function of ... gossip ... is to allow the

---

[16] M. Segalen, *Love and Power in the Peasant Family* (1983), pp. 138–9.
[17] H. Dillard, *Daughters of the Reconquest* (1984), p. 150.

whole village to define itself'.[18] Whether this was also true in medieval England we cannot know; but it may be worth considering. Women – and, it must be said, men too – appear regularly in court rolls faced with defamation charges. Defamation mattered. The defamation fines in the rolls of Warboys in Huntingdonshire, though of average rate, are assessed with greater regularity than those for assault.

We may leave the peasant women on firmer ground. Time and again they appear in court rolls for illegal gleaning, sometimes combined with petty theft. In 1313, for example, in Warboys we find such entries: 'they say that Agnes Malitraz does not deserve to stay in the village because she gleans wrongly taking sheaves and other small things; therefore she is prohibited the village'; 'and they say that Eleanor Baroun is of the same sort; therefore she is prohibited the village.'[19] In so far as women like Agnes and Eleanor moved on to try their luck in towns we will meet them again, but we should first consider briefly the problem of peasant women, poverty and crime.

Differences in peasant wealth were very great: the richest peasant families of Halesowen, according to Zvi Razi, might have 25–30 acres of arable; the poorest had to make do with a quarter of that or even less. They were unlikely to have animals beyond some poultry and maybe a sheep or a pig. For such, illegal gleaning could be a necessity. By no means all crimes committed by women can be attributed to poverty but, as the work of Barbara Hanawalt has shown, although women feature less frequently than men in medieval criminal records, when they do they are more likely to have committed petty theft than any other crime. What they steal is primarily food, clothing and household goods, grain and also vegetables, taken by night, from the gardens of neighbours.[20] (Even one of the servants of the holy woman Christina of Markyate could not resist pinching salad ingredients from a nearby garden. Some crimes, on the other hand, were on a professional scale, even family concerns. More typical is the plight of Alice de Schischurst of Halesowen; declared 'persona non grata' in

[18] J. Berger, *Pig-Earth* (1979), p. 9.
[19] For Warboys, see J. A. Raftis, *Warboys: Two Hundred Years in the Life of an English Medieval Village* (1974).
[20] B. Hanawalt, 'The Peasant Family and Crime in Fourteenth Century England', *Journal of British Studies* 13, no. 2 (1974), pp. 1–18.

1275, Alice managed to find refuge for a further year, but then she stole a measure of corn and half a measure of peas, set her house on fire and fled. A few years earlier, an old woman, Sabillia, had spent the day begging for bread. On her way home she slipped into a stream and drowned. There is no need to believe the chronicle report that during the great famine of the early fourteenth century mothers ate their babies in order to register the poverty and desperation of women like Alice or Sabillia. Nor do we need to construct any particularly vicious system of patriarchy to imagine that it was peasant women such as they who in those years would have suffered the most.

Townswomen

The distinction between town and country was not as sharp in medieval England as it is today. Within the boundaries of any borough might be plots of land where burgesses would keep horses and sheep, their town gardens housing their hens and pigs. Town wives, like their country counterparts, cared for such livestock; frequently, too, they brewed ale, as peasant women did, though since courts in towns, as in villages, levied fines in a husband's name, the identity of the family's brewer is often hidden. Despite this overlap, town life was otherwise based on trade and manufacturing and it was within this economy that many women hoped to find themselves a niche.

In the hard-pressed years of the late thirteenth century, towns were already drawing in women from the surrounding countryside. Such women came, often as illegal immigrants, hoping they could set themselves up as traders; frequently the gamble paid off and they stayed. After the Black Death, the numbers of migrating women increased still further so that by the later Middle Ages it was quite possible for towns to have more women living in them than men. This has been clearly demonstrated in Yorkshire by Jeremy Goldberg through his analysis of poll tax returns.[21]

The right to trade in a town without paying market tolls was bestowed only on those who had the liberty of a borough; but this was an expensive privilege, carefully monitored and guarded. Men and women, but mostly the latter, therefore

---

[21] P. J. P. Goldberg, *Women, Work, and Life Cycle in a Medieval Economy: Women in York and Yorkshire c. 1300–1520* (1992).

attempted to bypass the regulations and to slip into boroughs unnoticed. In Halesowen, the Shropshire borough studied by Rodney Hilton, about three-quarters of those charged with lodging illegal immigrants between 1293 and 1349 had sheltered women.[22] Three such illegal immigrants were the sisters Alice, Cristina and Juliana from the neighbouring hamlet of Illey, all of whom were fined for dishonest trading. Alice, presumably the eldest, was the first to be charged, in 1281; her sisters, undeterred, followed in her wake. Accusations against them include trading without permission, selling flour and ale in false measures and forestalling. Both Juliana and Cristina had children, but whether they had husbands is unclear. In 1317 Juliana appears in the record charged with sheltering her daughter Margery, a stealer of sheaves.

The late thirteenth century and early fourteenth century saw what Goldberg has described as a 'feminisation of poverty' that was particularly acute in towns.[23] This is not to say that men did not suffer too; in 1322, a crowd seeking alms from Dominican monks in London got crushed to death; twenty-six were women, twenty-nine men. But it remains clear that a significant proportion of women lived on the margins of town life, treading a fine line between poverty and destitution. Such women clustered together in suburbs and poorer neighbourhoods, sharing houses, beds and strategies for survival.

What we do not know is at what point (if at all) such alliances of poor women merit the name of beguinages. Beguinages, groups of women living together to share both work and spirituality, are known in the Low Countries from the thirteenth century. They never appear by that name in England; Norman Tanner considers the small groups of women living together in late-medieval Norwich in two of the city's tenements to be related to the movement, but he also thinks that Norwich is unusual in this respect.[24] It is worth bearing in mind that at least some of the women known to be living together in the poorer parts of other towns, as, for example, at Bootham in the suburbs of York, or in Winchester where a number were employed by St Mary's Abbey, may

[22] R. Hilton, 'Small Town Society in England before the Black Death', *Past and Present* 105 (1984), pp. 53–78.
[23] P. J. P. Goldberg, 'The Public and the Private: Women in the Pre-Plague Economy' in P. R. Coss and S. Lloyd (eds), *Thirteenth Century England* 111 (1991), pp. 75–89.
[24] N. Tanner, *The Church in Late Medieval Norwich, 1370–1532* (1984), p. 64.

have shared a purpose as well as their poverty. Economic and spiritual needs do not have to be incompatible. Roberta Gilchrist has recently suggested that the houses of charity known as the *maisons dieux* in York may have resembled beguinages. She suggests as an example the community of poor women living in the house of Cecily Plater in St Andrewgate, who were left 6s 8d by Thomas de Kent in 1397; in 1532 there was still such a community in St Andrewgate, the recipients this time of 3 shillings from the will of Leonard Shaw.[25]

For many of the women who moved from country to town, finding accommodation was not the problem: a large number of single women came as living-in servants. Servants, of whom just under a half were likely to be women, might account for a third of a town's population by the late fourteenth century. Service was not seen as a lifetime vocation but rather as an appropriate occupation to be taken up between adolescence and marriage. Both the skills and finance necessary for setting up a household might thereby be acquired and, since servants frequently ended up marrying each other, so too might a partner.

For those servants who were apprentices there were far more opportunities in towns than in the country. Apprenticeship differed from 'normal' service in that specialised training was involved, together with a lengthy contract, usually of seven years. Formal apprenticeship, however, was only rarely an option for women. In Exeter, for example, apprenticeship gave entry to the freedom of the city, but since women were not allowed this privilege they could not become recognised apprentices. What evidence there is for female apprenticeship centres around London, particularly its silk trade, an occupation uniquely restricted to women, but even in London it is probable that there were more women apprentices than show up in the records. Barbara Hanawalt, in her recent study *Growing up in Medieval London*, has found that women apprentices were seldom enrolled as such in the city's records, possibly because there were no female guilds. None the less, the statutes of the city legislated equally for male and female apprentices, and provision was also made for those women

[25] R. Gilchrist, *Gender and Material Culture* (1994), pp. 170–2; for the bequests, see P. H. Cullum, ' "And Hir Name was Charite" ', in P. J. P. Goldberg (ed.), *Woman is a Worthy Wight*, p. 209, n. 120.

who themselves needed to employ apprentices to follow their 'mistery'. Apprenticeship arrangements made with women were sometimes more flexible and less formal than strictly allowed by custom. The daughter of John Catour of Reading, apprenticed in the mid-fourteenth century to a London embroiderer who allegedly ill-treated her, was, on examination of the case, found to be apprenticed for only five years rather than seven and her master had not registered her. Judging from other contracts made with women apprentices, it seems to have been envisaged that they might not always wish to complete their period of training. Some contracts allowed for this eventuality; a woman wanting to end her contract in order to marry could buy her way out for an agreed sum.

In the hierarchy of service, then, apprenticeship stood high; at the other end of the scale we may place those women who came to towns with expectations of finding a livelihood but with no prior arrangements or contacts. Hanawalt cites the example of a certain Joan Smyth who turned up on the doorstep of Robert Mascall of Aldenham 'in poor and simple array and almost perished for want of sustenance'. Joan was lucky; Robert took her in, 'having pity and out of alms more than any other reason', and he employed her for the next three years.[26] Such women were, of course, particularly vulnerable both to financial and sexual exploitation. So too were the very young: twelve was a common age for starting service. Added security was to be found in family arrangements: nieces might serve aunts and uncles, sisters might succeed each other in any household; brothers who already knew the lie of the land might report back on favourable posts.

Hiring fairs were held regularly throughout the country, often on Quarter Days. In Yorkshire, Martinmas fairs were customary but in other parts of the country Christmas, or St John the Baptist's Day, was preferred. Whatever the date, in line with the provision of the Statute of Labourers (1351) contracts were expected to last for twelve months and could often be renewed, though it was usual after a year or two for a servant to look for another post. Rates of pay varied; some women received wages, others only board and lodging. An interesting fifteenth-century case is that of Alice Shevington of London, hired at the rate of 16 shillings a year, who began

[26] B. Hanawalt, *Growing up in Medieval London* (1994), p. 176.

to earn more on the side through her 'cunning with sore eyes'. Her master tried to withhold her wages whereupon she sued him for debt.

Servants' occupations were as varied as those of their master or mistress. They were by no means confined to domestic jobs and duties. There is, according to Goldberg, a sex-specific pattern in that women were more normally employed in the victualling and mercantile trades than in textiles and clothing with leather and metal being the least common areas of occupation (though women often worked gold).[27] There is a chronological pattern, too: by the close of the fifteenth century far more male than female servants were being employed in artisanal households. Female service was beginning its association with, on the one hand, an improvement in the social status of the employer and, on the other, of a corresponding loss of status for the employee.

Generalisations about the relationship between servant and master or mistress are hard to come by. Evidence from wills of the period suggests that bonds of friendship were often formed; servants might be not only left money but also beds, clothing, and pots and pans, valuable items to enable them to set up house on their own. We may imagine, in the absence of proof, that essentially warm and untroubled relationships lie behind such bequests. In contrast are tales of excessive cruelty and abuse, notably stories of forced prostitution or rape. Since the 1285 Statute of Westminster, rape was an offence punishable by death (the earlier penalty had been castration) but prosecutions were rare. Juries might be unwilling to convict because of the status of the rapist, or unable to do so because of the confusion and uncertainty of the evidence. Compromises were often reached or cases dropped. The complaints of servants did not always go unheard. In her study of London, Hanawalt gives the example of a master imprisoned through the testimony of his servant – he had 'offended by force against her and because she feared him' – but such cases could be complex and, without witnesses, the truth difficult to ascertain. Another of Hanawalt's stories is of a London barber who took in for the night a neighbour's servant whom he had found shivering in the street; several days later her master accused

[27] P. J. P. Goldberg, *Women, Work and Life Cycle in a Medieval Economy* (1992), p. 187.

the barber of having sexually abused her. The ballad of *The Servant Girl's Holiday* – I've waited longing for today: / Spindle, bobbin and spool, away! / In joy and bliss I'm off to play / Upon this high holiday[28] – presents in light-hearted fashion sexual adventures which in reality, for the women concerned, may have had a much grimmer aspect. In 1461 Thomas Hull of Lichfield was accused of having made three of his mother's servants pregnant; the court directed that he had either to choose one of them to marry or accept that the one he next slept with would henceforth be considered his legal wife.

Just as towns needed sewers, so too, the traditional argument went, they needed brothels. Prostitution in medieval English towns was in one or two cases regulated and in others only half-heartedly condemned. Some female servants were undoubtedly sold into prostitution; others, who had come to town looking for employment and failed to find it, may have considered joining a brothel a better option than returning home penniless. A well-ordered house, such as was established at Southwark on land belonging to the Bishop of Winchester, had points in its favour. Fifteenth-century regulations aimed to stop the 'great multiplication of horrible sin upon the single women', to ensure that brothel-keepers did not exploit prostitutes by over-charging them for ale, or making them do extra work such as spinning in their spare time. The keepers were not allowed to beat the women or ensnare them by getting them into debt. Officials of the bishop were to check regularly that no woman was being kept in prostitution against her will. Sometimes, none the less, this is precisely what happened. Redress was possible in theory, but not in practice. Ruth Karras reports such a case from the late fifteenth century: Ellen Butler had been looking for employment as a servant when she had met Thomas Bowde. Thomas offered her what he claimed was a good job; it turned out to be prostitution. When Ellen refused to do 'such service as his other servants', Thomas managed to get her sent to prison for alleged debt. The outcome of Ellen's petition for release is unknown but on the face of it the only sure way she could have paid off the debt would have been by accepting her job as prostitute.[29]

[28] Trans. B. Stone, *Medieval English Verse* (1971), p. 104–5.
[29] R. Karras, 'The Regulation of Brothels in Later Medieval England', in J. Bennett *et al.* (eds), *Sisters and Workers in the Middle Ages* (1989), p. 119.

By the end of the fifteenth century however, the days of licensed brothels were numbered; they would be finally closed in 1546. Signs of a new climate were already evident in the Coventry ordinance of 1492 outlawing brothels and prostitution. 'Senglewoman' in future were 'to go into service until they be married'. Citizens, anxious for the moral well-being of their city, left dowries for poor brides and their household possessions to young couples to help them set up home. In contrast with the marriage and employment trends of earlier decades this new concern to domesticate young women is worth examining and, in particular, the hypothesis proposed by Jeremy Goldberg, based on evidence from Yorkshire, in his *Women, Work and Life Cycle*.

Goldberg's argument is essentially this: the slow rise in the population after the Black Death is to be attributed to a new-found capacity on the part of women to earn a satisfactory living for themselves. Not only did this economic independence give women the opportunity to develop a work identity for themselves; it made them both choosier about whom to marry and delayed the event; some even chose to remain single all their lives. As evidence of this parity, created by the shortage of labour and a booming post-plague economy, Goldberg cites the deposition in a matrimonial cause of a Yorkshire saddler: 'that Thomas did not surpass the said Margery in wealth, status or ability, either in respect of her standing in society or her craft, for he understood that just as Thomas was able to support himself from his craft so Margery was able as a servant.' These halcyon days for women came to an end in the late fifteenth century, when economic recession forced women back into marginal positions. A protest in 1461 by Bristol weavers against women workers in their midst was repeated in Norwich in 1511, and there was worse to come. Women once again had little choice but to marry: 'age at marriage *probably* fell, the marriage rate *probably* increased' (author's italics).[30]

The problem with Goldberg's thesis is not so much the fate of women in the late fifteenth and sixteenth centuries – which it would be hard to gainsay – but rather the difficulty of comparison between the pre- and post-plague positions of urban women. We still do not know the age at which most

---

[30] P. J. P. Goldberg, *Women, Work and Life Cycle*, p. 347.

women were married in thirteenth-century England since there is no earlier equivalent to the poll tax returns of the fourteenth century, but it may already have been comparatively late in life. Moreover, even during Goldberg's 'high point of female economic activity' there were still, as he himself admits, few apprenticeships open to women outside London. Women continued to hold no public role in craft guilds and only one per cent were ever admitted to the freedom of the city of York. Nor do we have to wait for events in Bristol in 1461, or even in Norwich in 1511, for evidence of hostility towards women weavers. Already in 1400 an ordinance from York had declared: 'henceforth no woman of whatever status or condition, shall be put among us to weave, in case they spoil the cloth and jeopardise the name of the craft and its income, unless they have been properly taught and are sufficiently knowledgeable to work in the craft.'

The statute of 1363 that exempted women from having to follow only one trade or craft clearly presupposes and endorses the continuation of a system whereby women will continue to do 'odd jobs'. It may well be, though further work will be needed to substantiate this, that Goldberg's contrast is thus too sharp. On the one hand, women in the post-plague economy can still be seen to be easily expendable; on the other, it may be that in the albeit very different pre-plague conditions their role was greater than is generally allowed. However, it must be acknowledged that Goldberg's thesis has gained recent support from the work of Charles Donahue on marriage litigation in the diocese of York in the fourteenth and fifteenth centuries. In the fourteenth century women seem to have been much more eager than men to enforce marriage contracts; in the early fifteenth century they were less persistent in their efforts, arguably because the improved economic climate had made them less dependent on marriage for their livelihood and their identity.[31]

Those who chose never to marry were still, in late medieval England, a very small minority. Often they worked quite literally as 'spinsters' (though this is not, of course, to suggest that all spinsters were unmarried). Carding and combing wool

[31] C. Donahue, 'Female Plaintiffs in Marriage Cases in the Court of York in the Later Middle Ages: What can we learn from the Numbers?', in S. Walker (ed.), *Wife and Widow in Medieval England* (1993), pp. 183–212.

were also, according to Heather Swanson, jobs primarily done by women; weaving, by contrast, was in the hands of men.[32] Looms were costly and they took up space few women had at their disposal. A spinner might not even have her own wheel but would have to hire it. Female textile workers seldom figure among the more affluent section of the working population. They appear rather as objects of charity in the wills of their rich masters. Thus William Crosby, a dyer, left 20 shillings 'to be divided among the poor women working for me, preparing and carding my wool'. William Shipley, a draper (d. 1435), left 6d 'to each poor woman who works and spins for me'. Similarly, 'poor women' may be found in other trades, curry-ing leather, sewing up shoes and gloves, knitting caps. As piece-workers, they represent an elusive and precarious work-force, surfacing from time to time as beneficiaries of the gen-erosity of former masters. For a single woman to attempt to set up a more secure trade of her own required a capital outlay seldom available to her; with rare exceptions the women who prospered in business did so not on their own but as wives and widows.

For women, and for men too, marriage often saw the begin-ning of a new professional as well as a new familial life. Busi-ness from the start could be based on this partnership, the commitment of the wife as essential to the success of the enter-prise as the co-operation of the peasant wife to the man-agement of a rural croft. Again this system creates problems for the historian in that it makes it difficult to identify the role of wives. By way of example, Heather Swanson has drawn attention to the Ordinance of Founders of 1390 which stipu-lated that each master was to have only one apprentice; an exception was made in the case of Giles Bonoyne who was allowed two 'because he has no wife'. The expectation that both wives and daughters would be engaged in the work of the household, whatever it was, goes far towards explaining the wide variety of work carried out by women and the absence of prohibitions on grounds of gender. Traditional roles did not exclude others. A woman might be a huckster selling ale, bread, fish; she might also be an armourer, a book-binder, a merchant, a fletcher. She was not considered too weak to undertake jobs requiring physical strength, such as carrying

[32] H. Swanson, *Medieval Artisans* (1989).

thatch, turves, or tiles, or loading wool on to ships. Very occasionally, her role beside her husband is acknowledged. Thus we hear of the wife of Roger del Grene, Juliana, a comber, who in 1393 also 'practices the craft of saddler with her husband'. As Eileen Power pointed out in her seminal work *Medieval Women*, even guild regulations, which prohibited women from entering trades, allowed for the contributions of wives.[33] The Lincoln Fullers in 1297 demanded that 'no one of craft shall work at wooden bar with a woman unless with wife of master or her handmaid'. In London in 1344 the Girdlers excluded all but wives and daughters from working with them; again in London, in 1372, we find the wives of dyers of leather sworn with their husbands to do their calling.

It was the wife's familiarity with her husband's trade which gave her the expertise to carry it on should she be left a widow (see below, pp. 178–9). On the other hand, in certain circumstances opportunities existed for women to follow paths of their own; if she lived in London and in a number of other towns too – Lincoln, for example, or Exeter – a married woman could choose to adopt the status of *femme sole*. A *femme sole* had full responsibility for the management of her own business – for better or for worse. Whereas, as a wife, a woman was immune from prosecution for debt since by law she had no goods and chattels – they all belonged to her husband – as *femme sole*, a woman had to face charges concerning her business herself. An early-fourteenth-century London ruling, as quoted by Kay Lacey, is as follows:

where a woman *couverte de baron* [i.e. married] follows any craft within the city by herself apart, with which the husband in no way intermeddles, such a woman should be bound as a single woman as to all that concerns her said craft. And if the husband and wife are impleaded, in such case the wife shall plead as a single person in a Court of Record and shall have her law and other advantages by way of plea just as a single woman. And if she is condemned, she shall be committed to prison until she shall have made satisfaction; and neither the husband nor his goods shall in such case be charged or interfered with.[34]

The privileges of the *femme sole* may date, according to

[33] E. Power, *Medieval Women* (1975).
[34] K. E. Lacey, 'Women and Work in Fourteenth and Fifteenth Century London', in L. Charles and L. Duffin (eds), *Women and Work in Pre-Industrial England* (1985), p. 43.

Caroline Barron, from as early as the thirteenth century.[35] Many of those taking up the option in London were regrators or hucksters, a predominantly female occupation throughout the country and in fact one regularly operating on the wrong side of the law. In York in 1304 eighteen out of twenty seven regrators charged with malpractice were women. In 1395 complaints were lodged against the women poulterers of Nottingham for overpricing their garlic, flour, salt, butter, cheese and tallow. In 1422 London women were charged with forestalling cheese and butter. It is not clear that in such instances women working as *femmes soles* necessarily had the best of the bargain; their husbands could – and did – repudiate their debts, suggesting that the origins of the status lay rather with the safeguarding of male property than with any concern for female emancipation.

No account of the work of women in towns can fail to mention the activities of Margery Kempe. Celebrated as she is for the exuberance of her religious experiences (to which we shall return in a later chapter), her forays into trade in her native town of Lynn, as she tells them in *The Book of Margery Kempe*, have their own drama. Margery, we may suppose, was a woman with some capital – her father had been mayor of Lynn five times and she goes into business 'out of pure covetousness'. The brewery which she established was no kitchen enterprise, but a major venture which for three or four years made her 'one of the greatest brewers in town'. And then things begin to go wrong: 'when the ale had as fine a head of froth on it as any-one might see, suddenly the froth would go flat, and all the ale was lost in one brewing after another.' Her servants leave her and Margery, who by now has lost a large sum of money, has to shut up shop. Undeterred, she acquires a servant with two horses and a horse-mill for the purpose of grinding corn, confident that in this way she can make a living – but the horses refuse to co-operate and the servant moved seemingly by a mixture of exasperation and anxiety, reckons Margery is not someone to work for.

Margery's tribulations in business serve the purpose of curing her of false pride and vanity and setting her on the right path 'to enter the way of everlasting life'. None the less,

[35] C. Barron, 'The "Golden Age" of Women in Medieval London', *Reading Medieval Studies* 15 (1989), pp. 39–40.

it is worth noticing that, in 1438, when Margery is set to finish the dictation of her autobiography, she becomes a member of that prestigious economic body of Lynn, the Guild of the Holy Trinity. Despite her conversion, God and Mammon are not as far apart as all those gallons of flat ale and bushels of unground corn have led us to believe. Throughout her narrative, moreover, Margery does not behave as a woman whose ventures in any way implicate her husband: not only are the debts she incurs described as her own but we also find her taking responsibility for those of her husband. She does so as part of a bargain: *he* is to release her from her marriage debt, the obligation to have sex with him, if *she* pays his bills. Before embarking on a pilgrimage to Jerusalem Margery invites all her husband's debtors - through an announcement by the parish priest – to come and settle up with her. It is likely that she could afford to do this because of a legacy recently inherited from her father, but, as the mark of a financially independent woman, the action is nonetheless striking.

The Aristocracy

The popular definition of work as 'productive activity' does much to mask and devalue many of the day-to-day occupations with which women have traditionally been associated; this is as true for women of the landed aristocracy and gentry as it is for townswomen and peasants. Comparatively rich, and sometimes very rich, though upper-class women may have been, they were not idle. In the administration of households and estates they had a full part to play; the regular appointment of wives as executors of their husbands' wills testifies as much to their proven expertise as it does to marital affection. Some women were literally called upon to defend hearth and home when their menfolk were away. One such woman was Margaret Paston who can be found in *The Paston Letters* requisitioning crossbows and poleaxes from her absent husband so that she could defend their home from hostile neighbours; another was the Countess of Chester, left behind by her husband to face the siege of Lincoln Castle during the civil war of the twelfth century between King Stephen and Matilda, daughter of Henry I. When Stephen himself was captured, his wife, also called Matilda, took command, 'a woman of subtlety and a man's resolution' leading 'a magnificent body of troops' whom she ordered to 'rage most furiously [around London] with plunder and arson, violence and the sword'.[36]

The everyday activities of such women may have been both less onerous and less exciting than those of their husbands but, for all that, they were still exacting. Although the masculine character of aristocratic households has long been recognised (in the fifteenth century the Earl of Northumberland employed 166 men and only 9 women) the discussion of women's spaces within such establishments is now receiving fresh attention. According to Roberta Gilchrist, excavations at Pickering in North Yorkshire, where Countess Alice, wife of Thomas of Lancaster, ordered lavish new buildings for herself, suggest that increased status was marked by the stricter segregation of women's quarters, so that 'residences of the highest status saw the duplication of households for male and female members of the castle'.[37] A noblewoman was thus likely to have charge of her own household all the time, as well as that of her husband during his many absences. The numbers that made up such households naturally varied according to rank and wealth; few were as large, or indeed as masculine, as the Earl of Northumberland's, although Elizabeth Berkeley, Countess of Warwick in the early fifteenth century, had a household of about fifty, only nine of whom were women. Elizabeth, an heiress in her own right and one who, in a display of independence, kept the income from her natal lands separate from her husband's, in one year spent £511 6s 8d on provisions alone. It was not only Elizabeth's own household that had to be fed; hospitality was expected to be given to family, friends, and as a part of religious practice, to strangers.

The task of providing for the needs of even a relatively modest household was sufficiently daunting to have been described recently as a 'major business enterprise'.[38] Yet it should not be thought that the management of estates and households amounted to no more than provisioning and accounting, however formidable those tasks were, and however skilfully they needed to be executed. Debarred

---

[36] *Deeds of Stephen*, ed. K. Potter (1955), p. 81.

[37] R. Gilchrist, 'Medieval Bodies in the Material World', in S. Kay and M. Rubin (eds), *Framing Medieval Bodies* (1994), p. 53.

[38] J. Ward, *English Noblewomen in the Later Middle Ages* (1992), p. 57.

though they might have been from many more formal positions of authority, women's voices were still heard and heeded
on contentious matters. If we look at *The Paston Letters*, in the
1480s we find Margery Paston, her mother-in-law Margaret
and a family friend planning a visit to the dowager duchess
of Norfolk to ask her to support Margery's husband John in a
dispute about land. The idea of the delegation had evidently
come from Margery's cousin on the grounds that 'one word of
a woman should do more than the words of twenty men'.[39]
Knowing the Paston women as we do from their letters gives
us no grounds for thinking them to be by nature a peaceable
lot. In a patriarchical society even such forceful women as the
Pastons occupied a liminal space; but this was space that could
nevertheless be used to the advantage of the whole family. As
Philippa Maddern has pointed out, the role of the Paston
women was crucial in 'the bloodless battles of land transactions, county rumour-mongering and client maintenance'.[40]
Any assessment of women's work in medieval society must
allow for just this kind of social manoeuvring and bonding
which it fell to the lot of women to perform precisely because
in other respects their work identity was so labile.

[39] *Paston Letters*, vol. I, pp. 664–6; cited F. Riddy, 'Women Talking about the Things
of God' in C. Meale (ed.), *Women and Literature in Britain, 1150–1500* (1993), p. 126,
n. 85.

[40] P. Maddern, 'Honour among the Pastons: Gender and Integrity in Fifteenth
Century English Provincial Society', *Journal of Medieval History* 14 (1988), p. 366.

CHAPTER EIGHT

Widows

Widows deserve separate consideration not only because there were so many of them – conservative estimates put widows in charge of at least 10 per cent of medieval English households – but also because their status exemplifies many of the paradoxes of being a woman in a medieval society. Their image and status was full of variation, contradiction, ambivalence. On the one hand, widows were perceived in biblical terms as objects of respect and charity; on the other hand, like Chaucer's Wife of Bath, they were expected to be avaricious and sexually greedy. The widow who remarried was not allowed the nuptial blessing that was part of the liturgy in a first-time wedding; the widow who did not marry again now fulfilled many traditionally masculine roles. Naming practices throw into relief some of the identity problems experienced by widows. A woman who had previously been known as 'X, the wife of ...' might now become 'X, the widow of'; she could also take on her husband's name as her own; alternatively she might choose to revert to her maiden surname. We must look first at the rights which the law gave to widows and at the choices which they made within this framework.

Widowhood was anticipated at the moment of marriage. 'At the church door' (according to the twelfth-century legal text known as *Glanvill*) a man was to endow his wife with her dower. This endowment might take the form of 'nominated dower', that is, of specifically named property – usually but not exclusively land – or it would be calculated at the standard rate of a third of the husband's holding on the day of the marriage. Should she be left a widow, a wife was given full rights over her dower for the rest of her lifetime. She retained it whether she remarried or not, according to the thirteenth-century legal text attributed to Bracton, 'because of the burden of matrimony ... for the maintenance of the wife and the nurture of the children when they are born, should the husband pre-decease her'. She lost it only if it transpired that the marriage itself was invalid (for example, on grounds of consanguinity) or in the case of a divorce following her bad behaviour (generally taken to mean adultery) or if her husband committed treason. A widow was also entitled to *legitim*, that is, a third of her husband's goods or chattels. These, on her own death, she could leave to whomever she chose. Of the other two-thirds, one went to any children of the marriage, the other was set aside to be used for the benefit of the dead man's soul.

Although this may seem to be relatively straightforward, it was not. The first proviso that needs to be made is that both Bracton and *Glanvill* were primarily concerned with the workings of common law; customary law might, and did, make different dower arrangements, to which we will return. Secondly, there was the much debated question as to whether the *legitim* should be calculated according to the husband's property and land at the time of his marriage or at the time of his death. Thirdly, no guarantee was written into the agreement to ensure that the husband would honour his gift. The land in question only became the wife's in the event of her widowhood. Until then, she could lay no claim to it and, at least according to *Glanvill*, she did not even have the right to protest if her husband should decide to sell it. Once widowed, she would have to rely on whoever was heir either to buy the land back or to give her 'reasonable lands in exchange'. Even if the original, nominated dower had been kept intact she still needed the co-operation of the heir both to enter the land if it was vacant, and to reclaim it from any tenant if it were not. The heir, as *Glanvill* well knew, might be awkward:

when eventually the heir of the demandant woman's husband appears in court, either he will attest the claim and admit that the land is part of the woman's dower, and that she was endowed with it and that his ancestor was seised of it at the time when he endowed her with it as part of the land which he nominated as her principal dower; or else he will not ... if the heir neither attests nor admits the claim stated by the woman against the tenant, then the plea can be between the woman and the heir. For a woman cannot effectively prosecute any plea against another concerning her dower without her warrantor ... So if the heir denies to the woman all the right she claims, by saying in court that she was never endowed with it by his ancestor, the case may be settled by battle if the woman has there persons who heard and saw, and one of them is a suitable witness who heard and saw her endowed by the heir's ancestor at the church door at the time of her marriage and is ready to prove it against the heir. If the woman succeeds by battle against the heir, then he must deliver the land claimed to the woman, or else assign her equivalent lands in exchange.[1]

Glanvill, in the words of Janet Senderowitz Loengard, is 'black-letter law'.[2] Trial by battle was a rarity; protracted litigation, on the other hand, was not. Every year, a steady stream of cases came before the king's court. According to Loengard, during three years of Henry III's reign, from 1227–30, the king's court heard almost five hundred suits concerning dower.[3] Those years were not exceptional. The range of possible complications in such suits was endless. Was the husband legally entitled to the land claimed or was there some fault in his title? Was the husband truly dead? (There could reasonably be doubt in the cases of those claiming to be war widows.) What if he had become a monk? A wife had committed adultery; was she divorced or had her husband truly forgiven her? Had the wife already traded her dower rights for rents, either in money, or as in one case, for an alleged annuity of wheat?

Despite the difficulties which women might have in claiming their dower, they were not ineffective in doing so. In 1199 Alice, widow of Ralph Fitz Hugh, successfully sued her son and eleven other men (Ralph's grantees) for her dower. Women might act through an attorney but they are also to be found conducting their cases themselves. Evidence from London suggests that they were least successful when their adversary was the Church. We should not allow our sympathies to be always with the woman, however. Women might accumulate dowries through frequent remarriages: Isolda, daughter and heir of William Pantolf, married five times between 1180 and 1223. Such women might attempt to defraud the heir or they might live for an inconveniently long time. Take the case of Maud de Bohun, a twelfth-century octa-

[1] *Glanvill*, ed. D. Hall (1965), p. 64.
[2] J. S. Loengard, 'English Dower in the Year 1200', in J. Kirshner and S. Wemple (eds), p. 229.
[3] J. S. Loengard, '*Rationabilis Dos*', in S. S. Walker (ed.), *Wife and Widow*, p. 73, n.1.

genarian. Widowed at the age of ten, she subsequently remarried but retained all her long life, to the considerable impoverishment of her first in-laws, the dowry she had inherited as a child. Another formidable dowager, studied by Rowena Archer, was Margaret of Brotherton who outlived two husbands, four children and a grandson; the surviving heir made hopeful promises to be fulfilled 'when the inheritance shall be increased'.[4] Grandmother and grandson died in the same year, 1399. Deaths could indeed be unfairly distributed, causing hardship all round. In 1180, Roger Pinel died leaving a young widow of twenty but no children. His heir was his brother who, four years later, also died, leaving a widow of seventeen and two small children. The holding, not over-large in the first place, somehow had to support two widows and two children.

The impoverished widow got by as best she could; the rich widow had problems of her own. She could be as desirable as her dower. To Anglo-Norman and Angevin kings she was a profitable asset. Just as under-age heirs and heiresses became wards of court so, too, did widows. The king could give them in marriage to whomever he pleased, collecting a hefty fine for the privilege of this favour. Widows' grievances against this use of royal power surface in the coronation charter of Henry I, where promises are made both to respect their rights of dower and not to give them in marriage against their will. The 1130 pipe roll shows how little such promises were worth. Fines were collected both in respect of dower and marriage and from suitors. During subsequent reigns, the fines became more and more exorbitant. As Loengard had pointed out, this system effectively denied many women any choice at all. To raise the money necessary for the right to refuse to remarry, the woman might have to sell her one means of support as single woman: her dower.

The distaste which the 1185 *Register of Rich Widows and of Orphaned Heirs and Heiresses* arouses in the modern reader with its list of widows 'in the king's gift', is neither misplaced nor anachronistic. The barons of King John's reign were of much the same mind: clauses 7 and 8 of Magna Carta were not only explicit, they were also reasonably effective. Henceforth,

---

[4] R. Archer, 'The Estates and Finances of Margaret of Brotherton, *c.* 1320–1399', *Historical Research* 60 (1987), pp. 264–80.

widows were to pay nothing for their dower and they were not to be compelled to remarry. The reissue of Magna Carta in 1225 further clarifies the position of the widow's housing. She may stay for forty days in her husband's 'capital mesuage ... unless that house is a castle; and if she leaves the castle let there be provided for her at once a competent house in which she can live decently, until her dower is assigned to her, and let her have reasonable estovers [subsistence] of the common in the meantime.' After Magna Carta, dower came more and more frequently to be calculated according to the land held on the day of the husband's death. This, with the growing practice dating from around 1300 of holding lands in jointure, gave many widows considerable financial security, at the same time as raising their desirability as new wives.

Pressure to remarry was not every widow's problem; the terms of a number of wills make it clear that husbands were not always in favour of such a prospect and that they had taken steps to make the event unlikely. The will of the Earl of Pembroke (d. 1461) was not untypical: 'and wyfe ... remembre your promise to me take the ordre of wydowhood, as ye may be the better mayster of your owne, to performe my wille and to help my children, as I love and trust you.'[5] A new marriage could severely diminish a widow's legacy. In a will dated 1504, for example, Robert Clarivaux of Eyeworth left his house, land, leases, 100 marks and all his household goods to his wife Alice; but if she remarried 'she is to have £40 and 10 marks of household stuff only and she is to enter bond in £200 to co-exors and supervisors to this effect before entering administration.' Forbidding though these clauses may sound, they should not be seen simply as arbitrary attempts to exercise sexual control over wives from beyond the grave, but also viewed as measures designed to protect first families from the claims of stepfathers or half-siblings and to avoid the kind of hardships which an over-endowered widow could cause for the next generation. Thus it is worth bearing in mind that at the time of making their wills the Earl of Pembroke had seven children and Robert Clarivaux six.

The 'ordre of wydowhood' enjoined by her husband on the Countess of Pembroke was not simply a figure of speech.

---

[5] Cited in J. Rosenthal, 'Fifteenth-Century Widows and Widowhood', in S. S. Walker (ed.), *Wife and Widow in Medieval England* (1993), p. 46.

The widow who chose not to remarry but who, for whatever reason, did not want to enter a convent, could make public her resolution by taking a vow of chastity (hence the name of 'vowess') in the presence of a bishop; the ring and mantle she was to wear were blessed as part of the vowing ceremony, though in other respects they were no different from the sober clothing which any widow was expected to wear. Exceptionally, this vow was taken by Margaret Beaufort when her fourth husband Thomas Stanley was still alive (on his death in 1504 she confirmed it). Margaret's position, as the mother of Henry VII, can in no way be taken as normative, none the less the use she made of the channels of independence open to other women is instructive. Not only did Margaret assume the status of a vowess; she also, in Henry's first parliament, elected to become *femme sole*. This was an option which, as we have seen, was normally taken up by wives in business; there was no precedent for its assumption by a woman of the aristocracy but the freedom it gave Margaret suited her new role as the leading lady of the country.

In many ways Margaret's experiences of widowhood and subsequent remarriages, shaped as they were by the turmoil of the Wars of the Roses, read like highly coloured versions of the less dramatic but otherwise comparable stories shared by the women of her class. Margaret's first marriage to John de la Pole, and its dissolution, are events we have witnessed already. Her first widowhood is equally poignant: aged only thirteen, she was six months' pregnant when her second husband, Edmund Tudor, died of the plague. Margaret's landed wealth made her a coveted bride and a third husband, Henry Stafford, was chosen for her with precipitate speed; her riches were to be set alongside his need for political influence. What was important for Margaret about this third marriage was the protection it gave to her and her son Henry through her new father-in-law, the Duke of Buckingham. On Stafford's death in 1471 Margaret married again within months rather than years; once more, she would seem to have been buying a protector for herself and the young Henry with the lure of her estates. These were administered by Margaret herself with rigorous care. Her estate documents were stored in cupboards in the room next to her bedroom in order that they should be available for speedy consultation. Every page of her surviving accounts bears her signature.

Margaret and Henry emerged from the Wars of the Roses in triumph but it could well have been otherwise. Widows who took their sons' part in any kind of intrigue ran the risk of ending up destitute and in prison, a fate which Margaret had brought on herself for the part she had played in the conspiracy against Richard III in 1483. Another Margaret, Margaret de Fiennes, wife of the Marcher baron Edmund Mortimer and his widow for thirty years, was the undoubted victim of her son's failed ambition and Linda Mitchell has recently traced her family's story.[6] Both Margaret and her son Roger lost their lands in 1322 (Roger having run off with Edward II's queen) despite the fact that Margaret had loyally answered the king's summons of that year to send 200 men-at-arms from her dower lands. In 1330 Roger was executed; Margaret spent the rest of her days closely guarded and watched. Widows of traitors at best could negotiate some kind of landed settlement with the king; at worst, like the widows of the Scottish rebels of Edward I's reign, they might be (literally) caged and displayed for public scorn.

As the summons of 1322 suggests, dowagers such as Margaret de Fiennes were as liable as any other landowner to fulfil the obligations of their holdings. Margaret's mother-in-law, Maud, herself a widow for nineteen years, had had to play an active role in the campaigns of Edward I in Wales by providing him with soldiers – and their food – as well as with horses. Although it is possible that Maud and her peers, as honorary barons, were expected to attend the king's court in person to hear pleas – and they are known to have been excused from this duty on occasion – it seems more probable that they would have sent deputies. While we must be careful not to presume that women would have been totally out of place on such occasions, it is significant that when, in 1335, Margaret, widow of Edmund, Earl of Kent, was asked to prepare her men for war, she was requested to send a member of her household to London to discuss the defence of the realm. The judicial role of Margaret Beaufort, exercised personally in her court at Collyweston in Northamptonshire, arose from her particular role as the king's mother but subsequent debate in the Inner Temple concluded that women as *femmes soles* could indeed, through royal commission, be appointed justices of the peace. In contrast to Margaret, no special circumstances surrounded the position of Ela, Countess of Lacock, (d. 1261) who, widowed in 1226, put in a successful bid in 1231 to become sheriff of Wiltshire. Ela ended her days in a convent founded on her own land, and was buried in the abbey church surrounded by the remains (hearts and bones) of three of her sons.

The examples of Margaret de Fiennes or Margaret Beaufort should not delude us into assuming that medieval widows defined themselves only in relation to the sons and husbands of the family. Maud, the mother-in-law of Margaret de Fiennes, passed a widowhood marked by embittered battles with her son over her dower; Margaret Beaufort herself, for all her unswerving and ruthless dedication to Henry's cause, remained at the same time deeply committed to the memory of her mother's family and to the furtherance of her maternal kin, even when this conflicted with the king's expressed policies. Her devotion here may remind us of the wishes of that other formidable matriarch, Margaret Paston, widowed for eighteen years, who asked in her will of 1482 to be buried not beside her husband, but in the church of her childhood: 'I betake my soul to God ... and my body to be buried in the aisle of the church of Mautby before the image of Our Lady there, in which aisle rest the bodies of divers of my ancestors ...' Every one of Margaret's tenants was remembered in her will, but it was the Mautby householders who received the most. In life and in death widows such as Margaret knew how to demonstrate and register their complex identities.

Urban Widows

If we look next at the position of urban widows we will find much that is already familiar. In London, at least, city law and common law combined to give the widow a comfortable enough package. The widow had a share of the matrimonial home for life unless she remarried. It she did, it was assumed that she would set up a new home with her second husband. Her entitlement then became the standard third of the other properties owned by her former husband. The relevant clause in the city's custumal is as follows:

Wives, on the death of their husbands, by the custom of the city shall have their free bench. That is to say, that after the death of her husband the wife shall have of the tenement in the said city, whereof her husband died seised in fee, and in which tenement the said husband and wife dwelt together at the time of the husband's death, the hall, the principal private chamber, and the cellar wholly, and her use of the kitchen, stable, privy and curtilage in common with the other necessaries appurtenant thereto, for the term of her life. And when she marries again, she shall lose the free bench and her dower therein, saving to her her dower of the other tenements as the law requires.[7]

The generosity of these terms notwithstanding, London widows, like widows elsewhere, might have to fight for their rights. The same queries resurface: could the marriage be shown to have been valid? could the deceased husband's ownership of the land be proved? As already mentioned, widows tended to fare badly in disputes involving the Church, probably, as Barbara Hanawalt argues, winning their cases only 25 per cent of the time, because of the clergy's legal expertise. However, as Hanawalt's own analysis of dower cases for the years 1301–1433 also reveals, this is not a representative figure; overall, during this period, widows lost outright in only 13 per cent of cases.

London was unusual in one respect: the practice of *legitim* in the city assumed an importance not to be found in the rest of the country (with the exception of York and in Wales). *Legitim*, as we have seen, arose from the customary division of a man's goods and chattels into thirds. Even in her husband's lifetime, or so it seemed to *Glanvill*, it was 'kind and creditable in a husband' to allow a wife a third share of his goods to bequeath as she wished; 'many husbands', he wrote, 'do in fact do this which is much to their credit.' But by law rather than uxorial benevolence, on the death of a husband and once all debts had been paid, the widow was assured of her third of the residue, any children another; the final third was at the free disposition of the testator. By the fourteenth century, however, the distribution of chattels had fallen into the purview of ecclesiastical rather then secular courts. Custom rather than law now made it likely that a wife would inherit her third, but what this was depended on the husband's will. In 1366 parliament denied that *legitim* had any standing in

[7] Cited in B. Hanawalt, 'The Widow's Mite: Provision for Medieval London Widows', in L. Mirrer (ed.), *Upon My Husband's Death* (1992), p. 23.

common law and yet, according to London custom, claims for *legitim* could be entertained until as late as 1725. As Caroline Barron has suggested, this persistence of *legitim* was greatly to the advantage of a London widow since much of her husband's wealth was likely to have been in goods and chattels rather than in landed property; moreover, whatever goods and chattels she acquired in this way were hers outright (unlike dower) to spend, invest or bequeath as she chose.[8]

Assured of a roof over her head, and with capital behind her, the London widow had a number of options. The rich widow could expect a string of suitors, though she might fend them off by becoming a 'vowess' or by taking celibacy vows. Joan, fifteenth-century widow of the stapler Robert Byfield and heiress of 1,800 marks of dower, caused quite a stir in the city by taking 'the mantle and the ring' within a day of her husband's funeral. Otherwise, she was likely to have been in as much demand as, notably, was Margery Rygon, the young widow of a prosperous London draper of the late fifteenth century. Margery was wooed successfully and with alacrity by George Cely, himself a London merchant – much to the chagrin of the woman who became her sister-in-law, who later claimed that George had wasted too much of the family's substance on 'jewels diverse and many rich gifts and pleasures given to ... Margery Rygon, then widow, and other of her friends, time of his wooing, expenses of his marriage and household, and in lands [bought] to have the 'expedition of his said marriage'. True or otherwise, there can be no doubt that when it came to the celebration of the wedding no expense was spared. In the estimation of Alison Hanham, as much as six months' normal household expenditure was spent in that one week. To a modern reader, the quantities of fish and meat ordered are no less surprising than the variety; herons and wrens were included in the bill of fare as well as turbot, chickens and pheasants and three live rabbits, to be let loose, Hanham suggests, as both fertility symbol and as 'a medieval equivalent of balloons'.[9]

As many as 50 per cent of London widows may have remarried, even if rather less grandiosely than Margery Rygon.

---

[8] C. Barron, 'The "Golden Age" of Women in Medieval London', *op. cit.*, p. 43.
[9] A. Hanham, *The Celys and their World: An English Merchant Family of the Fifteenth Century* (1985), p. 314.

Hanawalt's study of Husting Court Wills revealed that only 3 per cent of London wills contained any stipulation that the widow was *not* to remarry; indeed, in 1403 a certain skinner left his business and his apprentices to his wife, with specific instructions that she was to run the enterprise herself or else, within three years, to marry someone who would keep it going. Business as usual was expected.[10] Widows of freemen who remained unmarried were now entitled to take up the freedom of the city for themselves. This was a privilege well worth having. It gave women in business the right to carry on their trade, freedom from tolls throughout England and permission to maintain apprentices, as indeed many did. Joan, widow of the London founder Richard Hille (d. 1440), took over her husband's foundry and responsibility for four male apprentices. Eileen Power also gives examples of widows of merchants actively pursuing their rights and the trades of their former husbands: in 1370 Alice, widow of John de Horsford, successfully claimed her share in the ownership of a vessel known as the *Seynte Mariebot*; earlier in the fourteenth century Rose of Burford, widow of a former sheriff of London, re-claimed money which the king owed her husband through a remission of customs duties otherwise payable on the export of her wool.

Working widows should not, of course, be regarded as a London speciality. In Shrewsbury Petronilla, widow of the tanner William Balle (d. 1313), kept up his business; at about the same time we find the widow of Peter the Potter making pots. A number of butchers' widows kept trade going at least, according to Diane Hutton, until their sons were old enough to take over.[11] In York, widows had the benefit of *legitim* but they do not always seem to have been assured of a life interest in the main tenement. Ellen, widow of the cordwainer Thomas Lynland (d. 1394), was to have only a third of his goods unless she accepted administration of his will. Other widows might be housed, but not in the main tenement. Emma Huntyngton, on the other hand, on the death of her husband in 1362 inherited both house and shop where, for the rest of her life, she continued work as an apothecary. Isabella, widow of John

[10] B. Hanawalt, 'The Widow's Mite: Provisions for Medieval London Widows', in L. Hirrer (ed.), *Upon My Husband's Death* (1992), p. 26.

[11] D. Hutton, 'Women in Fourteenth Century Shrewsbury', in L. Charles and L. Duffin (eds), *Women and Work in Pre-Industrial England* (1985), pp. 83–99.

Right: A sixth-century female burial from Lechlade, Gloucestershire. Grave goods here included jewellery, a wooden bowl, a bone spindle whorl and a bone comb.

Below: Aldhelm presents his book, *On Virginity*, to Abbess Hildelith and the nuns of Barking. From a tenth-century copy of the work.

Queen Emma and King Cnut
presenting a cross to New Minster,
Winchester. From an eleventh-
century Book of Life belonging to
New Minster.

An enigmatic scene from the
Bayeux Tapestry. Eleventh-
century 'readers' of the tapestry
might have known the details of
the scandal alluded to here. We
can only guess.

A woman milking a cow from a thirteenth-century bestiary. Dairy products were not highly prized foods in the middle ages but for a peasant family the cheese (about 80lbs) that could be made in a year from the milk of a single cow was a valuable supplement to bread and potage.

This late thirteenth-century depiction of a doctor at the bedside of a female patient may express horror not only at the state of her urine but also (to judge from the sequence of illustrations to which it belongs) at the kind of medical advice her women friends have been giving her.

Some of the tasks shared by men and women peasants – harvesting, stone-breaking and weeding – illustrated in the Luttrell Psalter (c. 1325–35).

The birth of the Virgin in a late medieval setting. Angels rock the cradle, but it is women who attend St Anne.

The diabolic associations of women and gossip is given lurid depiction in this early fourteenth-century stained glass window from Stanford, Northamptonshire.

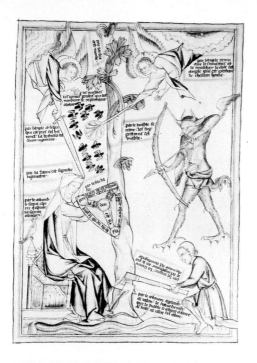

The first appearance in English art of a guardian angel, from the Lambeth Apocalypse (*c*. 1275), swatting flies which might otherwise distract the woman from her devotions. The woman is thought to be either Mary Magdalene or, more likely, Lady Eleanor de Quincy for whom the book was made.

St Anne teaching the Virgin to read, from the Douce Book of Hours (*c*.1325–30). The letters spell Domine – O, Lord.

Left: The owner of the de Brailes Hours, thought to be a certain Susanna, a parishioner of North Hinksey, Oxfordshire. The de Brailes Hours, called after its illuminator, William de Brailes, can be dated to *c.* 1240. It is the earliest Book of Hours to have survived and possibly the earliest to have been made.

Below: A late medieval illustration of Poor Clares in chapel. Although nuns needed priests for the administration of the sacraments, they could themselves make liturgical innovations. Notable are the arrangements for Easter celebrations at Barking under Abbess Katherine of Sutton (1363–76).

Above: Chaucer's Wife of Bath from the fifteenth-century Ellesmere manuscript. The glosses in this manuscript are thought by some scholars to suggest contemporary sympathy for the stance taken by the Wife.

Left: Matrimony, as depicted on one of the faces of a late medieval font at Gresham, Norfolk. Much as the Church tried to encourage marriage in church before a crowd of witnesses, as here, many marriages in the middle ages continued to be contracted in private.

Nonhouse, was given the freedom of the city and earned her living as a weaver; several other widows inherited looms. Other bequests to wives included anvils and a horse-mill. Alice Byngley (d. 1464) kept up her husband's business as shearman; Elena Couper continued the making of pins and Isabella de Copgrave (d. 1400) the manufacture of bricks. In Wakefield, in the late fourteenth century, the widow Emma Erle ran a thriving business trading cloth. In Wells, property left by her husband to Margery Moniers to administer included a whole street.

Such women have been described as 'the goodwives' of late medieval England. The late-twentieth-century obsession with work identity has given them a heroic stature which they might not themselves have recognised. It is not known whether they necessarily took over their husbands' trades willingly: in many cases this may have been a duty, not a choice, the work a chore rather than a source of pleasure. In 1429 the London apprentice of an ironmonger sued his widow, Beatrix Goscelyn, 'who by the law and custom of the city and will of the deceased ought to have kept up his household and instructed his apprentices' because she had sold the business 'to his manifest danger of falling into destruction and desolation'.[12] This is not an isolated case and should put us on our guard against regarding all work, however tedious, as a sign of liberation.

Widows who, for whatever reason, could not work or who were homeless had some chance of receiving urban charity: at the least some share in the distribution of 'doorstep' alms, of food or of money, at best a place in an almshouse or hospital. Almshouses, as Gary Shaw's recent work on Wells in Somerset has suggested, may have favoured a predominantly male 'aristocracy of beggars'; hospitals, on the other hand, came to provide widows both with a refuge and a source of employment.[13] St John's, Reading, for example, was staffed by 'certain religious women, chaste widows, living in God's service, praying night and day'. A *maison dieu* in St Andrewgate, York, took in only women, many of whom evidently were widows; a bequest of 1407 is for 'the poor widows and my tenants in St

[12] K. Lacey, 'Women and Work in Fourteenth and Fifteenth Century London', in L. Charles and L. Duffin (eds), *Women and Work in Pre-Industrial England* (1985), p. 47.
[13] G. Shaw, *The Creation of a Community: The City of Wells in the Middle Ages* (1993), pp. 242–3.

Andrewgate, 13s 4d between them'.[14] Such institutions hover between poorhouse, hospital and beguinage; they may serve as reminder of the difficulty and danger of attempting to fit the experiences of marginal groups, like poor widows, into formally recognised and designated slots.

Peasant Widows

Peasant widows took over tenements with varying degrees of ease; those who held by jointure could take up the holding without further ado, avoiding even an entry fine. Others might be the beneficiaries of 'deathbed' transfers, a last-minute bequest by which a husband could divest himself of his property before it became liable for 'death duties'. On the whole such widows did rather better under customary law than their common law sisters, but much depended on whether they chose to remarry and on the changing circumstances created by the Black Death, and also on regional variation. At Kibworth Harcourt in Leicestershire, for example, after the Black Death a widow on remarriage could keep land she would previously have forfeited. Terms were also generous at Islip in Oxfordshire: here, in the event of remarriage a widow could keep her tenement and on payment of a fine the new husband was admitted as a joint tenant. At nearby Launton, however, a widow could keep her holding for no longer than a year and a day unless she remarried; if she stayed single then she was to be content with her dower of a third.

The Launton logic presupposed that tenurial obligations would be more efficiently fulfilled by husband and wife than by a widow on her own. Such an assumption was not necessarily correct; many widows seem to have been quite capable of organising any necessary labour. At Cuxham, also in Oxfordshire, Alice, widow of Robert Beneyt, held her tenement on her own for thirty-two years. She had no son and two of her daughters married outside the manor; on her death in 1343 her holding went to an unmarried daughter whose entry fee covered, but did not compel, a future marriage. None the less, as Peter Franklin has suggested, convenience and convention

[14] P. H. Cullum,' "And Hir Name was Charite": Charitable Giving by and for Women in Late Medieval Yorkshire', in P. J. P. Goldberg (ed.), *Woman is a Worthy Wight*, p. 199.

seems to have encouraged a number of widows to remarry, sometimes picking a former live-in servant; the ploughing got done and both lord and local gossip were quieted.[15] The Black Death affected such remarriages in a number of divergent ways. Widows now found it harder to employ extra labour and, if figures for Kibworth Harcourt are anything to go by, they were consequently more likely to look for new husbands. Conversely, if the Halesowen evidence is at all representative, they were less likely to find them; land being plentiful, the attractions of the widows and their holdings waned.

Customary law apart, a widow's portion might be settled by the terms of her husband's will. That a villein could leave his property by will may seem strangely at variance with the servility of his status, but as with *inter vivos* settlements (to be considered below) the interests of lords were best served by allowing their peasants such freedom. Their concern was with the smooth running of their estates rather than with the personal details of land transactions; it was enough that they claimed the profits of any deed to be registered and had the final say in its implementation. Wills do not become common among the peasantry until the fifteenth century, but surviving examples suggest that they were generally designed for the benefit of the wife who also was likely to be the executor. In well over a half of those surveyed by Barbara Hanawalt the widow was given the main tenement for her lifetime. Provision for children did not necessarily take precedence. In the will of the Ulting fuller John Nele (1518) his wife inherited the house, and their son his father's tools and 'a shop to work in and a chamber in the house ... during his mother's life as long as he is good and gentle to his mother; otherwise she may shut him out of it for the rest of her life.'

A similar lack of sentimentality informs contracts *inter vivos*. These might be made by both husbands and wives eager to retire so long as they could arrange for maintenance in their old age and a decent funeral. In pre-plague years such contracts helped to release land to younger couples; later, they provided security for older couples, widows and widowers at a time when labour was both expensive and scarce. *Inter vivos* contracts provide a wealth of evidence on a wide range of topics:

[15] P. Franklin, 'Peasant Widows' "Liberation" and Remarriage before the Black Death', *Economic History Review* 2nd series 39 (1986), pp. 186–204.

relationships, both social and familial, standards of living and housing. Nothing was left to chance: Anicia atte Hegge of Crondall in Hampshire, on surrendering her holding to her daughter and son-in-law in 1313 expected in return an annual allowance of grain, a chemise worth 8d and a pair of shoes worth 6d each year, and every other year a woollen garment costing 3 shillings; in 1437/8 Emma del Rood of Cranfield was to have twelve bushels of wheat, two quarts of malt and a peck of oatmeal for porridge each year; in 1281 Agnes of Ridgeacre, Halesowen, wanted a house built for her that was to measure 30 × 14 foot, with three doors and two windows. The following further examples of the idiosyncrasies and complexities of the settlements relating to widows appeared in Elaine Clark's work on East Anglian court rolls:[16]

South Elmham: Ninth Year of Henry IV's reign: ... the jury presented that Henry Pekke died seised of I messuage, 10 acres, half a rod of customary land. His grandson, Henry Pekke, is his heir and is of legal age. He requests admittance to the tenement. But Joan Recher, the late Henry's widow, requests half of the tenement as dower. She is admitted. Henry is admitted to the other half with reversion of dower etc. to hold to himself and his heirs for services etc. Henry surrenders his half to the use of Joan for life. She resurrenders the entire tenement to him and to his heirs, but reserves 1 lower room and 1 upper room, also a parcel of land, with free entry for herself and her friends for life. Conditions: she is to receive yearly at 30 November 1 quarter of faggots valued at 12d; yearly for life, 8s paid in quarterly installments at 30 November, Easter, 24 June, 29 September; Henry to keep her two rooms fully repaired; he is to provide her with the same food and drink that he himself has, and if she is not pleased with this fare she is to have 12d yearly on account of her displeasure; entry to the main house whenever she wishes.

Wymondham: Fifth year of Henry VI's reign ... From Richard Sothereye, when dying, to Nicholas Blithe and Alice his wife, 2 acres, half a rod of customary land of the tenement 'Eliot' and one built up property with appurtenances in Sutton. Conditions: they pay to his wife, Alice, 6 li. in yearly installments of 13s 4d at 29 September; reservation to his widow of 1 room at south end of the hall; she may warm herself by their fire as often as she wishes; they will build for her a 'chymne' of clay; if the new tenants predecease the widow, or if the husband dies and his wife remarries, still a room must be reserved for the widow. Entry fine 6s 8d.

[16] E. Clark, 'Some Aspects of Social Security in Medieval England', *Journal of Family History* 7 (1982), pp. 307–19.

Horsham St Faith. Seventeenth year of Henry VI's reign ... From Margaret, widow of Clement Chapelyn, to John Chapelyn and his heirs 1 acre, 1 rod of 'werkland' and three acres called 'molon'. Conditions: widow to have for life 1 hall called 'la newhalle', a storeroom at the east end of the hall; easement in the bake-house for malting 32 bushels of barley with John's kiln; half of 1 'golfstede' in the west part of the grange, a stable at the west end of the messuage except during the fair of St Faith when its use is reserved for John; easement to a well for drawing water; free ingress and egress in the garden for visiting bees; 1 cow, 1 pig, 1 cock, 6 hens kept in the some messuage; if John predeceases the widow then his heirs or assigns to pay her for life 6s 8d at Michaelmas; John to have free entry and exit in the widow's upper room in order to enter his own upper room; John to have easement in the kitchen. Entry fine 26s 8d.

As the second of the above examples makes clear, *inter vivos* contracts were not always made with kin; this is particularly true of the post-plague era, although whether because children had moved away or had died prematurely is uncertain. In the late fourteenth and early fifteenth century as many as 30 per cent of parents apparently had no surviving children at the time of their death. That children were expected to care for their parents in their old age, and equally that everyone knew they might fail to fulfil such an obligation, seems clear from the practice described by Elaine Clark whereby children registered their promise to do so before the manorial court; parents, for their part, showed no hesitation in disinheriting children who neglected to look after them. A case from Great Waltham in Essex, of 1327, described by Richard Smith, sees Estrilda Nenour, widow, claiming back from her daughter Agnes land contracted five years earlier in return for accommodation, food and clothing. The court accepted Estrilda's complaints against her daughter and voided the contract. A year later Estrilda made a new bargain, this time with a couple, Alice and Robert, who do not seem to have been related to her; the terms were as before but with the addition of a safety clause: if Alice and Robert failed to satisfy Estrilda's needs then they were to pay her 20s 8d four times a year.[17]

The widows we meet in *inter vivos* contracts are assertive and confident of their rights. That not all were of the same

[17] R. Smith, 'The Manorial Court and the Elderly Tenant in Late Medieval England', in M. Pelling and R. Smith (eds), *Life, Death and the Elderly: Historical Perspectives* (1991), p. 54.

mettle, or as fortunate in their circumstances, is evident from the accounts in coroners' rolls of their sufferings and their fate. However, as Clark notes, known cases of hardship could provoke manorial action; not everything was left to the individual initiative of widows or the providence of their husbands. Thus in 1382 at Hindolveston in Norfolk the jurymen reported that a widow in the village with a holding of about eighteen acres of arable was no longer able to look after herself, let alone to fulfil her tenurial obligations; she was 'feeble of body and simple of mind'. Her land was accordingly assigned to her nearest kin with orders that he take responsibility for the widow for the rest of her life. Hard-luck cases might be heard and settled with compassion. When, in 1312–3, the house of Joan Bovecheriche, widow of Cuxham, burnt down, she also lost the cow she was due to pay as her husband's heriot, or death duty. She was excused the heriot and the four bushels of wheat due as rent at Michaelmas and given a quarter of wheat 'so that she might the better rebuild her house'.

Widows in villages, unless they had reached a retirement settlement of the kind we have seen above, had by the nature of their holdings to continue their work. They were given neither time nor opportunity to do otherwise; 'on the day after the husband's death [she] will find enough ploughmen to take the dead man's place' (Ramsey custumal). But as heads of households the profile of such women within their communities could, if they so wished, alter significantly: these widows must now come to the manorial court as a matter of duty, they must answer for their own debts and transgressions, conduct their own litigation and land transactions. For a number of them this was not an entirely new role; they were resuming responsibilities they had already shouldered as adolescents and relinquished only on marriage, and in certain cases they seem to have done so with zest. The response of the widows of Brigstock to the change and challenge of their circumstances has been studied by Judith Bennett.[18] In her terms 'the public reticence' of women such as Alice, widow of Peter Avice, is replaced by 'public assertion'. Alice comes to court to buy and sell land, to complain about other villagers, to act as pledge. The women who send their apologies for absence at court exist, but they are in the minority: only 10 out

---

[18] J. Bennett, *Women in the Medieval English Countryside* (1987), ch. 6, pp. 142–76.

of Bennett's sample of 101 show any signs of unwillingness to take up their new responsibilities.

None the less, it would be misleading to suggest that most widows simply stepped into their husbands' shoes, for several reasons. The manorial court remained a masculine space; women, as widows, still did not hold office. Moreover, as Bennett has pointed out, although widows developed a 'court network' close in its range to that of a man, the pattern of their transactions was, overall, different. The court life of the 'average' widow was not as busy as a man's and she was more likely to be concerned with the dispersal of property to her children than with increasing the size of the holding. What are we to make of this? According to Bennett, despite the relative inactivity of widows within Brigstock society we can be sure 'that these widows probably spoke with their neighbours and cultivated friendships outside of their families, but such associations, as indicated by the silence of the record, were comparatively limited in both breadth and depth'. This suggest astonishing confidence in the ability of the evidence to give an impression of the workings of an essentially oral society. How far we can ever fill the 'silence' is, of course, doubtful; but we can avoid disadvantageously placing women on ground that is not theirs.

We must look at what women are doing that is singular instead of concerning ourselves only with what they are failing to do. Thus it is not simply idle curiosity to wonder why widows in particular (as Bennett's analysis shows) are to be found harbouring strangers. Was this the case also in other manors? How are we to explain the difference between the culpable offence of harbouring strangers and the laudable virtue of welcoming them? Joan Clopton, a widow who died in 1419, was remembered in her parish church precisely for being 'unstinting to strangers'. How do court-roll networks compare with the networks revealed by the wills of peasant women? To ask these questions is not to advocate a return to a public/private dichotomy – the dividing line here has been shown by historians and anthropologists alike to be artificially constructed – but it is to suggest that we reconsider the relative value of the formal and the informal. Widows' circles of friends, acquaintances and strangers may well have provided forums of considerable influence and power, as anyone familiar with the workings of rural society even today can attest.

To favour the formal at the expense of the informal has its analogy in the belief that because medieval women were unlikely to know Latin they were therefore 'uneducated', and necessarily excluded from the intellectual and spiritual life around them. While further research is clearly needed to substantiate the hypothesis that widowed village women were figures of significant authority, the role that even women without a knowledge of Latin played in the culture and religious life of medieval England has already been established. It is to this that we must turn next.

PART FOUR

Culture and Spirituality

CHAPTER NINE

Female Monasticism

The convents of Anglo-Norman and Angevin England for a long time lacked their historians: Eileen Power began her major study of nunneries only in the late thirteenth century while David Knowles, in *The Monastic Order in England*, found the evidence for women's monasticism seemingly inadequate to make the topic worth his while. Recent work has significantly compensated for this neglect; contributions from both historians and archaeologists are now making it clear that if communities of religious women have not until now been as visible as those of men, this is primarily because they did not fit into male-imposed categories. 'Medieval female religious experience', to quote Roberta Gilchrist, 'was *different* from that of men, not *less successful*'.[1]

If we are to stress the differences between male and female monasticism, it may none the less be as well to start on common ground. Firstly, the pre-Conquest houses, both for men and for women, remained throughout the Middle Ages pre-eminent in wealth and prestige. In social standing, no post-Conquest nunnery ever rivalled the ancient Wessex foundations such as Wilton, Shaftesbury and Romsey; houses like these that had acquired fame and riches in the tenth century kept their cachet throughout the Middle Ages and their abbesses were usually women of considerable stature and influence. Likewise, despite royal patronage of new houses of monks such as the Cluniac house at Reading, it was the Anglo-Saxon cult centres of Winchester, Westminster and Canterbury which remained

---

[1] R. Gilchrist, *Gender and Material Culture: The Archaelogy of Religious Women* (1994), p. 191.

189

dominant in the religious landscape of medieval England. Secondly, as far as new houses were concerned, men and women alike participated, in the twelfth century, in a monastic renaissance that was marked by an exceptional degree of co-operation and friendship between the sexes. But there the similarities end and the differences begin.

Women religious in medieval England needed the support of men both for their material existence and for the provision of sacraments, but it was not up to them to fix the price. Men, for their part, needed women for spiritual inspiration and guidance – an example being the relationship of Christina of Markyate with Geoffrey of St Albans – but they dictated the terms. With rare exceptions, or so the sources suggest, men remained ambivalent about their female colleagues. In heady moments of religious renewal, such as the twelfth century, caution went to the winds; but not for long. Anxiety would resurface, and it would begin to seem more comfortable to love women from a distance, to keep them suitably clothed and properly locked up. This was, after all, St Francis's solution for Clare and it is paralleled all over Europe. Women from new, originally mixed communities came to be settled in houses miles away from the first foundations. In Rome, Pope Innocent III rigorously reorganised the informal groups of holy women living in the city into cloistered communities; likewise, at St Albans, 'half-secular nuns' were brought to book, rehoused, made to wear black and to live under a rule; 'for their reputation and well-being' they were given a house where they were enclosed 'under lock and door-bolt and the seal of the abbot'.[2] However, as we shall see, to be disciplined was not the same as to be discounted. But that is to anticipate events. Let us first look in more detail at the choices for religious women that opened up in the course of the twelfth century.

The monastic renaissance of the twelfth century saw the foundation of well over a hundred houses for women, pro-viding for around three thousand vocations. The fact that there were perhaps only nine houses at the time of the Conquest, and a meagre seven or eight founded during the following fifty years, gives some idea of the unprecedented scale of twelfth-century developments. A woman wanting to enter

[2] S. Elkins, *Holy Women of Twelfth Century England* (1988), p. 47.

the religious life not only now had more opportunity to do so; she also had unaccustomed choice. The new foundations represented the astonishing diversity of the movement. A postulant might become a Cluniac, a Cistercian, a Gilbertine, an Augustinian, a hospitaller, a Praemonstratensian, a Fontevraldine, an Arrouaisian, or, as before, a Benedictine, an anchorite or a hermit. While this list may accurately reflect a proliferation of labels that confuses the modern reader – it baffled contemporaries too – it does nothing to indicate the complexity behind them. For example, the two Cluniac houses seem to have had only the most tenuous links with the Order; the Cistercian communities were *ipso facto* out on a limb since it was only in 1213 that the Cistercian General Chapter began to accept any official responsibility for its women nuns and, by 1228, was already trying to prevent any more from joining; the Praemonstratensians for their part were every bit as hesitant as the Cistercians about acknowledging their sisters; the Gilbertines, on the other hand, would have become Cistercians if they had had their way; the Fontevraldines despite being an order with, initially, strong associations with prostitutes and the poor, had now become flagrantly aristocratic and highly independent; the Augustinians were joined by a house of hospitallers who had not realised that their original profession committed them to an overseas aid programme.

In addition to all those from the new orders and despite a papal ruling of 1139 designed to stop the practice, there were still women living in convents who called themselves nuns but who had taken no formal vows. There were also groups of women – for example, at Haliwell and Clerkenwell, in the suburbs of London – who are sometimes called Benedictines, at other times Augustinians. It is possible, as Sharon Elkins has suggested, that such communities did indeed have 'two identities'. Women had to be 'inventive and adaptive' and patterned their lives to suit the aspirations of their patrons quite as much as their own. It needs to be remembered that the new twelfth-century communities of religious men might show a similar lack of resolution as to which rule to adopt but they were freer than women to settle the matter on their own terms. Not needing the same kind of protection and support, men's communities were less likely to fall prey to the obligations of gratitude.

From the array of choices for women, let us look more closely at the Gilbertines and this for several reasons. They belong to the one wholly English order; it is an order founded specifically for women and its history graphically illustrates the needs fulfilled by such an order as well as the kinds of tensions it could generate. We have, moreover, a very full *Life* of the founder of the order, Gilbert of Sempringham, written around 1200 to promote his canonisation.[3]

According to this *Life*, Gilbert was born at Sempringham in Lincolnshire in the late eleventh century. His father was a Norman knight; his mother was Anglo-Saxon. This relatively humble parentage struck his biographer as noteworthy. The assumption that nobility of the soul presupposed nobility of birth was thus upset and needed explaining: it was, according to the *Life* (ch. 1), only 'by the special nature of his life' that Gilbert 'overcame both the world and his worldy origin'. On top of the disadvantage of his mother's 'inferior rank' there was, as far as hagiographical norms are concerned, another blow: 'his bodily form was misshapen and disfigured'. He did not even have a very promising childhood; no 'greatness of soul' was evident; on the contrary, the boy seemed both stupid and lazy. The singularity of Gilbert's background seemed appropriate for one who was destined to take responsibility for 'the firm direction of the weaker sex': here indeed was a new-style saint. Gilbert himself is presented as if he was in some ways like a woman: he was, perhaps in reference to the wise virgins of the New Testament, 'like a lamp ... prepared against a certain hour', and a clear example of God's preference for 'choosing the weak vessels of the world to confound those that are stronger'.

Gilbert's interest in 'the weaker sex' began after his appointment to the rectories of Sempringham and West Torrington. He had already shown an interest in teaching the local children; now he chose seven of the girls, and enclosed them by in an establishment adjacent to the parish church at Sempringham. (The enclosure was to the north of the church, an orientation which, as both Margaret Aston and Roberta Gilchrist have recently suggested, may have a cluster of associations for women: Lady Chapels, for example, are always to be found in the north of any church, a position corresponding

---

[3] The *Life* is part of *The Book of St Gilbert*, ed. R. Foreville and G. Keir (1987).

to Mary's stance at the right hand of Christ at the Crucifixion.[4]) Gilbert gave these disciples rules 'concerning their life and discipline' and arranged for them to have servants who would do their shopping and gather alms on their behalf, passing on to them what they needed through a window. In time the servant girls themselves, so the *Life* tells us, demanded and were granted their own vows and habits. It is not difficult to imagine that such recognition was precious; these women were poor and but for Gilbert's venture would have had few resources of their own to establish any kind of religious community. They had now, in the words of the *Life* (ch. 10), 'the chance of a permanent livelihood' and, like the enclosed sisters they served, a status as women of religion more normally reserved for their social superiors.

Seven women, their servants and Gilbert: it was still not enough. The reasoning of the *Life* is here of great significance: 'Now because women's efforts achieve little without help from men, he took on men, and put those he kept as servants about his house and on his land in charge of the nuns' external and more arduous tasks' (ch. 11). These men too had humble backgrounds. This is something it is important to consider; we need to recognise that the greater opportunities for women in the twelfth century have both a class as well as a gendered context. Gilbert's male recruits, like those of Bishop Aidan in the century of the conversion to Christianity, came from mixed backgrounds: 'some of them he had raised from his childhood at his own expense, others were fugitives from their masters freed in the name of religion and others again were destitute beggars ... because all these men, spurred both by the poverty of their human life and by their longing for the life of heaven wanted exactly what the lay sisters desired and requested, he took the same course of action in both their case as in the women's and finally bestowed the habit upon both.'

Thus constituted, the congregation was now ready to spread. By 1147 a new house was founded at Haverholme, in Lincolnshire, also staffed by lay brothers and sisters. Gilbert, at this point, would have willingly handed the enterprise over to the Cistercians. At the Cistercian General Chapter of 1147 he indeed asked for his two foundations to be affiliated to

---

[4] R. Gilchrist, *op. cit*; M. Aston, 'Segregation in Church', in W. Sheils and D. Wood (eds), *Women in the Church*, Studies in Church History 27 (1990), pp. 237–94.

their Order. The request was refused, possibly because the Cistercians were wary of female adherents, possibly also because they were even more wary of taking on houses which looked as if they might prove to be a financial liability. Faced with this rebuff, Gilbert added a further branch to his Order, comprised this time of 'educated men to share pastoral care' (ch. 15). Female communities were not expected to be self-sufficient. Just as they needed laymen to undertake for them 'arduous tasks', so too they needed clerks for their spiritual well-being: 'for as is laid down in the decrees of the fathers it is essential that communities of maidens be controlled through the support of monks and clerks. For it is beneficial for virgins who have given themselves to Christ if spiritual fathers are chosen for them so that they may not only be protected under their direction but also be fortified by their teaching.'

Gilbert's Order had now reached its final form; for a time, especially in the diocese of Lincoln, it flourished. When Gilbert died in 1188 there were about 1500 Gilbertines living in thirteen houses. But, by then, the Order had also suffered both scandal and dissension, the one in all probability fuelling the other. First the scandal: some time in 1166 a nun at the Gilbertine house of Watton in Yorkshire was found to be pregnant. Her lover was a lay brother. In the telling of the story as we have it from a letter written by the Cistercian abbot, Ailred of Rievaulx, God took pity on the nun to the extent of annulling the pregnancy but not before the nuns had ambushed their 'fallen sister', forced her to castrate her lover and 'had thrust the parts into her mouth'. This may strike twentieth-century readers as particularly savage; but castration was, at the time, the accepted penalty for rape and, judging from a case from Worcester at the turn of the century in which the (judicially) torn-off testicles of an adulterous male were tossed around an eager crowd of men and women, it may not have seemed wholly exceptional behaviour to the nuns or to anyone else. For Ailred, at any rate, the main question to be asked was how in the first place the situation could have arisen: 'Where then, Father Gilbert, was your most vigilant sense in the keeping of discipline? Where were those many well-thought-out mechanisms for keeping out the opportunity for failings? ... Where that watch so careful around all doors, windows, out of the way places so that evil spirits seem not to be able to enter?'[5]

[5] Cited in S. Elkins, *op. cit*, p. 109.

In Rome, at about the time when Ailred was writing his letter, a group of Gilbertine lay brothers were laying complaints about the Order before the Pope. They presented a number of grievances concerning the harshness of their way of life: it is likely that behind the grievances lay resentment at the increased influence of the clerical wing of the Order at their expense. Be that as it may, they added colour to their cause by casting aspersions on the sexual morality of the Order. Among others, King Henry II, the Archbishop of York and the Bishop of Winchester all rallied to Gilbert's defence, protesting the innocence of the Order, lauding its discipline, and affirming the strictness of segregation between the sexes. The crisis passed; but Gilbert's *Life* reflects continuing unease. The elaborate justification of the Order's constitution betrays the persistence of its critics. A story told by Gerald of Wales is instructive here. A nun in one of his communities fell in love with Gilbert. Gilbert's response was to show himself before the whole community, naked, 'hairy, emaciated, scabrous and wild', and to tell them, as he held up a crucifix, 'Behold the man who should be duly desired by a woman consecrated to God and a bride of Christ.'[6] Other texts, as we shall see, will show how fine could be the balance between earthly and divine love. For the nuns of Watton, the pregnant lay sister had impugned God's honour quite as much as their own.

The dramas of the Gilbertine Order and the fullness of the sources have tended to magnify its originality. It is not the least of the merits of the recent work on female monasticism by Sharon Elkins and Sally Thompson[7] that they have demonstrated that the twelfth century saw the establishment of a whole variety of double houses besides those founded by Gilbert. None had an enduring future; none the less these experimental communities were exceptional in suggesting a range of possibilities that later evidence has often obscured. Sometimes these foundations occurred as the result of family ties; in other cases links were created to solve financial pressures. Such arrangements might be fleeting; on the other hand, four houses usually listed as Cistercian nunneries turn out to

[6] Cited in G. Constable, *Medieval Women*, ed. D. Baker, Studies in Church History, *Subsidia* 1 (1978), p. 222.
[7] S. Elkins, *op. cit.*, and S. Thompson, *Women Religious: The Founding of English Nunneries after the Conquest* (1991).

have co-existed with Praemonstratensian canons for well over a hundred years.

What is also exceptional is the rapid spread of monasticism in the twelfth century. We must ask ourselves why female monasticism was given such support by men, and why, thereafter, there was only a trickle of new foundations.

Before 1100, as we have seen, there was no rush to found convents. All the more remarkable, then, is the initiative of Gundulph, Bishop of Rochester from 1077 to 1088, and formerly monk of Bec, the Norman house of Archbishops Lanfranc and Anselm. Gundulph was the first post-Conquest bishop to found a nunnery. This he did on his own land at West Malling, maybe modelling the building on the cathedral of Rochester (the archaeological evidence makes certainty here impossible), and the community remained under his personal supervision until shortly before his death. According to his *Life* he had a close friendship with Queen Matilda; he also took special care of pregnant women. What gives a particular edge to these concerns is that they seem to be related not so much to hagiographical conventions, but rather to innovative liturgical and devotional trends which Gundulph was supporting long before these became widespread. Thus Gundulph both displayed particular veneration for Mary Magdalene and celebrated the Feast of the Immaculate Conception at a time when the propriety of doing so was still under debate. Devotion to the two Marys, as practised by Gundulph, has rightly been seen as indicative of the new piety of the twelfth century, focused as it was on the humanity of Christ, on a God of compassion rather than of vengeance. The influence here of Archbishop Anselm's thinking on Gundulph, as developed by Anselm in his work on the incarnation – *Why God Became Man* – is apparent. At the same time it has often been noticed that while this new piety exalted both the Virgin and, through Mary Magdalene, the repentant sinner, it was perhaps of little use to 'actual' women. Gundulph's *Life* gives us cause for second thoughts.

Women, in twelfth-century texts, are praised for their 'more lively devotion' – the phrase (from the account of the canonisation process of Gilbert of Sempringham) implying that it is greater than men's; for their dedication, according to Ailred of Rievaulx, to 'spiritual offices and heavenly theories'; and for their capacity to be 'rapt in indescribable departures'.[8] They are not needed, as they had been during the age of the conversion to Christianity in the seventh and eighth centuries, as educators and teachers. In Gilbert of Sempringham's last years the University of Oxford was already in its infancy. High-level literacy became an all-male preserve but this privilege, it is sometimes forgotten, was bought at a price. In the age of the conversion, the word had unequivocally been the Word of God; by the twelfth and thirteenth centuries, words were recognised to be double-edged. Words could nourish faith; they could also destroy it: the cup of knowledge might turn out to be a poisoned chalice. The new learning had to be shared with the devil; he too, as Michael Clanchy has shown us, had by the thirteenth century learned to read and write. He is depicted now in manuscripts wielding pen and parchment.[9]

This new climate of anxiety about where education might lead the faithful, coinciding as it does with the development of christocentric piety, pushed to the fore the possibility of creating and exalting a new brand of female piety. We can see this in action, so to speak, in the *Life* of Christina of Markyate, written by someone who knew her well. Christina, somewhat misleadingly, is usually described as a hermit. She does indeed, when on the run, live for a time with hermits and like a hermit in a tiny cell, but it is circumstances – her need to go into hiding to escape the marriage being forced upon her by her parents (see page 122) – rather than choice which impose this life on her. Her final role as head of a small priory at Markyate probably corresponds more closely to the kind of life she had had in mind when she had first made the decision, as a young girl, to follow a religious vocation. Be that as it may, what matters about Christina is less the definition of her lifestyle than the nature of her spirituality and of her relationship with her patron Geoffrey, Abbot of St Albans.

In her early years of hiding, Christina is described as having a Psalter on her lap; huge toads come and squat on it, right in the middle of the page, frightening her with their huge and terrible eyes in an attempt to distract her psalm-singing. Here is a reference, in all probability, to the famous St Albans Psalter, one of the masterpieces of English Romanesque illumination.

---

[8] Cited in S. Elkins, *op. cit.*, p. 100.
[9] M. Clanchy, *From Memory to Written Record* (2nd edn 1993), pp. 187–8.

This Psalter, while not originally made for Christina – the prayers assume a male readership – seems to have been adapted at some stage for her use, possibly as a gift from Abbot Geoffrey. Her family and friends are now commemorated in the calendar; the feasts to be celebrated have been altered to include five female saints; illustrations that had particular meaning for Christina have been added: of the tale of Alexis, a romance story of a marriage purposefully unconsummated, and of Christ on the road to Emmaus, unrecognisable to his disciples as, in episodes in her *Life*, he was more than once to Christina herself. And for Psalm 105, an extra painting has been pasted in, a historiated initial illustrating Christina pleading with Christ for Abbot Geoffrey and his monks.

The Alexis and the Emmaus cycles are, according to C. Dodwell, 'apparently unique in Romanesque art in paying tribute to a local saint during that saint's life-time'; unique also is the 'sheer number' of historiated initials in the Psalter – there are in all 211.[10] This abundance of illumination is particularly apt in a Psalter that was to be Christina's. Christina herself was unlikely to have been literate; turning points in her life are marked by what she sees rather than the written word. Her vow of virginity is taken following a pilgrimage to St Albans 'where she had looked carefully at the place and observed the religious bearing of the monks' (ch. 4). While she is still a fugitive she is offered shelter by the hermit Roger; his anxieties about the arrangement are allayed in a scene of intense visual drama. Roger had at first thought it would be better if he had no direct contact with Christina; nevertheless, as the *Life* explains:

they saw each other the same day and it happened in this way. The virgin of God lay prostrate in the old man's chapel, with her face turned to the ground. The man of God stepped over her with his face averted in order not to see her. But as he passed by he looked over his shoulder to see how modestly the handmaid of Christ had composed herself for prayer, as this was one of the things which he thought those who pray ought to observe. Yet she at the same instant, glanced upwards to appraise the bearing and deportment of the old man, for in these she considered that some trace of his holiness was apparent. And so they saw each other, not by design and yet not by chance ... but by divine will, for ... the fire ... which had been kindled by the spirit of God and

[10] C. Dodwell, *The Pictorial Arts of the West 800–1200* (1993), pp. 329, 311.

burned in each cast its sparks into their hearts by the grace of that mutual glance; and so made one in heart and soul in chastity and charity in Christ they were not afraid to dwell together under the same roof. (ch. 38)

Time and again Christina's questions will be answered by visions from heaven: of Christ, of the Virgin, of St Margaret. As Christopher Holdsworth has pointed out, 'No one reading the *Life* can fail to be struck by the frequency with which visions or auditory experiences occur. Altogether forty-two are mentioned ... this means that the reader would have met almost one on each side of each of the twenty-two folios now occupied by the *Life*. Over two-thirds are reported as having been enjoyed by Christina herself; no one else gets much of a look-in, save Geoffrey the abbot who gets three.'[11]

Holdsworth explains Christina's visions by suggesting that they are the kind of thing we should expect in a 'recluse turned nun' who would have lacked precisely the 'discernment which wide reading and training in argument would have given to a university-trained man'. Moreover, because of the pre-cariousness of her position in her early years as a hermit, before her marriage contract had been annulled, she had, Holdsworth argues, a particularly strong need for reassurance and for her vocation to be thereby authenticated. The problem with this interpretation is that it fails to take into account the public esteem and acclaim accorded to these visions; thus, while there can be no doubt that medieval religious women did find empowerment through visionary experience, we must not overlook how often we know of these visions only because of the men who validated, admired and lived by them.

Such relationship between female seers and male devotees are particularly well attested for by continental examples – the reliance of the Dominican, Peter of Dacia (d. 1289), on the inspiration of the beguine Christine of Stommeln whom he met while searching for someone who would 'clear up all [his] doubts' is one instance among many[12] – but a similar relationship clearly existed between Geoffrey and Christina. Geoffrey, so Christina's *Life* tells us, 'had a deep respect for the maiden and saw in her something divine and extraordinary'

[11] C. Holdsworth, 'Christina of Markyate', in D. Baker (ed.), *Medieval Women* (1978), p. 198.
[12] J. Coakley, 'Friars as Confidants of Holy Women', in R. Blumenfeld-Kosinski and T. Szell (eds), *Images of Sainthood in Medieval Europe* (1991), pp. 222–46.

(ch. 60); in time he came to see that 'the virgin's pure heart had more power with God than the factious and shrewd cunning of the great ones of the world' (ch. 72). A bargain had been struck between them. Geoffrey, as abbot of one of England's richest monastic houses, was expected to keep it 'flourishing in possessions'; in such a post he was necessarily caught up both in the administration of the monastery's estates and in the ecclesiastical politics of the country. There had been a time when such power had made him haughty; but God, through Christina, brought about his conversion. A terrifying dream led him to promise Christina financial security:

> The virgin Christina, seeing that ... through the intervention of so lowly a person as herself the abbot had overcome evil and was now bent on doing good, cherished him with great affection and loved him with a pure and wonderful love ... Their affection was mutual, but different according to their standards of holiness. He supported her in worldly matters: she commended him to God more earnestly in her prayers (ch. 58) ... he centred his attention on providing the virgin with material assistance, she strove to enrich the man in virtue ... she would not cease until she was satisfied in her mind about [his] sure salvation ... (ch. 68)

The truly anxious figure in this scenario (*pace* Holdsworth) is not Christina but Geoffrey. It is Geoffrey who goes to Christina with his doubts and in search of her advice, Christina who perpetually 'labours to establish him in a state of peace'. This need cause us no surprise. Norman power in twelfth-century England was still viewed as sufficiently alien and ungodly to give those who exercised it any number of nightmares: Abbot Geoffrey, surrounded in the night by black creatures who suffocate and torment him, may remind us of the nightmares of King Henry I of peasants, clergy and barons advancing on him to seek revenge for his rapacity. Some kind of legitimation was to be sought in the co-opting of the support of native heiresses and saints. King Henry marries the Anglo-Saxon Matilda; Geoffrey puts his trust in Christina, his 'sweet and known remedy' (ch. 73); 'when he was supported by her he feared no difficulties for he had very often experienced her help in so many ways' (ch. 74).

The friendship of Geoffrey and Christina was none the less a subject of scandal, a cause for the 'wagging of spiteful tongues' (ch. 64); 'the abbot was slandered as a seducer and the maiden as a loose woman' (ch. 76). Such accusations are of particular interest in the light of the frank accounts in Christina's *Life* of her sexual temptations and of the rumours and innuendoes that surrounded the Gilbertines. The tenor of these is unlike anything we have met in the age of the conversion, an era otherwise comparable for friendships and co-operation between holy men and women when suspicion of contacts between them was couched, if at all, in quite different, less personal terms. The spotlight in twelfth-century texts shone on the nun in love with Gilbert of Sempringham, on Christina's desire for a tactfully unnamed cleric -- the mere thought of whom used to inflame her to such an extent that she feared her clothes would catch fire – and the subsequent intimacy between Geoffrey and Christina all testify to a heightened emotional climate that explains, even as it threatens to undermine, the bonds of spirituality such men and women shared.

In the age of the conversion, holy men and women were, at least initially, committed to an enterprise of equal opportunity based on teaching and learning the new faith together. In the twelfth century, on the other hand, devotional fashions stressed special relationships between holy women and Christ (to be examined further in the following chapter) – a feminised form of piety which many men found they could enjoy at best vicariously. For women, this became both a privilege and a burden. Elevated to spiritual pedestals, in charge of hot lines to heaven, such women were expected to lead lives charged with extraordinary emotional intensity and marked by spotless purity. A text such as the *Life* of Christina makes it plain that this was not a role to be borne without cost. The solution, as advocated by men, was to support strict rules of enclosure; by the thirteenth century these had become so much the norm that the contemporary historian of St Albans, in his account of Christina and Roger, rearranged their housing. Christina, in these pages, spent four years in a little hut near Roger but never once did she set eyes on him.

It will be remembered that Christina had become a hermit only because she had no choice, but she stayed on at Markyate after it had become a priory thanks to its endowment by Geoffrey, of her own volition. Archbishop Thurstan of York, the supporter of her original vocation, had meanwhile urged her to come north, to head his new nunnery of Clementhorpe. Christina refused. Her biographer notes with St Albans' pride how she 'had frequent visits from the heads of celebrated

monasteries in distant parts of England and from across the
sea, who wished to take her away with them and by her
presence add importance and prestige to their places'. Above
all, he continues, 'the archbishop of York tried very hard to do
her honour and make her superior over the virgins whom he
had gathered under his name at York ... but she preferred our
monastery' (ch. 50). The history of the foundation of Clementhorpe is worth tracing as an illustration of the functions of
a convent in the later Middle Ages.

Clementhorpe was an urban convent. It was founded some
time between c.1125 and 1133 just outside the city walls, only
a mile away from the cathedral of York, on a site where a
church may once have stood. It was the first of the Yorkshire
convents of the twelfth century – by 1160 there would be
another sixteen. Founded on the initiative of Archbishop Thurstan it was comfortably, if not lavishly, endowed; Thurstan
had given it an assortment of rents, tithes and land for a
guesthouse. It failed, as we have seen, to attract Christina as
its first prioress; thereafter no attempts seem to have been
made to look for another celebrity to fill the post. Both its
geographical position and the tenor of its way of life testify to
the role of Clementhorpe not as a place of high spirituality –
though it frequently housed an anchoress – but as an important
centre for the wider community of York. Prioresses were
usually chosen from among their own number; they might not
be famed for their visions, but they were respected and trusted
and, in their role as executors for the citizens of York, they
were left tokens of affection – a silver salt cellar, a pair of
sheets. The convent itself received bequests for the church –
an altar cloth, an image of the Virgin, silver beads for the statue
of St Sitha.

Children were brought up in the nunnery of Clementhorpe;
women retired there to live within the precincts, not necessarily as nuns but sometimes as vowesses. Both men and
women asked to be buried in the church and provided accordingly in their wills for their funeral expenses. Margaret Sta-
pilton (d. 1466) for example, left 13s 4d for wine and bread
for the service and 20 shillings for a funeral breakfast, to be
attended by everyone in the convent. Every now and then
there was a scandal – in 1318 the apostate nun Joanna was
ordered to return to Clementhorpe. The case was notable for

the ingeniousness of Joanna's defection – she had organised a mock funeral for herself - but nothing occurred that was sufficiently outrageous to seriously upset the respectability of the house. Between the time of its foundation and its dissolution in 1536 Clementhorpe became poorer in relative terms but with an income of £68 11s 8d (the dissolution estimate) it was still one of the richest of the Yorkshire nunneries. At the time of the dissolution there were said to be eight nuns and nine servants.

The convents of later medieval England have lived for years under the shadow cast over them by the work of an earlier generation of scholars who tended to see them, in derogatory terms, as refuge centres for poor aristocrats, undistinguished either in worldly or spiritual learning. Recent work has done much to challenge this verdict, making it clear that to judge convents in some league table alongside monasteries is an inappropriate exercise, masking as it does their special characteristics. Convents were indeed poor in comparison with monasteries but this was not a sign of negligence or apathy on the part of their inmates, it was because they were so often founded with different expectations and assumptions from monasteries. Nunneries like Clementhorpe catered for local needs. Their initial endowments were often modest, but none the less adequate for their purposes. Sometimes the endowment came from dowry land given by a woman founder who would herself enter the new house as its head. This was how Lacock – founded in 1232 by Ela, the widowed Countess of Salisbury – began. The inhabitants of the surrounding village became the abbey's tenants, its labourers and the recipients of its charity – bread and herrings, for example, for a hundred of the poor on the anniversary each year of Ela's death. Ela was buried in the abbey church; two of her granddaughters became canonesses and kept up the family connection. More modest families followed the same pattern.

Such 'small gentry foundations', often linked together by familial bonds, remained 'closely linked to gentry of their locality, people concerned with local parish and village affairs and local family ties'.[13] On the eve of the Reformation the recruitment in these houses was still strong, and indeed throughout the Middle Ages there was no falling off of convent

[13] R. Gilchrist, *Gender and Material Culture* (1994), p. 50.

numbers. The affection felt by nuns for their establishments is borne out by the attempts of several communities to keep together after the Dissolution by moving into family homes. It may not have been a severe transition to make. In their organisation, even in their layout, late medieval convents were not unlike private households. This should not be seen as a mark of decay, but as a further sign of the 'amorphous, a-institutional' quality of women's piety recognised and described by Caroline Walker Bynum.[14]

No account of female monasticism would be complete without some mention of the Brigittines, the Order founded by Bridget of Sweden in the mid-fourteenth century. Bridget belonged to the new breed of married holy women; she gave birth to eight children and it was only after her husband's death in 1344, in response to visions from the Virgin, that she founded a double house for monks and nuns placing the abbess in charge since, in the words of her *Rule*, 'the abbess out of reverence to the most blessed Virgin Mary to whom this order is hallowed, ought to be head and lady. For the Virgin, in whose stead the abbess is, was after Christ's ascension into heaven, head and queen of the apostles.'[15] No less revolutionary was Bridget's stress on learning. The nuns were to have as many books as they could use.

Bridget herself never became a nun – the abbess of her first house was her daughter – but she continued throughout her life to have visions, recorded first in Latin by her confessors and later translated into various vernaculars. These *Revelations* proved to be hugely popular throughout Europe, not least in England. As an Order, the Brigittines were taken up by King Henry V who, in 1415, founded a house for them at Syon in Middlesex, a community which pious aristocrats continued to favour throughout the fifteenth century. But the most striking testimony to Bridget's influence comes from the evidence of the circulation of her *Revelations* – commonly known as 'St Bride's book' – among lay men and women of quite modest means.

Bridget's popularity also brought her enemies. Jean Gerson,

[14] C. W. Bynum, *Fragmentation and Redemption: Essays on Gender and the Human Body in Medieval Religion* (1991), pp. 63–4.
[15] From the Middle English text of the *Rule* in A. Barratt (ed.), *Women's Writings in Middle English* (1992), pp. 92–3.

chancellor of the University of Paris and a renowned teacher of mystical theology, was bitterly opposed to her cult. For him, women's piety, as exemplified by Bridget, was 'overheated', its influence pernicious – 'there is hardly any other calamity more apt to do harm.'[16] What he called 'the itch to see and to speak, not to mention the itch to touch', he found deeply offensive. We shall encounter Gerson's attitude in England, among the clerical critics of Margery Kempe, in Chapter Eleven. The virulence of the attacks of such men is, of course, singular testimony to the potency of the religiosity they so disliked.

[16] Cited in B. Obrist, 'The Swedish Visionary: St Bridget', in K. Wilson (ed.), *Medieval Women Writers* (1984), p. 236.

CHAPTER TEN

Anchoresses and Recluses

The woman in medieval England who wanted to become a recluse or anchoress had to go through an arduous selection process. Her vocation had to be tested and approved by her bishop before there could be any possibility of allowing her enclosure to proceed. Once permission had been granted an awesome ceremony followed. The anchoress entered the church where she lay prostrate in the west end. A litany was recited by two clerks; the anchoress was blessed with water and incense and given two candles, representing love of God and the love of one's neighbour. There was a reading from scripture and a psalm; the candles were placed on the altar and Mass was celebrated. The anchoress was led towards a cell adjoining the church while Psalms from the Office of the Dead were sung; she was sprinkled with dust before entering her cell and the door was closed after her.

Ann Warren in her recent study *Medieval English Anchorites and their Patrons* has commented that, given the extent of the maintenance which a hermit needed, she can 'think of no modern equivalent with which to compare such a long-term commitment by so many to satisfy the religious compulsion of one'.[1] But the 'one' was, of course, as Warren herself shows, believed to be performing unseen and incalculable service on behalf of the many. In the words of the author of the early-thirteenth-century rule for anchoresses, *Ancrene Riwle*:

The night-raven under the eaves symbolises recluses who live under the eaves of the church because they know that they ought to be so holy in their lives that all Holy Church, that is Christian people, may lean

[1] A. Warren, *Anchorites and their Patrons in Medieval England* (1985), p. 15.

upon them, while they hold her up with the holiness of their lives and their blessed prayers. It is for this reason that an anchoress is called an anchoress and anchored under a church like an anchor under the side of a ship to hold it so that the waves and the storm do not pitch it over. So all Holy Church which is called a ship, shall be anchored to the anchoress and she shall hold it secure so that the puffing and blowing of the devil . . . do not pitch it over.[2]

This is not to be taken simply as poetic rhetoric. The well-being of recluses – anchorites and anchoresses – mattered not only to the parishes in which they lived but to the whole of society. Kings, bishops and aristocrats regularly endowed them in order to keep their good favour and to earn the benefit of their prayers. Among kings, Henry III was a particular friend and patron of recluses: twenty-seven received a main-tenance grant from him throughout his reign; many others received gifts of wheat or firewood. In 1245 all the anchoresses 'in or about London' were asked to pray for the soul of the King's father-in-law and rewarded for their labours with a meal. The same year he gave a certain recluse, Alice, three oaks to build herself a new home. Comparable beneficence was exercised among the nobility by, for example, Henry, first Duke of Lancaster, who not only supported two anchoresses at Pontefract in Yorkshire, ensuring them the services of a chaplain who would say Mass for them daily, but who also founded a reclusarium for the anchoress of his choice at Whalley in Lancashire. The monks of Whalley Abbey were to provide for both her spiritual and material needs.

An anchoress might be enclosed for twenty, thirty, even as many as fifty years. Occasionally her cell was tiny – a mere eight foot square sufficed for the anchoress of Leatherhead in Surrey. But anchor-holds could also be quite sumptuous, like that of Margaret White, the fifteenth-century anchoress of Stamford in Lincolnshire with whom Lady Margaret Beaufort sometimes shared wine and apples. Lady Margaret had herself provided Margaret with her cell, and furnished it with bedlinen and wall hangings. Contrary to expectations, more-over, many anchoresses lived not on their own in solitary confinement but with other anchoresses. They were likely to

---

[2] *Ancrene Riwle*, trans. M. B. Salu (1955), p. 63. References are to this edition but see now A. Savage and N. Watson (eds), *Anchoritic Spirituality* (1991).

have servants – who sometimes inherited the lifestyle and the cell – and they might even have a guest room.

Anchoresses – unlike anchorites – usually came straight from the world; some had first lived in a convent but even if this was so, as Warren points out, they did not advertise their conversion as a form of step up the spiritual ladder. This contrasts with the experience and stance of men. Men who became anchorites were often priests or monks; when they became recluses they are represented as having gained in stature whereas for women nothing they had been before their immurement seemed to matter. As anchoresses they could expect to be equally highly regarded whether they were lay, nun, virgin or widow. This coupling of spiritual exaltation with social levelling may be one of the reasons for the noticeable appeal of the vocation for women. According to Warren's calculations, anchoresses consistently outnumber anchorites, a trend particularly marked in the thirteenth century but still so in the fifteenth.

With the exception of Julian of Norwich's *Revelations*, to be considered below, we have for certain no other writings by English anchoresses. The possibility of anonymous devotional texts having been written by women, possibly anchoresses, as opposed to the assumed male authors of tradition, is now being considered but as Bella Millet has recently advised, care must be taken not to 'people the gaps in our knowledge with a phantom army of women writers; the assumption of female authorship remains no more than wishful thinking unless we are prepared to accept the burden of proof.'[3] Such proof is hard to find. The texts we will be examining are likely, then, to tell us in the first instance how men expected holy women to live – but this is not the least part of their interest. We will consider first three works of guidance written for particular recluses: for Eve of Wilton; for the sister of Ailred, twelfth-century abbot of the Cistercian house of Rievaulx in Yorkshire; and the *Ancrene Riwle*, for three sisters living together in an anchorhold somewhere in the West Midlands at the turn of the twelfth century.

Eve, originally a nun at the Anglo-Saxon convent of Wilton

[3] B. Millet, 'English Recluses and the Development of Vernacular Literature', in C. Meale (ed.), *Women and Literature in Britain 1150–1500* (1993), p. 98.

where she had been brought up – her parents had taken her there as a seven-year-old, just one year before the Norman Conquest – had as a young woman chosen to leave Wilton to live as a recluse in France. We know about her life from the letter written to her by the hagiographer Goscelin who, in his capacity as chaplain at Wilton, had formed a close attachment to Eve. Her departure from the community came as both a surprise to him and a source of sorrow. His letter is full of reproaches for what he takes as a betrayal of their friendship on her part, though such bitterness is tempered with respect for the way of life Eve has now chosen and for the sacrifices she has made, her renunciation of her 'sweet acquaintances, numerous friends, charming letters, her pious abbess, earnest teacher, agreeable sisters and diverse enjoyable things'.[4] Even has now a tiny (eight-foot) cell and only a window through which she can communicate with the world. But, suggests Goscelin, she has her role models – biblical heroines, the early Christian martyrs – and she can, and indeed must, read. The reading list which Goscelin suggests for her is formidable – St Augustine's *City of God* and his *Confessions*, Boethius's *Consolation of Philosophy*, the histories of Eusebius and Orosius – here clearly is a hermit whose classical education is far from rudimentary, as one might perhaps expect from a house such as Wilton which had a tradition of Latin learning that survived at least until the twelfth century. As we know from a different source, Eve found herself a 'soul-friend', the priest Hervey, with whom she spent her later years as a hermit. This relationship was not without its critics: 'I feel that you are troubled,' wrote a contemporary in an obituary for Eve, 'I feel that you are troubled who hear such talk. Brother, avoid all suspicious thought ... Such love was not in this world but in Christ.'[5]

The tenor of Ailred's letter to his sister, in effect an open letter to all recluses, stands in sharp contrast to Goscelin's letter to Eve. Although in Latin, it does not assume a readership of scholar-hermits (it was later translated into English) nor does it make any room for spiritual friendship. Ailred himself, in his relations with his monks, fostered just such bonds but

---

[4] Cited in S. Elkins, *Holy Women of Twelfth-Century England* (1988), p. 23.
[5] Cited J. Leclercq, 'Solitude and Solidarity: Medieval Women Recluses', in J. Nichols and L. T. Shanks (eds), *Peace Weavers; Medieval Religious Women*, vol. 2 (1987), p. 72.

in contrast Ailred's sister is warned insistently of the dangers of close relationships, notably with men but even with women. It becomes clear indeed from Ailred's exposition of the virtues of virginity that he is counting on the rigorous guarding of his sister's purity to compensate for his own sins of the flesh as a young man. The emotions she is not to feel for her fellow-beings are, in Ailred's scheme, to be directed towards the love of God with startling intensity; austerity and asceticism are combined with a fierce passion;

On your altar let it be enough for you to have a representative of Our Saviour hanging on the Cross; that will bring before your mind his Passion for you to imitate, his outspread arms will invite you to embrace him, his naked breasts will feed you with the milk of sweetness to console you.[6]

The recluse must nourish her spiritual life by actualising every moment of the Gospel life of Christ, from Annunciation to Crucifixion and Resurrection. She must share the joys and anxieties and anguish of Christ's mother; as Christ's side is pierced at the Crucifixion and blood and water pours forth, she is to

hasten, linger not ... The blood is changed into wine to gladden you, the water into milk to nourish you. From the rock streams have flowed for you, wounds have been made in his limbs, holes in the walls of his body, in which like a dove, you may hide while you kiss them one by one. Your lips, stained with his blood, will become like a scarlet ribbon and your word sweet.[7]

Ailred's letter to his sister is the 'first English meditative exercise', harbinger of a movement that has been described by Jack Bennett as 'one of the greatest revolutions in feeling that Europe has even witnessed'.[8] It was a movement which women were able to empathise with, and to make their own.

Our other treatise, the *Ancrene Riwle* or *Ancrene Wisse*, based in part on Ailred's letter, was written in the vernacular some time around 1200. It forms part of a corpus of what has been seen as 'women's literature'. The corpus consists of six major texts closely related to each other both in manuscript trans-

---

[6] Ailred of Rievaulx, *Treatises and the Pastoral Prayer*, Cistercian Fathers Series 11 (1971), p. 73.
[7] *Ibid.*, p. 91
[8] J. Bennett, *The Poetry of the Passion* (1982), pp. 39, 33.

mission and in the West Midland dialect they share. Its main, though not its only, audience is holy women. Apart from the *Ancrene Riwle* it includes a collection known as *The Katherine Group* made up of a homily on the custody of the soul (a translation of a contemporary Latin text), the treatise on virginity, *Holy Maidenhood*, and the *Lives* of three women saints – Katherine, Margaret and Juliana. To these we must add four meditations, generally known as *The Wooing Group*, whose primary focus is Christ's love for the soul. These texts have on the one hand aroused interest and admiration for their literary use of the vernacular and on the other various degrees of disquiet or dismay because of the 'manifest eroticism' and 'gross misogyny' they are thought to display. Both are issues we need to address.

As transmitters of spoken English vernacular women played a vital role in the generations after the Conquest, as we have seen. Their role in the survival of its use as a written language may have been no less significant. Anglo-Saxon vernacular, though displaced and altered, was never abandoned. While French might be the language of aristocratic circles, many women recluses – like Christina of Markyate – spoke English; Latin, the language so familiar to the recluse Eve, was becoming increasingly monopolised by a new breed of professionals - university men. By the thirteenth century Latin had come to be seen as a mark of clerical status and authority; the very fact that holy women were debarred from such positions made it imperative that their needs should be met in the vernacular. A work such as the *Ancrene Riwle* catered for such women and confirmed them in their place: excluded (like most of the laity) from the academy but included in the kingdom of God.

The *Ancrene Riwle*, composed though it initially was for three sisters – 'well-bred ... sought after for [their] goodness and kindness' – came to enjoy a wide circulation among men as well as women. The anchor-hold from which it originated likewise achieved fame, developing into a small community even within the lifetime of its author. None the less, he made no significant alterations to his text. He could still envisage within the anchor-hold a measure of informality and flexibility of a kind which an established convent might have had difficulty in tolerating. His stance suggests impatience with contemporary debates and wrangles about monastic rules. He goes out of his way to play down the minutiae of observance: 'outer' or 'exterior' rules should and will vary, and they are not to be the object of solemn promises; 'this applies to matters of eating and drinking, for example, of abstaining from meat or fish, and to all other kinds of things, clothing, rest, saying one's hours and other prayers, the number of them and the manner in which they are said.' The only vows an anchoress should take are those of obedience, chastity and stability of abode. She must obey not men's inventions but God's commands: 'charity, that is love, humility and patience, fidelity and the keeping of the ten commandments, confession and penance and other such matters.'[9]

'Confession and penance' lie at the heart of the *Ancrene Riwle*. Book IV contains a lengthy discussion of temptation in its various forms and suggests 'various comforts and remedies' to comfort them. Book V is entirely given over to the subject of confession. As a vernacular penitent's manual, the *Ancrene Riwle* is for its time unparalleled; no earlier discussion in the English language of 'inwit', or personal conscience, is known. The author's most important source, after the Bible, seems to be Peter the Chanter whose influence in England (through Thomas of Chobham) we observed in Chapter Six. Peter the Chanter and his circle are the 'think-tank' behind the Lateran decree of 1215 making annual confession mandatory and it is in the context of his work – the author's most important source after the Bible – that the deft handling of the controversial relationship between contrition and confession in the *Ancrene Riwle* must be understood.

Books IV and V of the *Ancrene Riwle* place the work at the forefront of early-thirteenth-century theology. It is important to stress this because there are passages in the work – on how beneficial it is for the anchoresses to mend church vestments, or the much-quoted advice on animals: 'you must not keep any animal except a cat ... it is odious, Christ knows, when there are complaints in a village about the anchoresses' animals' - which makes it sound as if the anchor-hold was nothing but a rather cosy shared residence, neither shockingly arduous nor spiritually very exciting. Books IV and V correct this impression. The women of the anchor-hold have not been shunted into a siding. They are the recipients of the most recent

[9] *Ancrene Riwle*, p. 3.

Paris teaching. The wide dissemination of the *Ancrene Riwle* was one of the ways in which such teaching spread to the laity.

The *Ancrene Riwle* has often been coupled with Ailred's treatise for his sister and there are indeed direct borrowings from it in the *Ancrene Riwle*. But as Linda Georgianna's work has shown, the contrast between the two rules is quite as striking as any similarity.[10] Ailred displays a much greater nervousness about worldly contamination than the *Ancrene Riwle*: everything worldly is possibly defiling and his sister's purity has to be guarded from it. The *Ancrene Riwle* on the other hand, displays a sense of the ways in which love of the world can lead to God rather than away from him; its author allows seemingly trivial incidents to have spiritual potential. Thus the sisters, faced with 'carnal temptations', rather than thinking about St Agnes and increasing their mortifications (Ailred's suggestion in such a situation) are, in the *Ancrene Riwle*, bidden to use quite random thoughts – about burglars, or fire, or someone they love drowning, or becoming pope – as spiritually useful distractions.

In Ailred's rule his sister was advised to love God as man and mother. The *Ancrene Riwle* introduces a new element of chivalry, both courtly and erotic. Christ is now the perfect knight, hero of a story that tells of a proud lady marooned and destitute in her castle, surrounded on all sides by implacable enemies. To save her life and win her love, the Christ-knight takes on his besiegers: single-handed he 'entered the tournament and like a brave knight had his shield pierced through and through ... his shield, concealing his God-head was his dead body.' The shield, as is customary, 'after the death of a brave knight is hung high in the church in his memory. And so is this shield which is a crucifix set in the church so that it may remind us of Jesus Christ's deed of knighthood on the cross.' As we read further, we find that the crucifix is to function not only as a reminder of Christ's love; it is also an invitation to the anchoress to love: 'with these two pieces of wood you should kindle the fire of love in your heart ... think how gladly you should love the king of glory who extends his arms towards you and bows down his head as if to ask for a kiss.' 'Stretch out your love to Jesus Christ,' the anchoresses are urged, 'you have won him. Touch him with as much love as

[10] L. Georgianna, *The Solitary Self: Individuality in the Ancrene Wisse* (1981).

you sometimes feel for a man. He is yours to do with all that you will.'[11]

The development of erotic language of the kind we find in the *Ancrene Riwle* has been traced by John Bugge in his study, *Virginitas*.[12] It is, in his words, a story of the 'transgression of the bounds of symbolism' whereby 'the metaphor of the spiritual marriage is literalised'. The use made in the mid-twelfth century, notably by the Cistercians, of a Origenist interpretation of the Song of Songs whereby the Bride of Christ is no longer taken to be the Church but rather the individual soul of man or woman, was, according to Bugge, prompted by a last-ditch attempt to revitalise monasticism in its struggle against university scholasticism. Unexpectedly this imagery became reshaped and sexualised in devotional literature and nowhere earlier or more explicitly than in *The Katherine Group* and *The Wooing Group*. In the meditation from *The Wooing Group*, 'The Wooing of our Lord', for example, an anchoress speaks in highly sensuous fashion to Christ:

My body will hang with your body, nailed on the cross, fastened, transfixed within four walls. And I will hang with you and nevermore come from my cross until I die ... Ah, Jesus, so sweet it is to hang with you. For when I look on you who hang beside me, your great sweetness snatches me strongly from pain.[13]

Commentators who have found such sexual imagery distasteful have done so particularly when viewed alongside the kind of denigration of earthly love and marriage that is found in *Holy Maidenhood*. In this diatribe, marriage is a very miserable second-best; it precludes the heights of heavenly bliss – reserved for virgins – and in recompense offers not even a modicum of earthly happiness. Sex is always disgusting and demeaning; animals at least copulate only once a year whereas men 'pursue filthiness at all times'. At night a woman will be constantly molested; in the daytime she will be shouted at and beaten and treated like a drudge. Pregnancy, child-care and housekeeping are (as we have seen on p. 123) represented as nauseous and exhausting. Although recently reclaimed as a charter for women's liberation, this text is more usually taken

[11] *Ancrene Riwle*, pp. 172–4; 177; 180.
[12] J. Bugge, *Virginitas: An Essay in the History of a Medieval Ideal* (1975).
[13] 'The Wooing of Our Lord', ed. A. Savage and N. Watson, *Anchoritic Spirituality* (1991), p. 256.

214

as illustrative of a strand of dualism recurrent in medieval thought. It is certainly not an original composition. It relies heavily on standard topoi of patristic teaching, but as such it needs to be read, as Nicholas Watson has pointed out, as a *pièce d'occasion*: '[it] does not necessarily represent the whole view of sex held either by its author or by its audience. It is, rather, an exercise written for those who have already repudiated sexual activity and family ties, intended to fortify them for the future.'[14]

The saints' *Lives* of *The Katherine Group*, in contrast to *Holy Maidenhood*, seem to have been written originally for a wider audience than just anchoresses. The *Life* of St Margaret, for example, is presented as if for oral delivery on Margaret's feast-day; married women, widows and virgins are all expected to be listening. St Margaret, as already noted, is the patron saint of childbirth despite her virgin status. In her *Life* the dragon who swallows her, – 'he stretched out his tongue to the soles of her feet and tossed her in' – is rendered powerless by the sign of the Cross and Margaret's 'rebirth' is celebrated by her promise to mothers in labour – 'in the house where a woman is lying in labour, as soon as she recalls my name and my passion, Lord, make haste to help her and listen to her prayer.'[15] But the *Life* of Margaret is also recommended reading for anchoresses. It is a text that bridges the very gulf which the author of *Holy Maidenhood* is seemingly at pains to emphasise. There are implications here which we must consider.

A recent examination of the *Life* of St Margaret, by Elizabeth Robertson, has stressed Margaret's 'corporeality' and takes this as indicative of the author's conception of female sanctity.[16] Thus, throughout the *Life*, Margaret's virginity is tested by the horrendous suffering inflicted on her body. Her enemies are similarly 'embodied': Olibrius, the governor of Antioch who desires her, the dragon who swallows her, the 'black, grisly and loathsome' demon who tempts her are all represented as physically menacing. Margaret can resist and

---

[14] N. Watson, 'The Methods and Objectives of Thirteenth-Century Anchoritic Devotion', in M. Glasscoe (ed.), *Medieval Mystical Tradition in England*, Exeter Symposium IV (1987), p. 137.

[15] 'Saint Margaret', in B. Millet and J. Wogan-Browne (eds), *Medieval English Prose for Women* (1990), pp. 61, 79.

[16] E. Robertson, 'The Corporeality of Female Sanctity in *The Life of St Margaret*', in R. Blumenfeld-Kosinski and T. Szell (eds), *Images of Sainthood in Medieval Europe* (1991), pp. 268–87.

endure because of her commitment to Christ in his body; he is her lover; as he suffered on the Cross for her, so she too can suffer in return. This is a story suffused with the erotic imagery of the *Ancrene Riwle* and *The Wooing Group*. Margaret is a saint anchoresses none the less share with their married sisters. How is this saintly physicality to be understood and what did it mean to the men who wrote these works?

Fundamental to any understanding of the religious symbolism of the body in the Middle Ages is the work of Caroline Walker Bynum. Bynum has illuminated the whole range of meaning which particular metaphor might have had for both men and women and has thereby demonstrated ways in which 'medieval thinkers used gender imagery fluidly, not literally'.[17] This usage sprang from a fusion of Aristotelian theories of generation in which woman provided matter and man provided spirit with the affective piety of the twelfth and thirteenth century centred on the humanity of Christ, from his birth to his Passion. Given that Christ's humanity came from his mother, his body, his flesh, was 'womanly': moreover, this flesh, when crucified, 'did womanly things: it bled . . .' And it did more: as distributed in the Eucharist it nourished, 'it bled food . . .'[18] Christ's blood was here analogous to a mother's milk. But if Christ's body could do 'womanly things', so too in certain ways could the bodies of all men. Both St Bernard and St Francis, notably among saints, saw themselves as 'mothers' of disciples to whom they gave birth and whom they nurtured. 'Actual' women could never lay claim to the exclusive use of feminine imagery; it belonged to all humanity. Nevertheless, it was women more than men who in the later Middle Ages developed forms of piety that were markedly somatic. Here St Francis is the exception that proves the rule. Francis was possibly the first stigmatic; he was also, until this century, the only man said to have been marked by all five of the visible wounds while allegedly 'dozens' of late medieval women received them.[19]

The stress placed by women on a physicality that linked them in this, as in other ways, to Christ as man, gave them claims to be powerful conduits of his grace; as such they

---

[17] C. W. Bynum, *Fragmentation and Redemption: Essays on Gender and the Human Body in Medieval Religion* (1991), p. 218.
[18] *Ibid.*, p. 101.
[19] *Ibid.*, p. 187.

attracted veneration and reverence on the one hand, envy and suspicion on the other. In England an official policy of caution seems to have been adopted. It would seem that, in a country long used to strong and intrusive government, it was possible for anchoresses to be carefully monitored and any visions discouraged. There is no other explanation for the fact that whereas female mysticism flourished on the Continent in the later Middle Ages, in England it lay dormant for the better part of the thirteenth and the opening decades of the fourteenth centuries, and this despite the passionate outpourings of the earlier anchoritic literature. The mid-fourteenth century, however, sees the beginnings of a change.

'An old woman,' wrote the fourteenth-century hermit and mystic Richard Rolle, 'can be more expert in the love of God ... than your theologian with his useless studying'.[20] Rolle himself had marked his conversion and withdrawal from the world by fashioning himself a habit made from two of his sisters' old dresses. His mystical experience, the foundation of his spiritual life, of warmth, sweetness and light came to him after nine months' gestation. His most steadfast patrons were the Cistercians nuns of Hampole Priory in West Yorkshire, among whom he made his home. It was for one of these nuns, Margaret Kirkby, who had left Hampole to become an anchoress at East Layton in North Yorkshire, that Rolle wrote his most influential treatise, *The Form of Living*, as well, it is now thought, as other vernacular works. Some time after Rolle's death in 1349, at the height of the Black Death, Margaret moved back to Hampole to be near his grave; it is likely that she took over his cell and certain that, together with her sisters at Hampole, she helped to compose a biographical *Office* to commemorate Rolle's life and to promote his cult. The intimacy between Margaret and Rolle has been captured in a much quoted passage from this *Office* which still bears repeating:

He came and found her mute, but when he had seated himself at her window and they had eaten together, it chanced that by the end of the dinner the recluse wished to sleep and oppressed by slumber her head drooped towards the window where God's saint, Richard, was reclining, and as she was leaning a little on the same Richard, suddenly, with a vehement onslaught, such a grave vexation took her in her sleep that she seemed to wish to break the window of her house, and in that

[20] Cited in M. Glasscoe, *English Medieval Mystics: Games of Faith* (1993), p. 60.

strong vexation she awoke and her speech was restored, and with great devotion she broke out into the words 'Gloria tibi Domine', and the blessed Richard completed the verse which she had begun.[21]

In Rolle's writings for Margaret, notably in *The Form of Living*, there is said to be a stress on the contemplative life of the anchoress that far exceeds anything to be found in the *Ancrene Riwle*. Such a judgement perhaps underestimates, on the one hand, the depths of ecstasy which the three sisters of the *Riwle* are expected to enjoy and, on the other, the caution with which Rolle advises Margaret to approach possible visionary experience. It none the less remains clear that the affective quality of Rolle's teaching was such that there were many among the clergy who worried that it could be misunderstood. Jonathan Hughes has recently shown how central a concern this was to the hierarchy and spiritual leaders in Yorkshire in the decades after Rolle's death.[22]

A leading critic of Rolle's influence was Walter Hilton, a writer whose major work *The Scale of Perfection* was, like Rolle's, dedicated to an anchoress but who was at the same time a passionate advocate of the mixed life, the 'medled lyf', that every lay man or woman could follow. Hilton was a moderate, anxious to make sure that Rolle's teaching was not taken too literally. Rolle's 'fire of love' was, Hilton assured his readers 'not physical ... it is only in the spiritual desire of the soul. Men and women who truly feel devotion are aware of this, but some people are simple and believe that because it is called fire, it should be hot like a physical fire.'[23]

In the practice of late medieval piety we can see from the works of both Rolle and Hilton how anchoresses provided inspiration as well as audience. The scripts are not untroubled; countless anxieties are seldom far below the surface – about the provenance of visions, or of the new heresy of Lollardy and the questions it raised, about the nature of the Mass, the use of the vernacular and the proper veneration to be shown towards images. It is, as Nicholas Watson has recently and so persuasively shown, against this background that we must approach the greatest of all the English women anchorites,

---

[21] Cited in M. Glasscoe, *English Medieval Mystics*. pp. 64–5.
[22] J. Hughes, *Pastors and Visionaries: Religion and Secular Life in Late Medieval Yorkshire* (1988).
[23] Cited by J. Hughes, *op. cit.*, p. 272.

Julian of Norwich, beloved in the twentieth century by theologians and poets alike.[24]

At the age of thirty Julian of Norwich, who seemed close to death, had a series of visions whose meanings were to occupy her for the rest of her life. It is not clear whether or not Julian was already an anchoress at the time of these visions but at some point she was enclosed in a cell belonging to Carrow Priory in Norfolk where she lived until her death shortly after 1416. Although Julian was revered in her lifetime, as evidenced by bequests in local wills and from the visit paid to her by Margery Kempe, her *Revelations* have only recently come to enjoy wide circulation. The *Revelations* – in vogue now not least because of Julian's conception of God as Mother – exist in two versions. Of the short text (S), one fifteenth-century manuscript survives; of the longer (L), only three post-Reformation manuscripts.

It is in the context of the relationship between S and L that Watson has placed his recent re-examination of Julian's work. It has long been held as axiomatic that S was written very soon after the actual visions whereas L – which is six times as long – was the fruit of Julian's interpretative meditations, spurred on by two further visions experienced in the years 1388 and 1393 and probably concluded shortly after the last of these. Watson, however, now argues that S for all its 'freshness', may have taken Julian some ten to fifteen years to write and that L likewise belongs to a later date than is usually assigned to it. The implications of his thesis are considerable.

Watson takes as his starting point the contrast to be observed in the recorded nature of female piety between thirteenth- and fourteenth-century England and the Continent: 'Julian's revelation of 1373 appears to be the first major English example of a female vision for two centuries: the same centuries which on the Continent constituted a golden age of women's mysticism.'[25] Not only is Julian marked out as singular by her visionary experience, she aggravates the situation by subsequently writing about it. The apologetic tone (in Chapter Six) with which she sets about this task, however contrived, is still a testimony to the novelty of what she is doing: 'But God

[24] N. Watson, 'The Composition of Julian of Norwich's *Revelation of Love*', *Speculum* 68 (1993), pp. 637–82.
[25] *Op. cit.*, p. 646.

forbid that you should say or take me for a teacher for I don't intend that nor ever did so, for I am a woman, ignorant, week and frail.' Her enterprise might have been seen as somewhat less daring by the last decade of the fourteenth century, by which time translations into Middle English of works by continental women mystics were becoming widely known, but even so Julian remains an isolated figure, without literary disciples. She also emerges, from Watson's analysis, as a figure acutely aware of the nature of the accusations which might be levelled against her; she is thus profoundly anxious lest her desire for an experience of the Passion, beyond that which 'paintings or crucifixes' could vouchsafe her, should lay her open to charges of Lollardy. This, as Watson points out, is an anxiety which makes sense only in the 1380s and the decades immediately following, when veneration of images had become a hotly debated issue.

If S belongs to the 1380s what, then, is its relationship to the vision of 1388 and indeed to L? S is a text imprinted with a deep sense of sin: the revelation of 1388, on the other hand, is renowned for a quite different understanding. Described at the end of L in Chapter 68, and coming fifteen years after Julian's first visions, it forms one of the most famous of all the passages she wrote:

From the time these things were first revealed I had often wanted to know what was our Lord's meaning. It was more than fifteen years after that I was answered in my spirit's understanding. 'You would know our Lord's meaning in this thing? Know it well. Love was his meaning. Who showed it to you? Love. What did he show you? Love. Why did he show it? For love. Hold on to this and you will know and understand love more and more. But you will not know or learn anything else – ever.'

This chapter both concludes L and explains the need to write it; the germ of the idea is, Watson argues, already present in the ending of S, containing as it does a hint of the new direction L had to take. The experience of 1388 had shown Julian that S, despite the years of reflection it had taken to write, was none the less, a 'failure'. Its theology was 'wrong'. She had to start again at the beginning. Even then she was in no rush to do so. L was just as slow to mature as S, perhaps not written in the fourteenth century at all but in the early years of the fifteenth, possibly given a final spur by the arrival of 228 books at the

cathedral priory of Norwich in 1407 – the bequest of Cardinal
Adam Easton, an erstwhile monk at the priory and a staunch
supporter of the canonisation of Bridget of Sweden. The books,
which are so formative in *The Book of Margery Kempe*, are likely
to have been in the priory's library at the time of her visit; they
may have been inspirational for Julian quite as much as for
the theologically less subtle Margery.

To locate Julian in the lay piety of her time and place does
her no disservice; it is a context which needs to be stressed and
which can be illustrated by the Norwich wills which included
bequests to her. The men and women who left her shillings and
pence were giving them not to 'the first English theologian', as
she has been hailed, but to their local holy woman. They too,
as Eamon Duffy in *The Stripping of the Altars* has reminded us,
could have expected on their deathbed a visit from a priest
who would hold before them, as he had held before Julian
when she was so critically ill, a crucifix, so that in the words
of the *Ordo Visitandi* 'in the image they may adore their
redeemer and have in mind his passion, which he endured for
their sins'. Julian herself, when she is describing the priest's
visit during her illness, does so in words taken from the *Ordo
Visitandi*. Likewise, and it is Duffy again who reminds us of
this, we need to consider those visions of Julian's in which she
sees the changing colour of Christ's body on the Cross as he
thirsts – 'the skin of his face ... was like a plank when it has
been planed and dried out'; his body is 'like some cloth hung
out to dry' – in the context of English devotional fascination
with the drying out of Christ on the Cross, a theme explored
in the *Fifteen Oes of St Bridget*.

The *Fifteen Oes* were perhaps the most popular prayers of
late-medieval England. Their origin is unknown, but the
legend surrounding them is telling: they were revealed by
Christ himself to a woman about whom we are told only that
she was 'a woman solitary and recluse'.[26] The woman is often
thought to have been St Bridget, but the uncertainty of the
attribution can stand as a reminder of the potential influence
of anchoresses on the piety of every man and woman up and
down the country.

---

[26] E. Duffy, *The Stripping of the Altars* (1992), p. 254.

CHAPTER ELEVEN

Lay Piety

In the early twelfth century a widow of Norfolk, Richelde de Faverches, had a vision of the Virgin; the Virgin told Richelde to build on her estates at Walsingham a wooden replica of the house in which she had been visited by Gabriel, angel of the Annunciation. The Virgin gave very precise instructions as to how, and exactly where, the house was to be built. Richelde did as she was told. Some time later a stone chapel was erected over the house; it acquired a phial containing drops of the Virgin's milk and the shrine was further embellished; images of saints and angels, *'alle clene gold'*, now surrounded the statue of the Virgin. Pilgrimages and healings followed apace. By the time of the Reformation, Our Lady of Walsingham had long become one of the most important cult centres in the country; in the *Valor Ecclesiasticus* of 1535 it was receiving a record £260 a year.

The shrine of Our Lady of Walsingham owed its origin, therefore, to a woman and many subsequent bequests – rings, rosaries, clothes and pictures. When John Paston fell ill around 1443, it was primarily from Walsingham that his wife Margaret sought help. A wax image of John, weighing as much as he did, was sent to the shrine by Margaret's mother and Margaret herself promised to make a pilgrimage to it. But despite all the evidence of female devotion to the shrine it would be singularly misleading either to overlook the fervour of its male adherents or to suppose that it was the sole focus of Marian piety for the people of Norfolk. Thus the early-sixteenth-century mayor of Norwich, Gregory Clark, left instructions in his will for pilgrimages to be made not only to Our Lady of Walsingham but also to Our Lady at 'Redybone' (according to

Norman Tanner this could refer to a shrine either in Lincolnshire or Hertfordshire), Our Lady of 'Armeburghe' (un-
identified), Our Lady of Grace at Ipswich, Our Lady of Grace
at Cambridge and Our Lady of the Mount at Lynn.[1]

The Virgin in medieval England had as many guises as she
had shrines. This is something which those who deplore her
status as a 'role model' for medieval women tend to overlook.
To argue that she represents a pinnacle of unattainable goodness is seriously to underestimate her versatility. Even if her
willingness to do Thomas Becket's mending may seem to be
taking charity too far, what remains remarkable is the range
of her acts of mercy: she not only acts as midwife and carer of
children, she also stands in for the sacristan of a convent who
has run off with her lover, comes to the rescue of women
who have committed murder and incest or both, and when
necessary can put on a good show as a knight at a tournament.
Mary's protection of women, symbolised by the seating
arrangements in those churches where women sat on her
'side', aligned with the Lady Chapel, did not, it goes without
saying, preclude her wider patronage of whole communities
in ways that were far from purely nominal. At Coventry, for
example, the cathedral was dedicated to Mary and housed 'a
piece of Our Lady's tomb; and Our Lady's milk in silver gilt'.
A local priest who criticised the recommended practice of the
daily saying of her Psalter was promptly ostracised.[2] Coventry's other patron is, of course, the legendary Lady Godiva
who saved the city from the oppressions of her husband by
taking him at his word and riding naked through the town.
Godiva herself was said to have been devoted to the Virgin;
her heroic ride earned her the sobriquet Dame Good Eve, a
reminder of a playfulness within the Eve/Mary dichotomy
which it is easy to forget.

Mary of the Gospels is given only few words; those anxious
to reinforce the Pauline message that women were to be silent
in church found this a reassuring precedent. But for many late
medieval men and women, the Virgin they knew stepped out
of vernacular drama not Latin Gospels. As Eamon Duffy has
recently pointed out, the seventeenth-century peasant whose

[1] N. Tanner, *The Church in Late Medieval Norwich* (1984), p. 85.
[2] C. Phythian-Adams, *Desolation of a City: Coventry and the Urban Crisis of the Late Middle Ages* (1979), p. 172.

knowledge of Jesus came solely from the long-suppressed Corpus Christi play he had seen in his youth at Kendal is striking testimony not so much to his ignorance of Christianity as to the 'enormous didactic and imaginative effectiveness' of late medieval religious drama.[3] It is therefore worth looking more closely at the images of women presented in such plays and the kind of messages they gave their female viewers.

On a first reading these plays do little beyond reinforcing gender stereotypes; Noah's wife, in the Towneley play, is a tiresome and recalcitrant old gossip; Noah's final success in getting her aboard the Ark is a triumph both of God's will and his own. Again, in depictions of the Nativity, sympathies are elicited for Joseph as husband, an old man married to a young woman whom he has every reason to suppose has been unfaithful to him. The comic nature of these representations, akin as it is to the tradition of the fabliau, may seem to be primarily concerned with establishing the rightness of the (gendered) social order, with teaching lessons of correct behaviour, rather than with instilling any devotional fervour or lore. The N-Town cycle, for example, includes *The Trial of Joseph and Mary*, a play set in a medieval ecclesiastical court, convened to establish whether one, or both of them had broken the vows of virginity they were said to have taken; Joseph is here taunted with the possibility that he may have to pay the cost of raising a child who is not his own. At York, the play of Joseph's troubles, in which Joseph returns home to find his wife pregnant, is likely to have provided the occasion for a dramatic rendering of charivari, put on as it was by the Pewterers and Founders, the 'makers of metal domestic utensils, the kettles, pans and dishes through which the "rough music" of charivari was expressed'.[4] The marriage between a young woman and a man too old (on his own admission) to be able to impregnate her was just the kind of match likely to provoke such a display.

But it is, of course, precisely the 'this worldly' character of such plays which made them so potent a vehicle for Christian teachings in which the social context was itself grounded and which it in turn moulded. The women of these plays struggle, however comically, just as much as do the men to make some

[3] E. Duffy, *The Stripping of the Altars* (1992), p. 68.
[4] T. Coletti, 'The Paradox of Mary's Body', in L. Lomperis and S. Stanbury (eds), *Feminist Approaches to the Body in Medieval Literature* (1993), pp. 78–9.

kind of sense of the story of salvation. Sometimes it is a woman who is obtuse, like Noah's wife; sometimes it is a man, like Joseph. The foibles of both are exposed; at the same time their concerns are not simply ludicrous. Above all, they speak. Silent characters – mostly women – of Old and New Testaments are now heard and elicit sympathy. Sarah, mother of Isaac taken off to be sacrificed by his father Abraham, is wordless in *Genesis*; in contrast, in five of the six English renderings of this episode Sarah has a part to play. The Digby play of *The Massacre of the Innocents* features a large cast of women who both speak and act. The figure of fun here is Watkyn, Herod's messenger, sent to kill their children, who swears he will be brave but dreads 'nothing more than a woman with her spindle' and ends up having to be rescued from the women's furious onslaughts. This is a play which, according to Gail Gibson, needs to be understood not only in relation to the Feast of the Innocents of 7 January but also to the celebration on the same date of St Distaff's Day, which marked the return to work of women after their Christmas holiday. It was a day of carnival, an occasion for 'misrule', for 'comic battles between the sexes' in which men set fire to women's flax and women made sure men got soaked.[5] The linking here of biblical history with contemporary experience is a leitmotif of late medieval piety. The Bible was not a collection of tales of long ago, but of constant recurrences. The gap between 'then' and 'now' could always be bridged.

Evidence of female participation in these plays is nevertheless small, limited to dances and processions, minor interludes, however spectacular. The parts of female characters, even of Mary or of her mother Anne, were played by young men. Customarily this has been taken as further evidence of the exclusion of women from public roles; and so it may be, though recent suggestions that we must also take into account the subversive potential of these cross-dressed men, as illustrative of the instability of gender roles, need to be considered. Of special relevance here is the part played – or not played – by women in religious drama in relation to their roles in liturgy. The notion that women, debarred by their sex from priestly functions and by their education from the language of the liturgy, could therefore take part only as spectators, has been

[5] G. Mc. Gibson, *The Theater of Devotion* (1989), pp. 42–3.

finally laid to rest by Eamon Duffy in *The Stripping of the Altars*. By way of example, it is worth looking at one particular drama described by Duffy. This is the case of the quarrelsome John Sharp, a merchant who owed rent to his local church for a shop he leased. When peace was made at last between Sharp and the church, this was publicised through Sharp's wife, Elizabeth, in a gesture of high theatre. The Sunday after the reconciliation it was Elizabeth's turn to provide the holy loaf for Mass. This in itself was a function of considerable importance, shared it would seem by men and women alike. Such bread was a vital commodity, to be baked even in times of famine. Blessed and distributed after communion, it was meant to be the first food of the day; in cases of emergency it could be given to dying persons instead of the Host. On the day in question, having presented her loaf Elizabeth Sharp called a meeting of parson and parishioners to tell them that she wished to celebrate the ending of the quarrel by making a present of an embroidered towel to be used as a napkin during the distribution of Easter communion. When she died the towel would go to the church; until then it must be fetched from her house each year. The resolution of a quarrel of purely secular origin was thus to be commemorated by a gesture which would recall, at the highpoint of the Church's year, the generosity and magnanimity of Elizabeth Sharp.

The confidence of Elizabeth Sharp is striking; her piety, none the less, eludes us. Was it, one might wonder, any greater than that of her husband John? Is it justifiable, in any case, to single out the piety of lay women for separate treatment? And can it be done? One approach to the problem might be to consider whether the spiritual experiences of Margery Kempe, as told in her autobiography, *The Book of Margery Kempe*, are representative of late medieval piety, or only of women's piety, or whether they are too idiosyncratic to be either.

Margery Kempe (born c.1373) in her day played many roles, as we have seen. Daughter of the local mayor, a brewer, wife of a burgess, mother of fourteen children, she was also pilgrim, journeying to Jerusalem and to Rome, mystic and vowess. In her relations with Christ she sees herself as daughter, mother, bride and sister. After her 'call' she starts to experience uncontrollable fits of weeping. The extravagant nature of her piety as she herself presents it, manifested through these noisy outbursts of tears, in turn infuriate, impress and perplex everyone she meets. Who was she? Was she 'truly good or truly wicked'? Crowds flock to hear her; others clamour to have her silenced. Illiterate, her story, ghost-written by priests, is an astonishing amalgam of daily experience and literary allusions. It is a work as full of earthiness as it is of heavenly vision. Scenes change with startling rapidity. Margery is as much at home searching out swaddling clothes for the Virgin as she is journeying along country roads with her husband, beer and cake.

Margery goes out of her way to tell us, on more than one occasion, which books she knows. For seven or eight years, she tells us, a certain priest read to her 'many a book of high contemplation, such as the Bible with doctors' commentaries on it, St Bride's book, Hilton's book, Bonaventura's *Stimulus Amoris (The Prick of Love), Incendium Amoris (The Fire of Love)* and others similar' (ch. 58). (The inaccurate attribution here of Richard Rolle's work, *The Fire of Love*, to Bonaventura, was at the time common.) The *Life* of the beguine Mary of Oignies was also known to her; likewise the *Revelations* of Elizabeth of Hungary. The list gives an interesting insight into the circulation of works newly available in Middle English which could, and did, provide Margery with inspiration. Mary of Oignies, St Bride (Bridget) and Elizabeth were, like Margery, all married women. Of these role models it is perhaps Bridget who most influenced Margery. Margery's friend the Carmelite friar Alan of Lynn was a fervent admirer of Bridget's work and the compiler of an index of her revelations. Margery herself literally walks in Bridget's footsteps, travelling like her both to the Holy Land and to the shrine of St James of Compostella in Spain; on pilgrimage to Rome in 1414 she makes a point of following up Brigittine links. She speaks to those who had known Bridget, she visits the spot where she had died, she emulates, promotes and competes with Bridget. Christ tells her, 'every word that is written in St Bridget's book is true and through you shall be recognised as truth indeed.' At the same time when, at Mass, she receives a vision of the sacrament at the moment of consecration 'fluttering to and fro just as a dove flutters her wings', she is assured by Christ, 'My daughter Bridget never saw me in this way' (ch. 20).

Female mystics both inspire and validate Margery's own visions and her tears. The priest who becomes in time her amanuensis is convinced of the authenticity of her feelings by his own reading of just those works which Margery claims had been read to her. Through this he comes to understand that Margery's weeping is a mark of grace, not an embarrassing affliction, a gift he would like to share. But it would be a mistake to imagine that the context of Margery's sobbing is entirely bookish; on the contrary, she cries so much and so often precisely because it is everyday sights and sounds that release her tears. However extreme Margery's behaviour, the appeal of her piety lies, paradoxically, in its very ordinariness. Because she has 'so much feeling for the manhood of Christ', tears well up at the mere sight of baby boys and handsome young men; devotional practices shared with friends cause her to cry. What marks Margery out is not the practice of this piety but the intensity of her response. Accompanying her on pilgrimage, for example, was a woman who carried around with her 'a chest containing an image of Our Lord ... [and] when they came into fine cities the women took the image out of her chest and set it on the laps of respectable wives. And they would dress it up in shirts and kiss it as though it had been God himself.' Margery would then begin to weep with 'great sobbing and loud crying' (ch. 30). At home, it is the ceremonies and feasts of the Church which cause her to cry – Corpus Christi processions, Candlemas celebrations, the liturgy of Easter – the sense they engender in her that she is an actual witness of the events commemorated. The sight of a *Pieta* during a chance visit with an acquaintance to a nearby church fills her with such compassion for Our Lady that 'she wept so bitterly as though she would have died'. The priest of the church comes to tell her, 'Woman, Jesus is long since dead.' She replies: 'Sir, his death is as fresh to me as if he had died this same day, and so I think it ought to be to you and to all Christian people.' Her companion is duly impressed and invites her back home for a meal (ch. 60).

Margery has friends and enemies in equal numbers. Bitter as the accounts of those who try to silence her are, it would be as well not to imagine her as a marginal figure or a social outcast. Rather, allowance must be made for Margery's need to experience persecution as a form of martyrdom. It was, she explained, 'a joyous thing to be reproved for God's love' (ch. 14). When she went to visit Julian of Norwich, Julian told her, she says, not to fear the talk of the world 'for the more contempt, shame and reproof that you have in this world, the more is your merit in the sight of God' (ch. 18). There are clear echoes here of Luke 6: 22: 'Happy are you when people hate you, drive you out, abuse you.' This is not to suggest that all Margery's talk of persecution is fantastical; or, indeed, without some cause. It is difficult not to feel some sympathy for the friar who found her tears so vexing an interruption to his sermons that he banned her from attending them. The suspicion that she might be a Lollard (see below, p. 238), and the angry accusations these give rise to, are equally understandable when we remember that the first Lollard to be burnt, in 1401, came from Margery's own parish church of St Margaret's in Lynn.

However, it is just as important to notice how many allies Margery found among both people and clergy: the Archbishop of Canterbury gives her the rare privilege of choosing her own confessor and the right to take communion every Sunday (as a general rule the laity communicated only at Easter); the confessor she then chooses, vicar of St Stephen's church in Norwich, 'always took her side' (ch. 17); the Bishop of Lincoln gives her 26s 8d to buy her vowess's mantle and ring. Time and again her prayers are sought for the dying. In 1438, when *The Book of Margery Kempe* was still in the throes of composition, Margery was elected to the Guild of the Holy Trinity, the highly influential body which effectively controlled all the municipal and mercantile business of her native town of Lynn. Later, the *Book* found favour with the Carthusian monks of the house of Mount Grace in Yorkshire. The annotations four of the monks made to their copy suggest that they found nothing untoward in her weepings or her visions, except for her claim to have made Mary some hot broth to comfort her after the crucifixion: a passage they chose to cross out. The sexual language with which Margery expressed her relationship to Christ - 'when you are in bed,' he tells her, 'you may take me as your wedded husband . . . take me boldly in the arms of your soul' – had too long a pedigree to be troubling. The prior of Mount Grace, Richard Methley, was thought to be a kindred spirit.

What is striking about Margery is, in fact, not so much the affectivity of her piety as the model she puts forward of 'a mixed life' of action and contemplation, the very model advocated for the laity of the fifteenth century, notably by Nicholas Love, prior of Mount Grace from 1410–17, in his *Mirror of the Life of Jesus Christ*. For Margery does much more than weep: she gives away all her money in alms; she visits the sick; during her time in Rome she spends six weeks living in considerable squalor ('full of vermin') looking after an old woman, serving her 'as she would have done Our Lady' (ch. 34). At home, she seeks and gets a legal separation from John, her husband, but she still cares for him in his last illness. He becomes incontinent; he causes Margery work and expense – 'in washing and wringing ... and keeping the fire going', all of which hinders her 'a great deal from contemplation'. But it is a task she has to do because of Christ's instructions:

You shall have as much reward for looking after him and helping him in his need at home, as if you were in church to say your prayers. And you have said many times that you would gladly look after me. I pray you now look after him for love of me, for he has sometime fulfilled both your will and my will and he has made your body freely available to me, so that you should serve me and live chaste and clean and therefore I wish you to be available to help him in his need and in my name. (ch. 76)

Family life is not something normally associated with Margery; we hear next to nothing of her fourteen children, and she tends to see her husband as a problem in her life rather than as a companion. All the more reason, then, to be struck, by the care for him enjoined on her by Christ. Married though she be to Christ, she still has obligations towards her earthly husband that she must not shirk. To be a good Christian she must also be a good wife to John.

The respect accorded to family life in late medieval piety is most forcibly brought home to us by the increased veneration shown, in England, for the mother of the Virgin, St Anne. Since 1382, as part of the celebrations of the marriage of Richard II and Anne of Bohemia, her feast-day had become part of the English calendar. Chapels and altars came to be dedicated to her, poems and plays were written in her honour. She is provided with an elaborate, even exotic genealogy, with parents called Izakar and Nazaphat, as well as three husbands by whom she has two more daughters who between them give birth to six of the Apostles. Her *Life*, written by the Suffolk friar Osbern Bokenham (b. 1393) for his patrons John and Katherine Denstone – who themselves have a child called Anne and hope now for a son – is a tale adapted from the *Golden Legend* of the shame and despair of Anne's first husband, Joachim, at the barrenness of their marriage. He 'waters his apple-tree daily and nothing grows.' The conception and birth of Mary cheers Anne and Joachim, hitherto a despised couple, quite as much as it heralds a new age for mankind: 'Not only from shameful barrenness has God delivered me,' says Anne, 'but also his people who were in distress he has visited so mercifully that through my fruit – thank the Lord – not I alone but all mankind shall find eternal comfort.'[6]

Bokenham's *Life* of Anne is only one in the series of thirteen saints' *Lives* that make up his *Legend of Holy Women*, a work which has been acclaimed as 'the first all-female hagiography in any language'.[7] Sheila Delany's recent suggestion is that the selection is the religious counterpart to Chaucer's *Legend of Good Women*.[8] This may be so, but it is also worth pointing to Duffy's observation that out of the saints whom Bokenham chose to write about, all except Lucy were already familiar from the rood screens of his native county.[9] This does not, of course, vitiate Delany's thesis; but it does draw attention to the high profile which women saints already enjoyed even before Bokenham gave further advertisement to their virtues. These saints, often positioned on north screens, faced that part of the church where women customarily sat though this identification in no way precluded the availability of their merits to men. Two of Bokenham's *Lives* were commissioned by women – those of Mary Magdalene and Elizabeth of Hungary (the saint who had inspired Margery Kempe). A third, the *Life* of St Margaret, patron saint though she was of childbirth, was written for a man friend of Bokenham's and in thanksgiving for a miracle worked by a ring with which Bokenham had touched a local relic of Margaret's foot.

Female piety in late medieval England, as promoted by Bokenham, or indeed as exemplified by Margery Kempe, in no way represented some kind of sub-culture. In so far as women held no office in the church, the extent of their influence could prove an embarrassment to the clergy, as the hostility of a number of priests towards Margery Kempe amply

---

[6] Osbern Bokenham, *A Legend of Holy Women*, trans. S. Delany (1992), pp. 40–1.
[7] *Ibid.*, p. xxvii.
[8] *Ibid.*, pp. xxi–xxvi.
[9] E. Duffy, 'Women Saints in Fifteenth and Sixteenth Century England', in W. J. Sheils and D. Wood (eds), *Women in the Church*, Studies in Church History 27 (1990), p. 185.

shows, but this was not felt at large by the body of the faithful, clerical or lay. Late medieval wills give evidence of a religious culture shared by both men and women. The Suffolk merchant John Baret (d. 1467) left elaborate instructions that bear witness to his Marian devotions and to his friendship with a certain Dame Margaret Spurdaunce (or Purdan). She is to receive from him a rosary and crucifix by way of remembrance of 'an old love, virtuously set at all times to the pleasure of God'. His funeral Mass is to be attended by 'five men clad in black in worship of Jesus' five wounds and five women clad in white in worship of Our Lady's five joys, each of them holding a torch of clean wax'.[10]

Margaret Spurdaunce was a widow; in her own will of 1481 she remembers local hermits and anchoresses and arranges for the disposal of her books. She leaves an English Psalter to a priest, her 'small Psalter' goes to her son. The Benedictine nuns of Thetford receive her 'English book of St Bridget', one Alice Barly is bequeathed 'a book called Hilton'. The works of St Bridget and of Hilton were, as we have seen, both formative for Margery Kempe and her circle. Their appeal, moreover, cut across all social barriers; they have long held a place in the historiography of the piety of the aristocracy of late medieval England due to their use in the devotions of Cicely, Duchess of York (1415–95). Eamon Duffy's warning against too exclusive a focus on the piety of such as Cicely, 'leisured aristocratic ladies',[11] is not intended as a licence to ignore it, all the more so because it was a piety that transcended class. The description of Cicely's day is therefore worth repeating:

She is accustomed to rise at seven o'clock and has ready her chaplain to say with her matins of the day, and matins of Our Lady; and when she is fully ready she has a low mass in her chamber, and after mass she takes something to recreate nature; and so goes to her chapel, hearing the divine service and two low masses; thence to dinner, during the time thereof she has a reading of holy matter, either Hilton of contemplative and active life, Bonaventura, *On the Infancy* [of the Saviour], *The Golden Legend*, St Matilda, St Katharine of Sienna or *The Revelations of St Bridget*.

After dinner, she gives audience to all such as has any matter to show to her by the space of one hour; and then she sleeps one quarter of an hour, and after she has slept she continues in prayer to the first peal of

[10] G. Mc. Gibson, *The Theater of Devotion* (1989), pp. 78–9.
[11] E. Duffy, *The Stripping of the Altars*, p. 2.

232

evensong; then she drinks wine or ale at her pleasure. Forthwith, her chaplain is ready to say with her both evensongs; and after the last peal she goes to the chapel and hears evensong by note; from thence to supper, and in the time of supper she recites the reading that was had at dinner to those that be in her presence.

After supper she disposes herself to be familiar with her gentlewomen, to the following of honest mirth; and one hour before going to her bed, she takes a cup of wine, and after that goes to her private closet, and takes her leave of God for all the night, making end of her prayers for that day; and by eight o'clock she is in bed.[12]

Cicely's routine, as has often been observed, gives an indication of how little the lay and monastic life styles differed from each other, all the more so because of the fifteenth-century tendency for convents to fragment into separate households. Many communities of nuns no longer ate together; convent buildings came to look more and more, according to Roberta Gilchrist, like the houses of the gentry. This is not necessarily to suggest 'decline': the new books of devotion to which Cicely was so attached were as avidly read within the cloister as without, though perhaps nowhere so keenly – apart from the Carthusian house of Mount Grace – as in the one convent founded for women in the fifteenth century, Syon, where indeed Cicely's own daughter, Anne, became prioress and which inherited all her books.

Even before the arrival of printing in the 1470s, women's piety in the fifteenth century was, then, bookish in unaccustomed ways. More women owned books; more of these books had women authors. Half of Cicely's reading list was by, or about, women mystics. Apart from Bridget there is Matilda, more commonly known now as Mechtild of Hackerborn, the thirteenth-century Cistercian nun whose visions were recorded in *The Book of Special Grace* which became available in English in the first half of the fifteenth century. 'St Katherine' is likely to refer to the *Life* of Catherine of Siena (1347?–80) by her Dominican confessor, Raymond of Capua, a work chosen for printing by Wynkyn de Worde as early as 1493.

It is not perhaps too fanciful to imagine that a reflection of the confidence women gained from the high value placed on

---

[12] *English Historical Documents*, vol. 4, ed. A. R. Myers (1969), p. 837; emended following C. A. J. Armstrong, *England, France and Burgundy in the Fifteenth Century* (1983), p. 141, n. 13.

their words and experiences can be glimpsed in the tomb in which Isabella, Countess of Warwick, hoped to be buried. Isabella, a friend and patron of the English devotional poet John Lydgate, planned an effigy centred on her relationship with Mary Magdalene. Mary Magdalene, identified in the Middle Ages as the repentant prostitute of the Gospels, the contemplative sister of Martha and the first witness of the Resurrection, provided a role model of dramatic potential which Isabella seized upon with particular aplomb. According to her will of 1439, money was to be left to the monks of Tewkesbury to silence any complaints they might have about her wishes, which were as follows:

And my Image to be made all naked, and no thyng on my hede byt myn here cast bakwardys ... and at my hede Mary Mawdelen leyng my handes a-cross, and seynt Iohn the Evangelyst on the ryght syde of my hede; and on the left side, Seynt Anton, and at my fete a Skochen of myn Armes departyd with my lordys, and ii Greffons to bere hit vppe; And all a-bowt my tumbe, to be made pore men a[n]d wemen In theire pore Array, with their bedys In theire handes.[13]

The theatricality of Isabella's projected tomb, of Margery Kempe's ecstatic tears, the unremitting devotionalism of Cicely's day suggest a heightened form of piety confined in earlier centuries to the cloister or the anchor-hold. The contrast has been drawn, and rightly, between earlier patterns of female lay piety, centred around formal observances with the 'personal, meditative prayer life' now advocated. But in making such a judgement it is important not to suggest that these earlier observances were either jejune or perfunctorily performed, or indeed to minimise the part played in them by the appropriate books – in this case by Books of Hours.

Books of Hours have been described as being 'books for everybody' – as indeed they became, particularly after the advent of printing. The first copies we know of were de luxe editions, however, and all of them were made for women. The earliest dates from c.1240 and was the work of the Oxford illuminator, William de Brailes. His patron, according to Claire Donovan, was a woman of whom we know little beyond the fact that she was probably called Susanna, that she lived in Oxford in the parish of St Laurence, and was a friend of the newly arrived Dominicans.[14] Susanna is depicted four times in her book, recognisable by her pink robe, red cloak, white hat and flowing hair, a sign of her status as an unmarried woman. In each of the pictures Susanna is at prayer.

Books of Hours were made up of extracts from the Psalter, long used in the devotions of the laity, and the breviary, a clerical book. Such books can be seen therefore as paving the way to that fusing of lay and monastic traditions which we have met already in the household of Cicely. They provided for a routine of prayer following the monastic services of Matins, Laud, Prime, Terce, Sext, None, Vespers and Compline that commemorated Christ's Passion, from the hour of his betrayal in the garden of Gethsemane to his crucifixion. The corresponding Hours of the Virgin, a new addition in the thirteenth century, recalled the life of the Virgin from the time of the Annunciation to her assumption into heaven. In Susanna's book it is these Hours of the Virgin that have pride of place, opening the book and accompanied by lavish illustrations. The main text is in Latin but captions in French provide hints on how the scenes are to be interpreted. At appropriate junctures, prayers of particular relevance to Susanna are included: for example, to the Dominicans, three of whom are mentioned by name, and to saints of Oxford churches – St Laurence and St Frideswide. A sequence of prayers in French adds what would now be regarded as a further customised touch to this book, a recognition of Susanna's need to make personal prayers in the vernacular. There is also the addition at Prime of a meditation on the Passion; at the time of the making of Susanna's book this was a relatively new rite, though by the end of the century it had become widely adopted among the laity.

Despite its formally liturgical nature, Susanna's book was both a new and adventurous devotional aid and a highly personal possession. It is a small book, measuring about 7 × 6 inches, the size therefore of a modern paperback and easily portable. We do not know whether Susanna's meditations were marked by the affectivity already considered appropriate for her contemporaries, those sisters of the *Ancrene Riwle* – who were also expected to recite the Hours of the Virgin – but it is worth pointing out that the design of the daily routine is

[14] C. Donovan, *The de Brailes Hours* (1991).

such as to encourage precisely that sense of the recurrence of Christ's Nativity, death and Passion found later in such moments as Margery Kempe's outburst on Christ's death – 'his death is as fresh to me as if he had died on this same day'. Time, in Books of Hours, is cyclical, and God is ever present; in the Egerton Hours, made also for a woman, the Holy Spirit casts a watchful eye as her pillows are straightened out before she goes to bed.

In Susanna's book, William de Brailes paints himself being snatched at the last moment from the jaws of hell by an angel bearing a scroll which explains his deliverance: he has been 'saved by virtue of his art'. Faith needed substantiation by good deeds; these amounted, often enough, to the financing of the prayers of others, a form of vicarious piety which enabled women to contribute not only towards the salvation of their own souls and the souls of the nearest and dearest, but also to a whole range of clerical enterprises in which they might otherwise have had no active part. The arrival and prosperity of the friars, in the thirteenth-century England, for example, was facilitated in no small measure by the support and generosity of female patrons. Equally, the future of the Oxford Dominicans, to whom Susanna was so attached, was secured in the 1230s and 1240s by the gifts of Isabel de Bolbec, Countess of Oxford, whom the Dominicans came to consider as their founder and whom they commemorated as such in their liturgy. Several Oxford and Cambridge colleges likewise owed their existence to the desires of women to secure adequate prayer provision for their kin. Balliol College, Oxford, owed its future to the fidelity with which Devorguilla of Galloway sought to ensure that the penance imposed on her husband John Balliol some years before his death was fully observed. Thanks to her efforts, Balliol College was given permanent endowments in return for three requiem Masses a year for Devorguilla and her family.

Oxford colleges were not within the means of every woman. Spiritual coats to keep out the devil had to be cut according to their owner's cloth. On the whole these were unisex garments: husbands and wives alike founded charities for each others' souls, provided candles for shrines, undertook pilgrimages. There is, however, some indication that women may have been expected to be, and perhaps in fact were, the more charitable sex. The obligation to fulfil the works of mercy laid upon every

Christian in Matthew 25 may in practice have fallen more heavily on women than men. In his month-mind sermon for her, Bishop Fisher presented Margaret Beaufort, mother of Henry VII, as a paragon in this respect – as indeed in others – a woman whose hands were ever busy in 'giving alms to the poor and needy, and dressing them also when they were sick, and ministering unto them meat and drink'.[15] It is clear from what we know of Margaret's activities that this eulogy was justified; but it is also clear that we must not attribute such exemplary characteristics only to the aristocracy. In an early-thirteenth-century vision story, a Sussex peasant by the name of Thurkill, approached by a saint in disguise seeking for shelter, is chivvied into offering help only after the saint has told him that his wife has already given hospitality to two poor women. P. H. Cullum's recent work on Yorkshire wills suggests that 'women were more likely to give charitably than men' and that the Sussex peasant was not just a hagiographical invention. In the 1388 will of the Yorkshire woman Cecily Giry, for example, the three feather beds and the bedclothes in her guestroom were to remain there for use of the poor.[16] Such deathbed piety can be matched by the activities of the living. In recent work on conviviality and charity Judith Bennett has shown how fifteenth-century women fund-raisers of St Mary-at-Hill, London, collected two to three times the amount raised by men. She suggests we consider a reciprocity between the 'desperate need' of many women to receive charity and the manifest willingness of others to provide it.[17]

The virtues of charity were, of course, also extolled by the Lollards - it being much better in their eyes to spend money on the poor than on pilgrimages – and it is to the problem of Lollardy and its connection with women that we should now turn. Lollardy, the first outbreak of heresy in the late fourteenth century in a country until then free of such problems, traumatised the English ecclesiastical establishment and led to a witch hunt which has made it extraordinarily difficult for

[15] Cited in M. Jones and M. Underwood, *The King's Mother: Lady Margaret Beaufort, Countess of Richmond and Derby* (1992), p. 179.
[16] P. H. Cullum, ' "And Hir Name was Charite": Charitable Giving by and for Women in Late Medieval Yorkshire', in P. J. P. Goldberg (ed.), *Woman is a Worthy Wight*, pp. 182–211.
[17] J. Bennett, 'Conviviality and Charity in Medieval and Early Modern England', *Past and Present* 134 (1992), pp. 19–41.

historians to sort out Lollard goats from orthodox sheep. Supposed Lollards, rounded up for questioning, themselves never offered any definition of their faith, except by way of response to their inquisitors. The role of women in supporting and disseminating the heresy may have been exaggerated – the association of women with heretical movements, whether in England or on the Continent, used as a rhetorical ploy designed to discredit heresy by appealing to misogynistic instincts – but all the same it was not merely chimerical. Women were Lollards, gave instruction in Lollard teachings, and in Lollard theology held a place equal to men. Walter Brut, arrested in 1391, claimed at his trial two years later that 'women have power and authority to preach and make the body of Christ, and they have the power of the keys of the church, of binding and loosing'.[18] This was a claim which, even in the absence of any evidence of women actually officiating, caused considerable anxiety and nervousness on the part of the authorities. Some thirty years later Lollards, both men and women, were again preaching the same message. 'Every faithful man and every faithful woman is a good priest and has as good power to make the body of Christ as any ordained priest': so said Sybil Godsell, disciple of the Lollard leader William White. Sybil was sentenced for her beliefs to seven years' imprisonment. White himself was sent to the stake, at Norwich, in 1428.

Against this background of Norwich heresy it can hardly come as a surprise that East Anglian Margery Kempe was called upon to defend herself against the charge of being a Lollard on at least four separate occasions – at Leicester, York, Bristol and Hull. Although Margery was able each time to prove her orthodoxy, her insistence on her right to 'speak of God' seemed to the authorities to be a stance uncomfortably close to that advocated by Brut and White. In fact, in the context of late medieval piety Margery should be hailed as a successful pupil rather than a threatening dissident. Her devotions and her lifestyle follow so closely the ideal of the 'mixed life' proposed for the laity by Nicholas Love and by Hilton that her notion of herself as 'a mirror ... so that [all] men] should take example from you to have some little sorrow in their hearts for their sins, so that they might through that

---

[18] Cited in M. Aston, *Lollards and Reformers* (1984), p. 52.

be saved' (ch. 78) comes to seem no more than due recognition for lessons carefully learned, internalised and lived. If Margery, none the less, was not the role model every woman wanted to follow, there were plenty of others to choose from the rich selection that was on offer in late medieval England.

CHAPTER TWELVE

Literary Interests and Images

Aristocratic women were expected and encouraged to be connoisseurs and patrons of the arts. The generosity such women lavished on the writers, musicians and artists of their courts redounded to the credit of their houses and to the honour of every man and woman associated with them. It was not that such patronage was exclusively a woman's prerogative – far from it – but whereas their menfolk could be excused if they neglected to do their bit, for a woman to show a comparable lack of concern or largesse would have been to demonstrate a shocking lack of decorum and finesse. Thus, however great the renown of William the Conqueror, his daughter, Adela, Countess of Blois, could with impunity put him in the shade. This was the 'one way daughter excels her father – she will favour verses and she knows how to have leisure for books. She also knows how to reward poets: no-one returns empty-handed from her uprightness . . . she possesses copious powers of composition, and she knows how to distinguish one poem from another.'

This is how Baudri, Bishop of Dol, eulogises his patron, Adela. Adela in Baudri's imagination, sits in her bedchamber, reading his poems; the walls are hung with tapestries that placed her father's victory at Hastings in 1066 and his conquest of England into a context of biblical and classical history, but these are only one part of the decor. On Adela's bed are carved the signs of philosophy and the seven liberal arts; signs of the zodiac and the planets are painted on the ceiling; the whole world, in the shape of a map made in marble is set into the floor at her feet. Adela herself, as ethereal as the new moon, is depicted as being the source of Baudri's inspiration and poetic confidence:

I speak on a mighty topic indeed, but I have known how to speak on a mighty topic since the time when I took my material from the countess. You yourself suggest to me my poem, you yourself furnish me with my pen, you yourself will give me inspiration, you yourself will fill my gaping mouth.

As Adela sits in her bedchamber while Baudri 'sweats' out poems for her, an elaborate game of patronage is played out. On the one hand, Baudri has no hesitation in asking for a lavish cope in reward for spreading her fame ('Don't forget the fringe' is his passing shot); on the other, Adela herself has interests beyond flattery: her patronage extends to works of history – Hugh of Fleury's chronicle is dedicated to her – and her influence goes far beyond the confines of her bedchamber. Adela was a believer in fine deeds as well as words: her husband, Stephen, deserted the First Crusade during the siege of Antioch in 1098 to return home; Adela would have none of it and sent him back to the fray (and in fact to his death in battle in 1101).

Adela's bedchamber has many fictional analogues; a woman's bedchamber functioned both as literary salon and literary topos. The lady of the house entertained herself here with her woman friends, but it was not an exclusively feminine world. It was also the place where women could choose to be on show to their men friends in a setting which was itself a display of their patronage and good taste. The narrator of the love story, the *Conte de Floire et Blancheflor*, describes how, one afternoon, the count visited a chamber 'to amuse [himself] with the damsels, of which there were beauties in the room. In the room there was a bed which was adorned with a spread. The spread was beautiful and costly, no better ever came from Thessaly. It was worked in flowers of blue silken bands and borders.' In *The Romance of Horn* the chamber of a princess is described; it has a ceiling 'carved by the art of a sculptor into a beautifully-made vault'; the floor beneath 'was completely strewn with flowers – yellow, blue, red, releasing a cloud of perfume'. It was there that the princes of the court and their followers went for entertainment, to 'drink wine, spiced and unspiced ... play chess and listen to the harp.'

How women are represented in such tales will be considered

below. The point to be made here is that the site of the telling of such tales is not a private world; nor are the tales themselves concerned as much with the experience of individuals as they are an expression of shared values. The attributes and interests which a woman might cultivate in her bedchamber were not a form of escapism; they complemented the activities of fathers, brothers, husbands and lovers. A woman's fostering of poets and artists was a way of advertising the nobility of her lineage. The new Queen Matilda, wife of King Henry I (1100–1135), is described as having fulfilled her role as patron with notable *éclat*:

She dwelt at Westminster for many years. She lacked nothing of regal magnificence ... She took a unique pleasure in hearing the service of God, and thus she provided unsparingly for clerics with melodious voices, all of whom she spoke courteously to, bestowed many gifts on, and promised more. With her liberality thus planted throughout the world, scholars celebrated not only for their songs but also for their verses came hither in throngs; and he who could soothe the ears of his lady by the newness of his song thought himself a happy man. She lavished money not only on these, but also on all kinds of men, especially strangers; and they, having received her gifts, proclaimed her fame far and wide throughout the lands.[1]

So wrote the contemporary historian William of Malmesbury; behind the praise lay, it must be said, William's anxieties about the cost of Matilda's generosity, a suspicion that the 'strangers' were getting more than their fair share, but in the new Norman England Matilda's role as queen had a special edge to it. She was, we must remember, of Anglo-Saxon birth, descended through her mother Margaret, queen of Malcolm of Scotland, from the royal house of Wessex. Matilda's marriage to Henry was both sign and promise of reconciliation between the vanquished and their conquerors. She had, therefore, divided responsibilities; even though the consort of a Norman king, Matilda had still to transmit and preserve her native inheritance. Her consciousness of her ancestry is reflected through her patronage: she commissioned William of Malmesbury, himself of mixed parentage, to write his *Deeds of the Kings of the English* while the monks of Malmesbury made for her a genealogical table of her ancestry. (It

[1] For the citations from Baudri of Dol and William of Malmesbury, see E. Salter, *English and International*, in D. Pearsall and N. Zeeman (eds), *Studies in the Literature, Art and Patronage of Medieval England* (1988), pp. 12–14.

may be noted that William was careful not to criticise his patron in her lifetime; his reservations about how much Matilda spent appeared only after her death.)

As Lois Huneycutt has recently argued, the *Life* of her mother, Margaret of Scotland, seems also to have been written at Matilda's behest, explicitly to provide her with guidelines for her task. According to the *Life*, reminiscences were not enough; Matilda wanted a biography: 'you desire not only to hear of the queen your mother . . . but also to have it constantly before you in writing: so that although you knew but little your mother's face, you may have more fully the knowledge of her virtues.' In this *Life* Margaret is represented as the civilising force at an otherwise barbarian and 'foreign' Scottish court. Margaret is both pious and learned while Malcolm, fond husband as he is, is the illiterate and grateful beneficiary of the superior culture introduced to his court by his wife. Palace and church are enriched with beautiful treasures – Margaret's room becomes 'a kind of workshop . . . of celestial art', an atelier where beautiful embroideries are made for churches; the country becomes richer, grander, holier; king and people are introduced to 'a better way of life'.[2]

To press analogies between Margaret and Malcolm and Matilda and Henry too far would be absurd; but it is not beyond the bounds of possibility that aspersions on Scottish barbarism were meant to allude to the philistinism of the Normans. As erstwhile Vikings, settlers in France only since the tenth century, the Normans had reason to be touchy about such charges; their claims in 1066 to be the rightful heirs and rulers of the most ancient kingdom of Western Europe needed not only the underpinning of military victory but also cultural validation. This was a programme that came to be developed on two fronts. On the one hand, the Normans aimed to appropriate the Anglo-Saxon past – rewriting its history, rehousing its saints in newly built cathedrals; on the other, as we have seen, they tried to supplant Anglo-Saxon literary culture with a written vernacular of their own: Old French. Recent work emphasises how negligible is the evidence of early French literature in France whereas in England it developed apace as a way of creating cultural bonds among the conquerors in a

---

[2] L. Huneycutt, 'The Idea of the Perfect Princess: The Life of St Margaret in the Reign of Matilda II, 1100–1118', *Anglo-Norman Studies* 12 (1989), pp. 81–97.

land that already had a venerable and particularly rich tradition of vernacular learning and lore.[3] Just as the Saxon invaders of the fifth and sixth centuries had adopted a new religion to give cohesion and legitimacy to the kingdoms they hoped to establish, so now for similar reasons the Normans put their faith in a new literature. Before long, Anglo-Norman, a distinctive dialect of this new vernacular, emerged in England alongside Old French; for the purposes of what follows, however, 'French' covers all works known to have been composed, copied or read in England, whether in Anglo-Norman dialect or in Old French.

A fashion for French literature was set by the court of Henry I and Matilda. *The Voyage of St Brendan*, a fantastical adventure story of the travels of a holy man, was translated on the orders of Matilda from Latin into French, possibly as early as 1106. The same work was re-dedicated after Matilda's death to Henry's new queen, Adela of Louvain. Adela was patron also of Philip de Thaon who, at her request, turned a Latin bestiary into French rhyming couplets. What makes such patronage particularly interesting is that it is unlikely that Adela (a Flemish princess) was a native French speaker and certain that the Anglo-Saxon Matilda was not, confirmation that it was cultural needs rather than preference for a known tongue that lay behind the writing of French.

The impetus given to the production of French works through the patronage of the royal court was crucial; at the same time the influence of provincial courts up and down the country must not be overlooked. Here, too, French literary culture found favour. Among the entourage of noblewomen were chaplains and clerks whose tasks could extend far beyond the strictly ecclesiastical; in any household they might be called upon to fill the role of tutor, musician or even composer. In the mid-twelfth century Alice de Condet, 'a beautiful and learned lady', mistress of Thorngate Castle near Lincoln, asked the clerk and poet Sanson de Nantuil – he was probably her chaplain – to put the *Proverbs of Solomon* into French verse for her. A yet more renowned patron is Alice's Lincolnshire neighbour, Constance FitzGilbert; it was for Constance that the clerk Gaimar wrote his *History of the English* and but for

---

[3] I. Short, 'Patrons and Polyglots: French Literature in Twelfth-Century England', *Anglo-Norman Studies* 14 (1991), pp. 231–49.

her help – or so Gaimar assures us – the work would never have been completed.

Gaimar's was a romance history composed in verse in French. The first half is lost but we know from his acknow-ledgements that he made considerable use of Geoffrey of Mon-mouth's celebrated *History of the Kings of Britain*. Geoffrey's *History*, through its retelling of the story of King Arthur and of Merlin, had succeeded both in establishing fictional continuity between Celtic Britain and its new rulers and in securing for England a European cultural classic; as a Latin work it was a rich quarry for vernacular renderings, such as Gaimar's. Gaimar, however, takes his story of England further than Geof-frey's, up to the death of King William Rufus (d. 1100). There he stops because, or so he tells us, the reign of Henry I which followed had already been covered by a certain David, writing under the patronage of Henry's wife, Adela. This work, now lost, had apparently been set to music by David; Constance herself had a copy – it had cost her a silver mark – and she read it often, though Gaimar himself considered it a bit on the dull side; a few jokes and some love interest would, he intimated, have livened it up.

The dazzling splendours of the court of Henry II and Eleanor of Aquitaine during the next decades have over-shadowed the achievements of earlier patrons such as Con-stance, but there is continuity here through the glamorous new styles introduced from Eleanor's homelands of southern France. Eleanor is famed as a patron of the latest artistic fashions, queen of the ethic of 'courtly love', and of troubadour poetry; like Constance, she was also the recipient of a French vernacular history, complete with Arthurian heroes, based on Geoffrey of Monmouth's rendition. This was the *Roman de Brut*, written by a clerk named Wace and dedicated to 'the noble Eleanor, high King Henry's queen'. It may have been through the marriage of Eleanor's daughter, Matilda, to Duke Henry of Saxony that such Arthurian stories first reached Germany. By a neat twist of literary history, Wace's work was in turn, around 1200, reshaped by the poet Layamon for his Arthurian tale, *Brut*, a tale now told in English. Layamon's style was deliberately archaic and, as such, looked back to the traditions of Anglo-Saxon poetry; it was at the same time an avant-garde work, a pointer to the eventual triumph of Middle English, the vernacular which by the fourteenth century had supplanted French as the literary language of England.

Layamon claimed to have had three sources: 'the English book which Bede had made; another ... in Latin made by St Albin and the fair Augustine and the third which a French clerk had made'; out of these he had fashioned his account of 'the noble deeds of the English, what they were named and whence they came'. The French clerk is Wace; we do not need to worry about the identity of the Latin source and its relationship to Bede (it is generally thought that Layamon is in fact referring simply to an English and a Latin version of Bede's *History*) to see that there is a recognition of the tri-linguality of Layamon's England not just as empirical fact but as the essential ingredient of its history. Unless these languages were acknowledged, no history of England as Layamon conceived it would have been possible; its identity lay precisely in the hybrid culture they had created. An understanding of their uses, and the tensions between the three languages, remains fundamental for any history of medieval England. We must therefore take a close look both at Layamon's England and the place in it of female literacy.

By the late twelfth and early thirteenth centuries, when Layamon was writing, there was no longer the same unity of interests and aspirations between crown and aristocracy as had existed in the century following the Norman Conquest. A sense of national identity now developed despite, rather than because of, the doings of the crown. The royal court was, and was perceived to be, full of 'foreigners': Poitevins, Provencals, Limousins. Henry II's queen, from Aquitaine, was followed by a succession of queens who likewise tended to surround themselves both with relatives and writers from their native lands. There was still room to try to 'frenchify' the Anglo-Saxon past – a notable example from the court of Henry III, the *Life* of Edward the Confessor in French, was dedicated to his queen, Eleanor, and passed to her women friends, the Countesses of Arundel and Cornwall – but it was already clear that although the ability to read French would remain a mark of high birth and breeding, it could no longer be used as a vehicle of cultural unity. Court French had come to differ notably from country French, and there was growing recognition of the importance of works written in English vernacular, by now the first tongue of the majority of the population.

Among the audience and patrons of English vernacular, a

vital role was played by holy women – nuns and anchoresses – as we have already seen. The literature written expressly for these women was considered in Chapter Ten. Here we must turn to the 'wives, maidens and all men' addressed in the prologue of *Havelok*, who supported the writing and telling of stories, romances and Arthurian tales both in English and in French. If Chaucer is to be believed, women became particularly attached to these tales of romance; and there is no reason to disbelieve him, despite attempts in recent years to stress the masculinity of Chaucer's own circle and of the court of his king, Richard II (a trend summed up by Felicity Riddy: 'the whole place presumably smelt of horses, sweat and unwashed feet'[4]). When all allowances have been made for what have been called 'implied and inscribed' women readers, fictional characters such as the 'wise wives' addressed by Alison in Chaucer's *The Wife of Bath's Prologue*, whose role must be understood primarily as rhetorical, there is still a place for 'actual' women readers. Chaucer himself was perhaps jolted into writing his *Legend of Good Women* by an 'actual' woman, Queen Anne, wife of Richard II, in response to her criticism of what she perceived as the misogyny of his earlier work, *Troilus and Criseyde*. Anne's influence on artistic taste in England – whatever the ambience of the court – seems indeed to have been considerable; she brought to the English court the literary traditions of her own vernaculars, both Czech and German, and many books and illustrators from her native Bohemia.

The evidence of women's wills in Chaucer's day, when books were becoming somewhat cheaper and more widely owned, reveals a network of women readers who bequeathed books from one generation to another. These included, along with devotional books, the works of romance which Chaucer depicted women reading to one another. Such books were frequently passed from mother to daughter, sister to sister, godmother to goddaughter, but it was not considered essential to keep them in the female line; women's reading tastes were catholic and they shared them with men. Elizabeth la Zouche, for example, in 1380 left her copies of *Lancelot* and *Tristram* to her husband. The Countess of Devon, Margaret Courtenay, on the other hand, in her will of 1390/91 left her books – primers, a book of medicine, tales of Merlin and Arthur of Brittany, and

---

[4] *Women and Literature in Britain*, ed. C. Meale (1993), p. 104.

Tristram – to her daughters and a woman friend. Margaret's husband, who had predeceased her, had also left books to their daughters but not to their sons.

Bequests are, of course, by their nature selective and there is every likelihood that testators have singled out only their favourite titles. But two works thought to have been owned by women – the Vernon and the Findern manuscripts – throw further light on female reading habits. The Vernon manuscript composed largely in English, with a little Latin and French, is primarily a collection of devotional works, including a large number of Marian legends and the A-text of *Piers Plowman*. It is a large book, and cannot have been intended for private reading but whether it belonged to a convent, or to the women of a lay household, is not clear. It has no liturgical content and it could have been equally at home in either. The Findern MS, on the other hand, is markedly secular, full of lyrics, romance tales and extracts from Chaucer. Women's names, possibly autographs, appear in parts of the manuscript, but whether these women were owners, scribes or poets has not been settled. Four of the love lyrics purport to be written by 'actual' women but opinion on this remains divided.[5]

Even though there are still many questions to be answered about the full extent of the relationship between women and books, recent research has added new dimensions to old debates on the representation of women in medieval literature and how they responded to what they read. It was standard practice, once upon a time, to contrast the epics of early medieval literature with the romances of the later period and to conclude that the change from one genre to the other signalled a real and significant change in the position of women. Epics, it was argued, were male-centred stories of prowess in battle; romances were heroine-centred and mirrored reality in showing women in the courtly worlds of the later Middle Ages as the privileged and adored mistresses of all they surveyed. More recent criticism has come to make this view seem singularly naive; the romance heroine on her pedestal is, if anything, worse off than her epic predecessor who had at least some part to play in the thick of the fighting, even if it amounted to

---

[5] See D. Pearsall (ed.), *Studies in the Vernon MS* (1990); S. McNamer, 'Female Authors, Provincial Settings: the Re-Versing of Courtly Love in the Findern MS', *Viator* 22 (1991), pp. 279–310.

no more than providing sustenance and delivering comforting exhortations (as for example in the Old French *Song of William*). The romance heroine, on the other hand, derives her identity from the colour of her lips and the shape of her bosom; a sexual object, she inspires not veneration but lecherous fantasy and desire. The celebrated twelfth-century invention of romantic love turns out to be nothing but a game for the glamorisation of rape.

Such a revisionist rereading of medieval literature, the insistence that misogyny, whether blatant or covert, is ever present in all medieval literary texts, may make any explanation of the violent outbreaks of medieval misogyny of the kind that we find, for example, in the Middle English poem *Gawain and the Green Knight*, seem superfluous; but it remains worth while to look again at such seemingly straightforward examples of misogyny and its critics. In the closing stanzas of *Gawain and the Green Knight* the shamefaced hero blames his failings on a woman:

... if a dullard should dote, deem it no wonder,
And through the wiles of a woman be wooed into sorrow
For so was Adam by one, when the world began,
And Solomon by many more, and Samson the mighty –
Delilah was his doom, and David thereafter
Was beguiled by Bathsheba, and bore much distress;
Now these were vexed by their devices – 'twere a very
    joy
Could one but learn to love, and believe them not.
For these were proud princes, most prosperous of old,
Past all lovers lucky, that languished under heaven,
    bemused.
        And one and all fell prey
        To women that they had used;
        If I be led astray,
        Methinks I may be excused.[6]

Gawain's outburst belongs to a recognisable tradition. What he has to say tallies with the description given by Chaucer's Wife of Bath of the reading matter of her husband, Jankyn. Jankyn has a book of 'wicked wives' featuring all the standard harridans of the past; his avid reading of the 'damned book'

[6] *Sir Gawain and the Green Knight*, ll. 2414–2428, trans. M. Borroff (1967).

leads to the Wife of Bath to seize it from him one evening, tear three pages out of it and thump him in the face. Such fictional exasperation has its counterpart in 'real life' in the response of the French writer Christine de Pisan, whose work has already been mentioned (see p. 139). Christine's *The City of Ladies* was born out of her deep anguish at the continual misrepresentation of women, out of her concern 'that so many different men – and learned men among them - have been and are so inclined to express both in speaking and in their treatises and writings, so many wicked insults about women and their behaviour.'[7]

On further examination there is, of course, nothing straightforward either about the misogyny of Gawain, or about the responses of the Wife of Bath or even of Christine de Pisan. Gawain's diatribe shocks not least because it is singularly gratuitous; his failing has been to accept from his hostess the secret gift of a green girdle whose magic powers will protect him in his forthcoming fight against the Green Knight. It is his love of his own life, not of a woman, that leads him to act deceitfully in not disclosing his gift when called upon to do so; the 'uncourtliness' of his behaviour is compounded rather than excused by his misogynistic tirade. The Wife of Bath, meanwhile, herself becomes a caricature of precisely the kind of stereotyped woman whose image she so bemoans. Even in the case of the 'real-life' Christine, complications arise: Christine had been provoked in large measure by the misogyny of Jehan Le Fèvre's *Lamentations* but in her defence of women she herself used many of the arguments which this same Jehan put forward in his sequel to *Lamentations*, rebutting every one of his earlier accusations.

In writing both a diatribe against women and a work in their praise, Le Fèvre was following an established literary convention that by its reductive nature reinforced, in each instance, the discourse of misogyny. Twentieth-century feminists have often felt similarly concerned by the conservatism inherent in oppositional policies. Without wishing to suggest that this was a worry shared by medieval women, it remains legitimate to ask whether there were other messages in the books they read, beyond the calls to pit or pedestal, to which

---

[7] Christine de Pisan, in A. Blamires (ed.), *Woman Defamed and Woman Defended* (1992), p. 290.

they were able to respond either by their patronage, their interpretative stance or, occasionally, by their own authorship. These are huge questions; what follows is an attempt to outline critical approaches which recent work has opened up, and which suggest that there is more to medieval literature than 'the monotonous persistence ... of the topoi of misogyny'.[8]

In the first place we have to consider how to explain the long-perceived differences between romances composed in France and many of those written in England, whether in French or, as became customary from the mid-thirteenth century, in Middle English. English romance has been characterised as being much less 'courtly', more interested in plot and place than in love and its attendant suffering. These stories, moreover, centring around problems of inheritance, depend heavily for their resolution on both the rights and the resourcefulness of women. In *Havelok the Dane*, a Middle English version of the French *Lai* included by Gaimar in his *History of the English*, the hero Havelok is consistently urged and aided by his wife Argentille to reclaim both his and her inheritance. She it is who learns from the flame that comes from his mouth as he sleeps that far from being the scullion given to her in marriage by her wicked uncle in order to dishonour her, he is in fact a prince, and it is through a deception of her devising that the final victory against the wicked uncle is won. *The Romance of Horn* and *Horn* (the Middle English version) is likewise concerned with the restoration of the hero's birthright, allied here to the consummation of his love with the faithful and doughty heroine, Rigmel. These are stories which, as Susan Crane has demonstrated, need to be read with the concerns of the English baronage for inheritance and legitimacy of title in mind. There is no conflict here between the aims and desires of hero and heroine. Both are concerned with, and both can contribute to, justice and a happy ending.

Very different in tone, even flagrantly misogynistic, is Hue de Rotelande's *Ipomedon*, a tale written in Herefordshire but set in Apulia, Calabria and Sicily, a backdrop likely to have been suggested by the marriage in 1177 of Joan, daughter of Henry II and Eleanor, to William II of Sicily. The hero, Ipomedon, is set to work by the heroine, La Fière (The Proud), to prove himself to be a worthy knight. Bold and bloody exploits

---

[8] R. Howard Bloch, *Medieval Misogyny* (1991), p. 3.

follow, but recognition is delayed by the various disguises adopted by Ipomedon. La Fière's subsequent confusion is mocked and made the opportunity for generalisations on the capacity of women to look after themselves by their own propensity to trick others. The eventual marriage of La Fière and Ipomedon is presented less as a romantic finale, more as a piece of sexual burlesque: 'Now they love each other so passionately that they fuck all day.' In his epilogue Hue invites the women of his audience to come to his house to see 'the charter of absolution' he has for reluctant lovers: 'if there is any lady or maiden or rich widow or damsel who does not want to believe that I have it, let her come there, and I will show her; the charter will be inscribed in a register [on her?] before she leaves, and it won't be too great harm if the seal hangs from the ass.'

In her recent analysis of *Ipomedon* Roberta Krueger asks: 'What might the female readers expressly addressed in the conclusions have made of this romance?'[9] Were they, like La Fière, manipulated, edged towards complicity with the hero's tricks? Only, argues Krueger, if we assume that women necessarily identified with La Fière, and we have no grounds for believing that they did. It is just as possible that *Ipomedon* worked for women as a kind of cautionary tale; it becomes then, according to Krueger, 'an object lesson in the dangers romance might hold for women. He [Hue de Rotelande] traces the steps by which a female heroine is deprived of her autonomy to become a victim of male machinations, and this he does with admirable clarity.' At the same time, fun is poked at the whole system of chivalric feats and the code of courtesy through the casting of Ipomedon as a prankster whose exploits become increasingly futile and wasteful of life. Such a critique of chivalry is by no means unparalleled and indeed is likely to provide a better clue to the understanding of many romances than can too narrow a concentration on gender issues. None the less, it is worth noting how deeply the misogyny of *Ipomedon* seems to have troubled its Middle English redactor. His retelling of the tale *Ipomadon, c.*1375, amounts, in Crane's words, to 'a rescue operation'; Hue's slanderous comments about women are removed and both hero and

---

[9] For citations from *Ipomedon* and for what follows, see R. Krueger, *Women Readers and the Ideology of Gender*, pp. 73–82.

heroine now credited with noble and generous motives.[10]

If Hue's *Ipomedon* is problematic entertainment for women, what, one might ask, did men make of *Partonopeu*, an anonymous late-twelfth-century romance, so successful as to be translated or adapted into nine different languages (English included)? On the surface at least, *Partonopeu* is the tale of an eponymous hero, constantly manipulated by women. Partonopeu is only thirteen when Melior, Empress of Byzantium, a woman of power, intelligence and magic powers is smitten by his great beauty. She falls passionately in love with him and plans to keep him with her until he is old enough to marry her. For the time being, Partonopeu is not to be allowed to see Melior who by her magic makes herself invisible to him and yet available for nights of love. On a trip home to France he is persuaded by his mother to break his promise to Melior and to attempt to see her by the light of a magic lantern. This act of betrayal is followed by banishment for Partonopeu and, for Melior, the loss of her magic powers. Partonopeu retreats to the Ardennes where he goes into a decline, to be rescued only through the intervention of a third woman, Uraque, Melior's sister, who tricks him into believing that Melior has pardoned him, when in fact she has done nothing of the sort and is about to hold a competition to find the husband her barons are now insisting she should have. The competition consists of a tournament, followed by a beauty contest: 'I care a lot about beauty,' Melior tells her men, 'you shouldn't be surprised, since that's the way you choose among us.'[11] As readers, however, we cannot but be surprised by such explicit games of gender reversal.

What difference does it make, if any, that *Partonopeu* is allegedly written for a woman, the poet's desired lover? Joan Ferrante[12] has suggested that the pairing of competent women with vulnerable men occurs with notable frequency precisely in works written for women; perhaps this is so, though it is a hard conclusion to sustain given that the women in question (as in *Partonopeu*) are often not named and may serve as rhetorical topoi rather than as actual sources of inspiration. A question of equal, if not greater importance, but no easier to

---

[10] S. Crane, *Insular Romance* (1986), p. 202–11.

[11] Cited in J. Ferrante, 'The Influence of Women Patrons', in D. Maddox and S. Sturm-Maddox (eds), *Literary Aspects of Courtly Culture*, p. 15.

[12] *Ibid.*, p. 7.

answer is: what difference does it make if the poet happens to be a woman?

A poet known to be a woman, probably writing in England in the mid-twelfth century, is Marie de France. Marie's identity is still uncertain though she is often thought to be an illegitimate daughter of the father of Henry II, and an abbess of Shaftesbury in Wiltshire. As a writer Marie is very conscious of her gender, and of how she may be effaced by men plagiarising her work. Her epilogue to her *Fables* states her case:

> I am from France, my name's Marie
> And it may hap that many a clerk
> Will claim as his what is my work
> But such pronouncements I want not!
> It's folly to become forgot.[13]

Her *Lais*, according to her contemporary Denis Piramus, appealed particularly to women, although men enjoyed them too. But where did the appeal lie? Can Marie's work be claimed for *écriture feminine*? In one sense, yes: the effectiveness of Marie's *Lais*, twelve short stories bounded by prologue and (brief) epilogue depend heavily, as Matilda Bruckner has shown, on the maintenance of the fiction that these are oral tales, stories dependent not on Latin texts but on lived experience. Marie thereby upsets the boundaries which convention has laid 'between folkloric culture and clerical culture ... between male cleric and female layperson'. She describes her work literally as a labour; it is a task that keeps her awake at night and leads to her 'giving birth from great pain'.[14]

Two of Marie's *lais* take their titles from the names of their heroines. Both are concerned with self-sacrifice and substitution. In *Le Fresne* a baby (Le Fresne) is abandoned at birth, and brought up as an orphan by nuns. As a young woman Le Fresne becomes the mistress of a neighbouring lord but is prepared to step aside to allow her nobly born twin to become his bride. Only as she prepares their wedding bed is the foundling's true identity revealed. The *lai* originally (and often still) known as *Eliduc*, changed its title to *Guildeluec and Guilliadun*, according to Marie, 'because the adventure on which it is based

---

[13] Marie de France, *Fables*, ed. and trans. H. Spiegel (1987).
[14] For citations and critical approach, see M. Bruckner, *Shaping Romance* (1993), ch. 5.

concerns the ladies'. The adventure tells of how the lawful wife (Guildeluec) makes way for the mistress (Guilliadun) of her husband (Eliduc) by retiring to a convent; in later years Guilliadun joins Guildeluec in her convent; Eliduc becomes a monk. All three live happily ever after.

Le Fresne and *Eliduc* can be, and have been, read as stories of sisterhood, tales of women who face the constraints and humiliations of patriarchal society by putting the happiness of other women before their own. There is no reason to deny such readings but, at the same time, room must be found for others: for the concerns of Marie de France with the identities and problems of both men and women in her society. Eliduc, as Bruckner has pointed out, is a name found in *Guildeluec*; gender identity in medieval stories is not as fixed as a first reading might imply. To look in them for 'good' or 'bad' women can be to miss the point. The heroine of a story may be no more than a symbol of the hero's 'potential excellence'; 'his final union with her (if he can achieve it) represents the completion of himself.'[15] Marie's opening lay, *Guigemar* (a name that has Marie in it), is the tale of a valiant young knight who none the less is 'incomplete'; 'nature has done him such a grievous wrong that he never displayed the slightest interest in love'. One day when out hunting he receives a wound from an arrow that rebounds from his quarry, a hind whose sexuality, like his own, is clearly problematic: 'the beast was completely white with the antlers of a stag on its head.' This creature tells him that he can be healed only by a woman who loves him and suffers for him and whose love he reciprocates. The woman is indeed found, lost, and found again, the ending dependent on the fastening of exchanged tokens – knots in Guigemar's shirt and in the woman's belt that no one but the lovers can untie – 'parallel objects that retain the essentials of sameness and difference that mark the male/female couple as a unit within society'.[16]

A recent study of Chaucer has suggested that we should divert attention away from Chaucer's attitude towards women and consider instead his attitude towards men, or more specifically towards masculinity, and his anxieties about its possible feminisation. This is a subject far too large to be

[15] J. Ferrante, *Woman as Image* (1975), p. 74.
[16] M. Bruckner, *Shaping Romance*, pp. 163–70.

broached here but it will be clear from the bibliography that the problem has already exercised a number of writers. Chivalry, the attempt to create an 'anti-yob' culture, soon raised several spectres. Did making love rather than war make men effeminate? This is precisely the question posed by Chrétien de Troyes, the poet favoured by Marie, Countess of Champagne, the daughter of Eleanor of Aquitaine, in *Erec and Enide*. Eric has lost all interest in tournaments; 'he preferred to spar with his wife.' Enide herself becomes troubled: 'the earth should swallow me up since the best knight, the boldest and bravest, the most loyal and courtly who ever was either count or king has, because of me, abandoned all chivalry.'[17] The part played by Enide in finding an honourable resolution to this conflict between the delights of tournaments and matrimony is told with deft irony. Erec considers he has put his wife's loyalty to the test; the audience cannot but be aware that what was at stake was in fact not Enide's loyalty but rather Erec's reputation as a knight and that he has regained this only with the help of Enide acting regularly against his instructions. It is Enide both in bed and in combat who has 'made a man of him'.

A final question: what separated the effeminate man from the homosexual? It is in the twelfth century that homophobia first appears in vernacular literature, according to Raymond Cormier, in the *Roman d'Eneas* at the moment when the mother of the heroine, Lavine, tries to dissuade her from loving Aeneas on the grounds that he is both stranger and sodomite.[18] This again is not a topic that can be pursued here, but since the publication of R. I. Moore's *Origins of a Persecuting Society* we have learned to associate outbreaks of homophobia in the twelfth century with a corresponding growth in misogynistic sentiment. Medieval attempts to wrestle with problems of gender none the less did not always follow these paths; its literature offered a space for the exploration of sexual difference quite as much as it provided a platform for the airing of prejudice.

---

[17] Cited in E. J. Burns, *Body Talk* (1993), p. 171. For further literature on Chrétien see the bibliography.
[18] R. Cormier, 'Taming the Warrior' in D. Maddox and S. Sturm-Maddox (eds), *Literary Aspects of Court Culture* (1994), p. 153–69.

Extracts from Primary Sources

The following extracts have been chosen to give the reader some idea of the range of primary material used in the writing of this book and to whet his or her appetite for further reading of the sources. There is one for each chapter, except for Chapter 1 (none) and Chapter 3 (two). Footnotes have not been included but no alterations have been made to the actual texts of the translations beyond the anglicising of names in the extract for Chapter 5.

For Chapter 2: The Life of Leoba

The Life of Leoba was written by Rudolph, monk of the German monastery of Fulda. It was completed by 837, within some 50 years of Leoba's death. In writing it, Rudolph was drawing on the written reminiscences of four of Leoba's pupils. (Source: C. H. Talbot, *The Anglo-Saxon Missionaries in Germany* (1954), pp. 213–21.)

At the time when the blessed virgin Leoba was pursuing her quest for perfection in the monastery the holy martyr Boniface was being ordained by Gregory, Bishop of Rome and successor to Constantine, in the Apostolic See. His mission was to preach the Word of God to the people in Germany. When Boniface found that the people were ready to receive the faith and that, though the harvest was great, the labourers who worked with him were few, he sent messengers and letters to England, his native land, summoning from different ranks of the clergy many who were learned in the divine law and fitted both by their character and good works to preach the Word of God. With their assistance he zealously carried out the mission with which he was charged, and by sound doctrine and miracles converted a large part of Germany to the faith. As the days went by, multitudes of people were instructed in the mysteries of the faith and the Gospel was preached not only in the churches but also in the towns and villages. Thus the Catholics were strengthened in their belief by constant exhortation, the wicked submitted to correction, and the heathen, enlightened by the Gospel, flocked to receive the grace of Baptism. When the blessed man saw that the Church of God was increasing and that the desire of perfection was firmly rooted he established two means by which religious progress should be ensured. He began to build monasteries, so that the people would be attracted to the church not only by the beauty of its religion but also by the communities of monks and nuns. And as he wished the observance in both cases to be kept according to the Holy Rule, he endeavoured to obtain suitable superiors for both houses. For this purpose he sent his disciple Sturm, a man of noble family and sterling character, to Monte Cassino, so that he could study the regular discipline, the observance and the monastic customs which had been established there by St Benedict. As the future superior, he wished him to become a novice and in this way learn in humble submission how to rule over others. Likewise, he sent messengers with letters to the abbess Tetta, of whom we have already spoken, asking her to send Leoba to accompany him on this journey and to take part in this embassy: for Leoba's reputation for learning and holiness had spread far and wide and her praise was on everyone's lips. The abbess Tetta was exceedingly displeased at her departure, but because she could not gainsay the dispositions of divine providence she agreed to his request and sent Leoba to the blessed man. Thus it was that the interpretation of the dream which she had previously received was fulfilled. When she came, the man of God received her with the deepest reverence, holding her in great affection, not so much because she was related to him on his mother's side as because he knew that by her holiness and wisdom she would confer many benefits by her word and example.

In furtherance of his aims he appointed persons in authority over the monasteries and established the observance of the Rule: he placed Sturm as abbot over the monks and Leoba as abbess over the nuns. He gave her the monastery at a place called Bischofsheim, where there was a large community of nuns. These were trained according to her principles in the discipline of monastic life and made such progress in her teaching that many of them afterwards became superiors of others, so that there was hardly a convent of nuns in that part which had not one of her disciples as abbess. She was a woman of great virtue and was so strongly attached to the way of life she had vowed that she never gave thought to her native country or her relatives. She expended all her energies on the work she had undertaken in order to appear blameless before God and to become a pattern of perfection to those who obeyed her in word and action. She was ever on her guard not to teach others what she did not carry out herself. In her conduct there was no arrogance or pride; she was no distinguisher of persons, but showed herself affable and kindly to all. In appearance she was angelic, in word pleasant, clear in mind, great in prudence, Catholic in faith, most patient in hope, universal in her charity. But though she was always cheerful, she never broke out into laughter through excessive hilarity. No one ever heard a bad word from her lips; the sun never went down upon her anger. In the matter of food and drink she always showed the utmost understanding for others but was most sparing in her own use of them. She had a small cup from which she used to drink and which, because of the meagre quantity it would hold, was called by the sisters 'the Beloved's little one'. So great was her zeal for reading that she discontinued it only for prayer or for the refreshment of her body with food or sleep: the Scriptures were never out of her hands. For, since she had been trained from infancy in the rudiments of grammar and the study of the other liberal arts, she tried by constant reflection to attain a perfect knowledge of divine things so that through the combination of her reading with her quick intelligence, by natural gifts and hard work, she became extremely learned. She read with attention all the books of the Old and New Testaments and learned by heart all the commandments of God. To these she added by way of completion the writings of the church Fathers, the decrees of the Councils and the whole of ecclesiastical law. She observed great moderation in all her acts and arrangements and always kept the practical end in view, so that she would never have to repent of her actions through having been guided by impulse. She was deeply aware of the necessity for concentration of mind in prayer and study, and for this reason took care not to go to excess either in watching or in other spiritual exercises. Throughout the summer both she and all the sisters under her rule went to rest after the midday meal, and she would never give permission to any of them to stay up late, for she said that lack of sleep dulled the mind, especially for study. When she lay down to rest, whether at night or in the afternoon, she used to have the Sacred Scriptures read out at her bedside, a duty which the younger nuns carried out in turn without grumbling. It seems difficult to believe, but even when she seemed to be asleep they could not skip over any word or syllable whilst they were reading without her immediately correcting them. Those on whom this duty fell used afterwards to confess that often when they saw her becoming drowsy they made a mistake on purpose to see if she noticed it, but they were never able to escape undetected. Yet it is not surprising that she could not be deceived even in her sleep, since He who keeps watch over Israel and neither slumbers nor sleeps possessed her heart, and she was able to say with the spouse in the Song of Songs: 'I sleep, but my heart watcheth.'

She preserved the virtue of humility with such care that, though she had been appointed to govern others because of her holiness and wisdom, she believed in her heart that she was the least of all. This she showed both in her speech and behaviour. She was extremely hospitable. She kept open house for all without exception, and even when she was fasting gave banquets and washed the feet of the guests with her own hands, at once the guardian and the minister of the practice instituted by our Lord.

Whilst the virgin of Christ was acting in this way and attracting to herself everyone's affection, the devil, who is the foe of all Christians, viewed with impatience her own great virtue and the progress made by her disciples. He therefore attacked them constantly with evil thoughts and temptations of the flesh, trying to turn some of them aside from the path they had chosen. But when he saw that all his efforts were brought to nought by their prayers, fasting and chaste lives, the wily tempter turned his attention to other means, hoping at least to destroy their good reputation, even if he could not break down their integrity by his foul suggestions.

There was a certain poor little crippled girl, who sat near the gate of the monastery begging alms. Every day she received her food from the abbess's table, her clothing from the nuns and all other necessities from them; these were given to her from divine charity. It happened that after some time, deceived by the suggestions of the devil, she committed fornication, and when her appearance made it impossible for her to conceal that she had conceived a child she covered up her guilt by pretending to be ill. When her time came, she wrapped the child in swaddling clothes and cast it at night into a pool by the river which flowed through that place. In this way she added crime to crime, for she not only followed fleshly sin by murder, but also combined murder with the poisoning of the water. When day dawned, another woman came to draw water and, seeing the corpse of the child, was struck with horror. Burning with womanly rage, she filled the whole village with her uncontrollable cries and reproached the holy nuns with these indignant words: 'Oh, what a chaste community! How admirable is the life of nuns, who beneath their veils gave birth to children and exercise at one and the same time the function of mothers and priests, baptising those to whom they have given birth. For, fellow-citizens, you have drawn off this water to make a pool, not merely for the purpose of grinding corn, but unwittingly for a new and unheard-of kind of Baptism. Now go and ask those women, whom you compliment by calling them virgins, to remove this corpse from the river and make it fit for us to use again. Look for the one who is missing from the monastery and then you will find out who is responsible for this crime.' At these words all the crowd was set in uproar and everybody, of whatever age or sex, ran in one great mass to see what had happened. As soon as they saw the corpse they denounced the crime and reviled the nuns. When the abbess heard the uproar and learned what was afoot she called the nuns together, told them the reason, and discovered that no one was absent except Agatha, who a few days before had been summoned to her parents' house on urgent business: but she had gone with full permission. A messenger was sent to her without delay to recall her to the monastery, as Leoba could not endure the accusation of so great a crime to hang over them. When Agatha returned and heard of the deed that was charged against her she fell on her knees and gazed up to heaven, crying: 'Almighty God, who knowest all things before they come to pass, from whom nothing is hid and who hast delivered Susanna from false accusations when she trusted in Thee, show Thy mercy to this community gathered together in Thy name and let it not be besmirched by filthy rumours on account of my sins; but do Thou deign to unmask and make known for the praise and glory of Thy name the person who has committed this misdeed.'

On hearing this, the venerable superior, being assured of her innocence, ordered them all to go to the chapel and to stand with their arms extended in the form of a cross until each one of them had sung through the whole psalter, then three times each day, at Tierce, Sext and None, to go round the monastic buildings in procession with the crucifix at their head, calling upon God to free them, in His mercy, from this accusation. When they had done this and they were going into the church at None, having completed two rounds, the blessed Leoba went straight to the altar and, standing before the cross, which was being prepared for the third procession, stretched out her hands towards heaven, and with tears and groans prayed, saying: 'O Lord Jesus Christ, King of virgins, Lover of chastity, unconquerable God, manifest Thy power and deliver us from this charge, because the reproaches of those who reproached Thee have fallen upon us.' Immediately after she had said this, that wretched little woman, the dupe and the tool of the devil, seemed to be surrounded by flames, and, calling out the name of the abbess, confessed to the crime she had committed. Then a great shout rose to heaven: the vast crowd was astounded at the miracle, the nuns began to weep with joy, and all of them with one voice gave expression to the merits of Leoba and of Christ our Saviour.

So it came about that the reputation of the nuns, which the devil had tried to ruin by his sinister rumour, was greatly enhanced, and praise was showered on them in every place. But the wretched woman did not deserve to escape scot-free and for the rest of her life she remained in the power of the devil. Even before this God had performed many miracles through Leoba, but they had been kept secret. This one was her first in Germany and, because it was done in public, it came to the ears of everyone.

On another occasion, when she sat down as usual to give spiritual instruction to her disciples, a fire broke out in a part of the village. As the houses have roofs of wood and thatch, they were soon consumed by the flames, and the conflagration spread with increasing rapidity towards the monastery, so that it threatened to destroy not only the buildings but also the men and beasts. Then could be heard the mingled shouts of the terrified villagers as they ran in a mob to the abbess and begged her to avert the danger which threatened them. Unruffled and with great self-control, she calmed their fears and, without being influenced by their trust in her, ordered them to take a bucket and bring some water from the upper part of the stream that flowed by the monastery. As soon as they had brought it, she took some salt which had been blessed by St Boniface and which she always kept by her, and sprinkled it in the water. Then she said: 'Go and pour back this water into the river and then let all the people draw water lower down the stream and throw it on the fire.' After they had done this the violence of the conflagration died down and the fire was extinguished just as if a flood had fallen from the skies. So the buildings were saved. At this miracle the whole crowd stood amazed and broke out into the praise of God, who through the faith and prayers of his handmaid had delivered them so extraordinarily from a terrible danger.

I think it should be counted amongst her virtues also that one day, when a wild storm arose and the whole sky was obscured by such dark clouds that day seemed turned into night, terrible lightning and falling thunderbolts struck terror into the stoutest hearts and everyone was shaking with fear. At first the people drove their flocks into the houses for shelter so that they should not perish; then, when the danger increased and threatened them all with death, they took refuge with their wives and children in the church, despairing of their lives. They locked all the doors and waited there trembling, thinking that the last judgment was at hand. In this state of panic they filled the air with the din of their mingled cries. Then the holy virgin went out to them and urged them all to have patience. She promised them that no harm would come to them; and after exhorting them to join with her in prayer, she fell prostrate at the foot of the altar. In the meantime the storm raged, the roofs of the houses were torn off by the violence of the wind, the ground shook with the repeated shocks of the thunderbolts, and the thick darkness, intensified by the incessant flicker of lightning which flashed through the windows, redoubled their terror. Then the mob, unable to endure the suspense any longer, rushed to the altar to rouse her from prayer and seek her protection. Thecla, her kinswoman, spoke to her first, saying: 'Beloved, all the hopes of these people lie in you: you are their only support. Arise, then, and pray to the Mother of God, your mistress, for us, that by her intercession we may be delivered from this fearful storm.' At these words Leoba rose up from prayer and, as if she had been challenged to a contest, flung off the cloak which she was wearing and boldly opened the doors of the church. Standing on the threshold, she made a sign of the cross, opposing to the fury of the storm the name of the High God. Then she stretched out her hands towards heaven and three times invoked the mercy of Christ, praying that through the intercession of Holy Mary, the Virgin. He would quickly come to the help of His people. Suddenly God came to their aid. The sound of thunder died away, the winds changed direction and dispersed the heavy clouds, the darkness rolled back and the sun shone, bringing calm and peace. Thus did divine power make manifest the merits of His handmaid. Unexpected peace came to His people and fear was banished.

There was also another of her deeds which everyone agrees was outstanding and memorable, and which I think it would be wrong to pass over in silence. One of the sisters of the monastery named Williswind, of excellent character and edifying conduct, was attacked by a grave illness; she suffered from what the doctors call haemorrhoids, and through loss of blood from her privy parts was racked by severe pains of the bowel. As the ailment continued and increased from day to day in severity, her strength ebbed away until she could neither turn over on her side nor get out of bed and walk without leaning on someone else. When she was no longer able to remain in the common dormitory of the monastery because of the stench, her parents who lived close by asked and obtained permission for her to be taken on a litter to their house across the river Tuberaha. Not long afterwards, as the sickness gained hold, she rapidly drew near her end. As the lower part of her body had lost all sense of feeling and she was barely able to breathe, the abbess was asked by her parents not to come and visit the sick nun but to pray to God for her happy decease. When Leoba came, she approached the bed, now surrounded by a weeping throng of neighbours, and ordered the covering to be removed, for the patient was already enveloped in a linen cloth, as corpses usually are. When it was taken away she placed her hand on her breast and said: 'Cease your weeping, for her soul is still in her.' Then she sent to the monastery and ordered them to bring the little spoon which she usually used at table; and when it was brought to her she blessed milk and poured it drop by drop down the throat of the sick nun. At its touch, her throat and vitals recovered; she moved her tongue to speak and began to look round. Next day she had made such progress that she was able to take food, and before the end of the week she walked on her own feet to the monastery, whence she had previously been carried on a litter. She lived for several years afterwards and remained in the service of God until the days of Lewis, King of the Franks, always strong and healthy, even after the death of Leoba.

The people's faith was stimulated by such tokens of holiness, and as religious feeling increased so did contempt of the world. Many nobles and influential men gave their daughters to God to live in the monastery in perpetual chastity; many widows also forsook their homes, made vows of chastity and took the veil in the cloister. To all of these the holy virgin pointed out both by word and example how to reach the heights of perfection.

For Chapter 3: King Alfred's law-code and The Penitential of Theodore

Alfred's law-code is thought to date from the last decade of his reign. It is a work heavily influenced not only by earlier Anglo-Saxon law but also by Old Testament traditions of law-making. (Source: *The Laws of the Earliest English Kings*, ed. and trans. F. L. Attenborough (1922), pp. 69, 71, 73, 75, 76.)

8. If anyone takes a nun from a nunnery without the permission of the king or bishop, he shall pay 120 shillings, half to the king, and half to the bishop and the lord of the church, under whose charge the nun is.

   §1. If she lives longer than he who abducted her, she shall inherit nothing of his property.
   §2. If she bears a child, it shall inherit no more of the property than its mother.
   §3. If her child is slain, the share of the wergeld due to the mother's kindred shall be paid to the king, but the father's kindred shall be paid the share due to them.

9. If anyone slays a woman with child, while the child is in her womb, he shall pay the full wergeld for the woman, and half the wergeld for the child, [which shall be] in accordance with the wergeld of the father's kindred.

   §1. Until the value amounts to 30 shillings, the fine shall be 60 shillings in every case. When the [said] value amounts to this sum, the fine shall be 120 shillings.
   §2. Formerly the fines to be paid by those who stole gold and horses and bees, and many other fines, were greater than the rest. Now all fines, with the exception of that for stealing men, are alike – 120 shillings.

10. If anyone lies with the wife of a man whose wergeld is 1200 shillings, he shall pay 120 shillings compensation to the husband; to a husband whose wergeld is 600 shillings, he shall pay 100 shillings compensation; to a commoner he shall pay 40 shillings compensation [for a similar offence].

11. If anyone seizes by the breast a young woman belonging to the

commons, he shall pay her 5 shillings compensation.

§1. If he throws her down but does not lie with her, he shall pay [her] 10 shillings compensation.

§2. If he lies with her, he shall pay [her] 60 shillings compensation.

§3. If another man has previously lain with her, then the compensation shall be half this [amount].

§4. If she is accused [of having previously lain with a man], she shall clear herself by [an oath of] 60 hides, or lose half the compensation due to her.

§5. If this [outrage] is done to a woman of higher birth, the compensation to be paid shall increase according to the wergeld....

18. If anyone lustfully seizes a nun, either by her clothes or by her breast, without her permission, he shall pay as compensation twice the sum we have fixed in the case of a woman belonging to the laity.

§1. If a young woman who is betrothed commits fornication, she shall pay compensation to the amount of 60 shillings to the surety [of the marriage], if she is a commoner. This sum shall be [paid] in livestock, cattle being the property tendered, and no slave shall be given in such a payment.

§2. If her wergeld is 600 shillings, she shall pay 100 shillings to the surety [of the marriage].

§3. If her wergeld is 1200 shillings, she shall pay 120 shillings to the surety [of the marriage]....

25. If anyone rapes the slave of a commoner, he shall pay 5 shillings to the commoner, and a fine of 60 shillings.

§1. If a slave rapes a slave, castration shall be required as compensation....

29. If anyone rapes a girl who is not of age, the same compensation shall be paid to her as is paid to an adult.

The Penitential of Theodore is thought to have been compiled about 50 years after the death of Theodore in 690. It was put together by a Northumbrian disciple of Theodore's; despite the complexities of the manuscript tradition it is generally believed to contain an authentic record of his teaching. (Source: *Medieval Handbooks of Penance*, trans. J. T. McNeill and H. M. Gamer (1990), pp. 195–8.)

XIV. Of the Penance for Special Irregularities in Marriage

1. In a first marriage the presbyter ought to perform Mass and bless them both, and afterward they shall absent themselves from church for thirty days. Having done this, they shall do penance for forty days, and

absent themselves from the prayer; and afterwards they shall communicate with the oblation.

2. One who is twice married shall do penance for a year; on Wednesdays and Fridays and during the three forty-day periods he shall abstain from flesh; however, he shall not put away his wife.

3. He that is married three times, or more, that is in a fourth or fifth marriage, or beyond that number, for seven years on Wednesdays and Fridays and during the three forty-day periods they shall abstain from flesh; yet they shall not be separated. Basil so determined, but in the canon four years [are indicated].

4. If anyone finds his wife to be an adulteress and does not wish to put her away but has had her in the matrimonial relation to that time, he shall do penance for two years on two days in the week and [shall perform] the fasts of religion; or as long as she herself does penance he shall avoid the matrimonial relation with her, because she has committed adultery.

5. If any man or woman who has taken the vow of virginity is joined in marriage, he shall not set aside the marriage but shall do penance for three years.

6. Foolish vows and those incapable of being performed are to be set aside.

7. A woman may not take a vow without the consent of her husband; but if she does take a vow she can be released, and she shall do penance according to the decision of a priest.

8. He who puts away his wife and marries another shall do penance with tribulation for seven years or a lighter penance for fifteen years.

9. He who defiles his neighbor's wife, deprived of his own wife, shall fast for three years two days a week and in the three forty-day periods.

10. If [the woman] is a virgin, he shall do penance for one year without meat and wine and mead.

11. If he defiles a vowed virgin, he shall do penance for three years, as we said above, whether a child is born of her or not.

12. If she is his slave, he shall set her free and fast for six months.

13. If the wife of anyone deserts him and returns to him undishonored, she shall do penance for one year; otherwise for three years. If he takes another wife he shall do penance for one year.

14. An adulterous woman shall do penance for seven years. And this matter is stated in the same way in the canon.

15. A woman who commits adultery shall do penance for three years as a fornicator. So also shall she do penance who makes an unclean mixture of food for the increase of love.

16. A wife who tastes her husband's blood as a remedy shall fast for forty days, more or less.

17. Moreover, women shall not in the time of impurity enter into a church, or communicate – neither nuns nor laywomen; if they presume [to do this] they shall fast for three weeks.

18. In the same way shall they do penance who enter a church before purification after childbirth, that is, forty days.
19. But he who has intercourse at these seasons shall do penance for twenty days.
20. He who has intercourse on the Lord's day shall seek pardon from God and do penance for one or two or three days.
21. In case of unnatural intercourse with his wife, he shall be penance for forty days the first time.
22. For a graver offense of this kind he ought to do penance as one who offends with animals.
23. For intercourse at the improper season he shall fast for forty days.
24. Women who commit abortion before [the foetus] has life, shall do penance for one year or for the three forty-day periods or for forty days, according to the nature of the offense; and if later, that is, more than forty days after conception, they shall do penance as murderesses, that is for three years on Wednesdays and Fridays and in the three forty-day periods. This according to the canons is judged [punishable by] ten years.
25. If a mother slays her child, if she commits homicide, she shall do penance for fifteen years, and never change except on Sunday.
26. If a poor woman slays her child, she shall do penance for seven years. In the canon it is said that if it is a case of homicide, she shall do penance for ten years.
27. A woman who conceives and slays her child in the womb within forty days shall do penance for one year; but if later than forty days, she shall do penance as a murderess.
28. If an infant that is weak and is a pagan has been recommended to a presbyter [for baptism] and dies [unbaptised], the presbyter shall be deposed.
29. If the neglect is on the part of the parents, they shall do penance for one year; and if a child of three years dies without baptism, the father and the mother shall do penance for three years. He gave this decision at a certain time because it happened to be referred to him.
30. In the canon, he who slays his child without baptism [is required to do penance for] ten years, but under advisement he shall do penance for seven years.

For Chapter 4: Judith

Nearly all the Anglo-Saxon poetry that has survived is to be found in four late-Anglo-Saxon manuscripts: the Exeter book, containing over a hundred poems; the Junius MS, with *Genesis A* and *B*, *Daniel*, *Exodus*, *Christ and Satan*; the Vercelli book, which includes *The Dream of the Rood* and *Elene*; and the

Beowulf MS, in which is to be found not only *Beowulf* but
also all that we have of *Judith*. Although the dating of the
composition of these poems remains controversial, there is
general agreement that the Beowulf MS itself dates from the
tenth rather than the eleventh century. (Source: S. Bradley,
Anglo-Saxon Poetry (1982), pp. 496–504.)

... she was suspicious of gifts in this wide world. So she readily met
with a helping hand from the glorious Prince when she had most need
of the supreme Judge's support and that he, the Prime Mover, should
protect her against this supreme danger. The illustrious Father in the
skies granted her request in this because she always had firm faith in
the Almighty.

I have heard, then, that Holofernes cordially issued invitations to a
banquet and had dishes splendidly prepared with all sorts of wonderful
things, and to it this lord over men summoned all the most senior
functionaries. With great alacrity those shield-wielders complied and
came wending to the puissant prince, the nation's chief person. That
was on the fourth day after Judith, shrewd of purpose, the woman of
elfin beauty first visited him.

X

So they went and settled down to the feasting, insolent men to the
wine-drinking, all those brash armoured warriors, his confederates in
evil. Deep bowls were borne continually along the benches there and
brimming goblets and pitchers as well to the hall-guests. They drank it
down as doomed men, those celebrated shield-wielders – though the
great man, the awesome lord over evils, did not foresee it. Then Holofernes, the bountiful lord of his men, grew merry with tippling. He
laughed and bawled and roared and made a racket so that the children
of men could hear from far away how the stern-minded man bellowed
and yelled, insolent and flown with mead, and frequently exhorted the
guests on the benches to enjoy themselves well. So the whole day long
the villain, the stern-minded dispenser of treasure, plied his retainers
with wine until they lay unconscious, the whole of his retinue drunk as
though they had been struck dead, drained of every faculty.

Thus the men's elder commanded the hall-guests to be ministered to
until the dark night closed in on the children of men. Then, being
wickedly promiscuous, he commanded the blessed virgin, decked with
bracelets and adorned with rings, to be fetched in a hurry to his bed.
The attendants promptly did as their master, the ruler of armoured
warriors, required them. They went upon the instant to the guest-
hall where they found the astute Judith, and then the shield-wielding
warriors speedily conducted the noble virgin to the lofty pavilion where

the great man always rested of a night, Holofernes, abhorrent to the Saviour.

There was an elegant all-golden fly-net there, hung about the commandant's bed so that the debauched hero of his soldiers could spy through on every one of the sons of men who came in there, but no one of humankind on him, unless, brave man, he summoned one of his evilly-renowned soldiers to go nearer to him for a confidential talk.

Hastily, then, they brought the shrewd lady to bed. Then they went, stout-hearted heroes, to inform their master that the holy woman had been brought to his pavilion. The man of mark, lord over cities, then grew jovial of mood: he meant to defile the noble lady with filth and with pollution. To that heaven's Judge, Shepherd of the celestial multitude, would not consent but rather he, the Lord, Ruler of the hosts, prevented him from the act.

So this species of fiend, licentious, debauched, went with a crowd of his men to seek his bed – where he was to lose his life, swiftly, within the one night: he had then come to his violent end upon earth, such as he had previously deserved, the stern-minded prince over men, while he lived in this world under the roof of the skies.

Then the great man collapsed in the midst of his bed, so drunk with wine that he was oblivious in mind of any of his designs. The soldiers stepped out of his quarters with great alacrity, wine-glutted men who had put the perjurer, the odious persecutor, to bed for the last time.

Then the glorious handmaid of the Saviour was sorely preoccupied as to how she might most easily deprive the monster of his life before the sordid fellow, full of corruption, awoke. Then the ringletted girl, the Maker's maiden, grasped a sharp sword, hardy in the storms of battle, and drew it from its sheath with her right hand. Then she called by name upon the Guardian of heaven, the Saviour of all the world's inhabitants, and spoke these words:

'God of beginnings, Spirit of comfort, Son of the universal Ruler, I desire to entreat you for your grace upon me in my need, Majesty of the Trinity. My heart is now sorely anguished and my mind troubled and much afflicted with anxieties. Give me, Lord of heaven, victory and true faith so that with this sword I may hew down this dispenser of violent death. Grant me my safe deliverance, stern-minded Prince over men. Never have I had greater need of your grace. Avenge now, mighty Lord, illustrious Dispenser of glory, that which is so bitter to my mind, so burning in my breast.'

Then the supreme Judge at once inspired her with courage – as he does every single man dwelling here who looks to him for help with resolve and with true faith. So hope was abundantly renewed in the holy woman's heart. She then took the heathen man firmly by his hair, dragged him ignominiously toward her with her hands and carefully laid out the debauched and odious man so as she could most easily manage the wretch efficiently. Then the ringletted woman struck the malignant-minded enemy with the gleaming sword so that she sliced through half his neck, so that he lay unconscious, drunk and mutilated.

He was not then yet dead, not quite lifeless. In earnest then the courageous woman struck the heathen dog a second time so that his head flew off on to the floor. His foul carcass lay behind, dead; his spirit departed elsewhere beneath the deep ground and was there prostrated and chained in torment ever after, coiled about by snakes, trussed up in tortures and cruelly prisoned in hellfire after his going hence. Never would he have cause to hope, engulfed in darkness, that he might get out of that snake-infested prison, but there he shall remain for ever to eternity henceforth without end in that murky abode, deprived of the joys of hope.

XI

Judith then had won outstanding glory in the struggle according as God the Lord of heaven, who gave her the victory, granted her. Then the clever woman swiftly put the harrier's head, all bloody, into the bag in which her attendant, a pale-cheeked woman, one proved excellent in her ways, had brought food there for them both; and then Judith put it, all gory, into her hands for her discreet servant to carry home. From there the two women then proceeded onwards, emboldened by courage, until they had escaped, brave, triumphant virgins, from among the army, so that they could clearly see the walls of the beautiful city, Bethulia, shining. Then the ring-adorned women hurried forward on their way until, cheered at heart, they had reached the rampart gate.

There were soldiers, vigilant men, sitting and keeping watch in the fortress just as Judith the artful-minded virgin had enjoined the despondent folk when she set out on her mission, courageous lady. Now she had returned, their darling, to her people, and quickly then the shrewd woman summoned one of the men to come out from the spacious city to meet her and speedily to let them in through the gate of the rampart; and to the victorious people she spoke these words:

'I can tell you something worthy of thanksgiving: that you need no longer grieve in spirit. The ordaining Lord, the Glory of kings, is gracious to you. It has been revealed abroad through the world that dazzling and glorious success is impending for you and triumph is granted you over those injuries which you long have suffered.'

Then the citizens were merry when they heard how the saintly woman spoke across the high rampart. The army was in ecstasies and the people rushed towards the fortress gate, men and women together, in flocks and droves; in throngs and troops they surged forward and ran towards the handmaid of the Lord, both old and young in their thousands. The heart of each person in that city of mead-halls was exhilarated when they realised that Judith had returned home; and then with humility they hastily let her in.

Then the clever woman ornamented with gold directed her attentive servant-girl to unwrap the harrier's head and to display the bloody object to the citizens as proof of how she had fared in the struggle. The noble lady then spoke to the whole populace:

'Victorious heroes, leaders of the people; here you may openly gaze upon the head of that most odious heathen warrior, the dead Holofernes, who perpetrated upon us the utmost number of violent killings of men and painful miseries, and who intended to add to it even further, but God did not grant him longer life so that he might plague us with afflictions. I took his life, with God's help. Now I want to urge each man among these citizens, each shield-wielding soldier, that you immediately get yourselves ready for battle. Once the God of beginnings, the steadfastly gracious King, has sent the radiant light from the east, go forth bearing shields, bucklers in front of your breasts and mail-coats and shining helmets into the ravagers' midst; cut down the commanders, the doomed leaders, with gleaming swords. Your enemies are sentenced to death and you shall have honour and glory in the fight according as the mighty Lord has signified to you by my hand.'

Then an army of brave and keen men was quickly got ready for the battle. Renowned nobles and their companions advanced; they carried victory-banners; beneath their helms the heroes issued forth straight into battle from out of the holy city upon the very dawning of the day. Shields clattered, loudly resonated. At that, the lean wolf in the wood rejoiced, and that bird greedy for carrion, the black raven. Both knew that the men of that nation meant to procure them their fill among these doomed to die; but in their wake flew the eagle, eager for food, speckled-winged; the dark-feathered, hook-beaked bird sang a battle-chant.

On marched the soldiers, warriors to the warfare, protected by their shields, hollowed linden bucklers, they who a while previously had been suffering the abuse of aliens, the blasphemy of heathens. This was strictly repaid to all the Assyrians in the spear-fight once the Israelites under their battle-ensigns had reached the camp. Firmly entrenched, they vigorously let fly from the curved bow showers of darts, arrows, the serpents of battle. Loudly the fierce fighting-men roared and sent spears into their cruel enemies' midst. The heroes, the in-dwellers of the land, were enraged against the odious race. Stern of mood they advanced; hardened of heart they roughly roused their drink-stupefied enemies of old. With their hands, retainers unsheathed from scabbards bright-ornamented swords, proved of edge, and set about the Assyrian warriors in earnest, intending to spite them. Of that army they spared not one of the men alive, neither the lowly nor the mighty, whom they could overpower.

Thus in the hour of morn those comrades in arms the whole time harried the aliens until those who were their adversaries, the chief sentries of the army, acknowledged that the Hebrew people were showing them very intensive sword-play. They went to inform the most senior offices of this by word of mouth and they roused those warriors and fearfully announced to them in their drunken stupor the dreadful news, the terror of the morning, the frightful sword-encounter.

Then, I have heard, those death-doomed heroes quickly shook off their sleep and thronged in flocks, demoralised men, to the pavilion of the debauched Holofernes. They meant to give their lord warning of battle at once, before the terror and the force of the Hebrews descended upon him; all supposed that the men's leader and that beautiful woman were together in the handsome tent, the noble Judith and the lecher, fearsome and ferocious. Yet there was not one of the nobles who dared awaken the warrior to enquire how it had turned out for the soldier with the holy virgin, the woman of the Lord.

The might of the Hebrews, their army, was drawing closer; vehemently they fought with tough and bloody weapons and violently they indemnified with gleaming swords their former quarrels and old insults: in that day's work the Assyrians' repute was withered, their arrogance abased. The men stood around their lord's tent, extremely agitated and growing gloomier in spirit. Then all together they began to cough and loudly make noises and, having no success, to chew the grist with their teeth, suffering agonies. The time of their glory, good fortune and valorous doings was at an end. The nobles thought to awaken their lord and friend; they succeeded not at all.

Then one of the soldiers belatedly and tardily grew so bold that he ventured pluckily into the pavilion as necessity compelled him. Then he found his lord lying pallid on the bed, deprived of his spirit, dispossessed of life. Straightaway then he fell chilled to the ground, and distraught in mind he began to tear his hair and his clothing alike and he uttered these words to the soldiers who were waiting there miserably outside:

'Here is made manifest our own perdition, and here it is imminently signalled that the time is drawn near, along with its tribulations, when we must perish and be destroyed together in the strife. Here, hacked by the sword, decapitated, lies our lord.'

Then distraught in mind they threw down their weapons; demoralised they went scurrying away in flight. The nation magnified in strength attacked them in the rear until the greatest part of the army lay on the field of victory levelled by battle, hacked by swords, as a treat for the wolves and a joy to the carrion-greedy birds. Those who survived fled from the linden spears of their foes. In their wake advanced the troop of Hebrews, honoured with the victory and glorified in the judgment: the Lord God, the almighty Lord, had come handsomely to their aid. Swiftly then with their gleaming swords those valiant heroes made an inroad through the thick of their foes; they hacked at targes and sheared through the shield-wall. The Hebrew spear-throwers were wrought up to the fray; the soldiers lusted mightily after a spear-contest on that occasion. There in the dust fell the main part of the muster-roll of the Assyrian nobility, of that odious race. Few survivors reached their native land.

The soldiers of royal renown turned back in retirement amidst carnage and reeking corpses. That was the opportunity for the land's in-dwellers to seize from those most odious foes, their old dead enemies, bloodied booty, resplendent accoutrements, shield and broad sword, burnished helmets, costly treasures. The guardians of their homeland had honourably conquered their enemies on the battlefield and destroyed with swords their old persecutors. In their trail lay dead those who of living peoples had been most inimical to their existence.

Then the whole nation, most famous of races, proud, curled-locked, for the duration of one month were carrying and conveying into the beautiful city, Bethulia, helmets and hip-swords, grey mail-coats, and men's battle-dress ornamented with gold, more glorious treasures than any man among ingenious men can tell. All that the people splendidly gained, brave beneath their banners in the fray, through the shrewd advice of Judith, the courageous woman. As a reward the celebrated spear-men brought back for her from the expedition the sword and the bloodied helmet of Holofernes as well as his huge mail-coat adorned with red gold; and everything the ruthless lord of the warriors owned of riches or personal wealth, or rings and of beautiful treasures, they gave it to that beautiful and resourceful lady.

For all this Judith gave glory to the Lord of hosts who granted her esteem and renown in the realm of earth and likewise too a reward in heaven, the prize of victory in the glory of the sky because she always had truth faith in the Almighty. Certainly at the end she did not doubt the reward for which she long had yearned.

For this be glory into eternity to the dear Lord who created the wind and the clouds, the skies and the spacious plains and likewise the cruel seas and the joys of heaven, through his peculiar mercy.

For Chapter 5: Encomium Emmae

The *Encomium*, as both the title and introduction of the work make clear, is a book 'devoted entirely to the praise of Queen Emma'. Who the author was we do not know, though it seems likely that he was a cleric belonging to a Flemish community (either St Omer or St Bertin) and that he was writing during the reign of Emma's son Harthacnut (1040–2), to fulfil a commission laid upon him by Emma before she returned to

England after her spell as an exile in Flanders. The following extract is taken from Book 3, chapters 1–12 of the *Encominum Emmae*. (Source: *Encomium Emmae Reginae*, ed. A. Campbell (1949), pp. 39–53.)

1. When Cnut was dead and honourably buried in the monastery built at Winchester in honour of St Peter, the lady, Queen Emma, remained alone in the kingdom, sorrowing for the bitter death of her lord and alarmed at the absence of her sons. For one of them, namely Harthacnut, whom his father had made king of the Danes, was in his own kingdom, and two others were residing with their relative Robert, for they had been sent to the country of Normandy to be brought up. And so it came to pass that certain Englishmen, forgetting the piety of their lately deceased king, preferred to dishonour their country than to ornament it, and deserted the noble sons of the excellent Queen Emma, choosing as their king one Harold, who is declared, owing to a false estimation of the matter, to be a son of a certain concubine of the above-mentioned King Cnut; as a matter of fact, the assertion of very many people has it that the same Harold was secretly taken from a servant who was in childbed, and put in the chamber of the concubine, who was indisposed; and this can be believed as the more truthful account. Soon after being chosen, this man, fearing for the future, summoned Archbishop Æthelnoth, a man gifted with high courage and wisdom, and commanded and prayed to be consecrated king, and that the royal sceptre, which was committed to the archbishop's custody, should be given to him together with the crown, and that he should be led by the archbishop, since it was not legal that this should be done by another, to the lofty throne of the kingdom. The archbishop refused, declaring by oath that while the sons of Queen Emma lived he would approve or consecrate no other man as king: 'Them Cnut entrusted to my good faith; to them I owe fidelity, and with them I shall maintain faith. I lay the sceptre and crown upon the holy altar, and to you I neither refuse nor give them; but by my apostolic authority, I forbid all bishops that any one of them should remove these things, or give them to you or consecrate you. As for you, if you dare, lay hands upon what I have committed to God and his table.' He, wretched man, did not know what to do or whither to turn. He used threats and it did not avail him, he promised gifts and sorrowed to gain nothing, for that apostolic man could not be dislodged by threats or diverted by gifts. At length he departed in despair, and so despised the episcopal benediction, that he hated not only the benediction itself, but indeed even turned from the whole Christian religion. For when others entered church to hear mass, as is the Christian custom, he either surrounded the glades with dogs for the chase, or occupied himself with any other utterly paltry matters, wishing only to be able to avoid what he hated. When the English observed his behaviour they sorrowed, but since they had chosen him

to be their king, they were ashamed to reject him, and accordingly
decided that he should be their king to the end.

2. But Emma, the queen of the kingdom, silently awaited the end of
the matter, and for some little time was in her anxiety daily gaining
God's help by prayer. But the usurper was secretly laying traps for the
queen, since as yet he dared not act openly, but he was allowed to hurt
her by nobody. Accordingly, he devised an unrighteous scheme with
his companions, and proposed to kill the children of his lady, that
henceforth he might be able to reign in security and live in his sins. He
would, however, have effected nothing whatever in this matter if,
helped by the deceit of fraudulent men, he had not devised what we are
about to narrate. For having hit upon a trick, he had a letter composed as
if from the queen to her sons, who were resident in Normandy, and of
this I do not hesitate to subjoin a copy:

3. 'Emma, queen in name only, imparts motherly salutation to her
sons, Edward and Alfred. Since we severally lament the death of our
lord, the king, most dear sons, and since daily you are deprived more
and more of the kingdom, your inheritance, I wonder what plan you
are adopting, since you are aware that the delay arising from your
procrastination is becoming from day to day a support to the usurper
of your rule. For he goes round hamlets and cities ceaselessly, and
makes the chief men his friends by gifts, threats and prayers. But they
would prefer that one of you should rule over them, than that they
should be held in the power of him who now commands them. I
entreat, therefore, that one of you come to me speedily and privately,
to receive from me wholesome counsel, and to know in what manner
this matter, which I desire, must be brought to pass. Send back word
what you are going to do about these matters by the present messenger, whoever he may be. Farewell, beloved ones of my heart.'

4. This forgery, when it had been composed at the command of
Harold the tyrant, was sent to the royal youths by means of deceitful
couriers, presented to them as being from their unwitting mother, and
received by them with honour, as a gift from their parent. They read its
wiles in their innocence, and alas too trustful of the fabrication, they
unwisely replied to their parent that one of them would come to her,
and determined upon day and time and place for her. The messengers,
accordingly, returned and told the foes of God what answer had been
made to them by the most noble youths. And so they awaited the
prince's arrival, and schemed what they should do to him to injure him.
Now on the fixed day Alfred, the younger prince, selected companions
with his brother's approval, and beginning his journey came into the
country of Flanders. There he lingered a little with Marquis Baldwin,
and when asked by him to lead some part of his forces with him as a
precaution against the snares of the enemy, was unwilling to do so, but
taking only a few men of Boulogne, boarded ship and crossed the sea.

But when he came near to the shore, he was soon recognised by the enemy, who came and intended to attack him, but he recognised them and ordered the ships to be pushed off from that shore. He landed, however, at another port, and attempted to go to his mother, deeming that he had entirely evaded the bane of the ambush. But when he was already near his goal, Earl Godwine met him and took him under his protection, and forthwith became his soldier by averment under oath. Diverting him from London, he led him into the town called Guildford, and lodged his soldiers there in separate billets by twenties, twelves and tens, leaving a few with the young man, whose duty was to be in attendance upon him. And he gave them food and drink in plenty, and withdrew personally to his own lodging, until he should return in the morning to wait upon his lord with due honour.

5. But after they had eaten and drunk, and being weary, had gladly ascended their couches, behold, men leagued with the most abominable tyrant Harold appeared, entered the various billets, secretly removed the arms of the innocent men, confined them with iron manacles and fetters, and kept them till the morrow to be tortured. But when it was morning, the innocent men were led out, and were iniquitously condemned without a hearing. For they were all disarmed and delivered with their hands bound behind their backs to most vicious executioners, who were ordered, furthermore, to spare no man unless the tenth lot should reprieve him. Then the torturers made the bound men sit in a row, and reviling them beyond measure, followed the example of that murderer of the Theban Legion, who first decimated guiltless men, though more mercifully than they did. For that utterly pagan ruler spared nine of the Christians and killed the tenth, but these most profane and false Christians killed nine of the good Christians and let the tenth go. That pagan, though he massacred Christians, nevertheless ordered that they should be beheaded on an open plain unfettered by bonds, like glorious soldiers. But these, though they were in name Christians, were nevertheless in their actions totally pagan, and butchered the innocent heroes with blows from their spears bound as they were, like swine. Hence all ages will justly call such torturers worse than dogs, since they brought to condemnation the worthy persons of so many soldiers not by soldierly force but by their treacherous snares. Some, as has been said, they slew, some they placed in slavery to themselves; others they sold, for they were in the grip of blind greed, but they kept a few loaded with bonds to be subjected to greater mockery. But the divine pity did not fail the innocent men who stood in such peril, for I myself have seen many whom it snatched from that derision, acting from heaven without the help of man, so that the impediments of manacles and fetters were shattered.

6. Therefore, since I am dealing briefly with the sufferings of the soldiers, it remains that I should curtail the course of my narrative in

telling of the martyrdom of their prince, that is to say the glorious Alfred, lest perchance if I should choose to go over all that was done to him in detail, I should multiply the grief of many people and particularly of you, Lady Queen. In this matter I beg you lady, not to ask more than this, which I, sparing your feelings, will briefly tell. For many things could be told if I were not sparing your sorrow. Indeed there is no greater sorrow for a mother than to see or hear of the death of a most dear son. The royal youth, then, was captured secretly in his lodging, and having been taken to the island called Ely, was first of all mocked by the most wicked soldiery. Then still more contemptible persons were selected, that the lamented youth might be condemned by them in their madness. When these men had been set up as judges, they decreed that first of all both his eyes should be put out as a sign of contempt. After they prepared to carry this out, two men were placed on his arms to hold them meanwhile, one on his breast, and one on his legs, in order that the punishment might be more easily inflicted on him. Why do I linger over this sorrow? As I write my pen trembles, and I am horror-stricken at what the most blessed youth suffered. Therefore I will the sooner turn away from the misery of so great a disaster, and touch upon the conclusion of this martyrdom as far as its consummation. For he was held fast, and after his eyes had been put out was most wickedly slain. When this murder had been performed, they left his lifeless body, which the servants of Christ, the monks, I mean, of the same Isle of Ely, took up and honourably interred. However, many miracles occur where his tomb is, as people report who even declare most repeatedly that they have seen them. And it is justly so: for he was martyred in his innocence, and therefore it is fitting that the might of the innocent should be exercised through him. So let Queen Emma rejoice in so great an intercessor, since him, who she formerly had as a son on earth, she now has as a patron in the heavens.

7. But the queen, smitten by so unheard-of a crime, considered in silent thought what it was needful that she should do. And so her mind was carried this way and that in uncertainty, and she was chary of trusting herself further to such perfidy, for she was dazed beyond consolation with sorrow for her murdered son, although she derived comfort in a much greater degree from his assured rest. And so she was, as we have said, distressed for a twofold reason, that is to say, because of misery and sadness at her son's death, and also because of uncertainty concerning what remained of her own life and her position. But perchance at this point some one, whom ill-will towards this lady has rendered spiteful and odious, will protest to me: 'Why did she refuse to die the same death, since she in no way doubted that her son, who had been slain under these conditions of treachery, enjoyed eternal rest?' To rebut this I consider that one must use such a reply as: 'If the persecutor of the Christian religion and faith had been present, she would not have

shrunk from encountering mortal danger. On the other hand it would have appeared wrong and abominable to all the orthodox, if a matron of such reputation had lost her life through desire for worldly dominion, and indeed death would not have been considered a worthy end to the fortunes of so great a lady.' Keeping these and similar arguments in mind, and considering advantageous to her fortunes that authentic injunction of the Lord's exhortation, in which, to wit, He says to the elect, 'If they should persecute you in one city, flee into another,' she acted upon a hope of saving what was left of her position, which was under the circumstances in which she was placed sufficiently sound, and at length followed a sagacious plan by the grace of the divine regard. She believed it expedient for her to seek foreign nations, and she brought this decision to consummation with shrewd judgment. However, she did not find that those nations which she sought were to be foreign to her, for while she sojourned among them she was honoured by them in a most proper manner, just as she was by her own followers. And so she assembled as many nobles who were faithful to herself as she could, in view of the circumstances and the time. When these were present, she told them her inmost thoughts. When they had proceeded to approve the plan put in train by their lady, their ships' supplies are prepared for exile. And so, having enjoyed favourable winds, they crossed the sea and touched at a certain port not far from the town of Bruges. The latter town is inhabited by Flemish settlers, and enjoys very great fame for the number of its merchants and for its affluence in all things upon which mankind places the greatest value. Here indeed she was, as she deserved, honourably received by Baldwin, the marquis of that same province, who was the son of a great and totally unconquered prince, and by his wife Athala (a name meaning 'most noble'), daughter of Robert, king of the French, and Queen Constance. By them, furthermore, a house in the above-named town, suitable for royal outlay, was allotted to the queen, and in addition a kind offer of entertainment was made. These kindnesses she partly accepted with the greatest thanksgiving, partly she shewed that up to a point she did not stand in need.

8. And so, being placed in such great security, she sent messengers to her son Edward to ask that he should come to her without delay. He obeyed them, mounted his horse and came to his mother. But when they had the opportunity for discussion, the son declared that he pitied his mother's misfortunes, but that he was able in no way to help, since the English nobles had sworn no oath to him, a circumstance indicating that help should be sought from his brother. Thereupon Edward returned to Normandy, and the queen still hesitated in her mind as to what she ought to do. After her son's departure, she dispatched messengers to her son Harthacnut who then held sway over the Danes, and through them revealed to him her unheard-of sorrow, and begged

him to hasten to come to her as soon as possible. The horror of so great a crime made his ears tremble, and first of all as he deliberated his spirits sank stunned by intolerable sorrow. For he burned in his heart to go and avenge his brother's injuries, nay more, to obey his mother's message.

9. Accordingly, providing for either eventuality, he got ready the greatest forces he could of ships and soldiers, and assembled the greater number of them in a certain inlet of the sea, to come to his support if on his journey the opportunity to give battle or the need for defence should befall him. For the rest, he set out accompanied by not more than ten ships to go to his mother, who was labouring under the very great distress of sorrow. When, therefore, they were absorbed in their prosperous voyage, and were not only eagerly ploughing the salt foam with brazen prows, but also raising their topsails to the favourable winds, whereas the surface of the sea is never dependable, but is always found to be unreliable and faithless, suddenly a murky tempest of winds and clouds was rolled up from behind, and the surface of the sea forthwith was agitated by overtaking south winds. And so the anchors were dropped from the prows, and caught in the sands of the bottom, which is what is wont to be done in such desperate straits. This incident, although it was distressing to them at the time, is not believed to have taken place without the consent of God, who disposes all things, as the issue of the affair afterwards proved, when the limbs of all yielded to quiet rest and sleep. For on the next night, when Harthacnut was at rest in his bed, by divine providence a vision appeared, which comforted and consoled him and bade him be of good cheer. Furthermore, it exhorted him not to desist from his undertaking, for after a space of a few days the unjust usurper of his kingdom, Harold, would perish, and the kingdom conquered by his father's strength would return safely by most rightful succession to himself, the rightful heir.

10. The dreamer accordingly, when he awoke, was enlightened by the signs described above, and returned thanks to Almighty God for such great consolation, and had at the same time not the slightest doubt about the coming events which the vision above described had foretold. Thereupon, the wrath of the sea having subsided, and the storm having dropped, he spread his bellying sails to the favourable winds; and thus, having enjoyed a successful voyage, he touched at Bruges. Here, having moored his ships with anchors and rods, and having commissioned sailors to look after them, he betook himself directly with chosen companions to the lodging of his mother. What grief and what joy sprang up at his arrival, no page shall ever unfold to you. There was no little pain when his mother beheld with some stretch of her imagination, the face of her lost one in his countenance; likewise she rejoiced with a great joy at seeing the survivor safe in her presence. And so she knew that the tender mercy of God had regard to her, since she was still undeprived of

279

such a consolation. And soon afterwards, while the son was lingering with his mother expecting the events promised by the vision above described, messengers arrived bearing glad tidings, and announced, to wit, that Harold was dead, reporting furthermore that the English nobles did not wish to oppose him, but to rejoice together with him in jubilation of every kind; therefore they begged him not to scorn to return to the kingdom which was his by hereditary right, but to take counsel for both his own position and their safety with regard to the common good.

11. Encouraged by these things, Harthacnut and his mother decided to return to the shores of the ancestral realm. When word of this matter smote the ears of the people, soon you would have seen pain and grief to be universal. For the rich mourned her departure, with whom they had ever enjoyed pleasant converse; the poor mourned her departure, by whose continual generosity they were relieved from the burden of want; the widows mourned with the orphans, whom she had freely enriched when they were taken from the holy baptismal font. Therefore I do not know with what praises to exalt her, who never failed to be immediately present with those being re-born in Christ. Her faith clearly calls for praise and at the same time her kindness is in every way to be extolled. If I should propose to discuss this matter with regard to her individual good deeds, I believe that my time would be exhausted before my subject, so I hasten to return to the course of our narrative.

12. While preparations were being made for the return of the queen and her son, the whole shore was perturbed by lamentation and groaning, and all raised angry right hands to the sky. They wept, in short, that she, whom during her whole exile they had regarded as a fellow citizen, was leaving them. She had not been a burden-some guest to any of the rich, nor had she been oppressive to the poor in any matter whatever. Therefore you would have thought that all were leaving their native soil, you would have said that all the women intended to seek foreign lands along with her. Such was the lamentation on the whole shore, such was the wailing of all the people standing by. Although they rejoiced with her to some extent at her recovery of her old position, nevertheless the matrons could not let her go with dry eyes. At last love of the homeland prevailed, and having kissed all severally and having said a tearful farewell to them, she sought the deep sea with her son and her followers after a great abundance of tears had been shed on both sides.

For Chapter 6: The Sickness of Women

The *Sickness of Women* is a translation of a late Middle English MS (Sloane 2463) itself based, in part, on a translation from a Latin medical textbook of Gilbert the Englishman, whose own work was in turn something of a miscellany. The extract should be read in conjunction with M. Green's article 'Obstetrical and Gynecological Texts in Middle English', *Studies in the Age of Chaucer* 14 (1992), pp. 53–88 and the review by J. Stannard and L. Voigts, *Speculum* 57 (1982), pp. 435–6.

Source: *Medieval Woman's Guide to Health*, ed B. Rowland (1981), pp. 147, 149, 151, 153, 155, 157.)

Excessive bleeding after childbirth.
Women sometimes bleed too much after childbirth, and this makes them very weak. But you should not in this case give her any medicines that are comforting, nor baths nor strong medicated compresses, but other medicines such as were described earlier in the chapter on hemorrhage. Have her bled under the ankle of one foot, and another day under the other ankle. Then give her other medicines as before stated here that we should give, such medicines as were described in the chapter on the retention of blood. And some women have decaying matter when they have a discharge, and sometimes such matter passes from them instead of blood; and sometimes bleeding comes with the blood that they should be purged of. And if they are old women or women that are barren, there is no need to give them medicines. If they are young women, boil watercress, septfoil, cinquefoil, or water parsnips in wine. And let her sit over the smoke of them so that it reaches her privy member.

Alternatively, take wild thyme, make a powder of it, and put it in a bag of sufficient breadth and length to cover both privy members of the woman. And put it on hot and fasten it securely so that it cannot fall off.

Sores of the womb are healed with the juice of plantain and morel, and 6 ounces each of white of egg, juice of purslane, gum tragacanth, and gum arabic. Let this medication be given, and it will act like an excellent mucilage, good for cooling and healing. And if the veins are broken, they should be healed with juice of centaury, Armenian bole, sandragon, myrtle seeds, round birthwort, and with other similar medicines. Also, take this as the main medicine for all kinds of sores in this place if they are due to excessive heat, as they usually are, rather than due to cold. Take 6 drachms each of gum arabic and white gum tragacanth, and steep the mixture in 2 ounces of water of roses, an ounce of myrtle oil, and 6 scruples each of powder of mastic and olibanum. And all these should be made into one preparation like an ointment. And let a discreet woman apply this medication where the sore is, not only to inflammation in this place but to all other places, lacerations, cracks in the lips, and the mouth. Another medicine for the same thing: take gum arabic, 4 drachms of gum tragacanth, 2 drachms of borax, 1 drachm each of camphor, Armenian bole, alkannet, sandragon, half a drachm each of mastic, myrtle, white lead, olibanum, litharge, 4 ounces of oil from the store, 8 drachms of water of roses. Put the gum tragacanth and the borax in the rose water, steep a day and a night until they are all dissolved; then strain them through a light cloth until they come through entirely clean; and have all the other spices made into a fine powder and mixed with the previously mentioned oil, as well as with this mucilage, until they are entirely blended, and then put to use when necessary. This medicine is good for all kinds of cancers, tumors, hot sores, erysipelas, that is, wildfire, sores, carbuncles, ulcers from a morbid secondary form of black bile, and all other such complaints. If the sores are the result of cold, take 4 drachms of mucilage of fenugreek, sarcocolla infused in a mixture of 1 scruple each of camomile, spikenard, mastic, myrrh, cinnamon, and castory, skillfully made into a powder. Mix them all together with 2½ drachms of woman's milk and juice of plantain; when they are well mixed, apply it to the disorder in the privy member because this medicine does away with all the maladies of that place if they can be cured by medicines.

Concerning cancers and ulcers of the womb.
Cancers and festerings of the womb come from old injuries of the womb that have not healed well, but that kind of sickness we will hardly mention because doctors say that, with regard to hidden cancers, it is better than they should be uncured rather than cured or treated. Nevertheless, this ointment is good for such things and for itching and blisters in the uterus. Take a ripe gourd, pare it and clean it inside, grind it very small, and put in a pot on the fire with oil of roses, wax, sheep's tallow, and when they are well boiled, throw in mastic powder and olibanum, and let them boil well together. And afterward strain through a cloth and anoint patients with the medicament inside. And this ointment is also good for burning and scalding; after using it on a sore, place icy leaves boiled in wine on top. A strengthening medicine for all kinds of cancerous complaints; take this medicine for them all. First take half a pound of roots of red dock, 1 pound of roots of iris, boil these roots in 3 quarts of clear water and a quart of white wine; boil them down to half a gallon. And add a little honey, say, 6 drachms with the whites of 16 eggs, clarify the mixture, and wash the privy member carefully with it; then take well-combed cotton and put the cotton gently into a linen bag; then wet the bag with the cotton, and it will clean the cancer without difficulty, and take away the dirt from it. Then make this plaster: take 2 drachms each of gum of white tragacanth and gum arabic, put them to steep in water of roses until they are very soft; then take also 2 drachms each of aloes, lotion of white lead, lotion of frankincense, sandragon, 1 drachm of litharge of gold, 2 drachms of wax, 6 drachms of oil of roses; make very hot a brass mortar and put in it the wax, the oil of tragacanth, and the gum arabic, mix them well

together, and let them cool slightly; then put in the oil of roses with the powders and mix them thoroughly. And when they are well blended and very cold, add camphor with a little more of the oil of crushed roses. And from this mixture make tested medical potions, for it is very good.

For swelling of women's legs when they are pregnant.
The legs of pregnant women will swell. Then take what lies in the smithy's trough beneath his grinding stone, dry it, make a powder of it, mix it with vinegar, and anoint the place that swells with it. Alternatively, lay it on like a plaster. Or take bean-meal flour, mix it with vinegar and oil, and put it on the swelling. Or else anoint it with black soap, and afterward lay a plaster on it of elder leaves fried by themselves in a pan without any other liquor. And the same medicines are good for swelling in a man's feet or for legs that travel by the roads.

To provoke menstruation: Take 1 handful each of parsley roots, fennel, half a handful each of hyssop leaves, savory, betony, laurel leaves, rosemary, lavender, 3 handfuls of catmint, 2½ drachms of dittany, rue, artemisia, 4 drachms each of caraway, polypody, and a flagon of white wine; [have the herbs] cut, cooked thoroughly, strained and again cooked with 1 scruple of saffron, 2 ounces of cloves, half a drachm of grains of paradise, 6 drachms of honey, fetid salt. Take 2 scruples each of white grains of terebinth, colocynth, pounded aloe, citron, ginger, thyme, 2 drachms of hemlock, half a scruple each of black and white hellebore, saffron, pellitory, hemlock seeds, anise seeds, bishop's-weed, caraway, mustard and nasturtium seed and rhubarb, 2½ drachms of parsley, galbanum, panax, vine-palm, and asafetida, 2 drachms each of myrrh, and drawn oil benedicta, 1 scruple each of gum arabic, castory, scammony, euphorbia, spurge, wood aloes, centaury, and French lavender, 2 scruples of larch fungus; let pills be made with leek juice in portions of 2½ drachms with the above-described mixture.

A plaster: Take 2 handfuls of mallows, 1 handful each of milfoil, fennel, and dwarf elder, 3 handfuls each of leaves of leeks; let them be cut very minutely, ground, and roasted with a little water, and let a circular plaster be put around the whole of the stomach up to the vulva.

Fermentation: Take 1 measure of roots of iris, 1 ounce of anise, 1 drachm each of rosemary, calamint, hyssop, savory, and origanum; let them be cooked in equal amounts of wine and water, and let the herbs be placed in a bag, and after fermentation let the bag be placed on the vulva for a mola of the womb and for a dead fetus. Take 2 drachms each of leek seeds, wild celery, myrrh, spikenard, calamint, camel's hay, and the rind of cassia fistula; have anise ground to powder, and let her take it early before having a bath, with water, wine, honey, and a decoction of 1 handful each of savory, hyssop, dittany, madder, elecampane, catmint, iris, dry salt, and southernwood. In like manner, according to

Rhazes, take 6 drachms each of hazelwort, round and long birthwort, 3 drachms each of myrrh, larch fungus, and spikenard; have pills made, each 3 drachms in weight, with a potion of junipers, and they greatly assist in bringing forth the embryo. Take 1 drachm and 18 grains each of iris, hazelwort, tree nightshade, and seeds of three-leaf fennel, 2 drachms of anise, 2 drachms, 2 scruples, and 2 grains each of long birthwort, artemisia, and wood of cassia, 1 drachm, 1 scruple, and 1 grain of lesser centaury, 2 drachms of greater centaury, 2 drachms of carrots, 1 ounce of black hellebore, 1 drachm and 9 grains of laurel leaves, 4 drachms of licorice, 1 ounce of lupins, 2 drachms of fennel, 6 drachms, 2 scruples, and 3 grains of myrrh, 3 drachms of carob, 6 drachms of styptic, 2 drachms, 2 scruples, and 2 grains of Macedonian pellitory, 5 drachms, 1 scruple, and 2 grains of black pepper, 1 drachm of galingale, 2 drachms, 2 scruples, and 2 grains of laurel seed, 2 drachms and 2 grains of spikenard, 2 drachms of potash, that is, gunpowder, 1 drachm, 2 scruples, and 2 grains of camel's hay, some parsley, 1 drachm of savin, 1 drachm, 2 scruples, and 2 grains of balsam wood, some fleawort, 2 drachms and 1 scruple of purified peonies, 2 drachms of cloves, 3 drachms each of roots of caper and cinnamon, honey as sufficient in portions of 4 drachms, with juice of catmint. The before-mentioned remedy of Master Edmund is the giving of a hemagoge, that is to say, a remedy that causes the flow of menstrual blood; for the many ailments of women and of the womb that are not usually purged, it is a marvelous purge. It purges the menstrual blood, and it kills the dead fetus in the uterus and expels it, and is conducive to health after childbirth, breaks the stone in the bladder, and ejects it, causes urination, heals strangury, makes euphrasy work, cures hardening of the spleen, and all things inside, and is most helpful in the case of disorders of the stomach; it cures those who cannot retain their food, vigorously expels phlegm, and cures those who are suffering from the colic disease of the kidneys; it is useful also to a man who wishes to be as healthy as possible. Nothing has been discovered that is more useful to women. For which reason the patients should beware lest it provokes hemorrhoids or flux of the womb or dysentery. It opens the passages of the whole body, brings out a dead fetus and the secundine and purges the bladder, warms the stomach, checks vomiting, destroys flatulence.

For Chapter 7: Christine de Pisan, *The Book of Three Virtues* (also known as *The Treasury of the City of Ladies*)

Christine de Pisan (or Pizan) (1365–c.1430) was of Italian birth; married to a French courtier at the age of 15, she was already a mother of three and a widow by the time she was 25. Her ability to support herself as a professional writer has led to her being a much-studied figure in feminist scholarship in recent years. Although she never came to England (despite invitations from King Henry IV), she had English friends and patrons; her son Jean spent three years in the household of the Earl of Salisbury. *The Book of Three Virtues* is one of her most popular works although unlike some of her other writings it has only recently been translated into English. The extracts which follow are from Book II, chapters 9–10, and Book III, chapters 8 and 12. (Source: *A Medieval Woman's Mirror of Honor: The Treasury of the City of Ladies,* trans. and ed. C. Willard and M. Cosman (1989), pp. 168–72, 209–10, 219–21.)

9. *Which speaks of the lady baronesses and the sort of knowledge which may be useful to them.*

Now it is time to speak to the ladies and demoiselles who live in castles or other sorts of *manors* on their own lands, in *walled cities*, or in smaller market towns. For them this advice should be helpful. Because their estates and powers vary, we must differentiate among them in our discussions of certain things: their status and their style of living. As for their morals and good deeds on God's behalf, certainly they can profit from our advice in the earlier chapters to princesses and women living at court. All women can learn to cultivate virtue and avoid vice. However, the women I address now are powerful women: baronesses and great land owners who nevertheless are not called princesses. Technically, the name 'princess' should not be applied to any but empresses, queens, and duchesses. Yet in Italy and elsewhere, wives of men who because of their land holdings are called princes, after the names of their territories, may be called princesses. Although countesses are not universally called princesses, because they follow duchesses in rank according to the importance of their lands, nonetheless we have included them among the princesses. First we address these baronesses of whom there are many in France, in Brittany, and elsewhere.

These baronesses surpass in honor and power many countesses, even though their titles are not as distinguished. Certain barons have enormous power because of their land, domains, and the nobility that goes with them. Thereby, their wives have considerable status. These women must be highly knowledgeable about government, and wise – in fact, far wiser than most other such women in power. The knowledge of a baroness must be so comprehensive that she can understand everything. Of her a philosopher might have said: 'No one is wise who does not know some part of everything.' Moreover, she must have the courage of a *man.* This means that she should not be brought up overmuch among women nor should she be indulged in extensive and feminine pampering. Why do I say that? If *barons* wish to be honored as they deserve, they spend very little time in their manors and on their own lands. Going to war, attending their prince's court, and traveling are the three primary duties of such a lord. So the lady, his companion, must represent him at home during his absences. Although her husband is served by bailiffs, provosts, *rent collectors*, and land governors, she must govern them all. To do this according to her right she must conduct herself with such wisdom that she will be both feared and loved. As we have said before, the best possible fear comes from love.

When wronged, her men must be able to turn to her for refuge. She must be so skilled and flexible that in each case she can respond suitably. Therefore, she must be knowledgeable in the mores of her locality and instructed in its usages, rights, and customs. She must be a good speaker, proud when pride is needed; circumspect with the scornful, surly, or rebellious; and charitably gentle and humble toward her good, obedient subjects. With the counsellors of her lord and with the advice of elder wise men, she ought to work directly with her people. No one should ever be able to say of her that she acts merely to have her own way. Again, she should have a man's heart. She must know the laws of arms and all things pertaining to warfare, ever prepared to command her men if there is need of it. She has to know both assault and *defense* tactics to insure that her fortresses are well defended, if she has any expectation of attack or believes she must initiate military action. Testing her men, she will discover their qualities of courage and determination before overly trusting them. She must know the number and strength of her men to gauge accurately her resources, so that she never will have to trust vain or feeble promises. Calculating what force she is capable of providing before her lord arrives with reinforcements, she also must know the financial resources she could call upon to sustain military action.

She should avoid oppressing her men, since this is the surest way to incur their hatred. She can best cultivate their loyalty by speaking boldly and consistently to them, according to her council, not giving one reason today and another tomorrow. Speaking words of good courage to her men-at-arms as well as to her other retainers, she will urge them to loyalty and their best efforts.

Such courses of action are suitable for the wise baroness whose absent husband has given her the responsibility and commission to take his place. This advice would be useful if an aggressor or some baron or powerful man should defy her. So, also, the baroness will find particularly expedient the advice in the chapter on widowed princesses. For if during a baron's lifetime his wife knows everything about the management of his affairs, then if left a widow, she will not be ignorant of her rights if anyone dares to try to take advantage of her and make away with her inheritance.

10. *Which explains how ladies and demoiselles who live on their lands should conduct themselves with respect to their households.*
A slightly different manner of life from that of the baronesses is suitable

for ladies and demoiselles living in fortified places or on their lands
outside of towns. Nevertheless, since, like barons, knights, squires, and
gentlemen also must travel and follow the wars, their wives, when they
are wise and capable, should be able to manage the family's affairs.
These women spend much of their lives in households without husbands. The men usually are at court or in distant countries. So the ladies
will have responsibilities for *managing their property*, their revenues, and
their lands. In order for such a woman to act with good judgment, she
must know the *yearly income* from her estate. She must manage it so
well that by conferring with her husband, her gentle words and good
counsel will lead to their agreement to follow a plan for the estate that
their revenues permit. This plan must not be so ambitious that at year's
end they find themselves in debt to their retainers or other creditors.
Surely there is no disgrace in living within one's income, however small
it may be. But it is shameful to live so extravagantly that creditors
daily shout and bellow outside the door, some even raising clubs and
threatening violence. It is also terrible to have to resort to extortion
from one's own men and tenants. The lady or demoiselle must be well
informed about the rights of domain of *fiefs* and secondary fiefs, about
contributions, the lord's *rights of harvest*, shared crops, and all other rights
of possession, and the customs both local and foreign. The world is full
of governors of lord's lands and jurisdictions who are intentionally
dishonest. Aware of this, the lady must be knowledgeable enough to
protect her interests so that she cannot be deceived. She should know
how to manage accounts and should attend to them often, also super-
intending her agents' treatment of her tenants and men. If they are being
deceived or harassed beyond reasonable bounds, both she and her
husband would suffer. As for penalties against poor people, she should
be more compassionate than rigorous.

Farming also is this good housekeeper's domain. In what weather
and in what season the fields should be fertilised; whether the land is
moist or dry; the best way to have furrows run according to the lay of
the land; their proper depth, straightness, and parallel layout; and the
favorable time for sowing with seed suited to the land – all these she
must know. Likewise, she must know about vineyards if the land lies
in a region where there are grapes. She requires good laborers
and supervisors in these activities, and she should not hire people
who change masters from season to season. It is a bad sign if workers are always on the move. Nor should she hire workers who are too
old, for they will be lazy and feeble, nor too young, for they will be
frivolous.

She will insist that her laborers get up early. If she is a good manager
she won't depend on anyone else to see to this but will arise early
herself, put on a cloak, go to the window, and watch there until she sees
them go out, for laborers usually are inclined to laziness. She should

often take her recreation in the fields to see just how they are working, for many willingly stop raking the ground beyond scratching the surface if they think nobody notices. There are plenty of workers capable of sleeping in the shade of a willow tree in the field, leaving the workhorses or the oxen to graze by themselves, caring only that by evening they can say they have put in their day. The good housekeeper must keep her eyes wide open....

8. Which speaks of artisans' wives and how they should conduct themselves.
Now we must speak of the lifestyle of women married to the artisans who live in the cities and good towns, both in Paris and elsewhere. Of course, these women will find valuable the good advice already given to others if they so wish. However, although certain trades are more highly regarded than others (for instance, goldsmiths, embroiderers, armorers, and tapestry weavers are thought more distinguished than masons and shoemakers), we address the wives of all craftsmen. All of them should be attentive and diligent.

If they wish to earn money honorably, they should urge their husbands and their workmen to take up their trade early in the morning and leave it late. No trade is so good that if one is not hard-working one barely lives from one crust of bread to the next. Urging the others to action, she herself should put her hand to the task, making sure that she knows the craft so well that she can direct the workmen if her husband is not there and reprove them if they do not work well. She must admonish them against laziness; a master often is deserted by irresponsible, lethargic workmen. When her husband gets a commission for some difficult and unusual task, she firmly must convince him not to accept any work through which he might suffer a loss. If he does not personally know his client, she should advise him to produce as little work as possible on *credit*. Several already have been ruined by this. Sometimes greed to earn more or the importance of the tendered offer tempts one to such risks.

The artisan's wife should keep her husband attracted to her by love, so that he will stay at home the more willingly, not tempted to join those foolish bands of *young men in taverns* and not likely to dissipate his earnings with superfluous, outrageous expenses, as many young artisans do, especially in Paris. Rather, treating him with tenderness, she should keep him nearby. Common wisdom has it that three things drive a man from his home: a quarrelsome wife, a smoking hearth, and a leaking roof.

Furthermore, she should be willing to stay home, not running here and there every day, gossiping in the neighborhood to find out what everybody else is doing, nor frequenting her cronies. All this makes for poor housekeeping. Neither is it good for her to go to so many gatherings across town, nor to go travelling off needlessly on pilgrimages, which invariably would cause unnecessary expense.

She also should encourage her husband to let them live within their income so that their expenses will not be greater than their earnings, which would force them into debt at the year's end. If she has children, she first should have them taught at school so that they will better know how to serve God; then she ought to have them apprenticed to some trade so that they can earn their living. For a great gift to one's child is knowledge, a skill, or a trade. Beyond these, the mother above all must protect the child from affectation and indulgence. These greatly discredit children of the good towns – and reflect badly on their fathers and mothers, otherwise expected to be the source of virtue and good habits. Sometimes, however, parents so spoil their children by pampering them during their years of growing up that they cause their offsprings' ultimate misfortune and ruination. . . .

12. *Which speaks to the wives of laborers.*

Now drawing close to the end of our discussion – for which the time has come – we will speak to the simple wives of village workers. For them it is hardly necessary to forbid expensive ornaments and extravagant clothes; for they are well protected from all that. Nevertheless, though commonly they are nourished with black bread, milk, bacon, and soup, their thirst quenched with water, and though they have heavy enough burdens to bear, still their lives often are more secure and better nourished than the lives of those seated in high places. Because all creatures, no matter what their estate, need instruction in living well, we wish these women to participate in our lessons.

Humble women living in the village, on the plains, or in the mountains! You often cannot hear what the church preaches about salvation except from your priest or chaplain in his brief Sunday instruction. If our lesson should reach your ears, remember it so that the ignorance which could mislead you will not hinder your salvation.

Know, first of all, that there is a single God: all powerful, completely good, just, wise, from whom nothing is hidden, and who rewards every being for good or evil according to what she deserves. He alone should be perfectly loved and served. Because He is so good, He holds agreeable all the service laid before Him with good heart. Because He is so wise, He recognises everyone's potentialities; if the heart is in it, it is enough for each to do for Him with pure devotion whatever she is able. Some among you, by whose labor the world gains its sustenance and nourishment, have neither leisure nor ability to serve Him through fasting, saying prayers, or attending church, as do the women in the larger towns. Yet you have as great a need of salvation as they. You must serve Him in another manner.

Whole-heartedly and willingly, as you love Him, you must be sure that you do not do unto your neighbors or others what you would not have them do unto you. You must admonish your husbands to do likewise. If working the land for others, they must do it well and loyally, as if for yourselves. At harvest time, they should pay the master with wheat that has been grown on the land, if such is the agreement, and not mix in oats, pretending that nothing else was grown there, not hide the good ewes or the best rams at their neighbor's in order to pay the master with inferior animals, and not pretend that his best ones are dead by showing him the skins of other animals, nor pay him with the worst fleeces. Nor should they give the master a dishonest accounting of his carts or other property, nor of his poultry.

Furthermore, they should not cut wood from another's property without permission to build houses. When they take responsibility for the vineyards, they should be diligent and thorough, and work at the proper season. When the master commissions them to hire helpers, if they are hired at four groats a day, they should not pretend they cost seven. In all such matters, good wives must encourage their husbands to prudence; otherwise they will damn themselves. Working with loyalty not only will make all your tasks more agreeable but also will assure your salvation by living a life pleasing to God.

You women, yourselves, should do what you can to help your husbands, neither breaking down hedges nor allowing the children to; not stealing grapes, fruit, vegetables, or anything else from someone else's garden either by night or day; not putting animals to graze in a neighbor's seeded fields or meadows; not stealing from anyone else or letting anyone else steal from you. Go to church whenever possible, pay *tithes* to God faithfully (and not with the worst things), and say *Pater Nosters*. Live in peace with the neighbors, without perpetual *lawsuits* over trifles – as has become the habit of many villagers who seem never happy unless they are in court. Believe in God, and pity those in trouble. By following these paths, all good people can ensure their salvation, men as well as women.

For Chapter 8: Glanvill

Glanvill is the name given to a legal treatise written c.1187–9 during the reign of Henry II. Although we do not know who the author was, it seems certain that he had close connections with the royal court and it is likely that he had had some professional training as a lawyer. The work is generally recognised as being 'the first text-book of common law'. This extract is from Book VI, chapters 15–18. (Source: *Glanvill*, ed. G. D. G. Hall (1965), pp. 65–9.)

It should be noted that a man may endow his wife in these words: 'I give you this land or vill by name, with all appurtenances'; if at that time some appurtenance was not in his demesne, nor was he seised of it at the time of the marriage, and during his life he recovered it by legal proceedings or acquired it lawfully in some other way, his wife can lawfully claim that appurtenance with the others as dower after her husband's death.

It should be known, moreover, that if any woman's husband sells his wife's dower to another after he has endowed her with it, his heir must, if he can, deliver that dower to the woman, and must give to the purchaser reasonable lands in exchange for what was sold or given by his ancestor; if he cannot deliver to the woman, he must give her reasonable lands in exchange.

When no part of a woman's dower is vacant, so that she has none of it, then the plea is dealt with from the beginning in the lord king's court, and he who is holding the dower shall be summoned by the following writ:

The writ for making a summons for dower where none is yet had

The king to the sheriff, greeting. Command N. justly and without delay to cause M., who was the wife of R., to have her reasonable dower in such-and-such a vill, which she claims to have as the gift of the said R. her husband and of which she has none, as she says, and which she alleges he is unjustly withholding from her. If he will not do this, summon him by good summoners to be before me or my justices on a certain day, to show why he has not done it. And have there the summoners and this writ. Witness, etc.

The presence of the heir is necessary

Whoever is holding the dower, whether the heir or some other person, the heir must in all cases be present to answer the demandant for her dower. If it is some person other than the heir who is withholding the dower from the woman, then he shall be summoned by the writ just given; and the heir shall be summoned by the writ given previously.

The plea between the heir and the woman can take many forms. The woman will claim her dower either as nominated dower or as reasonable dower which has not been nominated. Again, the heir will either admit that dower was nominated to her but was not the land which she claims, or will say that none was nominated. If, then, the dispute between them concerns the existence of nominated dower or conflicting views as to what dower was nominated, then procedure in this plea is in the manner set out above.

However, if reasonable dower with no specific nomination is claimed, it is clear law that the heir must assign to the woman as dower one third of the whole free tenement which his ancestor had in demesne on the day he married her, complete in all respects as to lands and tenements and advowsons of churches; so that, if there is only one church in the whole inheritance and it happens to fall vacant in the woman's lifetime after the death of her husband, the heir may not present a parson to that church without the woman's consent. The chief messuage is exempted because it cannot be given as dower; nor shall it be divided, but shall remain intact. Moreover, property held by women as dower from a previous endowment is not included in making the division. Furthermore, if two or more manors are to be divided, the chief manor shall not be divided but shall go intact together with the chief messuage to the heir, and satisfaction shall be made to the woman from the other manor or manors. It should be noted that assignment of dower to the woman shall not be postponed because the heir is under age.

It should also be noted that if land is given to any woman as nominated dower and a church has been founded in that fee, the woman shall have the free presentation to it after the death of her husband and can grant the church to any suitable clerk if it falls vacant; but she cannot grant it to a [religious] community, because this would take away for ever the right of the heir. However, if the woman's husband during his life grants the church to a clerk, the clerk can keep the church for the rest of his life even if it is done after the husband endowed his wife with that land. Of course, if the husband grants the church to a religious house, then after his death the church ought to be delivered to the woman and she shall have the free presentation to it during her life; after the woman and the clerk who was instituted parson by her presentation have both died, the church shall revert again to that religious house, to remain with it for ever.

It should be known also that if a man's wife is separated from him during his lifetime because of some shameful act, she cannot have any claim to dower. I state the same rule if she is divorced from him because of consanguinity, namely that she can claim no dower; and yet her children can be heirs and by the law of the realm they succeed to their father by hereditary right.

It should also be noted that when a son and heir marries a wife with his father's consent, and gives his wife as dower by assignment of his father a certain part of his father's land, she cannot ever in future claim more of it as dower. However, if her husband predeceases his father it is uncertain whether she can keep that land as dower and whether her husband's father is bound to warrant the land for her.

If a woman has more as dower than properly belongs to her, the sheriff shall be commanded by the following writ to have it measured:

The writ for measuring dower

The king to the sheriff, greeting. B. has complained to me that M. his mother has more of his inheritance as dower than she ought to have and belongs to her as reasonable dower. Therefore I command you justly and without delay to have it measured, and justly and without delay to cause the said B. to have what he ought to have as his right and inheritance, and justly and without delay to cause the said M. to have what she ought to have and belongs to her as her reasonable dower; that he need no longer complain for default of justice in this matter. Witness, etc.

For Chapter 9: The Book of St Gilbert

The Book of St Gilbert was composed by a canon of the Order of Sempringham as a compilation of all the documents necessary for the canonisation of Gilbert, founder of the order. Gilbert died in 1189; he was canonised in 1202. *The Book* includes a *Life*, a number of letters concerning a controversial period in the order's history, and accounts of miracles attributed to Gilbert. The following extract is taken from chapters 9–11 of the *Life*. (Source: *The Book of St Gilbert*, ed. R. de Foreville and G. Keir (1987), pp. 31, 33, 35, 37, 39.)

9. The origin of the Order of Sempringham and the enclosing of nuns

At that time, when Henry I reigned in England, as Gilbert says in the book which he wrote about the building of his monasteries, there were in the village of Sempringham some girls living a secular life; their minds had received the seed of God's word, which he had constantly supplied to them, and, with the help of moisture and warmth, they grew until white already to harvest. Wishing to overcome the temptations of their sex and of the world, these girls longed to cling without hindrance to a heavenly bridegroom. Holy Gilbert, filled with God's charity, had arranged to devote to His service the churches of Sempringham and [West] Torrington mentioned above, and to distribute his own possessions to the needy. When he found no men willing to lead such strict lives for God's sake, Gilbert thought it right to make over everything he owned to the use of such girls as, being truly poor in spirit, could obtain the kingdom of heaven for themselves and for others. Thus he made for himself friends of the mammon of unrighteousness that they might receive him into everlasting habitations. However, he did not at first make friends for himself of men, but, to rejoice with him over the coin which had been found, he called together women as his friends, who in their chastity later too brought him forth many men to share in this friendship. The natural law of pity instructs us, and divine counsel urges us, to do good without stinting to weaker folk, and for this a richer reward is to be expected. Because the fruit of virgins is one hundredfold, when he abandoned his own possessions in order to preserve their virgin status he received a hundredfold and possesses eternal life. Moreover, following the correct way of giving, he bestowed his goods upon the righteous, in accordance with the saying: 'Give to the good and do not harbour sinners.' From their number he consecrated seven virgins aflame with desire for heaven as temples to the sevenfold spirit, so that if adorned by virtue their virginity might win merit. For what use is a lamp which is empty of oil? And what advantage is it if the flesh is wholesome but the mind corrupt, or the body pure and the heart tainted? On this basis the heathen would be virtuous when their whole life is a sin. That the girls might become holy in mind and body he prepared for them and put forward the means of sanctity with which they might secure their own salvation. In order to please Him in whose service he has enlisted, he who fights on God's side never involves himself in secular business; and, if what is clear in Dinah's case applies to all women everywhere, tender virginity is frequently and easily tempted by the serpent's cunning; therefore he shut them away from the world's clamour and the sight of men, so that having entered the king's chamber they might be free in solitude for the embrace of the bridegroom alone. And since to obtain salvation it is not enough to desist from evil unless this is followed by the performance of good works, he dictated for them and taught them the law of holiness, by which they might please their heavenly bridegroom and, when they had become beloved, always remain in his chaste embrace. He gave them instructions concerning their life and discipline, urging and ordering them to preserve chastity, humility, obedience, charity, and the other rules of life, all of which they willingly accepted and devoutly kept.

In the minds of these women there gleamed the image of a valuable pearl, which they bought, giving themselves and their possessions for it. Further, although they lived in the flesh, their life transcended it; but because they did live in the flesh and could not exist outside it, he made available for their use all that the condition of fleshly need requires in the form of food, clothing, shelter, and the other necessities of life according to the degree judged right by his prudence. In this way dwellings suitable for the religious life were duly built, together with an enclosure sealed on every side. Then, with the aid and counsel of the venerable bishop Alexander, he enclosed the handmaidens of Christ to live a solitary life under the wall on the northern side of the church of St Andrew the Apostle in the village of Sempringham. Only a window was preserved which could be opened so that necessaries could be passed in through it. They lived in the world but he sought to set them apart from it, to exile them from their land, their kin, and their father's house, so that they should be like a church, or rather be made a church themselves, and oblivious of their families and homes – in other words leaving behind all curiosity, concupiscence, and ambition – might cause the highest King to feel desire of their beauty. I repeat he sought by imprisoning their bodies in this way to display, or rather bring about, the exiling of their souls to God, because the world's throng often makes a great barrier – very great indeed – separating us from a sense of God's presence. And as the women were not allowed to go out anywhere, even to perform or obtain necessities, he appointed to their service some poor girls, who served them dressed in secular attire; they were to transfer whatever had to be given or received through the window in a proper fashion. He had left this single opening to be used only at a suitable time; in fact he would have fastened it permanently if humans could have lived without human things. There was a door, but it was never unlocked except by his command, and it was not for the women to go out through but for him to go in to them when necessary. He himself was the keeper of this door and its key. For wherever he went and wherever he stayed, like an ardent and jealous lover he carried with him the key to that door as the seal of their purity.

10. *The calling of lay sisters*

Further, he took care that no trouble from outside should break in upon the peace and quiet of these women, because he learnt from wise religious that it is not safe for young girls in secular life who wander about everywhere to serve those in religious orders. Since evil conversation destroys good behaviour, he was anxious that they should not report or perform any worldly deed which might offend the nuns' minds. And so, on the persuasion and advice of such men, it came about that these serving women asked, along with the life of religion, for a habit to be granted them in which they could minister to the handmaidens of Christ, leading a poor but honourable existence. See how the grain of corn produced another shoot as it fell to the earth. When blessed Gilbert saw this, his heart was filled with joy because of their zeal for the faith. But he was unwilling hastily or lightly to impose the heavy yoke of a vow upon untried souls and especially upon simple and ignorant women, who commonly promise what they do not understand and more than they can perform. For he was afraid that later perhaps, overcome by regret, they would renounce their vow, bringing greater ruin upon themselves and destroying the holy life of religion. Truly the souls of novices must be tested lest Satan transform himself into an angel of light and the wolf put on sheep's clothing, the sparrow the feathers of a hawk, and the wild ass the limbs of a lion. So that they might understand what they were doing and reply for themselves as mature adults, he spoke to them in advance and laid before them all the rigour of monastic discipline and a way of life which was stricter than any that they had ever experienced or anywhere witnessed. He preached to them contempt for the world and the abandonment of all property; restraint upon the will and mortification of the flesh; continual work and infrequent rest; many vigils and little sleep; extended fasting and bad food; rough clothing with no adornment; confinement within the cloister to ensure that they did no evil and periods of silence lest they speak it; constant prayer and meditation to prevent them from thinking what was forbidden. The women claimed that for God's sake all these things pleased them and they reckoned austerity to be comfort, work rest, and tribulations a delight so long as they could attain what they had chosen. It is true that the want they suffered in their poverty and the labour of begging forced these women to undertake difficulties willingly so long as they were assured of a permanent livelihood. However, the love of God and their souls' salvation led them on to endure hardship for a time that they might earn everlasting rest. Thus virtue was made out of necessity and, although in some of them the object of their original resolution was perhaps less than ideal, this did not prevent but secured for them the accomplishment of good works. But even so, being a prudent man, Gilbert did not wish to bind them as yet with a vow, in order that they might undergo the usual probation; instead he told them to wait for a year to pass, that their desire might actually increase with the delay.

11. *The conversion of lay brethren*

Now because women's efforts achieve little without help from men, he took on men, and put those he kept as servants about his house and on his land in charge of the nuns' external and more arduous tasks; some of them he had raised from childhood at his own expense, others were fugitives from their masters freed in the name of religion, and others again were destitute beggars. For he was the true servant of the Gospels who, following his Lord's command, went out into the streets and open spaces of the city and forced all those that he found poor, weak, blind, and lame, to enter, that the Lord's house might be filled. Because all these men, spurred both by the poverty of their human life and by their longing for the life of heaven, wanted exactly what the lay sisters desired and requested, he took the same course of action in their case as in the women's, and finally bestowed the habit upon both in token of humility and renunciation of the world. He imposed on them many heavy tasks and a few light ones, which we have recorded above, as well as spiritual qualities like humility, obedience, and patience and the like, which are difficult to perform but are greatly rewarded; all these they accepted most willingly and promised under oath to observe. See how the talent was doubled, as if he received it single in the women and obtained it double from the women and men together. See how 'the joints of the thighs of the bride were linked together like a necklace made by a craftsman's hand'.

For Chapter 10: *Ailred of Rievaulx's Rule for the Life of a Recluse*

Ailred (or Aelred), abbot of the Cistercian house of Rievaulx in Yorkshire, wrote this rule for his sister in the early 1160s during the last decade of his life. It is composed in the form of a letter in which Ailred first gives practical advice – on food, clothing and the timetabling of the day – before moving on to discuss his sister's spiritual needs and obligations. We know nothing of this sister beyond what we can glean from the text, but the influence of Ailred's letter spread far beyond her own reclusorium, wherever that may have been. It was, for example, well-known by the author of the *Ancrene Riwle*.

This extract is taken from chapters 25–8 of the *Rule*. (Source: Aelred of Rievaulx, *Treatises and the Pastoral Prayer*, Cistercian Fathers Series: Number Two (1971), pp. 72–8.)

25. For all the glory of the king's daughter is within, clad as she is in robes decked with borders of woven gold. If you are already the King's daughter, since you are the bride of the King's Son, and have heard the Father's voice saying: 'Listen, daughter, and see and incline your ear,' let all your glory be from within. See that your glory be the witness of your conscience. There let there be the fair array of the virtues, let it be there that colors of one sort and another so blend in harmony that one may increase the beauty of another and that which of its own nature is less brilliant may shine more brightly in comparison with another. Let chastity be combined with humility and nothing could be more splendid. Let simplicity be added to prudence and nothing could be more dazzling. Let mercy be joined with justice and nothing could be more pleasing. Ally modesty with courage and nothing could be more useful. Keep the eyes of your mind occupied with this array of virtues, make it your whole concern to nurture it in your soul. Then if you attach borders of woven gold to it you will have made yourself a many-colored robe in which your Bridegroom will delight to see you. The border is the part at the edge, the end as it were of a garment. But the end of the Law is charity, coming from a pure heart and a good conscience and unfeigned faith.

26. Let it be in these that you glory and find your happiness; within, not without, in true virtues, not in paintings and statues.

Your altar should be covered with white linen cloths. Their whiteness will betoken chastity and display simplicity. Consider what toil, what poundings it took to rid the linen of the earthy color in which it grew up and to bring it to such whiteness that it could adorn an altar, cover Christ's body. We are all born with the color of earth since: 'I was conceived in iniquity and in my sins did my mother conceive me.' In the first place linen is steeped in water, and in the waters of baptism we are buried together with Christ. There sin is destroyed but infirmity remains unhealed. We are given some whiteness by the forgiveness of our sins, but because of our natural corruption, which remains, we are not yet fully rid of our earthy color. When it is taken out of the water

linen is dried, for after the waters of baptism the body has to be macer-
ated by fasting and so emptied of unlawful humors. Next linen is
pounded with hammers, and our flesh is wearied by many temptations.
After this linen is threshed with iron nails so that it may shed its
superfluous covering, and when we have been scraped with the teeth
of regular observance we are scarcely left with the necessaries. Then
linen passes through a gentler process of refining by means of softer
teeth, and we, having overcome the worst passions with great toil,
are cleansed from lighter and everyday sins by simple confession and
satisfaction. Then linen is drawn out in lengths by spinners and we are
drawn on to what lies ahead by patience and perseverance. Further, in
order that its beauty may be perfect, fire and water are applied to it,
and we have to pass through the fire of tribulations and the water of
compunction in order to arrive at the refreshing coolness of chastity.

Let these be the thoughts which the furnishings of your oratory
suggest to you, instead of feasting your eyes on unbecoming fantasies.
On your altar let it be enough for you to have a representation of our
Saviour hanging on the Cross; that will bring before your mind his
Passion for you to imitate, his outspread arms will invite you to embrace
him, his naked breasts will feed you with the milk of sweetness to
console you.

If you like, in order to bring home to you the excellence of virginity,
a picture of the Virgin Mother and one of the Virgin Disciple may stand
on either side of the Cross, so that you may consider how pleasing to
Christ is the virginity of both sexes, consecrated in his Mother and the
Disciple he loved more than the others. Therefore as he hung on the
cross he brought them together in so close a union as to give her to the
Disciple as a mother and him to his Mother as a son. O how blessed is
John in this legacy: with all the solemnity of a last will and testament
he is given the fair flower of the whole human race, the hope of the
world, the glory of heaven, the refuge of the wretched, the comfort of
the afflicted, the consolation of the poor, the salvation of the despairing,
the reconciliation of sinners, in a word the mistress of the world and the
queen of heaven.

Let these things serve to increase your charity, not to provide empty
show. From all of them you must ascend to unity, for only one thing is
necessary. That is the one thing, the unity which is found only in the
One, by the One, with the One with whom there is no variation, no
shadow of change. The man who unites himself with him becomes one
spirit with him, passing into that unity which is always the same and
whose years do not come to an end. This union is charity, as it were the
edge and border of the spiritual vesture.

27. Indeed the nuptial robe, woven out of all the array of the virtues,
ought to have borders of gold, that is, of charity in all its brilliance. It
should contain all the virtues and bring them together into unity. It

should impart to one and all its own splendor and make the many into one, uniting with the many to the One, so that all may no longer be many but one.

Now charity has two divisions, love of God and love of one's neighbor. Further, love of one's neighbor has two subdivisions, innocence and beneficence, that is, to do no harm to anyone and to do good to those to whom you are able. It is written: 'What you would not have done to yourself do not to another' – and this is innocence. Our Lord says in the Gospel: 'Everything that you would have men do to you, do you also to them' – and this is beneficence.

Take good heed how these two things concern you. First you are to harm no one, then you are not to desire to harm anyone. The first is easy for you, since it is something not in your power to do, unless perhaps you inflict injury with your tongue. The second will not be difficult if you keep your way of life and love the poverty which you have vowed. For there cannot be any ground for ill will towards anyone when there is no covetousness, when nothing is loved that might be taken away, nothing taken away that ought to be loved.

Then wish well to everyone, be of service to those to whom you can. And how is that possible, you will say, since I am not allowed to possess the least thing which I might give to those in need.

28. Recognise the state in which you are, dearly beloved. There were two sisters, Martha and Mary. The one was busy, the other was at leisure. The one gave, the other asked. The one was anxious to serve, the other nourished her affections. She did not walk about or run hither and thither, was not concerned with the reception of guests, not distracted by household worries, not busy with answering cries of the poor. She just sat at Jesus' feet and listened to what he had to say. This is your portion, dearly beloved. Dead and buried to the world, you should be deaf to all that belongs to the world and unable to speak of it. You should not be distracted but absorbed, not emptied out but filled up. Let Martha carry out her part; although it is admitted to be good. Mary's is declared better. Did Mary envy Martha? Rather it was the other way about. So let those who seem to make the best out of living in the world envy your life; it is not for you to envy theirs.

The giving of alms belongs to those who have earthly possessions or who have been entrusted with the administration of Church property. For what was given to Holy Church by the faithful is handed over to bishops, priests and clerics to be distributed, not hidden away or appropriated, but given in alms. Whatever they have belongs to the poor, to widows and orphans, and to those who minister at the altar and so have the right to live from the altar. The gifts too which are made to monasteries for the use of Christ's servants should be administered by persons appointed for the purpose, so that what remains over when the needs of the brethren have been satisfied is not stored up in coffers but given away to guests, pilgrims and the poor. This is the concern of those who are entrusted with Martha's functions, not of those who with Mary are left free to enjoy a leisure that will be profitable to their souls. So monks of the cloister should not be troubled with any concern for the poor or distracted by the reception of guests; indeed they should not even have any care for the morrow, no anxiety over food and drink. Let them rather feed on saffron and take their pleasure in the things of the spirit. It is for those who are thought little of and therefore appointed as judges to betake themselves to the dungheap. They are the oxen with whose dung the slothful man is pelted. For there are some who grow weary of spiritual things like the Jews in the desert and feel a loathing for the manna from heaven. When they see others busy about temporal affairs they envy them, criticise them, complain of them and, on account of the dung which soils them, are pricked by bitter jealousy. If it should chance that any such should be charged with the administration of temporal affairs it is to them that the words can fittingly be applied: 'They who were fed with saffron have be taken themselves to the dungheap.'

If then even those who live in community and have not a little in common with Martha are not allowed to be busy about many things, how much less will it be allowed to you who have withdrawn from the world to the fullest extent and are forbidden not only to possess but even to see or hear what belongs to the world? For since no one gives you anything to distribute in alms, from what source will you come to possess anything you might give away? If your work yields something, give it away not by your own hand but by that of some other person. If your food comes from others what right have you to give away what belongs to them, since you are not allowed to take anything more than what you need for yourself?

What good then will you be able to do to your neighbor? Nothing is more valuable, a certain holy man has said, than good will. Let this be your offering.

What is more useful than prayer? Let this be your largesse. What is more humane than pity? Let this be your alms. So embrace the whole world with the arms of your love and in that act at once consider and congratulate the good, contemplate and mourn over the wicked. In that act look upon the afflicted and the oppressed and feel compassion for them. In that act call to mind the wretchedness of the poor, the groans of orphans, the abandonment of widows, the gloom of the sorrowful, the needs of travellers, the prayers of virgins, the perils of those at sea, the temptations of monks, the responsibilities of prelates, the labors of those waging war. In your love take them all to your heart, weep over them, offer your prayers for them.

Such alms are more pleasing to God, more acceptable to Christ, more becoming your profession, more fruitful to those who receive them. The performance of such good works as these help you to live out your profession instead of upsetting you; they increase the love you have for your neighbor instead of diminishing it; they are a safeguard, not an obstacle to tranquillity of mind.

What more can I say when holy men, in order to love their neighbors perfectly, made it their concern to have nothing in this world, to desire nothing, and not even to possess things without attachment. You will recognise the words: they come from St Gregory. See how many think the opposite. For in order to carry out the law of charity they seek to have something to give away, whereas St Gregory awards the perfection of charity to those who resolved to have nothing, to desire nothing, not to possess anything even without being attached to it.

For Chapter 11: Osbern Bokenham's Life of St Elizabeth of Hungary

Osbern Bokenham (b. 1393) was an Augustinian canon of Clare Priory, Suffolk, at a time when East Anglia was renowned as a centre of literary activity; contemporaries of Bokenham include the authors John Capgrave and John Lydgate. Bokenham's *Life of St Elizabeth* was one of the thirteen verse lives of female saints that make up his *Legend of Holy Women*, a work that has been hailed by Sheila Delany as 'unique in the history of hagiography, for it is the first all-female hagiography in any language'. (Source: Osbern Bokenham, *A Legend of Holy Women*, trans. with introduction, S. Delany (1993), pp. 177–86.)

This blessed Elizabeth was daughter to the king of Hungary, noble by birth but in religious learning more noble, for she enhanced her family tree with her examples of perfection and embellished it with miracles brighter than the sky, through the grace of her holiness.

And no wonder, for the sovereign author of nature extolled her high above nature when she – flower of beauty, nurtured with royal care with others of her family – despised all infantile things or else turned them to the service of God.

In this kind of behaviour we can see with what simplicity her child-hood began and with what devotion she occupied herself in the daily practices of goodness. Frivolous games she hated so as to avoid the favor of Fortune's fickleness, but she loved to perfect herself in reverence for God.

When she was five years old or less, as the *Legend* tells, her heart was so devoted to God that she would often go to church to pray, and when she was there she so desired to serve God that her playmates and servants could scarcely get her away without great difficulty.

When she was brought to play with her playmates and the children chased each other as children do, she fled to the church, looking for a way in, and when she entered she fell down on her knees, or on the tiled floor on her face, worshiping God.

And though she was unable to read, she would hold a psalter spread open before her and would pretend to read it, unwilling to give it up and making up an excuse not to be taken away from it too quickly.

Often in her playing she would fall down on the ground on her face, prostrate, as the game required; but her real intention in doing so was to have an occasion, under cover of the game, to worship God whom she loved above all.

She also had a noble habit that if she won something in a game, she would give it away to other little girls, poor ones, exhorting them to say their pater noster often and their Hail Mary, and thus she persuaded them to learn to pray.

So as she grew up her devotion also grew. Because she wished not to be overthrown by the devil's sleight or suggestion, she put herself under Our Lady's protection, beseeching her to be her advocate; and she chose Saint John the Evangelist as keeper of her virginity.

Therefore, on Saint Valentine's day, when, according to the custom of that country, the names of various apostles were written at random on altar candles and each girl took whichever one fell to her, three times Elizabeth got the candle inscribed to Saint John.

Thereafter her affection was so strongly set on this blessed apostle that she could deny no petition made her in his name. And so that no parade of worldly prosperity should make a fool of her, she made a point of throwing out some rich item every day.

In playing, when she saw wantonness follow mirth, as is the way with children, she would stop, saying seriously to her playmates: 'One song is enough, so for God's sake let's restrain ourselves from another song.' And with similar wise words she used to restrain her servants from vanity.

As for her outward manner, what more can I say than that in her dress she loved honesty and scorned fancy clothing? She also would say certain prayers every day, and if they were omitted because of other occupations, even though she were made to go to bed by those responsible for her, she wouldn't sleep until she had done her stint.

Solemn holy days this girl observed with such devotion that she would not permit anyone to lace up her sleeves until after mass. On Sundays she would not wear gloves until noon, no matter how cold it might be: this was in devoted reverence for the dominical solemnity.

And so that she should not be prevented from performing any of the special practices she was committed to, she often knelt down and vowed that she would never – despite the persuasion of man or woman, rich or poor – be deterred from these rituals until death prevented her.

She also heard divine service with such reverence that when the gospel was read or when Christ's body was present in the sacraments, she would stand up with sleeves unlaced and put aside her brooches, and anything else belonging to her head she would place on her shoulder instead.

When this innocent body had thus prudently governed the time of her virginity, and in the course of years attained the age of womanhood, she was compelled by her father to enter the state belonging to married people – matrimony, which in the faith of the trinity stands alongside the keeping of God's ten commandments.

Although she was reluctant to enter the state of matrimony, she did agree to it: not because of lust or physical attraction but to do her father's will and, also, if God should send her fruit, to educate them in his service. These considerations moved her to accept this conclusion.

But before she was bound to the law of marriage and still in her liberty, to show that no fleshly lust was to be found in her she had a vow written down: that if her husband should happen to die before her, she would observe perpetual chastity.

So Elizabeth, mirror of continence, was wedded to Landgrave, prince of Thuringia, as ceremoniously as her royal magnificence required and as God's providence had ordained so that through her prudence she might bring many to love God and teach them to serve him.

So that although this blessed Elizabeth changed her condition, by her father's decree, to one quite strange to her – I mean from virginity to matrimony – yet in her secret heart her unchangeable desire would have preferred to remain a maid than to be a princess, queen, or empress.

About her great devotion and reverence and meekness toward God; about her abstinence toward herself; about her generosity and piety toward the poor, and her tender care for the sick, and how she cheered and comforted the needy; all this the following account will declare.

To speak first of prayer: she was so fervent that she often preceded her servants to church by several hours. She spent the time there so devoutly that it seemed she intended to obtain with her private prayers some new grace from him who sends all goodness from heaven.

And she prayed this way not only in church, but also she would often arise at night to do the same, remaining an hour or two in such prayer as she thought best. Her husband often asked her to spare her body and give it some rest.

But because she wished to maintain this ritual and not be kept from it by chancing to oversleep, she commanded her favorite handmaiden to grasp her by the bare foot and shake her by the foot until she awoke.

One night it happened that this damsel came toward the bed without a light, and accidentally shook the prince's foot so that he suddenly awoke. But when he understood the reason, he forgave the intrusion and pretended it had never happened.

So by the tolerance of this good man the blessed Elizabeth arose every night. And that the sacrifice of her prayers to God might be ever more acceptable, she often used to water them with plentiful weeping.

Despite this copious weeping, the tears produced no disfiguration in her face, but rather gladness, and whoever saw her might truly guess that joy and sorrow had such balance in her that though she showed outward sadness, she had abundance of inward joy.

To speak of her meekness, there was never a meeker creature anywhere than she; I am sure there couldn't possibly be, for the more despised and contemptible a thing was, the more charitable she was toward it and the gladder to do it.

This was demonstrated when one of her servants became so terribly ill that people were terrified to look at him and would not touch him – except for her only; for she had such tender regard for him that she allowed him to lay his head in her lap.

And notwithstanding his horribleness, her grace in meekness was such that, when no handmaiden would come near him, she did not hesitate to open his sores with a pin or needle to let out the filth, and she clipped his ragged hair and with her own hands washed his head.

During rogations she always wore linen clothes and followed the procession barefoot, so grounded in humility was she. At stations where sermons were preached, she would not take her place among the upper ranks but would always sit among the poorest women.

In her purifications she would not cover herself with precious gems nor with brooches nor cloth of gold as is the custom of high-ranking ladies, but, following Mary's example and despising worldly pomp, she held her children in her own arms and dedicated them with a lamb and a candle.

And when she returned home from church, she quickly went to her chamber, took off all the clothes she had worn to church and, before she would sit down to dinner, gave every single one to some poor woman dwelling nearby.

It was also a token of great meekness in one who stood in such liberty as Elizabeth did, that she subjected herself to one Master Conrad, especially considering his poverty; but he was outstanding in erudition and doctrine, and perfect in his living.

To him, with her husband's permission, this meek and humble creature made a solemn vow to obey him in everything without fail while she lived; she did this to obtain the merit of pure obedience and to follow Christ's example in dying obedient.

Not long afterward, when Conrad had summoned her to his preaching, and the marquise of Miseno had kept her away so that she could not do his bidding, he took Elizabeth's absence so badly that he would not forgive her until, stripped to her smock, she was beaten with other guilty women.

O true meekness! O blessed obedience! What woman could now obey such a commandment without offense as did this mirror of patience: Behold! Scarcely any nun would do it meekly; and, to tell the whole truth, I believe that neither priest nor monk, canon nor friar would hear it without murmur and grudging too.

For these days the clay of both men and women is so badly alloyed with stubborn will that if they were assayed with such obediences, they would complain and be ill pleased. And this is one important reason, I dare say, why religious discipline is so deeply disturbed, for due corrections are all put away.

But I will walk no further in this matter nor make of it any longer clamor; for no doubt if I were to speak the whole truth some people would be highly indignant that I needlessly digressed from my material. Therefore I promise to cease and hasten back to Elizabeth.

I say this mirror of true obedience, this blessed Elizabeth, practiced great rigor of strict abstinence, and with vigils and disciplines pained her body. She also often kept from her husband's bed and secretly lay sleepless all night in her prayer.

And if, after long waking, she wished to grant her body some rest, forced by the common necessity of sleep as human frailty requires, she would not return to her lord's bed but would lie down to sleep on the floor, all dressed, on a rug.

She also used to make her maidservants beat her violently with large, thick rods. She did this to make recompense for the bitter pain of Christ's scourging, and also to control her flesh from wantonness.

Moreover, if we wish to know her abstinence in eating and drinking, and her temperance in all such things, I say that she often used to excuse herself from the table in order to refuse refined foods and be content with simple bread.

For Master Conrad had strictly ordered her to eat no household food except what was bought by her servants. Because she would not forget this order, she and her maidens often devoured the grossest possible foods, even when delicacies were available in plenty.

But despite the great strictness with which she treated herself, nonetheless she would serve and prepare food and distribute it plentifully throughout the hall. This was so that there would be no comments about overscrupulous or irrational religiosity in her, and so she courteously entertained all guests.

It happened once, after a long journey when she was faint and weary, that she and her lord sat down to dinner and were served with food that she believed was certainly not rightfully obtained; so she ate with her handmaidens and was content with hard black bread moistened in hot water.

For this reason her husband assigned a portion of his budget to support her and her maidens, who had agreed to live as their lady did;

but nonetheless she often left court food and ate the food of some good poor person.

When Landgrave heard about his wife's discipline, he patiently tolerated it, never begrudging it in word or behavior but, rather, approving it in his private thoughts. In fact, he often said sincerely that had it not been for the world's shame and the trouble of his household, he would gladly have done the same.

Notwithstanding her high dignity, Elizabeth desired the state of voluntary poverty. She did so for two reasons: first, to sympathise with Christ's poverty, and then that the world with its pompous array should find nothing of its own in her.

Therefore this blessed matron, when she was alone with her maidens in her chambers, would dress herself in poor people's ugly clothes, and put a foul kerchief on her head, saying, 'Look, this is how I'll go when I come to the state of poverty.'

And though she governed herself with the bridle of abstinence, as you have heard, yet she practiced such generosity of alms to the poor that she could not bear to see anyone fall into misery or trouble; so that throughout the country people called her 'mother of the poor.'

She attended diligently to the seven works of mercy and fulfilled them devoutly, so that she might achieve the friendly blessing that Christ shall send to his chosen children, when he shall specially commend them for these works and say, 'Come, take the eternal kingdom!'

To give a short summary of them, I say she would gladly clothe the naked poor, nor fail to bury poor pilgrims properly. She made christenings for poor children when they were baptised and was willing to be godmother the better to help them.

Often with her maidens she would spin and prepare cloth with her own hands, for three reasons: first, to exclude idleness by her labor; also to give the example of meekness; third, with the labor of her own hands to do alms for the poor who asked, and this was in honor of Christ.

Moreover, she used to feed the hungry, distributing victuals generously to the needy but most plentifully in times of famine. Once when her husband was with Emperor Frederick at Cremona, she completely emptied his warehouses to distribute grain where any needed it.

She gave drink to the thirsty, and in this connection a great miracle occurred, as you shall hear. Once she served beer to a large group with her own hands because of her meekness. When they had all drunk enough, there was no less beer in the cup.

To speak of her hospitality, she loved it so much that she harbored pilgrims and all poor people. She even built a hospital down in the valley below the castle, so that people who could not climb up could be received there and take their alms.

Notwithstanding the difficulty of going up and down, she would visit this hospital at least once a day and administer to the sick, giving them what they needed and exhorting them to patience.

And although she could barely stand the stinking exhalation of the air there, yet for God's love she did not abhor sick people's putridity but endured it, and diligently tried to help them and cure them even when her maidens could scarcely endure the patients' breath.

Poor women's children she sponsored at the hospital, showing them as much charity as if she had been their mother. When she came, some ran to her as children to a mother, and some crawled; but when she left, they all wept as if she had been their mother.

She once bought little glass pots and fragile trinkets for the children to play with, as was the custom in that country; and, as she brought them down from the hilltop in her skirt, they fell, but not one was broken, though they fell on great stones.

Her special pleasure was to visit bedridden women, young and old. She would peer into their rooms to learn their need and hasten to comfort them charitably with word and deed.

In these deeds she obtained God's eternal reward by a fivefold consideration: first by personal visitation; and by work in going back and forth; third is compassion and pity; fourth is spiritual consolation; fifth is abundance of temporal support.

She also loved to bury the poor, so that when she heard of one who needed it, she hurried to the place, carrying with her cloth of her own making in which she could lay the dead body; and until it were buried she would not go home again.

Once it happened that she could not find anything suitable to wrap a man's body in, for what she had asked for had been left behind in haste. She thought of her veil and tore it to wind the body in, and buried it.

So this blessed woman was accustomed to practice the seven works of bodily pity, in more ways than I can tell now. Her husband, too, may be commended for this, for he was very devoted to God; but because he couldn't himself perform this kind of work, he gave his wife permission and authority to do as she wished for both their benefit.

For Chapter 12: Le Fresne

Le Fresne belongs to a collection of twelve French poems, preserved in their entirety only in one thirteenth-century manuscript (Harley 978). In the prologue to the opening poem, the author claims to be a certain Marie; despite the possibility that this attribution is an interpolation, it is generally believed that this 'Marie' and the poet Marie referred to by the twelfth-century writer Denis Piramus are one and the same, but this does not, of course, tell us who she is. Current scholarship denies the once-cherished view that she was a daughter of Queen Eleanor of Aquitaine; other possible 'Maries' now include a half-sister of Henry II's; an abbess of Reading; a daughter of King Stephen.

In the early fourteenth century, *Le Fresne* was translated into Middle English. For an extract from this, the *Lay le Freine*, see *Women's Writing in Middle English*, ed. A. Barratt (1992), pp. 41–8.

(Source: *The Lais of Marie de France*, trans. G. Burgess and K. Busby (1986), pp. 61–7.)

I shall tell you the lay of *Le Fresne* according to the story which I know.

There once lived in Brittany two knights who were neighbours, rich and wealthy men, worthy and valiant knights from the same region. They had both taken a wife and one of the ladies conceived, giving birth to two children when her time came. Her husband was happy and joyful, and because of his joy sent word to his neighbour that his family was increased, as his wife had had two sons. He also said that he would present one of them to him so that he could stand godfather to the boy who would be named after him. The rich man was seated at table when the messenger arrived and knelt before the high table. He delivered his message fully, whereupon the lord gave thanks to God and offered him a fine horse. This knight's wife, who was sitting next to him at table, smiled, for she was deceitful and arrogant, prone to slander and envy. She spoke foolishly and said in front of the whole household: 'So help me God, I am astonished that this worthy man decided to inform my husband of his shame and dishonour, that his wife has had two sons. They have both incurred shame because of it, for we know what is at issue here: it has never occurred that a woman gave birth to two sons at once, nor ever will, unless two men are the cause of it.' Her husband stared at her and reproached her severely. 'Lady,' he said, 'no more! You should not speak thus! The truth is that this lady has been of good repute.' Those in the house took note of these words which were repeated and became widely known throughout all Brittany: the lady was much hated and later suffered because of them, for all women who heard these words, both poor and rich, hated her as a result. The bearer of the message told his lord everything and when he heard the account he was saddened and did not know what to do. For this reason he hated the worthy woman and was highly mistrustful of her, keeping her in close custody without her having deserved it.

The same year the slanderer herself conceived twins and now her neighbour was avenged. She carried them until her time came and then had two daughters, which grieved and distressed her greatly. She lamented to herself: 'Alas!' she said, 'what shall I do? Now I shall never have esteem or honour! I am shamed, in truth, for neither my husband nor all his family will ever believe me, to be sure, when they hear of this adventure. I have been my own judge: I spoke ill of all women. Did I not say that it has never been the case and we had never seen it happen that a woman has had two children unless she has known two men? Now I have twins and it seems that I am paying the price. Whoever slanders and lies about others does not know what retribution awaits him. One can speak ill of someone who is more praiseworthy than oneself. To ward off shame, I shall have to murder one of the children: I would rather make amends with God than shame and dishonour myself.' Those who were in the chamber comforted her and said that they would not allow it, for killing was not a trifle.

The lady had a maid of very noble birth who had long taken care of her and brought her up, loved her and cherished her greatly. The girl heard her lady crying, lamenting grievously and moaning, and this caused her great anguish. She came and comforted her: 'Lady,' she said, 'it is no use. You will do well to abandon this sadness! Let me have one of the children and I shall rid you of her so that you will never be shamed or see her ever again. I shall abandon her in a church to which I shall carry her safe and sound. Some worthy man will find her and, if it please God, raise her.' The lady heard what she said and was overjoyed, promising her that she would receive a good reward if she performed this service. They wrapped the noble child in a cloth of fine linen and then placed over her the finest piece of striped brocade which her husband had brought from Constantinople, where he had been. With a piece of her ribbon, the lady attached to the child's arm a large ring made from an ounce of pure gold, with a ruby set in it and lettering on the band. Wherever she was found, people would then truly know that she was of noble birth. The damsel took the child and left the chamber forthwith. That night, when all was dark, she left the town and took to a wide path which led her into the forest, and making her way through the wood by keeping to the main path, she emerged on the other side with the child. Far away to the right she had heard dogs barking and cocks crowing, and there she knew she could find a town. The damsel went quickly in the direction of the barking and entered a rich and fair town where there was an exceptionally wealthy and well-endowed abbey. I think it housed nuns with an abbess to watch over them. The girl saw the church, the towers, the walls and the bell-tower, and approached hurriedly, stopping before the door. She put down the child she was carrying, knelt humbly and began her prayer: 'God,' she said, 'by your holy name, if it please you, Lord, keep this infant from perishing.' When she had finished her prayer, she looked behind her and saw a wide ash-tree, luxuriant and with many boughs. It branched out into four forks and had been planted there as a source of shade. She took the child in her arms, ran up to the ash-tree, placed the child in it

and then left her, commending her to the one true God. The damsel
returned and told her lady what she had done.

There was a porter at the abbey who opened the outer door of the
church by which people entered to hear the service. That night he arose
early, lit candles and lamps, rang the bells and opened the door. When
he saw the garments on the ash-tree his only thought was that someone
had stolen them and put them there. He made his way over to the tree
as soon as he could, felt with his hand and thus found the child. He
then gave thanks to God, took the child and returned home, not wanting
to leave it there. He had a widowed daughter who had in the cradle a
baby she was suckling. The worthy man called out: 'Daughter, arise,
arise! Light a fire and candles! I have brought here a child which I found
outside in the ash-tree. Suckle it with your milk for me, keep it warm,
and bathe it!' She obeyed him and lit the fire, taking the child and
making it warm. She bathed it well and then suckled it with her milk.
On its arm she found the ring, and when they saw the rich and beautiful
cloth of silk, they were sure that she was born of high degree. That day
after the service, when the abbess left the church, the porter went to talk
to her, for he wanted to tell her the story of how he had found the child.
The abbess commanded it to be brought before her just as it had been
found and so the porter went to his house and willingly brought the
child to show her. She looked at the girl intently and said she would
have her brought up as her niece, forbidding the porter to say anything
about it. She herself raised the child and because she had been found in
the ash-tree, they named her Le Fresne, which was what people then
called her.

The lady kept her secretly for a while as her niece and the girl was
raised within the bounds of the abbey. When she reached the age when
Nature forms beauty, there was no fairer, no more courtly girl in Brittany,
for she was noble and cultivated, both in appearance and in speech. No
one who had seen her would have failed to love and admire her greatly.

In Dol there lived the best lord there has ever been. I shall now tell
you his name: in his country they called him Gurun, and he had heard
tell of the maiden and began to love her. He went to a tournament and
returned by way of the abbey, asking to see the girl. The abbess showed
her to him, and when he saw that she was very beautiful and well
educated, wise, courtly and well brought-up, he said to himself that he
would henceforth consider himself unfortunate if he did not have her
love. He was distraught and did not know what to do, for if he were to
return too often the abbess would notice and he would never see the
girl again. He thought of a solution; he would increase the wealth of
the abbey and give it a great deal of his land, thereby enriching it for all
time, for he wanted to have a lord's rights to a dwelling-place and
residence. In order to join their community he gave them a generous
portion of his wealth, but his motive was other than remission for his

sins. He went there often to talk to the girl, and begged her and promised her so much that she granted what he sought. When he was sure of her love, he spoke to her one day: 'Fair one, you have now made me your love. Come away with me for good! I assure you that should your aunt notice she would be most aggrieved and extremely angry if you became pregnant in her house. If you accept my advice, you will come away with me. Be sure I shall never fail you and shall provide for you well.' As she loved him deeply, she granted him his request and went away with him: he took her to his castle. She took her brocade and ring, for that might yet turn out to her advantage. The abbess had given them to her and told her what had happened when first she had been sent to her and placed in the ash-tree. Whoever had sent her in the first place had given her the brocade and the ring, but no other riches accompanied her; she had then raised her as her niece. The girl kept the brocade and ring and put them in a casket which she carried with her, for she did not want to leave or forget it. The knight who took her away cherished and loved her greatly, as did all his men and his servants. There was not one, humble or great, who did not love and honour her for her nobility.

After she had been with Gurun for some time, the landed knights reproached him for it severely, and they often spoke to him saying that he should take a noble wife and free himself from Le Fresne. They would be happier if he had an heir to inherit his land and it would be a grievous loss if he did not have a child by a wife on account of his concubine. They would never more consider him their lord, nor serve him willingly, if he did not do their bidding. The knight agreed to take a wife on their advice and so they looked to see where one might be found. 'Lord,' they said, 'close to us here is a worthy man quite your equal who has a daughter as his heir: much land will come with her. The damsel is called La Codre and in all the land there is none so fair. In exchange for Le Fresne, whom you will give up, you will have La Codre. On the hazel there are nuts to be enjoyed, but the ash never bears fruit. We shall seek to obtain the damsel, and if it please God, we shall give her to you.' Thus they sought this marriage and assent was given by all parties. Alas! what a misfortune that the worthy men did not know their story of these damsels who were twin sisters! Le Fresne was kept hidden from the other girl, who was then married to Le Fresne's beloved. When she learned of the marriage, Le Fresne showed no displeasure but served her lord properly and honoured all his people. The knights of his household, the squires and the serving-boys, grieved much because they were going to lose her.

On the day set for their marriage Gurun summoned his friends, and his vassal the Archbishop of Dol was there. They brought Gurun's wife to him, but her mother, who accompanied her, was afraid of the girl whom he loved so much, lest she try to cause ill-will between her daughter and her husband. She planned to cast her out of her own house and advise her son-in-law to marry her to a worthy man, for in this way she could be rid of her.

The wedding was richly celebrated and there was much merry-making. The damsel was in the bedchamber but gave no sign that anything she had seen had upset her, not even sufficiently to anger her. She served the lady willingly and properly so that those who saw her, both men and women, marvelled at it. Her mother looked at her intently, and esteemed and loved her in her heart. She thought and said to herself that if she had known the kind of person Le Fresne was, she would not have suffered harm because of her daughter La Codre, nor would her lord have been taken from her.

That night, when the bed in which the wife was to lie was being prepared, the damsel went there and took off her cloak. She summoned the chamberlains and showed them how her lord wanted the bed made, for she had often seen it done. When they had made the bed ready, they covered it with a sheet made from old dress-material. The damsel saw it and was dissatisfied, for it did not seem right to her. She opened a chest, took out her brocade and, to honour him, put it on her lord's bed. The Archbishop was there to bless them and make the sign of the cross over them, for this was part of his duty. When the chamber was empty, the lady brought her daughter, whom she wanted to get ready for bed, and told her to undress. She saw the brocade on the bed, the like of which she had never seen, save for the one she had given away with the daughter she had concealed. Then she remembered her and trembled in her heart. She called the chamberlain to her. 'Tell me,' she said, 'on your faith, where was this fine brocade found?' 'Lady,' he said, 'I shall tell you: the damsel brought it and cast it over this coverlet which she did not like. I think that the brocade is hers.' The lady called her and she came. When she had taken off her cloak, her mother spoke to her: 'Fair friend, do not conceal it from me. Where was this good brocade found? How did you acquire it? Who gave it to you? Tell me from whom you received it!' The girl answered her: 'Lady, my aunt, the abbess, who raised me, gave it to me and ordered me to keep it. Those who sent me to be brought up gave me that and a ring.' 'Fair one, may I see the ring?' 'Yes, my lady, with pleasure.' She brought her the ring and the lady looked at it carefully, easily recognising it and the brocade. She had no doubt, for she now knew for sure that this was indeed her daughter, and, for all to hear, she said openly: 'You are my daughter, fair friend!' Because of the emotion she felt she fell back and fainted. When she arose from her swoon, she sent for her husband straightaway and he came, quite frightened. When he had entered the chamber, the lady fell at his feet and embraced him closely, begging his pardon for her crime. He had no part in this affair. 'Lady,' he said, 'what are you saying? There is nothing but good between us. Whatever you wish, let it be pardoned!

Tell me your will!' 'Lord, since you have forgiven me, listen to what I have to tell you! Once, in my great wickedness, I slandered my neighbour. I spoke ill of her two children, but in fact I did myself harm. The truth is that I became with child and had two daughters, one of whom I hid. I had her abandoned at a church and sent with her our brocade and the ring you gave me when you first spoke with me. It can be hidden from you no longer: I have found the cloth and the ring, and have recognised here our daughter whom I had lost by my folly. This is the damsel, so worthy, wise and fair, whom the knight loved and whose sister he has married!' The lord said: 'I was never as happy as I am now that we have found our daughter. God has given us great joy rather than allowing the sin to be doubled. Daughter, come here!' The girl rejoiced when she heard the story. Her father wanted to wait no longer and went to fetch his son-in-law himself to tell him the story, taking the archbishop with him. The knight was never so joyful as when he learnt about it. The archbishop recommended that things be left as they were that night; the next day he would unjoin those he had married. Thus they agreed and the following day the two were separated. Gurun then married his beloved and her father gave her to him as a mark of affection. He gave her half his inheritance and he and her mother were present at the wedding with their other daughter, as was fitting. When they returned to their own country, they took their daughter La Codre with them. She later made a rich marriage.

When the truth of this adventure was known, they composed the lay of *Le Fresne*. It was given this title on account of its heroine.

Bibliography

Chapter 1: Archaeology

C. J. Arnold, *An Archaeology of the Early Anglo-Saxon Kingdoms* (1988).
S. Bassett (ed.), *The Origins of Anglo-Saxon Kingdoms* (1992).
M. L. Cameron, *Anglo-Saxon Medicine* (1993).
J. Campbell *et al.* (eds), *The Anglo-Saxons* (1982).
M. Carver (ed.), *The Age of Sutton Hoo* (1992).
T. M. Dickinson, 'An Anglo-Saxon "Cunning Woman" from Bidford-on-Avon' in M. Carver (ed.), *In Search of Cult* (1993), pp. 45–54.
S. C. Hawkes, 'The Archaeology of Conversion: Cemeteries' in J. Campbell *et al.* (eds), *The Anglo-Saxons*.
A. L. Meaney, *Anglo-Saxon Amulets and Curing Stones* (1981).
D. Miles and S. Palmer, *Invested in Mother Earth* (n.d.).
G. Owen-Crocker, *Dress in Anglo-Saxon England* (1984).
E. J. Pader, *Symbolism, Social Relations and the Interpretation of Mortuary Remains* (1982).
P. Rahtz, T. M. Dickinson and L. Watts (eds), *Anglo-Saxon Cemeteries* (1979).
G. Speake, *A Saxon Bed Burial on Swallowcliffe Down* (1989).
E. A. Thompson, *St Germanus of Auxerre and the End of Roman Britain* (1984).
D. Wilson, *Anglo-Saxon Paganism* (1992).

Chapter 2: History and Hagiography

PRIMARY SOURCES
B. Colgrave and R. Mynors (ed. and trans.), *Bede's Ecclesiastical History* (1969).
B. Colgrave (ed. and trans.), *Two Lives of Saint Cuthbert* (1927, pb. 1985).
B. Colgrave (ed. and trans.), *The Life of Bishop Wilfrid by Eddius Stephanus* (1940, pb. 1985).

Bibliography

E. Emerton (ed. and trans.), *St Boniface: the Letters* (1940).

M. Lapidge and M. Herren (trans.), *Aldhelm: The Prose Works* (1979).

M. Lapidge and J. Rosier (trans.), *Aldhelm: The Poetic Works* (1985).

J. McNeill and H. Gamer (trans.), *Medieval Handbooks of Penance* (1990).

C. H. Talbot (ed. and trans.), 'The Life of St Boniface'; 'The Life of Leoba'; and 'The Correspondence of St Boniface', in *The Anglo-Saxon Missionaries in Germany* (1954).

See also in Penguin Classics, *The Age of Bede*, trans. J. F. Webb and D. H. Farmer (1988), and Bede, *The Ecclesiastical History of the English People*, trans. S. Price and D. H. Farmer (1990).

SECONDARY WORKS

J. Blair and R. Sharpe (eds), *Pastoral Care Before the Parish* (1992).

N. Brooks, *The Early History of the Church of Canterbury* (1984).

J. Campbell, *Essays in Anglo-Saxon History* (1986).

C. Fell, 'Some Implications of the Boniface Correspondence', in H. Damico and A. Hennessey Olsen (eds), *New Readings On Women in Old English Literature* (1990).

S. Hollis, *Anglo-Saxon Women and the Church: Sharing a Common Fate* (1992).

H. Mayr-Harting, *The Coming of Christianity to England* (3rd edn 1991).

H. Mayr-Harting, *The Venerable Bede, the Rule of St Benedict and Social Class* (Jarrow Lecture, 1976).

P. Sims-Williams, *Religion and Literature in Western England, 600–800* (1990).

L. Webster and J. Backhouse (eds), *The Making of England, Anglo-Saxon Art and Culture* (1991).

Chapter 3: Law Codes

PRIMARY SOURCES

English Historical Documents, vol. 1, *c.500–1042* ed. D. Whitelock (1979).

The Laws of the Earliest English Kings, ed. and trans. F. L. Attenborough (1922).

The Law of Hywel Dda, ed. and trans. D. Jenkins (1986).

Medieval Handbooks of Penance, ed. and trans. J. McNeill and H. Gamer (1990).

SECONDARY WORKS

J. Blair and R. Sharpe (eds), *Pastoral Care Before the Parish* (1982).

T. Charles-Edwards, *Early Irish and Welsh Kinship* (1993).

M. Clunies Ross, 'Concubinage in Anglo-Saxon England', *Past and Present* 108 (1985), pp. 3–34.

C. Fell, *Women in Anglo-Saxon England and the Impact of 1066* (1984).

C. Fell, 'Some Implications of the Boniface Correspondence' in H. Damico and A. H. Olsen (eds), *New Readings on Women in Old English Literature* (1990), pp. 29–43.

J. Goody, *The Development of the Family and Marriage in Europe* (1983).

A. Klinck, 'Anglo-Saxon Women and the Law', *Journal of Medieval History* 8 (1982), pp. 107–19.

M. Meyer, 'Early Anglo-Saxon Penitentials and the Position of Women', *The Haskins Society Journal, Studies in Medieval History*, ed. R. Patterson, vol. 2 (1990), pp. 47–61.

A. W. B. Simpson, 'The Laws of Ethelbert', in M. Arnold, T. Green, S. Scully and S. White (eds), *On the Laws and Customs of England* (1981).

D. Whitelock, *The Beginnings of English Society* (1952).

Chapter 4: Vernacular Literature

PRIMARY SOURCES
The most convenient anthology in translation remains S. A. Bradley, *Anglo-Saxon Poetry* (1982); but see also the Bibliography in M. Godden and M. Lapidge (eds), below, for details of further editions and translations.

SECONDARY WORKS
E. Anderson, *Cynewulf: Structure, Style and Theme in his Poetry* (1983).

J. Chance, *Woman as Hero in Old English Literature* (1986).

H. Damico, *Beowulf's Wealhtheow and the Valkyrie Tradition* (1984).

H. Damico and J. Leyerle (eds), *Heroic Poetry in the Anglo-Saxon Period: Studies in Honour of Jess B. Bessinger, Jr* (1993).

H. Damico and A. H. Olsen (eds), *New Readings on Women in Old English Literature* (1990).

M. Enright, 'Lady with a Mead-Cup: Ritual, Group Cohesion and Hierarchy in the Germanic World', *Fruhmittelalterliche Studien*, 22 (1988), pp. 170–203.

M. Godden and M. Lapidge (eds), *The Cambridge Companion to Old English Literature* (1991).

S. Greenfield and D. Calder, *A New Critical History of Old English Literature* (1986).

B. Kliman, 'Women in Early English Literature, "Beowulf" to the "Ancrene Wisse" ', *Nottingham Medieval Studies* 21 (1977), pp. 32–49.

A. Klinck, 'Female Characterisation in Old English Poetry and the

Growth of Psychological Realism: *Genesis B* and *Christ 1'*, *Neo-philologus* 63 (1979), pp. 597–610.
A. Meaney, 'The *Ides* of the Cotton Gnomic Poem', *Medium Aevum* 48 (1979), pp. 23–29.
(B. Harwood and G. Overing (eds), *Class and Gender in Early English Literature: Intersections* (1994) came to my attention too late for me to be able to benefit from its insights.)

Chapter 5: 1066 for Women
PRIMARY SOURCES
English Historical Documents, vol. I, *c.500–1042*, ed. D. Whitelock (1979); vol. II, *1042–1189*, ed. D. Douglas (1981).
Encomium Emmae Reginae, ed. A. Campbell, Camden Society, 3rd. series lxxii (1949).
The Life of Edward the Confessor, ed. F. Barlow (1962).
The Carmen de Hastingae Proelio of Guy Bishop of Amiens (The Song of the Battle of Hastings), ed. C. Morton and H. Muntz (1972).

SECONDARY WORKS
B. Bandel, 'The English Chroniclers' Attitude Towards Women', *Journal of the History of Ideas* 16 (1955), pp. 113–18.
D. Bernstein, *The Mystery of the Bayeux Tapestry* (1986).
M. Chibnall, *The Empress Matilda: Queen Consort, Queen Mother and Lady of the English* (1991).
M. Clanchy, *England and its Rulers 1066–1272* (2nd edn 1992).
C. Clark, 'Women's Names in Post-Conquest England: Observations and Speculations', *Speculum* 53 (1978), pp. 223–51.
C. Fell, *Women in Anglo-Saxon England and the Impact of 1066* (1984).
J. Holt, 'Feudal Society and the Family in Early Medieval England', *The Transactions of the Royal Historical Society*, Fifth series, 32 (1982), pp. 193–212; 33 (1983), pp. 193–220; 34 (1984), pp. 1–26; 35 (1985), pp. 1–28.
M. Meyer, 'Women's Estates in Later Anglo-Saxon England: The Politics of Possession', *Haskins Society Journal* 3 (1991), pp. 111–29.
S. F. C. Milsom, 'Inheritance by Women in the Twelfth and Early Thirteenth Centuries', in M. Arnold *et al.* (eds), *On the Laws and Customs of England* (1981), pp. 60–89.
J. Nelson, *Politics and Ritual in Early Medieval Europe* (1986).
John Carmi Parsons, 'Ritual and Symbol in the English Medieval Queenship to 1500', in L. Fradenburg (ed.), *Women and Sovereignty* (1992), pp. 60–77.
David Parsons (ed.), *Eleanor of Castile, 1290–1990* (1991).
John Carmi Parsons, *Medieval Queenship* (1994).
E. Searle, 'Women and the Legitimisation of Succession at the

Bibliography

Norman Conquest', *Proceedings of the Battle Conference* 3 (1981), pp. 159–70.

P. Stafford, 'The King's Wife in Wessex', *Past and Present* 91 (1981), pp. 3–27.

P. Stafford, 'Women in Domesday', *Reading Medieval Studies* 15 (1989), pp. 75–94.

P. Stafford, *Unification and Conquest: A Political and Social History of England in the Early Middle Ages* (1989).

P. Strohm, *Hochon's Arrow: the Social Imagination of Fourteenth-Century Texts* (1992).

Chapter 6: Sex, Marriage and Motherhood
(1) Sexual Debates

PRIMARY SOURCES
A. Barratt (ed.), *Women's Writing in Middle English* (1992).
B. Rowland (ed.), *Medieval Woman's Guide to Health* (1981).

SECONDARY WORKS
J. Benton, 'Trotula, Women's Problems, and the Professionalization of Medicine in the Middle Ages', *Bulletin of the History of Medicine* 59 (1985), pp. 30–53.

P. Biller, 'Marriage Patterns and Women's Lives: A Sketch of Pastoral Geography', in P. J. P. Goldberg (ed.), *Woman is a Worthy Wight* (1992), pp. 60–107.

V. Bullough, 'Medieval Medical and Scientic Views of Women', *Viator* 4 (1973), pp. 485–502.

J. Cadden, *Meanings of Sex Difference in the Middle Ages: Medicine, Science and Culture* (1993).

M. Green, 'Women's Medical Practice and Health Care in Medieval Europe', in J. Bennett *et al.* (eds), *Sisters and Workers in the Middle Ages* (1989), pp. 39–78.

M. Green, 'Female Sexuality in the Medieval West', *Trends in History* 4 (1990), pp. 127–58.

M. Green, 'Obstetrical and Gynecological Texts in Middle English', *Studies in the Age of Chaucer* 14 (1992), pp. 53–88.

D. Jacquart and C. Thomasset, *Sexuality and Medicine in the Middle Ages* (1988).

H. Mayr-Harting, 'Functions of a Twelfth-Century Shrine: The Miracles of St Frideswide', *Studies in Medieval History Presented to R. H. C. Davis*, ed. H. Mayr-Harting and R. I. Moore (1985), pp. 193–206.

E. Makowski, 'The Conjugal Debt and Medieval Canon Law', *Journal of Medieval History* 3 (1977), pp. 99–114.

319

P. Payer, *The Bridling of Desire: Views of Sex in the Later Middle Ages* (1993).
N. Siraisi, *Medieval and Early Renaissance Medicine* (1990).

(2) Marriage

PRIMARY SOURCES
N. Davis (ed.), *Paston Papers and Letters of the Fifteenth Century,* 2 vols. (1971–6).
C. H. Talbot (ed.), *The Life of Christina of Markyate* (1959).

SECONDARY WORKS
C. Brooke, *The Medieval Idea of Marriage* (1989).
E. Clark, 'The Decision to Marry in Thirteenth and Early Fourteenth Century Norfolk', *Medieval Studies* 49 (1987), pp. 496–516.
P. J. P. Goldberg, ' "For Better, For Worse": Marriage and Economic Opportunity for Women in Town and Country', in P. J. P. Goldberg (ed.), *Woman is a Worthy Wight* (1992), pp. 108–25.
T. Head, 'The Marriages of Christina of Markyate', *Viator* 21 (1990), pp. 75–101.
R. Helmholz, *Marriage Litigation in Medieval England* (1974).
G. Homans, *English Villagers of the Thirteenth Century* (1960).
M. Jones and M. Underwood, *The King's Mother: Lady Margaret Beaufort, Countess of Richmond and Derby* (1992).
J. Murray, 'On the Origins and Role of "Wise Women" in Cases of Annulment on the Grounds of Male Impotence', *Journal of Medieval History* 16 (1990), pp. 235–49.
T. North, 'Legerwite in the Thirteenth and Fourteenth Centuries', *Past and Present* 111 (1986), pp. 3–16.
R. C. Palmer, 'Contexts of Marriage in Medieval England', *Speculum* 59 (1984), pp. 42–67.
C. Richmond, 'The Pastons Revisited: Marriage and the Family in Fifteenth Century England', *Bulletin of the Institute of Historical Research* 58 (1985), pp. 25–36.
J. Rosenthal, 'Aristocratic Marriage and the English Peerage, 1350–1550: Social Institution and Personal Bond', *Journal of Medieval History* 10 (1984), pp. 184–94.
J. Scammell, 'Freedom and Marriage in Medieval England', *Economic History Review* 27 (1974), pp. 523–37; for the subsequent debate, see *ibid.*, 29 (1976), pp. 482–90.
E. Searle, 'Seigneurial Control of Women's Marriage', *Past and Present* 82 (1979), pp. 3–43.
M. M. Sheehan, 'Choice of Marriage Partner in the Middle Ages: Development and Mode of Application of a Theory of Marriage',

Studies in Medieval and Renaissance History, new series 1 (1978), pp. 1–34.

M. M. Sheehan, 'The Formation and Stability of Marriage in Fourteenth Century England: Evidence of an Ely Register', *Medieval Studies* 33 (1971), pp. 228–63.

E. J. Smith, 'The Medieval Merchet: A Late Contribution to the Debate', *Medieval History* 2 (1992), pp. 26–35.

J. Ward, *English Noblewomen in the Later Middle Ages* (1992).

S. L. Waugh, *The Lordship of England: Royal Wardships and Marriages in English Society, 1217–1327* (1988).

J. Wogan-Browne, 'Saints' Lives and the Female Reader', *Forum for Modern Language Studies* 27 (1991), pp. 314–29.

(3) Motherhood

PRIMARY SOURCES

M. Goodrich (trans.), 'Bartholomaeus Anglicus on Child-Rearing', *History of Childhood Quarterly* 3 (1975), pp. 75–84.

S. Roche-Mahdi (ed.), *Silence: A Thirteenth-Century French Romance* (1992).

SECONDARY WORKS

P. Ariès, *Centuries of Childhood: A Social History of the Family* (1962).

C. Atkinson, *The Oldest Vocation: Christian Motherhood in the Middle Ages* (1991).

P. Biller, 'Childbirth in the Middle Ages', *History Today* (August 1986), pp. 42–9.

P. Biller, 'Marriage Patterns and Women's Lives: A Sketch of Pastoral Geography', in J. P. J. Goldberg (ed.), *Woman is a Worthy Wight* (1992).

P. Biller, 'Birth-Control in the Medieval West', *Past and Present* 94 (1982), pp. 3–26.

R. Blumenfeld-Kosinski, *Not of Woman Born: Representations of Caesarean Birth in Medieval and Renaissance Culture* (1990).

C. Buhler, 'Prayers and Charms in Certain Middle English Scrolls', *Speculum* 39 (1964), pp. 270–78.

M. L. Cameron, *Anglo-Saxon Medicine* (1993).

M. Clanchy, *From Memory to Written Record: England 1066–1307* (2nd edn 1993).

V. Fildes, *Wet-Nursing: A History from Antiquity to the Present* (1988).

G. Mc. Gibson, *The Theater of Devotion* (1989).

B. Hanawalt, *The Ties That Bound: Peasant Families in Medieval England* (1986).

B. Hanawalt, 'Childrearing Among the Lower Classes of Late

Medieval England', *Journal of Interdisciplinary History* 8 (1977), pp. 1–22.

B. Hanawalt, *Growing Up in Medieval London* (1993).

L. Haas, 'Social Connections between Parents and Godparents in Late Medieval Yorkshire', *Medieval Prosopography* 10 (1989), pp. 1–21.

R. Helmholz, 'Infanticide in the Province of Canterbury During the Fifteenth Century', *History of Childhood Quarterly* 2 (1974–5), pp. 282–390.

P. Niles, 'Baptism and the Naming of Children in Late Medieval England', *Medieval Prosopography* 3 (1982), pp. 95–108.

N. Orme, *From Childhood to Chivalry: The Education of English Kings and Aristocracy, 1066–1530* (1984).

V. Sekules, 'Women's Piety and Patronage', in N. Saul (ed.), *Age of Chivalry* (1992).

S. Shahar, *Childhood in the Middle Ages* (1990).

Chapter 7: Women at Work

PRIMARY SOURCES
English Historical Documents, vol. 3: 1327–1485, ed. A. R. Myers (1969).
Christine de Pisan, *A Medieval Woman's Mirror of Honour*, ed. and trans. C. Willard and M. Cosman (1989).

SECONDARY WORKS
R. Archer, ' "How ladies ... who live on their manors ought to manage their households and estates": Women as Landholders and Administrators in the Later Middle Ages', in P. J. P. Goldberg (ed.), *Woman is a Worthy Wight* (1992), pp. 149–81.

C. Barron, 'The "Golden Age" of Women in Medieval London', *Reading Medieval Studies* 15 (1990), pp. 35–58.

J. Bennett, *Women in the Medieval English Countryside: Gender and Household in Brigstock before the Plague* (1987).

J. Bennett, 'Public Power and Authority in the Medieval English Countryside', in M. Erler and M. Kowaleski (eds), *Women and Power in the Middle Ages* (1988), pp. 18–36.

L. Charles and L. Duffin (eds), *Women and Work in Pre-Industrial England* (1985).

H. Dillard, *Daughters of the Reconquest: Women in Castilian Town Society* (1984).

P. J. P. Goldberg, 'Female Labour, Service and Marriage in the Late Medieval Urban North', *Northern History* 22 (1986), pp. 18–38.

P. J. P. Goldberg, 'The Public and the Private: Women in the Pre-Plague Economy', in P. R. Cross and S. Lloyd (eds), *Thirteenth Century England III* (1991), pp. 75–89.

Bibliography

P. J. P. Goldberg, *Women, Work and Life Cycle in a Medieval Economy: Women in York and Yorkshire, c.1300–1520* (1992).

P. J. P. Goldberg, ' "For Better, For Worse": Marriage and Economic Opportunity for Women in Town and Country', in P. J. P. Goldberg (ed.), *Woman is a Worthy Wight* (1992), pp. 108–25.

H. Graham, ' "A Woman's Work . . ." Labour and Gender in the Late Medieval Countryside', in P. J. P. Goldberg (ed.), *op. cit.*

B. Hanawalt, *The Ties that Bound: Peasant Families in Medieval England* (1986).

B. Hanawalt, *Growing up in Medieval London* (1994).

B. Hanawalt (ed.), *Women and Work in Pre-Industrial Europe* (1986).

B. Harvey, *Westminster Abbey and its Estates in the Middle Ages* (1977).

R. Hilton, *The English Peasantry in the Later Middle Ages* (1975).

R. Hilton, 'Small Town Society in England before the Black Death', *Past and Present* 105 (1984), pp. 53–78.

G. Homans, *English Villagers of the Thirteenth Century* (1941).

C. Howell, *Land, Family and Inheritance in Transition* (1983).

H. Jewell, 'Women at the Courts of the Manor of Wakefield, 1348–1350', *Northern History* 26 (1990), pp. 59–81.

R. Karras, 'The Regulation of Brothels in Later Medieval England', in J. Bennett *et al.* (eds), *Sisters and Workers in the Middle Ages* (1989), pp. 100–34.

M. Kowaleski, 'The History of Urban Families in Medieval England', *Journal of Medieval History* 14 (1988), pp. 47–63.

K. Mertes, *The English Noble Household 1250–1600* (1988).

S. Penn, 'Female Wage-Earners in Late Fourteenth Century England', *Agricultural History Review* 35 (1987), pp. 1–14.

C. Phythian-Adams, *Desolation of a City: Coventry and the Urban Crisis of the Late Middle Ages* (1979).

L. Poos, *A Rural Society after the Black Death: Essex 1350–1525* (1991).

E. Power, *Medieval Women* (1975).

J. A. Raftis, *Warboys: Two Hundred Years in the Life of an English Medieval Village* (1974).

Z. Razi, *Life, Marriage and Death in a Medieval Parish* (1980).

E. Searle, *Lordship and Community: Battle Abbey and its Banlieu, 1066–1538* (1974).

M. Segalen, *Love and Power in the Peasant Family: Rural France in the Nineteenth Century*, trans. S. Mathews (1983).

R. Smith, 'Women's Property Rights under Customary Law: Some Developments in the Thirteenth and Fourteenth Centuries', *Transactions of the Royal Historical Society*, 5th series, 36 (1986), pp. 165–94.

R. Smith, 'Coping with Uncertainty: Women's Tenure of Customary Land in England c.1370–1430', in J. Kermode (ed.), *Enterprise and Individuals in Fifteenth Century England* (1991), pp. 43–67.

Bibliography

H. Swanson, *Medieval Artisans* (1989).
J. Ward, *English Noblewomen in the Later Middle Ages* (1992).

Chapter 8: Widows

PRIMARY SOURCES
The Household Book of Dame Alice de Bryene, ed. M. K. Dale and V. Redstone (1931).
The Treatise on the Laws and Customs of England commonly called Glanvill, ed. D. Hall (1965).

SECONDARY WORKS

R. Archer, 'Rich Old Ladies: The Problem of Late Medieval Dowagers', in A. Pollard (ed.), *Property and Politics: Essays in Late Medieval History* (1984), pp. 15–35.
R. Archer, 'The Estates and Finances of Margaret of Brotherton, c.1320–1399', *Historical Research* 60 (1987), pp. 264–80.
R. Archer and B. Ferme, 'Testamentary Procedure with Special Reference to the Executrix', *Reading Medieval Studies* 15 (1989), pp. 3–34.
C. Barron and A. Sutton (eds), *Medieval London Widows 1300–1500* (1994).
J. Bennett, *Women in the Medieval English Countryside: Gender and Household in Brigstock before the Plague* (1987).
E. Clark, 'Some Aspects of Social Security in Medieval England', *Journal of Family History* 7 (1982), pp. 307–19.
C. Dyer, *Standards of Living in the Later Middle Ages: Social Change in England, c.1200–1500* (1989).
P. Franklin, 'Peasant Widows' "Liberation" and Remarriage before the Black Death', *Economic History Review* 2nd series, 39 (1986), pp. 186–204.
M. Jones and M. Underwood, *The King's Mother: Lady Margaret Beaufort, Countess of Richmond and Derby* (1992).
M. Labarge, 'Three Medieval Widows and a Second Career', in M. Sheehan (ed.), *Aging and the Aged in Medieval Europe* (1990), pp. 160–72.
S. Loengard, 'Of the Gift of her Husband': English Dower and its Consequences in the Year 1200', in J. Kirshner and S. Wemple (eds), *Women of the Medieval World* (1985), pp. 215–55.
L. Mirrer (ed.), *Upon My Husband's Death: Widows in the Literature and Histories of Medieval Europe* (1992).
R. M. Smith, 'The Manorial Court and the Elderly Tenant in Late Medieval England', in M. Pelling and R. Smith (eds), *Life, Death and the Elderly: Historical Perspectives* (1991), pp. 39–61.
J. Rosenthal, *Patriarchy and Families of Privilege in Fifteenth Century England* (1991).

S. Sheridan Walker (ed.), *Wife and Widow in Medieval England* (1993).
J. Ward, *English Noblewomen in the Later Middle Ages* (1992).

Chapter 9: Female Monasticism

PRIMARY SOURCES
The Book of St Gilbert, ed. R. Foreville and G. Keir (1987).
The Life of Christina of Markyate, ed. C. H. Talbot (1959).

SECONDARY WORKS
D. Baker (ed.), *Medieval Women* (1978).
J. Burton, *The Yorkshire Nunneries in the Twelfth and Thirteenth Centuries* (1979).
J. Burton, *Monastic and Religious Orders in Britain 1000–1300* (1994).
C. W. Bynum, *Fragmentation and Redemption: Essays on Gender and the Human Body in Medieval Religion* (1991).
B. Dobson and S. Donaghey, *The History of Clementhorpe Nunnery* (1984).
C. Dodwell, *The Pictorial Arts of the West 800–1200* (1993).
S. Elkins, *Holy Women of Twelfth Century England* (1988).
R. Gilchrist, *Gender and Material Culture: The Archaeology of Religious Women* (1994).
O. Pacht, C. Dodwell and F. Wormald, *The St Albans Psalter* (1960).
S. Thompson, *Women Religious: The Founding of English Nunneries after the Conquest* (1991).

Chapter 10: Anchoresses and Recluses

PRIMARY SOURCES
Ailred of Rievaulx, *Treatises and the Pastoral Prayer*, Cistercian Fathers Series 11 (1971).
Anchoritic Spirituality, trans. A. Savage and N. Watson (1991).
Julian of Norwich, *Showings*, trans. E. Colledge and J. Walsh (1978).
B. Millett and J. Wogan-Browne (eds), *Medieval English Prose for Women* (1990).

SECONDARY WORKS
J. Bugge, *Virginitas: An Essay in the History of a Medieval Ideal* (1975).
C. W. Bynum, *Fragmentation and Redemption: Essays on Gender and the Human Body in Medieval Religion* (1991).
S. Elkins, *Holy Women of Twelfth Century England* (1988).
L. Georgianna, *The Solitary Self: Individuality in the Ancrene Wisse* (1981).
M. Glasscoe, *English Medieval Mystics: Games of Faith* (1993).
J. Hughes, *Pastors and Visionaries: Religion and Secular Life in Late Medieval Yorkshire* (1988).
A. Warren, *Anchorites and their Patrons in Medieval England* (1985).

N. Watson, 'The Composition of Julian of Norwich's *Revelation of Love*', *Speculum* 68 (1993), pp. 637–82.

Chapter 11: Lay Piety

PRIMARY SOURCES

The Book of Margery Kempe, trans. B. A. Windeatt (1985).
Osbern Bokenham, *A Legend of Holy Women*, trans. S. Delany (1992).
Everyman and Medieval Miracle Plays, ed. A. C. Cawley (1993).
Trans. and annotated R. N. Swanson, *Catholic England: Faith, Religion and Observance before the Reformation* (1993).

SECONDARY WORKS

K. Ashley and P. Sheingorn (eds), *Interpreting Cultural Symbols: St Anne in Late Medieval Society* (1990).
M. Aston, *Lollards and Reformers* (1984).
C. Atkinson, *Mystic and Pilgrim: The Book and the World of Margery Kempe* (1983).
R. Beadle (ed.), *Medieval English Theatre* (1994).
S. G. Bell, 'Medieval Women Book Owners: Arbiters of Lay Piety and Ambassadors of Culture', in M. Erler and M. Kowaleski (eds), *Women and Power in the Middle Ages* (1988).
C. Cross, ' "Great Reasoners in Scripture": The Activities of Women Lollards, 1380–1530', in D. Baker (ed.), *Medieval Women* (1978).
P. H. Cullum, ' "And Hir Name was Charite": Charitable Giving by and for Women in Late Medieval Yorkshire', in P. J. P. Goldberg (ed.), *Woman is a Worthy Wight* (1992), pp. 182–211.
C. Donovan, *The de Brailes Hours* (1991).
E. Duffy, *The Stripping of the Altars* (1992).
G. Mc. Gibson, *The Theater of Devotion: East Anglian Drama and Society in the Late Middle Ages* (1989).
J. Hughes, *Pastors and Visionaries: Religion and Secular Life in Late Medieval Yorkshire* (1988).
K. Lochrie, *Margery Kempe and the Translations of the Flesh* (1991).
V. Sekules, 'Women's piety and patronage', in N. Saul (ed.), *Age of Chivalry* (1992), pp. 180–31.

Chapter 12: Literary Interests and Images

PRIMARY SOURCES

A. Barratt (ed.), *Women's Writing in Middle English* (1992).
A. Blamires (ed.), *Woman Defamed and Woman Defended* (1992).
Chrétien de Troyes, ed. and trans. D. Owen, *Arthurian Romances* (1993).

Hue de Rotelande, Ed. A. J. Holden, *Ipomedon: poeme de Hue de Rotelande* (1979).

Marie de France, trans. G. Burgess and K. Busby, *The Lais of Marie de France* (1986).

Marie de France, ed. and trans. H. Spiegel, *Fables* (1987).

Partonopeu de Blois, ed. J. Gildea, *A French Romance of the Twelfth Century* (1967).

J. Weiss (ed.), *The Birth of Romance: An Anthology*.

SECONDARY WORKS

R. H. Bloch, *Medieval Misogyny and the Invention of Western Romantic Love* (1991).

M. T. Bruckner, *Shaping Romance: Interpretation, Truth and Closure in Twelfth-Century Fictions* (1993).

E. Jane Burns, *Bodytalk: When Women Speak in Old French Literature* (1993).

S. Crane, *Insular Romance: Politics, Faith and Culture in Anglo-Norman and Middle English Literature* (1986).

S. Crane, *Gender and Romance in Chaucer's Canterbury Tales* (1994).

S. Delany, *The Naked Text: Chaucer's Legend of Good Women* (1994).

C. Dinshaw, *Chaucer's Sexual Poetics* (1989).

J. Ferrante, *Woman as Image in Medieval Literature* (1975).

A. Gransden, *Historical Writing in England, c.550–1307* (1974).

K. Gravdal, *Ravishing Maidens: Writing Rape in Medieval French Literature and Law* (1991).

E. T. Hansen, *Chaucer and the Fictions of Gender* (1992).

R. Krueger, *Women Readers and the Ideology of Gender in Old French Verse Romance* (1993).

M. D. Legge, *Anglo-Norman Literature and its Background* (1963).

L. Lomperis and S. Stanbury (eds), *Feminist Approaches to the Body in Medieval Literature* (1993).

J. Mann, *Geoffrey Chaucer* (1991).

P. Martin, *Chaucer's Women: Nuns, Wives and Amazons* (1990).

P. Noble, *Love and Marriage in Chrétien of Troyes* (1982).

D. Maddox and S. Sturm-Maddox (eds), *Literary Aspects of Courtly Culture* (1994).

C. Meale (ed.), *Women and Literature in Britain, 1150–1500* (1993).

M. Mills *et al.* (eds), *Romance in Medieval England* (1991).

E. Salter, D. Pearsall and N. Zeeman (eds), *English and International Studies in the Literature, Art and Patronage of Medieval England* (1988).

Addendum to the Bibliography

Since the publication of the hardback edition, the following new titles have appeared:

J. Carpenter and S. MacLean (eds), *Power of the Weak: Studies on Medieval Women* (1995) – a collection of essays, several relating to England.

J. Hannam, A. Hughes and P. Stafford (eds), *British Women's History: a Bibliographical Guide* (1996) – a bibliography of books and articles published before 1992.

Two source collections:

J. Ward (trans. and ed.), *Women of the English Nobility and Gentry 1066–1500* (1995).

P. J. P. Goldberg (trans. and ed.), *Women in England c. 1275–1525* (1995).

Index

329

Index

baptisms 126, 127, 129
Baret, John 232
Barking (Essex) 32–3, 34, 37
Barratt, Alexandra 99, 100
Barron, Caroline 165, 177
Bartholomew the Englishman
124–5, 134, 135
Baudri of Dol 240, 241
Bayeux tapestry 69, 71, 79
Becket, Thomas, archbishop 129,
223
Bede 19, 20, 21, 22, 23, 24, 25, 26,
27, 28, 34, 35, 36, 37, 39, 40, 41,
50, 246
Beguinages 155, 156, 180
Benedict Biscop 26
Benedictional of Aethelwold 77, 85
Bennett, Jack 210
Bennett, Judith 143, 146, 184, 185,
237
Benton, John 99
Beowulf 54–7, 59–60, 64, 65
Berger, John 142, 152
Berhtgyth 26
Bernard, St 216
Bernstein, David 71
Bertha, queen 21, 22, 57
Bertila, abbess 32
Bidford-on-Avon (Warwick) 17
Bifrons (Kent) 11
bigamy 111–13
Biller, Peter 94, 127, 129, 131
Bischofsheim (Mainz) 29
Black Death 160, 180, 181
Bokenham, Osbern 230–1
Bonaventura, *The Prick of Love* 227;
On the Infancy 232
Boniface V, pope 21
Boniface, St 29, 30, 31, 32, 38, 42,
43, 47, 51; 'Boniface
correspondence' 31, 37–8
Books of Hours 234–6; Egerton
Hours 236; *see also* de Brailes
Books owned/read by/to women
198, 204, 209, 211, 221, 227, 232,
233, 234–5; ch.12 *passim*
Bracton 107, 169

Brandon (Suffolk) 27
breast-feeding 134, 135, 136, 137
Breedon (Leics.) 62
Bridget, St, of Sweden 129, 204,
221, 227, 232
Brighthampton (Oxon.) 11
Brigitines, Order of 204
Brigstock (Northants) 143, 144,
146, 147, 148, 184
Bristol 160, 161
Brittany 151, 152
brothels 120, 159, 160; *see also*
prostitution
Broughton (Huntingdon) 149
Bruckner, Matilda 254
Brythnoth 71
Buckland (Kent) 7, 11
Bugga, abbess 24, 38
Bugge, John 214
burial practices 4f
Bury St Edmunds (Suffolk) 122
Bynum, Caroline Walker 204, 216

Caedmon 25, 35
Calle, Richard 117
Camerton (Somerset) 11
Canterbury (Kent) 21, 71, 89, 114,
116
Carrow Priory (Norfolk) 219
Catherine of Sienna 233
Cely, George 177
Cenwealh, king 13
Chance, Jane 53
Chaucer, Geoffrey 168, 231, 247,
249–50, 255
Chelles (Francia) 24, 31
Chessel Down (Isle of Wight) 7
Chidewite 120
child-birth 16, 100, 123, 124, 125,
126, 128–9, 137, 215
children 45, 133f
Chrétien de Troyes, *Erec and Enide*
256
Christianisation, effects of 5, 7, 8,
9, 16, 20f, 41, 43, 48–52
Christina of Markyate 122, 153,
190, 197, 198, 199–202, 211

330

Index